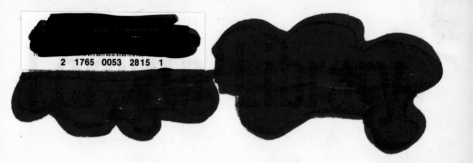

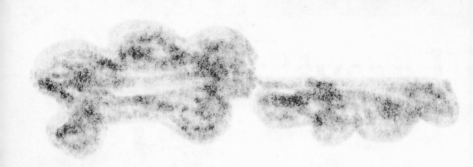

The Frankenstein Legend:

A Tribute to Mary Shelley and Boris Karloff

by
DONALD F. GLUT

The Scarecrow Press, Inc.
Metuchen, N. J.   1973

Library of Congress Cataloging in Publication Data

Glut, Donald F
    The Frankenstein legend.

    1.   Shelley, Mary Wollstonecraft (Godwin) 1797–1851.
Frankenstein.   2.   Karloff, Boris, 1887–1969.
3.   Frankenstein films.   I.   Title.
PR5397.F73G4   791.43'0909'351   73–944
ISBN 0-8108-0589-8

Cover illustration, of Boris Karloff as the
Monster, by courtesy of the artist Larry M. Byrd.

to **FORREST J ACKERMAN**

whose efforts have helped to keep the memories of
Mrs. Shelley and Mr. Karloff alive
and to perpetuate the Frankenstein legend.

ACKNOWLEDGMENTS

My sincerest thanks to the following people, all of whom contributed directly to this book:

John Abbott; Richard Andersen, my co-editor of the fan publication Shazam; Bebe Bergsten of Historical Films; Calvin T. Beck of Castle of Frankenstein; Bernhardt of Moewig-Verlag; Otto O. Binder; Robert Bloch; Bill Blackbeard; Richard Bojarski; Jean-Pierre Bouyxou; Sol Brodsky of Skywald Publishing Corporation; Bob Burns; Larry Byrd, my art director on Modern Monsters magazine; M. J. Campbell and Helene Moschedlover of the Literature and Philosophy Department of the Los Angeles Public Library; Fred Clarke, publisher of Cinefantastique; Chris Collier; Del Connell and Chase Craig of Western Publishing Company; Roger Corman; Ralph Costantino; Steve Dalen; Maurine Dawson; Katherine C. Egan of General Foods Kitchens; Harlan Ellison; Victor Fabian; Robbie Franklin and Eric Moon of Scarecrow Press; Bill Gaines of EC Publications; Luis Gasca of Buru Lan Ediciones; Martin Goodman, Stan Lee, and Roy Thomas of Marvel Comics Group; Bob Greenberg; Richard Hagopian; Curtis Harrington; Ron Haydock; Arlene M. Hermann of Helfgott & Partners; Eric Hoffman; Cortlandt B. Hull; Carmine Infantino of National Periodical Publications; Larry Ivie, editor and publisher of Monsters and Heroes; David Jones; Marvin Jones; George Junger of Doyle Dane Bernbach; Ross Kight; David Kinoshita of International Toho; Jack Kirby; Allen G. Kracalik; S. Richard Krown of UPA Pictures; Stanley J. Kucaba of Ovaltine Food Products; Ingeborg Kurtze of the German Consulate; Elsa Lanchester; Walter Lantz; Andy Lee of Universal Pictures; Christopher Lee; Richard A. Lupoff; Amy P. Makar of the Marschalk Company, Inc. ; Esteban Maroto; Robert R. McCollough of the University of Oregon library; Don Megowan; Rick Mitchell; Douglas Moench; Philip Morris; Michael Nesmith; William G. Obbagy, President of the American Bela Lugosi Fan Club; Darlyne O'Brien; Gus Ocosta of Columbia Pictures; Don Post; Jean F. Preston of the Henry E. Huntington Library and Art Gallery; Basil Rathbone; Craig Reardon;

Marla Reitman of Hanna-Barbera Productions; Laurence E. Reynolds of J. Walter Thompson Company; Frank M. Robinson of Playboy magazine; Jesse Santos; Don Shay; Erik Shiozaki; Dick Smith; Jim Steranko; Glenn Strange; Don Thompson; Christine Trumble of Clinton E. Frank, Inc.; Dale Van Sickel; James Warren of Warren Publishing Company; Alan White; Don Willis, author of Horror and Science Fiction Films: A Checklist (Scarecrow Press, 1972); and to anyone I may have accidentally missed.

Special thanks to Jim Harmon, the world's leading authority on "old time" radio, author of The Great Radio Heroes and The Great Radio Comedians, who supplied all of the tapes available of Frankenstein radio programs; Walter W. Lee, author of the staggeringly comprehensive Reference Guide to Fantastic Films, which this writer often consulted prior to publication; and Bill Warren, both a fan and a scholar of the genre, who was so prompt on the telephone to report to me some newly discovered Frankenstein title.

And thanks most of all to Forry Ackerman, editor of Famous Monsters of Filmland and my literary agent, without whose help (as the old saying goes) this book would not have been possible. Most of the photographs in this book are from the Ackerman Archives. Much of the information related in the text comes from the Forrest J Ackerman collection, which includes such items as Bela Lugosi's personal scrap book.

TABLE OF CONTENTS

PREFACE

I never wanted to create life. But my interest in the Monster created by Victor Frankenstein has occupied the majority of my years. Perhaps it was my gradual discovery of just what Frankenstein had created on that bleak November night during the Eighteenth Century that aroused in me such an avid interest in the subject--enough of an interest to write this book.

My first hearing of the name "Frankenstein" was as a small boy in the 1950's. I was walking home with my mother from a Chicago motion picture theatre called the Music Box where we saw the film Tap Roots, made a few years before, which featured Boris Karloff as an Indian. During the film my mother had mentioned that the Indian was portrayed by Karloff, who had played "Frankenstein." I couldn't resist learning more about the intriguing three-syllable name.

"Frankenstein," she told me as we walked, "was a dead man who was brought back to life." That sounded incredible, but I suspected there was more to the story. I began to notice advertisements in the Chicago Sun-Times, our family newspaper, for Frankenstein movies with so many titles that I could not remember them all. Unfortunately most of these ads either featured artwork done by the local artists or showed the Monster in such shadowy detail that I had no idea as to how he looked.

It was during my early Cub Scout days, approximately in 1952, that I was told by a fellow Scout that "Frankenstein" was not only a revived deadman, but a creature made up from parts of different corpses. To make him even more of a monstrosity, he had a large nail sticking out of his head. A nail? This naturally made no sense to me.

About that time I became acquainted with the Dick Briefer Frankenstein comic book, never realizing that the

Monster (I still thought he was called "Frankenstein") shown on the gruesome covers looked any different on the screen, or never even knowing that there was a novel written by Mary Shelley. The Briefer Monster had no "nails" or whatever jutting from his head. But, to confuse me even more, the Classics Illustrated comic book Frankenstein also found its way into my hands. It had what might have looked like nails--actually, more like-bolts--on the neck and the sides of the knees.

In 1955 I was walking past a toy shop during the Halloween season and spotted a green half mask, vaguely resembling the Monster in the Briefer comic books. Someone had mentioned to me only a few days before that "Frankenstein" had a very high forehead with a scar. This rubber mask certainly fit the description and also had metal plugs and clips that made me recall that old story about the nails.

My luck reached new heights in 1956 when a local movie house called the Modé ran a triple horror bill: The Mummy, starring Karloff, House of Frankenstein, and House of Dracula. The posters stated that Karloff also starred in House of Frankenstein. At last I was going to see Boris Karloff as "Frankenstein!" When the picture started and Karloff appeared as the mad doctor I wondered if the actor were playing two parts. Furthermore, the early introduction of Count Dracula made me wonder if the projectionist had somehow interchanged the reels of the two films. It was then that I learned A) Frankenstein was the name of the scientist and not the Monster, B) Karloff was not the only actor to portray the Monster, C) in the later films other monsters joined in the horror festivities, and D) I was a Frankenstein fan.

I discovered the novel by Mary Shelley. But as a youth of twelve years it bored me. There were no hunchbacked assistants or fabulous laboratory scenes. It wouldn't be for years that I learned how immature were my first impressions.

I had legitimately got sick and stayed home from school the day Primo Carnero starred as the Monster in the "Matinee Theatre" version of Frankenstein in 1957. There was no use swearing that turning on the show and seeing the title Frankenstein was a total surprise to me. Soon I was seeing more Frankenstein films in theatres. Boris Karloff caused magic on television one night when he was the guest of honor on "This Is Your Life." "Shock Theatre,"

with bug-eyed Marvin gleefully kidding the macabre, premiered on WBKB-TV in Chicago at ten o'clock, 7 December
1957, with the original Boris Karloff <u>Frankenstein.</u> And
<u>Famous Monsters of Filmland</u>, with an article titled "The
Frankenstein Story," premiered on the newsstands. Possibly of equal importance was my learning that there were
<u>other</u> people in this world who loved these motion pictures.

THE FRANKENSTEIN LEGEND is the end result of
an interest that began on that warm Chicago night I first
heard the name "Frankenstein." I have attempted to chron-
icle the story of the Monster, making it as complete as
possible. It is unnerving to contemplate the time between
this writing and final publication, when there will probably
be some new titles that should be included.

If your spine thrills at the thought of an ambitious
scientist "tampering with the unknown" and "playing God"
... if you enjoy the countless reruns on television of <u>Frank-</u>
<u>enstein Meets the Wolf Man</u> and feel a nostalgic joy over a
performance by Boris Karloff, come with me into the laboratory and world of Frankenstein. Scientists will rob graves.
Brains will be switched from one skull to another. Laboratories will come alive with electrical madness to give life to
patched-together travesties of humanity. Angry villagers
will storm the castle with fiery torches and a ready battering ram. And Mary Shelley, the young woman responsible
for it all, will, like her creation, live again.

This is the world of Frankenstein, the scientist who
created a man and then left him to the mercies of a merci-
less humanity. Perhaps in this age of heart transplants
and electronic wonders, that world, of questionable merit,
is not too far off.

Donald F. Glut

May, 1972

INTRODUCTION: MY FRIEND, THE MONSTER

by Forrest J Ackerman

[Forrest Ackerman was a personal friend of the late Boris Karloff and continues this friendship with his daughter Sara and grandsons Michael and David. He wrote the script for the Karloff-narrated Decca record album "An Evening with Boris Karloff and His Friends" and shortly after the death of the actor, whom he often referred to in print as King Boris the Benign, Ackerman assembled the paperback tribute to his memory, The Frankenscience Monster (New York: Ace Pub. Co., c1969).

[Mr. Ackerman interviewed Mr. Karloff in one of his London flats, dined with him and Fritz Lang, director of M and Metropolis, in the home of Robert (Psycho) Blochs, chatted with him in his dressingroom during the making of the second version of The Raven (the color film co-starring Vincent Price and Peter Lorre) and spoke with him several times on the set during the filming of his final four films, of which The Incredible Invasion was to be the very last.

[As a young fan Ackerman saw Frankenstein the film and read Frankenstein the book before I was born. He considers it one of the major honors that have come to him in his lifetime that, together with Boris Karloff, he received the first Ann Radcliffe Award, the top recognition for excellence in the Gothic field, from the Count Dracula Society. He has also appeared, in regard to Frankenstein, on television's "To Tell the Truth" and also the "Merv Griffin Show," on which he gave a dramatic reading of some of Colin Clive's dialogue from Frankenstein.

[When Boris Karloff died, Editor Ackerman dedicated the 56th issue (July 1969) of Famous Monsters of Filmland magazine to the memory of "the

man who was made by a monster." Following is his
introduction to THE FRANKENSTEIN LEGEND. --DFG.]

The Frankenstein Monster was one of the best Christmas presents I ever had.

If memory serves me right across a span of more than 40 years, it would have been at the morning matinee on opening day, 24 December 1931, at the Orpheum theater in San Francisco that I first fell under the thrall of Frankenstein.

I was a 15-year-old boy then, steeped since six in the tradition of thrilling silent films of the fantastic such as Dante's Inferno, The Thief of Bagdad, The Hunchback of Notre Dame, Faust, Siegfried, The Phantom of the Opera, London After Midnight, Metropolis, The Monster, The Lost World and Seven Footprints to Satan, and the exciting new "talkies" such as The Terror, The Bat Whispers, High Treason, The Mysterious Island and ... Dracula.

When I was eight, I had the wits scared out of me when foolhardy Mary Philbin snatched off the mask of Erik of the catacombs and revealed, as Robert Bloch has put it best, "the naked face of horror" that was Lon Chaney Sr. at the zenith of his power, in the immortal characterization that was the supreme achievement of his make-up mastery, his greatest face of all the famous thousand, in the filmization of Gaston Leroux' ghastly masterpiece. Fortunately I gathered my wits together in time to be present at the Northern California premiere of Boris Karloff's "answer" to Erik. (Although there actually never was any question: Chaney's Phantom was the shining hour of the silent film era's horror history; Karloff's Monster, the pinnacle of perfection of all horrors created since sound began.)

The fright sequence in Phantom of the Opera remains a classic of instant Total Terror. In Frankenstein, canny director James Whale coolly prolonged the introduction of the Monster for all it was worth. Who, having once seen it, can ever forget the slowly opening door to Colin Clive's laboratory and the backward entrance of the Creation; how the great awkward man-made monster, an automaton of terror, slowly as a zombie turned about to reveal its shocking face and form to transfixed audiences. In my day there were genuine screams throughout the theater and a nurse in white uniform (real or phony?--I suspect, it being during the Depression, she was the manager's unemployed sister) running down the aisle to escort a fainting "patron" (a plant?) to the ambulance parked outside the movie house as a publicity gimmick. Hip promo men may have helped along a bit the reputation of the picture's horror elements by such pre-arranged stunts but there were plenty, as I said, of genuine screams throughout the theater. I could be dramatic, but false to reality, and report that my own screams were among those echoing in the auditorium but I think that instead I was probably gripped quietly with an inner delight as my sense-of-wonder nerves were stimulated by the unnerving sight before me!

There would be a few more memorable highlights of horror for me in fright films to come--the breaking of Lionel Atwill's mask by Fay Wray in Mystery of the Wax Museum; the power mad voice of The Invisible Man, Claude Rains, in his major outburst of megalomania ("To send thousands squealing in terror at the touch of my little invisible finger! The whole world's frightened of me--even the Moon's frightened of me!"); the first tree-crunching appearance of the sovereign of Skull Island: King Kong; but nothing ever again really to compare with the initial confrontation with Boris Karloff as Frankenstein's Monster. No, I haven't forgotten Henry Hull as the WereWolf of London, the lycanthrope of fang and fury, nor Fredric March's Oscar-winning portrayal of evil incarnate in Dr. Jekyll and Mr. Hyde, nor the hideous end of Dr. Moreau (Charles Laughton) in the House of Pain at the hands of the manimals at the climax of The Island of Lost Souls. But above them all: the Karloff Frankenstein.

Cleverly taking advantage of the commotion the Frankenstein movie caused, Weird Tales magazine began serializing Mary Shelley's novel with its May 1932 issue. The story kept readers on tenterhooks for an agonizing eight instalments!

In 1935 the president of Universal himself, Carl Laemmle Sr., arranged an invitation for me to visit the Studio to see a preview in a small projection room of The Bride of Frankenstein. Afterwards, as I was leaving the lot, I had a supreme thrill: in the outer office, as I was walking toward the receptionist's desk to relinquish my pass, Henry Frankenstein (Colin Clive) walked past me!

I think you may be interested in what my reaction was,

at the age of 18, to Boris Karloff's second portrayal of the Frankenstein Monster. Fortunately I typed out my thoughts at the time and they were published in an amateur periodical, a "fanzine" of the science fiction field called Fantasy Magazine. I quoted my review to members of the Count Dracula Society a couple of years ago during an evening devoted to the memory of the then-recently-dead Boris Karloff, when Robert Bloch, Walter J. Daugherty, Donald A. Reed, Eric Hoffman and others spoke about him. My talk was taped and transcribed and, through the courtesy of Morris Scott Dollens and Beverly Presar, I quote it to you now [complete with interpolations]:

> The startling sequel science film opens in 1816 with Elsa Lanchester as Mary Wollstonecraft Shelley, authoress of the original Frankenstein story, revealing the terrible truth--the monster was not killed in the burning mill--the monster still lives! The picture then fades into the conclusion of the original: The peasants morbidly lingering around the smoking ruins believed to be the funeral pyre of Dr. Frankenstein's awful creation.

> The father of a little girl drowned by the monster enters the wreckage for the grim satisfaction of seeing the bones of the destroyed blasphemy but comes face to face with the Monster, horribly burned but alive. It savagely drowns him in a cistern, then clambers out of the ruins and stumbles away.

> Dr. Frankenstein, convalescing from his fright and fall from the mill, at last recovers and is visited by sinister Dr. Pretorius, the erudite scientist from whom he first learned the rudimentary principles of the artificial creation of life. [Dr. Pretorius had appeared a couple of years earlier in The Ghoul--he was Ernest Thesiger, who also appeared with Karloff in The Old Dark House.] The teacher demands Frankenstein aid him in further experiments. Frankenstein, still awed by his own ability to bring forth life, accompanies Pretorius, who reveals to him a sight of super science--his astounding work of test tube men. An experiment of tiny living human beings created from culture. Fantastic figurines imprisoned alive in small glass bottles. All thought

of promise to Elizabeth, his wife, is swept away, Frankenstein becoming fanatically enthusiastic on the new project--that of creating a mate for the Monster.

While the pasty-faced phantom, more unbelievably ghastly than ever now, his head scorched, mis-shapen skull sutured together with strips of silver, knobbed rod piercing his neck just below a long, livid gash forming a hinge for his head, flame-seared arms, is brought to bay by bloodhounds, bound to a pole and carted into the village jail. The 7-foot creation, inhumanly strong, easily escapes, killing several people as it makes for the mountains.

The Monster is attracted to a hermit's hut by the strains of a violin. Upon entering the hut, the old man occupant, who is blind, greets it as a friend, but finally realizes his great guest cannot speak. The Monster is overcome by the first signs of kindness toward him, thus begins a close friend-ship. It is taught to talk in passing days. [When the monster learned to speak, this was a very important step in the development of its character. It became more sympathetic than ever.]

[When I was with Boris Karloff five years ago in his apartment, he was going to see Frankenstein that evening for the firstime since the original showing in 1931. He was reminiscing about it and he said that he was very pleased that after the film originally opened, he received letters from all over the world. He remembered youngsters in Australia writing to him, letters from Canada, from home in England. And universally they reacted to the Monster with sympathy. And he was very pleased, because he said that was exactly the way he saw the role and wished to play it, and that he in fact insisted on a certain scene being removed from the film. It was shot--as a matter of fact it slipped through onto the screem at least on one occasion. I saw it, feeling somewhat like I was in the Twilight Zone, out in the next town south of here. One evening I was out there and saw the Frankenstein film. We come to the sequence where the Monster is kneeling by the lake with the little girl, and she picks a daisy and says, "I can make a boat. Here, I'll show you how." And she picks a petal, throws it into the water. He finds that very amusing and he is throwing his petals in. Finally, he throws the flower in, and when he has nothing left he makes a gesture with his hand as if to say, "More, let's keep the game going." And finally, figuring that if flowers will float, little girls will float, that'll be fun, he picks up the girl and throws her in the lake. And is quite surprised when she screams and drowns.

[Well, Karloff himself felt that that scene made him appear to be extremely brutal and sadistic. I personally didn't interpret it that way. To me it seemed like it would simply have evidenced the ignorance of a burgeoning mind, and he was in effect just a newborn baby in a giant body. But he told me in his apartment that he played the role for sympathy and that's what it got him all over the world and that's what particularly pleased him. And when they made the sequel, it was even more evident that he was a sympathetic creature put upon by humanity, in his tender sequence first of all with the hermit.]

Unfortunately, several months later, the Monster is seen by hunters happening by, which have to kill it. Again it is forced to fight, then escaping to take refuge in a cemetery. The same night, Dr. Pretorius and two satanic servants creep into the burial vault, secure a woman's skeleton from which to fashion the body of the Monster's mate. There Pretorius meets the Monster, who carries on a halting conversation with him, delighted when it learns that a companion is to be created for it.

Dr. Frankenstein now attempts to back out of the weird second experiment but the Monster kidnaps his wife and he is forced to continue to insure her return unharmed. The picture is at its peak.

In a reduplication of the original sensational laboratory sequence, the body of the synthetic woman is raised to the tower top at the height of a terrific electrical storm, while the great ray-diffusing machinery roars and crackles--a cannonading, awe-inspiring spectacle. The swathed form is lowered--alive! It is the creature from the graveyard, towering above the impious scientists who have created it.

Hardly less terrifying than the Monster itself, seven feet tall, scarred neck showing where the head had been sewed to the body, electrically

xvii

Loyal Subject Ackerman with King Boris the Benign of Karloffornia, relaxing on set.

charged hair standing up upon the skull, gray
streaking up from each temple, the Creation
Macabre staggers toward the Monster man who
preceded her in assemblage and introduction to
life.

And then the crashing climax quickly occurs.

I remember the opening of the third Frankenstein
film, Son of Frankenstein, as an occasion. In Los Angeles,
all of us L. A. Science Fantasy Society fans who could do
so gathered for the morning matinee. It is possible that a
young Ray Bradbury, that day in 1939, sat in the same row
with me. Henry Kuttner could have been there too. Shortly
after, I saw the Pete Smith Novelty short, Third Dimensional

Murder, which featured Ed Payson in a Son of Frankenstein-type get-up doing a Quasimodo-like act of pouring molten metal into the laps of shrieking audiences via the old blue-and-red cellophane glasses technique of 3D. I somehow seem to have been the only fan who ever actually saw the short subject and for many years carefully guarded the only known still from it. I understand this present volume's author, through the good offices of make-up maestro Dick Smith, presents and preserves another scene for us.

The first time I met Boris Karloff was in Hollywood after seeing him in a stageplay of On Borrowed Time. I went backstage afterward to meet him and seek his autograph on an anthology of "masterpieces of horror and the super-natural" which he had compiled, And the Darkness Falls. (In this case I wouldn't be surprised if he did select the stories rather than merely lend his name to the book and turn the job over to a ghost.) In green ink (mine) he signed: "Best wishes, Boris Karloff." As the book was published in 1946, my meeting with him could have been no earlier than that. I didn't see him again (except in every screen appearance) for another 20 years but he was never far from my thoughts as his stature as Mr. Monster grew and grew.

In 1951, when I took my first trip to Europe, in Germany I made a point of seeking out the Frankenstein Castle, a morning's journey by car from Frankfurt. Constructed, fittingly enough, in the 13th century, the castle's ruins, about 1200 feet of them, still stand today. It was built about A.D. 1250 by a young Frankenstein on the side of a long, narrow range of hills. When new, the castle must have been strong enough to withstand--almost--the attack of even a mythical monster, fortified as it was by a whole system of moats, drawbridges and outer walls. The tomb of a Knight George actually exists near the castle and legend has him killed by "a terrible man-eating monster in the neighborhood of the Katzenborn (Cat's Well), which frightened the whole valley of Niederbeerbach below." There are rumors that the castle conceals a treasure; certainly the Frankenstein legend itself is a literary treasure which has rarely failed to produce profit for film-makers who explore its theme.

In February 1958, when the first issue of the periodical I still edit, Famous Monsters of Filmland, appeared, no less than 15 photos of Frankenstein's Monster were featured and a leading article, "The Frankenstein Story."

It was in 1965 that I next saw Boris Karloff. I was now nearing 50 and he was beyond his mid-70s. The occasion was pleasant but frustrating. A meeting in Mr. Karloff's own London flat had been arranged for me by my late good journalist friend Peter J. Jarman. Unlike Bela Lugosi, who had a healthy ego, Boris Karloff seemed disinterested in keepsakes, mementoes, trophies, etc. I had hoped to see scrapbooks galore, rare photos, awards, but there was nothing of his past accomplishments on display. Mr. Karloff and Peter, who had met several times before, were soon engaged in a leisurely chat about what, to me, was total trivia, although I realize that cricket, gardening and such mundane matters were of absorbing interest to my host. Little time was left for me to query Mr. Karloff directly about matters cinematic as his wife appeared before long to apologize to us because she had to whisk him away soon to see a revival of Frankenstein. My tendrils stood on end when I heard that--I wanted to see the picture in his presence so much that I could taste it--but it seemed to me it would be impolite to try to get Mrs. Ackerman, myself and my friend invited to this special showing if it didn't occur to Mr. Karloff to volunteer. Mrs. Ackerman attempted to take some snapshots of my hero and myself in his own surroundings and great was my aggravation as flashbulb after flashbulb failed to function on this critical occasion. Finally, just as I was making some exaggerated motion toward the camera, clowning that I was not ready to be photographed yet, the flash inadvertently went off; it was the last shot and I was captured for all eternity with a ludicrous expression on my face, albeit Mr. K. came out OK.

Outside the Karloff apartment, directly we were out of earshot, I groaned; "Oh, God, I sure wish I could be at that Frankenstein showing!" Peter reacted as though struck by a bolt of lightning. He pulled his pipe out of his mouth. "Some journalist I am! But, of course! The thought should have occurred to me!" Quickly, much hunting about was done to find a phone, calls were made and delays endured, until finally the sands of time ran out; finally I got the full picture: people had been invited to a formal dinner, after which the showing would take place and then Mr. Karloff would speak in reaction to seeing himself as the monster once again across a gulf of 35 years. That night I brooded about this miserable turn of fate--very likely there was somebody at the banquet simply out of duty, secretly bored at having to attend "a monster movie," who would have been glad of the excuse to relinquish his or her place to me; but, alas, it was not to be.

I understand that in the early part of this century there was a town or hamlet in the United States called Frankenstein. I believe it was in Vermont or New Hampshire and in fact was immortalized in the early film <u>Frankenstein's Trestle,</u> mistakenly believed for some to be an actual Frankenstein movie. In the summer of 1963 I spent five weeks behind the wheel of an automobile, driving 8700 miles from Los Angeles to Washington, D.C., and back, for no other reason than to meet fans of monster movies. Early one morning, concentrating on the road ahead, I happened to glance to the right. I was electrified by what I saw! A sign reading: "Frankenstein 9 mi." Rubber skidmarks are still visible on that highway, marking my screeching halt, and my hasty U-turn. This was too good to miss! Already I had visions of buying half a hundred postcards and spending half a day sending fiend-friends greetings postmarked <u>Frankenstein!</u>

As we neared the little village (brave Mrs. A. was with me) I became more and more excited. I felt just like reporter David Manners in <u>The Black Cat</u>! The day was gray and overcast, perfect weather. Then the first evidence of humanity came into sight: a Gothic church on the outskirts of town.

The town was so tiny we were out of it before I had time to put on the brakes.

I turned around and drove back. We stopped at a little combination cafe and tobacco shop.

Floating in a jar was what I at first took to be disembodied eyes or perhaps cats' brains. Anyway, something directly out of the glass bowl in Dr. Waldman's lecture hall at the beginning of the first

Frankenstein--the one Fritz stole.   Actually the contents
were a specialty of the locality: hard-boiled pickled Polish
eggs.   I had a cup of coffee and a little conversation with
the proprietor.   Dashed was my dream of Frankenstein post-
marks for, though there had once been a postoffice there,
the population had dwindled so (ominous!) that a P.O. was
no longer justified.   Frankenstein: Pop. 26!

Wendayne and I went back to the nuns' quarters at
the side of the school.   There the Mother Superior gave us
cordial greeting.   When I asked if she had ever heard of
the Frankenstein Monster, she replied, "Yes, and I believe
some of our students are descended from him!"   Then she
produced a mimeographed fact sheet that had me bugeyed:
"History of Frankenstein"!   It was about the surrounding
terrortory and she explained that just 100 years before the
time of our visit a German family named Franken had settled locally.   The land was stony--the German word for
"stone" is "stein"--hence, the stony land of the Frankens
became ... Frankenstein!

(En passant: in 1926 when my grandmother was
reading Ghost Stories magazine to me regularly, I lived
with my parents in a Hollywood bungalow sandwiched between
neighbors with significant names: to the west, Mr. Canny,
the elderly neighborhood mystery man--surely he should have
been named Mr. Uncanny; and to the east, so help me Mary
Shelley there lived the Finkensteins!   Now what do you make
of that?)

I know you'd like to know but I'm not going to tell
you where the town of Frankenstein is, the one in the USA
that certainly wasn't contributing to the population explosion
at the time I visited it.   I made a mental promise to the
people there.   I have a hunch the poor villagers would have
no peace of mind if the mad mad world of filmonster fans
ever discovered their whereabouts.   The natives would be
restless tonight and every night.   They would curse my
name unto the 13th generation and rue the day that the
Ackermonster of Horrorwood turned off the beaten track and
visited their village, thereafter revealing their whereabouts
to souvenir hunters and journalists, who arrived like locusts
and stripped the land bare, stone by stone, so that in the
end there were no "steins" left and they had to rename the
town Franken....

1969:   Man on the Moon and Boris Karloff ... dead.

Is it sacrilegious to combine the two events in the same thought? There could, of course, be no comparison in their magnitude. But the lunar landing was something I had looked forward to for about 40 years and the death of Boris Karloff was something I had feared for about the same length of time. Tears were involved in both: the triumphant tears of vicarious vindication after 40 years of faith in the Space Dream; tears of sadness at the inevitable human loss of a cinema giant. Black Monday--2 February 1969-- the sad sad day the Frankenstein Monster died. Tears immediately came cascading out of my telephone and continued to dampen my mailbox for weeks afterward. I never experienced anything like the outpouring of sorrow over the death of Boris Karloff, as expressed by his fans to me as the only person they knew to whom they could directly communicate their feelings of loss. Later that year I was invited, along with 35 other fantasy film enthusiasts and filmmakers from various parts of the world, to a film festival in Brazil, where my suggestion that Elsa Lanchester, the Bride of Frankenstein, eulogize our demised "king" was not possible, the honor falling to me instead to open the Festival in the name of Boris Karloff and to dedicate it to his memory.

In 1970 at the Science Fiction Film Festival in Trieste I was approached by a young Italian who told me that later on that year he was to have an "All About Frankenstein" book published in Italy. He asked me to write a Foreword for it. I did but that is the last I have heard of it to date. The same year, in Paris, I was given a private showing by its producers of the legendary Torticola contre Frankensberg and was surprised to be told in my own home the following year by actor Michel Piccoli that it was he who played "Twisted Neck" in this curiosity.

1972: and on screens through the country I am being killed by the Frankenstein Monster! Greater love hath no man, or something. You can see it happen in Dracula vs. Frankenstein, which reunites Lon Chaney Jr. and J. Carrol Naish, who were together in House of Frankenstein in 1944. When I received a phone call asking me if I'd care to play the part of Dr. Beaumont in the picture (odd coincidence: I was the original agent of the late fantasy author Charles Beaumont) I at first declined when told that I would be killed by the Monster. It wasn't that the prospect didn't appeal to me but I had already been suffering for a month with a severely sprained shoulder and my arm was in a sling

and it hardly seemed like the thing for a man in pain to be
waltzing around with a monster. But the director assured
me, "It won't hurt a bit! You see, you're not killed in the
usual fashion"--at the mention of which visions from past
Frankenstein pictures were conjured up in my mind where
victims were choked, tromped, drowned, thrown from high
places, etc.--"something new has been added: Frankenstein
has been bitten by Dracula and himself becomes a vampire
and you'll very painlessly be fanged to death!" Well, that
sounded harmless enough, so I agreed to do the part. But
when it came time to die, the make-up artist had been
working on his Creation from about noon till 11 at night and
suddenly, to everyone's horror, it was discovered he's built
up his mouth in such a manner that it wasn't possible to
insert any fangs! Hasty conference and it's decided the
vampire angle will have to be dropped and Dr. Beaumont
will simply be killed in the old tried and true fashion, i.e.,
having every bone in his body broken. Hey!--wait a minute!
--I'm Dr. Beaumont! But the show must go on. Trooper
time. Stiff upper lip and all that. So the monster (and he
really was about 7' tall, a brawny young bruiser) lifts my
struggling form off the ground like I weighed no more than
a bag of marshmallows, squeezes the life from me (crunch!)
and lets my limp body fall to the concrete pavement (thump!).
I lie there turning blue in the face from a combination of
cold and asphyxiation while feigning death by holding my
breath because the director has forgotten to indicate the
scene's completion by calling "cut!" They like my death
scene so well that they decide to shoot it a couple more
times from different angles and each "take" takes a little
more out of me. Finally every bone in my body is broken
so the director is satisfied that he's got the realism he
wants and calls, "OK, wrap it up!" The nurse in attend-
ance thinks he's gotta mean me so I get the Mummy treatment. This Introduction has been typed with my left little
finger--the tip: the only bone in my body that wasn't
broken. (You think I'm joken?)

Don Glut has asked me to put absolutely everything
I can think of in this Introduction which in any way relates
to my relationship with Frankenstein. So--two final thoughts:

In 1965, in just about his last screen appearance, I
played Basil Rathbone's assistant in Queen of Blood, as it
was known on the screen and in paperback (Planet of Blood,
as it was called on TV). I have one nice eyeball-to-eye-
ball close-up with him; what thoughts were passing through

my mind as I did the scene? These: "Basil Rathbone, a quarter of a century ago you were playing Wolf von Frankenstein, bringing Boris Karloff back to life in Son of Frankenstein, and I was watching you in the audience. It's you, Basil Rathbone, and I'm standing opposite you now, in a science fiction picture."

Lastly, a revelation. I sat on a scoop about Life Without Soul too long and Carlos Clarens (whom I salute) broke into print with word about it first. There are yet certain information and stills I am hoarding against the day that a publisher invites me to do a really fabulous book on fantastic films. But now, exclusively for THE FRANKENSTEIN LEGEND, for the first time in English, you are about to read the name of a Frankenstein film made in 1920! To give credit where credit is due, I would not have known of this film if I had not learned of it from Italy's number one authority on fantastic movies, Luigi Cozzi. It was from my friend Luigi that I learned the title: Il Mostro di Frakestein [The Monster of Frankenstein]. And I have a picture of the Monster, too!

But for that revelation you'll have to buy my book. Or the second, revised, enlarged edition of THE FRANKENSTEIN LEGEND!

Forrest J Ackerman

Karloffornia

The Hydes of March 1972

Chapter 1

MARY SHELLEY AND HER ETERNAL CLASSIC

Mary Wollstonecraft Shelley was nineteen years old when on the night of 19 June 1816 she retired for bed at Lord Byron's Villa Diodati. Her controversial life had, to that date, provided her with more than enough research material to arrive at a gruesome story of horror to satisfy the request of Byron: "We will each write a ghost story," the free-living and loving poet told his assemblage of friends that included Mary's young husband Percy Bysshe Shelley, and Byron's handsome young physician and secretary Dr. John Polidori (affectionately referred to by Byron as "Polly-Dolly").

Dwarfed by the talents of the three men, youthful Mary retired for bed somewhat disheartened after days of questioning. "Have you thought of a story?" she had been asked each morning, forced to reply in the negative, and unaware that her own life had already laid the foundation for the world's most famous novel of horror, Frankenstein; or, The Modern Prometheus.

In the introduction Mary Shelley wrote to the 1831 edition of the book, she related:

> When I placed my head on the pillow, I did not sleep, nor could I be said to think. My imagination, unbidden, possessed and guided me, gifting the successive images that arose in my mind with a vividness far beyond the usual bounds of reverie. I saw--with shut eyes, but acute mental vision--I saw the pale student of unhallowed arts kneeling beside the thing he had put together. I saw the hideous phantasm of a man stretched out, and then, on the working of some powerful engine, show signs of life, and stir with an uneasy, half vital motion.

1

Portrait of Mary Wollstonecraft Shelley at the age she wrote her immortal novel.

Frightful must it be; for supremely frightful would
be the effect of any human endeavor to mock the
stupendous mechanism of the Creator of the world.
His success would terrify the artist; he would rush
away from his odious handiwork, horror-stricken.
He would hope that, left to itself, the slight spark
of light which he had communicated would fade;
that this thing, which had received such imperfect
animation, would subside into dead matter; and he
might sleep in the belief that the silence of the
grave would quench for ever the transient existence
of the hideous corpse which he had looked upon as
the cradle of life. He sleeps; but he is awakened;
he opens his eyes; behold the horrid thing stands
at his bedside, opening his curtains, and looking
on him with yellow, watery, but speculative eyes.

In her mind, a young medical student had fashioned
a monstrous composite corpse from various alien organs,
and then endowed it with a terrible artificial life force. All
that remained was to scribe the horrifying tale. The story
had seemingly come to her miraculously. Actually the
origins of Frankenstein went back to the first gasps of life
breathed by Mary and to the influences of even earlier times.

The story of Mary Shelley proves to be as extraordinary as
that of Frankenstein. Mary was born in London in August
1797 to Mary Wollstonecraft, a staunch preacher of free
love and author of Vindication of the Rights of Women (1792),
now much quoted by the Women's Liberation movement, and
William Godwin, author of the famous anarchist utopia book,
An Enquiry Concerning Political Justice, a great document
of eighteenth-century political philosophy highly successful
in its day and since. He also wrote bizarre tales including
Adventures of Caleb Williams (1794) about a murderous
sadist, St. Leon (1799) about a disfigured Transylvanian
prince, and Fleetwood: or, The New Man of Feeling (1804)
about a criminal assassin. Both Mary Wollstonecraft and
Godwin were respected as England's most liberal intellectuals
and their thinking would greatly influence their daughter's
own mind and life.

Mary Wollstonecraft was a supporter of natural child-
birth. As a result of not calling in doctors to attend the
delivery until too much time had passed, the woman died
within ten days of giving birth to her baby daughter. God-

win never forgave his daughter for causing the death of his
wife.   Moreover, he decided the only thing to satisfy his
grief was the punishment of the child.   He named her Mary
Wollstonecraft Godwin as if the tolerated girl were a reincarnation of his spouse, then gave her to the care of an
unqualified stepmother.

His belief that Mary was a youthful projection of his
deceased wife was carried to the extremes.   Feverishly the
child attempted to overcome the growing shadow of her
mother by steeping herself in literature and listening to the
discussions carried on by her father and his group of intellectual friends.   She also began to write.

> The unfeeling, relentless pressures on Mary in
> the 'Godwin forcing-house' (Biographer Eileen Big-
> land's phrase) finally had its weird effect.   Mary
> Shelley never succeeded in matching the superior
> intellect and moral courage of Mary Wollstonecraft;
> and the incessant reading and writing under the
> cold shadow of her rival mother only served to
> condition her permanently to associate books and
> writing with her mother's 'resurrection.'[1]

Young Mary's attempts to compete with her dead
mother reached obsessive proportions by the time she turned
seventeen.   The melancholic teenager began to read and
write while seated beside the grave of Mary Wollstonecraft
which was just behind the Old St. Pancras Church where her
parents had been married.   The visitations were on a daily
basis.   But the corpse of Mary Wollstonecraft never rose.

While Mary continued to engage in such bizarre pas-
times, her father was arranging a scheme he hoped would
be beneficial to all involved.   Godwin had been corresponding
with the radical atheist and poet Percy Bysshe Shelley, a
professed heir to a considerable fortune.   This man of only
twenty years, while already married to Harriet Westbrook,
seemed to William Godwin the ideal husband for Mary.
Leaving his pregnant spouse, Shelley was convinced through
letters to join Godwin and help him financially.   As a result
of journeying to discuss the fine arts (and to loan money)
with the older man who had been kind enough to send him
so much advice, Percy met the radiant Mary.   They sup-
pressed their true mutual feelings until he followed her on
one of her depressing excursions to the graveyard.   There,
mimicking the boldness of her mother, she pronounced her

love for him.   The cemetery became their clandestine meeting place.

Shortly after this encounter Shelley and Mary left
England for the continent.   Eight months later a child,
William, was born to them.   As if further punishing Mary
for her mother's death, the child lived but a short time.
The couple eventually did marry in Scotland in 1816, two
years after meeting.   One year later they would take up
residence in Marlow, England, with two children, William
and Clara.

These events in the life of Mary Wollstonecraft Shelley,
although she had no idea at the time, were already amassing
toward the creation of the Frankenstein Monster.   Still there
were other factors that contributed to this most famous of
gothic horror stories.

Dating back centuries were the legends of the Golem,
the living creature of clay.   The story of the Golem had
been incorporated into a collection of ghostly stories called
Phantasmagoriana.   The book was a favorite of Mrs. Shelley's
and she often dwelled upon the idea of an inanimate figure
receiving life by mortal man.

Mary Shelley had also been fascinated by stories of
human-like robots.[2]   It is quite probable that she read the
writings of the German, E. T. A. Hoffman, whose stories,
"Automatons" (1812) and "The Sandman" (1814), both dealt
with very human-like machines.   The former involved a
mechanical dancing partner;   the latter, Olympia, an animated doll so alluring that it attracted the love of a madman.
Hoffman's stories considered the possibility of man and machine becoming interchangeable.   Mary also became en-
thralled by the real-life robot created by the Viennese mech-
anician, de Kempelen, in 1769 and which had defeated Em-
press Maria-Theresa of Austria in a game of chess.[3]   She
was well conditioned to the idea of giving some form of life
to inanimate creations.

Many of Percy Shelley's own interests proved to be
fertilizer for the forming entity that would someday become
the Frankenstein Monster.   Shelley had particular fascination
for the Greek myth about Prometheus.   According to Aeschy-
lus' Prometheus Bound, Zeus had regarded the human beings
which he had created as worthy only of extinction.   Zeus decided to freeze the entire human race when Prometheus,

recognizing good in mankind, helped the mortals overcome
their condition by stealing for them the fire of lightning.
Furthermore Prometheus infuriated Zeus by infusing life into
men of clay which he had formed.   For his treachery Prometheus was eternally punished. [4]

In a sense Shelley regarded Dr. Benjamin Franklin as
a "modern Prometheus" (a term which Mary used as the sub-
title of Frankenstein) because he brought down the electrical
power of lightning for the benefit of mankind in much the
same manner as the Greek deity.   He often discussed the
Prometheus myth with Byron, while Mary listened attentively.

Shelley's fascinations that influenced Mary's writing
did not commence with Prometheus.   He had become engrossed
with the experiments of Philippus Aureolus Paracelsus of
Ingoldstadt, Germany (the town Mary chose for the creation
of the Monster in her novel) and those of Cornelius Agrippa
and Albertus Magnus, all of whom attempted to discover the
secrets of immortality during medieval times.   None of them
ever achieved success at their quest.   Paracelsus was only
forty-eight when he died in 1541.

The infamous Lord Byron had rented a home near
Lake Geneva in Switzerland called Villa Diodati.   Percy and
Mary Shelley followed suit by renting a nearby villa.   The
mutual acts were primarily intended to escape the curious
Swiss who just had to know what blasphemies and sexual
deviations were constantly performed by the troupe, which
also included Dr. Polidori and actress Claire Clairmont, a
step-daughter of Mary's father William Godwin, through his
re-marriage in 1801, now gotten pregnant by the already
married but unabashed Lord Byron.   It was at this villa that
the Monster of Victor Frankenstein was really created.

The dreary days and long periods of rain provided
little chance for the talked-about visitors to Geneva to enjoy
the countryside.   The weather was taking effect upon them
and giving them thoughts of ghosts and of stories to chill the
spine.   Byron added to the somber atmosphere by reading a
German ghost tale in which a man kissed his new bride at
which point she transformed into a rotting corpse.   To his
horror--and to that of Percy, who had abandoned his own
wife in favor of Mary Godwin--the bridegroom saw the carcass to be that of a previous love whom he had left behind.

Lord Byron delighted in his bits of sadism at the

expense of the others.   Then he gnawed even deeper into the
spirits of the Shelleys.   He began to read the poem Christabel, which seemed to have particular significance for the
young Mary.   Written just after her birth by Samuel Taylor
Coleridge, a friend of William Godwin, the poem told a story
similar to the real life relationship between Mary and her
mother.   Through supernatural power, the mother in the
poem took revenge upon her newly married daughter Christabel and her husband.

The young Mary remained surprisingly unaffected by
Byron's knife-twisting.   Percy's actions were quite the opposite.   Like a raving dog, Shelley erupted with foaming mouth
and wide open eyes, as Lord Byron gleefully pronounced the
line from Christabel, " ... a sight to dream of, not tell. "
When Byron went on to recite the later line, "There are
things born in the twilight hours more monstrous than nightmares, "[5] Percy was already bounding through the halls of
the villa, howling like a human wolf.   It took a furious chase,
plus cold water and potent ether administered by Lord Byron
and Dr. Polidori, to bring Shelley back to relative normalcy.
Later Percy told the assemblage that he was particularly
taken by the part of the poem concerning the breasts of a
witch that made him think of the grisly sight of a strange
woman with eyes where her nipples should have been.

The atmosphere was perfectly right for the group of
Percy, Mary, and Polidori to heed Lord Byron's suggestion
that each write a ghost story.   The most productive tale
spewing from that suggestion began as the basics of a plot
started by Lord Byron involving what sounded like the beginning of a vampire tale.   Leaving the theme, as his own ego
forbade him from doing such "lowbrow" writing, the idea was
snatched by Polidori who developed it into a novella he called
The Vampyre.   Polidori achieved some venegeance upon his
mentor by characterizing the vampiric Lord Ruthven as alike
Lord Byron.   The image of the suave vampire nobleman had
been born.   Most fictional vampires--primarily Count Dra-
cula--have been patterned after the image of Lord Ruthven.
In this sense Lord Byron did achieve somewhat of the eternal
life considered by Percy Shelley.   We might also say that
both Count Dracula and the Frankenstein Monster were created
as a result of the same nights at Villa Diodati.

Mary Shelley had been unable to think of a story that
would please and chill the others at the villa.   She listened
more than spoke as Lord Byron and her husband engaged in

some rather heavy conversations, first regarding Prometheus, both bound and unbound, and then the work of Dr. Erasmus Darwin (an ancestor of Charles Darwin). Dr. Darwin had performed experiments trying to give some type of simple life to inanimate objects. Rumor at the time said that he actually achieved the feat, getting movement from, according to Mrs. Shelley in her introduction, "a piece of vermicelli in a glass case."

With a life so far filled with legend and literature and obsessions with the macabre and with death, Mary Shelley tried that night of 19 June 1816 to go to sleep. By morning she had created the Frankenstein Monster.

"Frankenstein"

When Mary Shelley next addressed the assemblage of ghost story writers, her youthful eyes were sparked with ideas, although Frankenstein as the novel we know today had still not been entirely developed.

"Swift as light and as cheering was the idea that broke in upon me," Mary Shelley said in her 1831 introduction.

'I have found it! What terrified me will terrify others; and I need only describe the spectre which had haunted my midnight pillow.' On the morrow I announced that I had thought of a story. I began that day with the words, 'It was on a dreary night of November,' making only a transcript of the grim terrors of my waking dream.

The story of a scientist attempting to create human life was originally intended by Mary to be a relatively short story. Percy Shelley recognized in the theme an inherent scope and urged his wife to expand the story to a greater length. Mary was one to listen to the suggestions of her intellectual husband and proceeded to write the novel Frankenstein.

The very name of "Frankenstein" today is synonomous with horror. Certainly the name has a gutteral, powerful tone to it, making it at least plausible that Mary merely concocted it because of its ominous sound. Actually the name "Frankenstein" is a common one--it can be found today in most telephone directories--but it seems to have been well considered for Mary Shelley's book.

Title page of 1831 (standard) edition of <u>Frankenstein</u>.

In reply to a letter commenting upon his "Horrible Truth About Frankenstein" article for <u>Life</u> in the 5 April 1968 issue of that magazine, Samuel Rosenberg deduced that the name "Frankenstein" had two basic origins: Percy Shelley wrote "St. Irvyne" when eighteen years old, featuring a hero named Wolfstein, who, like so many real life characters of Shelley's interest, desired to find the secret of immortality. From "Wolfstein" Mary salvaged the last portion. "Franken" came from yet another source. Her husband had found extreme interest in the experiments of Benjamin Franklin, the contemporary Prometheus of his day. Mary, then, adapted the name "Frankenstein"[6] from the accomplishments and interests of her husband, who had inspired her to escape the confines of the short story.

A flood of gothic romance novels had already saturated the literary world by the time Mary Shelley began to write her work. She decided to give her readers something extra, an extremely complex story with a totally real horror that would not be written away as a bad dream or the plot of a scoundrel trying to steal some hapless governess' inheritance.

Mary Shelley had not thought it important enough to sign her name to the book. <u>Frankenstein</u> was published, after fifteen months in the writing, anonymously in 1818 by Lackington. Some of Percy Shelley's ideas had naturally become those of Mary herself. For that reason critics interpreted the book as being authored by Percy Shelley. (Percy wrote the preface to the novel. The implication was that both preface and novel were by the same author.) It was not until a later edition of <u>Frankenstein</u> that the book was revealed as the work of a young girl.

<u>Frankenstein</u> was originally published in three hardcover volumes, apparently as often as the publisher decided or could afford to release the latest installment. The tale began with the fifth chapter (as the book exists today), opening with the scene in which Victor Frankenstein brought his creature to life. The three-part story was told in the first person by Victor Frankenstein. Later his creature related a lengthy (over forty pages) uninterrupted flashback in the first person.

A later edition of <u>Frankenstein</u> brought the book to its present form. Mary had polished the previous draft, added chapters, and built a frame around what had already been written. [7] The novel now opened with Victor rescued by

The very first illustration of the Frankenstein Monster, from
the 1831 Standard Novels edition.

Captain Robert Walton (narrating in the first person). Frankenstein, aboard Walton's ship, told him his terrible story,
creating a flashback. The Monster's own seemingly endless
narration provided a flashback within a flashback. This format was extremely difficult to make believable, especially
considering the unrealistic verbosity of the characters. Yet
Mrs. Shelley managed to surmount her own imposition of
three first person accounts. The technique worked.

Mary Wollstonecraft Shelley's Frankenstein; or, The
Modern Prometheus, astounds many of today's readers accus-
tomed only to the motion picture versions. There are no
gothic castles with fantastic electrical apparatus crackling
away while a mad scientist raves maniacally and his grotesque
hunchbacked assistant warns him against trying to play at
being God. Victor Frankenstein was not, as is a common
disbelief, a baron or even a doctor. Although Victor's family
background included Frankensteins in high office, he was not
a nobleman. He was simply "Victor," a science student, and
not "Dr. Frankenstein. "

Captain Robert Walton had been making a voyage to explore
the North Pole during the Eighteenth Century (presumably
during the latter portion of the 1700s and not, as most people
think due to the publication date of the novel, in the early
1800s). A lonely man desiring a true friend, Walton thought
he had at last found such a companion when his ship was
caught in an ice flow and he had the opportunity to rescue a
dishevelled man made sick by the elements. The stranger
had been pursuing barely distinguishable yet obviously giant
creature by dogsled. The large man-like form had seemingly
escaped when the man was taken aboard Captain Walton's
vessel. When the strangely melancholic man was able to
speak freely he expressed fear over Walton's own inquisitive-
ness in desiring to learn the unknown. Then he proceeded to
tell Captain Walton the terrible story which brought him to
that sorry condition to the frozen regions of the Arctic. The
captain put down his story and later sent the manuscript to
his sister in England, Mrs. Saville.

The stranger was Victor Frankenstein, born in Geneva,
Switzerland, and in love since childhood with a golden-haired
girl with whom he had grown up, Elizabeth Lavenza. At age
fifteen, Frankenstein observed the tremendous power of electricity as a bolt of lightning destroyed a large oak tree. He
attended the University of Ingoldstadt in Germany when he

Original conception of the Monster by Nino Carbe--the first book version with electrodes on the neck.   From World Publishing Company's 1932 edition of <u>Frankenstein</u>.

turned seventeen years old.   He became, like Percy Bysshe
Shelley, fascinated by the work done in earlier centuries by
Albertus Magnus, Cornelius Agrippa, and Paracelsus.   Young
Frankenstein's genius and ambition to go beyond what science
had already discovered to get at more fundamental truths
caused one of the university's faculty, M. Waldman, to make
him his own disciple.

> 'I am happy,' said M. Waldman, 'to have gained a
> disciple; and if your application equals your ability,
> I have no doubt of your success.... If your wish is
> to become really a man of science, and not merely a
> petty experimentalist, I should advise you to apply to
> every branch of natural philosophy, including mathe-
> matics.'
>
> He then took me into his laboratory, and explained to
> me the uses of his various machines; instructing me
> as to what I ought to procure, and promising me the
> use of his own when I should have advanced far enough
> in the science not to derange their mechanism.   He
> also gave me the list of books which I had requested;
> and I took my leave.
>
> Thus ended a day memorable to me: it decided my
> future destiny.

Victor Frankenstein's interest became channeled into
various areas that would eventually lead him to a most astounding discovery.   He perfected some advanced designs of
chemical instruments and he became fascinated by the construction of the human body.   His studies went into deter-
mining the basic causes of life.   During his investigations
Victor became aware of the link between death and life and
how they were eternally joined.   The man dies, his body rots
away, and is eaten by the worm who propagates that stagnant
human body through its own being.   Frankenstein began to go
on field trips to graveyards and charnel houses.

Then, after many days and nights of scientific inves-
tigation and labor in his private laboratory (in an apartment,
not a castle), Frankenstein discovered the secret of life.
Here Mrs. Shelley's text is extremely unlike the later adaptations of the movies, television, and so forth.   In these versions the actual creation of the Monster usually takes up a
good portion of the story, with Frankenstein and/or his assistant rummaging through cemeteries and various places of

the dead with long scenes showing the alien organs being
joined to form the composite corpse.   With statements that
the creature was being formed as a result of the student's
visits to charnel houses and the like, Mary Shelley described
the discovery of the secret of life briefly.

> After days and nights of incredible labour and fatigue,
> I succeeded in discovering the cause of generation and
> life; nay, more, I became myself capable of bestowing
> animation upon lifeless matter.

Naturally inquisitive, Captain Walton requested Victor
to reveal the nature of his secret of life.   Frankenstein
denied his appeal, seeing in the captain a reflection of his
own ambition.   Nor did Victor give an accurate account of
the creation of his being.   He merely reported that in order
to make his task easier and to bypass the minuteness of some
of the parts, he fashioned a giant body, eight feet tall and
proportionally large.   His materials came from cemeteries,
dissecting rooms, and slaughter houses (implying the use,
perhaps, of some animal tissues).   Frankenstein worked upon
his creation for two years.   By the end of autumn his enormous being was complete.

Mary Shelley's description of the procedure by which
Frankenstein gave his being life is vague, purposely so in
that Victor did not want to betray his secret to Walton and
also because she was not herself a scientist.   From various
passages in the book mentioning electricity and chemistry it
is reasonable to assume that Victor Frankenstein infused the
artificial spark of life into his creation through galvanic
power and through injections, using some of the advanced
apparatus which he had himself designed.

The high point in most Frankenstein motion pictures
is the scene in which the Monster is given life.   There is
usually a terrific display of electrical power, with climbing,
crackling Jacob's ladders, great fingers of electricity jumping
from terminal to terminal, and a raging electrical storm
crashing the heavens.   The scene in the upstairs room of
his house, separated from the others rooms by a staircase
and gallery, Victor Frankenstein's life-giving act was described by Mary Shelley in but one paragraph.   What the
movies make an entire story out of, Mary almost threw
away.   It was with this paragraph that the first edition of
her novel originally began.

It was on a dreary night of November that I beheld the
accomplishment of my toils.   With an anxiety that almost amounted to agony, I collected the instruments of
life around me, that I might infuse a spark of being
into the lifeless thing that lay at my feet.   It was already one in the morning;   the rain pattered dismally
against the panes, and my candle was nearly burnt out,
when, by the glimmer of the half-extinguished light, I
saw the dull yellow eye of the creature open;   it
breathed hard, and a convulsive motion agitated the
limbs.

Almost equally vague was Mrs. Shelley's description
of the being created by Frankenstein.   She makes no reference
to the standard plug-like electrodes and numerous stitched
scars that have characterized the image of the Monster through
motion pictures, television, comic books, and the like.   Furthermore, as the being came to life, Victor seemed to discover that his handiwork was ugly.   His previous zeal to
create life had apparently blinded him to the repulsiveness of
that which he had hoped to make beautiful.

How can I describe my emotions at this catastrophe,
or how delineate the wretch whom with such infinite
plans and care I had endeavored to form?   His limbs
were in proportion, and I had selected his features as
beautiful.   Beautiful! ... Great God!   His yellow skin
scarcely covered the work of muscles and arteries beneath;   his hair was of a lustrous black, and flowing;
his teeth of a pearly whiteness;   but these luxuriances
only formed a more horrid contrast with his watery
eyes, that seemed almost of the same colour as the
dun white sockets in which they were set, his shrivelled complexion and straight black lips.

Aware of the ugliness he had created, Victor Frankenstein fled from his living brainchild.   Here the movie and
other adaptations missed the point.   Their main objective was
to show the creation of a monstrosity, while Mary Shelley
briefly passed over such scenes.   The creation of the Monster
is but a small fragment of Frankenstein.   What the story is
all about came after the being had been infused with life.

Victor Frankenstein fled.   He rejected his creature
in much the same way later existentialists believed God rejected man.   Although the creature later begged his creator
for love and understanding, Frankenstein continually denied

happiness to his being.   Therein lay the tragedies of Frankenstein and the Monster.   Having taken upon himself the role of
creator, Victor then refused to assume the accompanying re-
sponsibilities, setting his creature to grovel in its own miserable existence in a universe where other beings also rejected
it for its external ugliness.   Frankenstein never accepted the
fact that beneath the shrivelled yellow flesh of his creation
lay an emotional being that cried to give as well as receive
love.   It was for this rejection that the being eventually became a "monster," bent upon murderous revenge.

Frankenstein was an allegory and reflected the life of
Mary Shelley and her group of influential relatives and friends.
In the scene following the creature's artificial "birth," this
allegorical quality becomes especially obvious.   Victor
Frankenstein fled from his being to his bedroom.   Falling
asleep from exhaustion, he had the nightmare of embracing
and kissing his beloved Elizabeth.   When their lips met his
fiancée was horribly transformed into the decomposing corpse
of his mother.   Awakening in terror, he found the real life
form of his monstrous handiwork gaping down at him with the
watery yellow orbs.

In Victor Frankenstein we see the influences of both
Percy Shelley, who longed to discover the secret of immortality and the reality of the Promethian act of bestowing life
upon a lifeless form.   But we can also perceive the figure
of William Godwin (to whom Frankenstein was dedicated),
who rejected his daughter due to the death of his wife.

When Victor fled from his creation it was not unlike
Percy Shelley's own "mad dog" bounding through Lord Byron's
rented villa.   The terrible dream of kissing his fiancée only
to find her metamorphosed into a rotting carcass brings to
mind Byron's own story told to Mary and his other friends.
The fact that the corpse was that of Victor's mother is reminiscent of Mary Wollstonecraft Godwin, who was only returned
to life in the dream of her bereaved husband.   Victor's dream
blended into the reality of the composite corpse made by
Frankenstein.   The Monster, then, seems to be a literary
manifestation of Mary Shelley who was in a bizarre way a
monstrous reincarnation of her deceased mother.

One of the true tragic qualities of Frankenstein is that
the Monster exhibited more human qualities, more desires to
both give and receive compassion and love, than did Victor
Frankenstein.   In this sense the creature was more human

Illustration by courtesy of Corgi Books, London.

than the creator. Victor mechanically denied all the Monster's pleas for happiness; he had created a thing more human than himself.

Between Victor Frankenstein and his creation we can see two extremes. To provide an intermediary character, Mary Shelley thought of Captain Robert Walton. Like the Monster, Walton craved companionship; like Victor Frankenstein, he sought to learn that which was yet unknown. The inception of Captain Walton again stemmed from incidents in Mary's impressionable life. When she was only eight years old she listened to Samuel Taylor Coleridge dramatically recite his classic poem based upon the philosophy of William Godwin: Mary's father contended that once love died a man became unbearably lonely and destructive--Coleridge presented this idea in his immortal Rime of the Ancient Mariner. Victor quoted from the poem after the being came to life.

Robert Donald Spector of Long Island University stated:[8]

> Walton, like Coleridge's wedding guest in 'The Rime of the Ancient Mariner,' becomes the man to whom the story must be told, the man who listens in fascination to events that somehow involve his very being. Like Frankenstein, he would give all for scientific discovery; like the monster, he suffers desperate loneliness. Somehow, in their relationship to the captain, the experiences of Frankenstein and his monster become the hopes, desires, and fears of all men. That is Mary Shelley's finest achievement.

Victor Frankenstein fled from his apartment house, leaving his creation to fend for itself. During the next year he did not encounter the being. He received a letter from his father, Alphonse Frankenstein, stating that his own little brother William had been strangled by a powerful hand. With the body was a locket that seemed to be the object of the crime apparently committed by a servant girl, Justine Moritz. Though believed innocent by Victor, Justine was executed for the murder.

Wandering dejectedly through the hills, Victor encountered for the first time since his creation the giant figure of his being. Believing the creature guilty of two deaths he cursed it. To his horror the Monster spoke intelligently, fluently, the first words that would violate the ears of Frankenstein.

'I expected this reception,' said the daemon.   'All
men hate the wretched; how, then, must I be hated,
who am miserable beyond all living things!   Yet you,
my creator, detest and spurn me, thy creature, to
whom thou art bound by ties only dissoluble by the
annihilation of one of us.   You purpose to kill me.
How dare you sport thus with life?   Do your duty
towards me, and I will do mine towards you and the
rest of mankind.   If you will comply with my condi-
tions, I will leave them and you at peace; but if you
refuse, I will glut the maw of death, until it be
satiated with blood of your remaining friends.'

The Monster then related the incidents in his life that
followed his unnatural creation.   At first he merely explored
and revelled in the spectacular displays of nature.   In a
strange way he was like Adam in the Garden of Eden, innocent and totally responsive to the elements.   Again this
showed Percy Shelley's influence on his wife's writing.   He
is reported to have read John Milton's Paradise Lost to her
while she plotted Frankenstein.   It is not surprising that her
novel opened with an appropriate quotation from it:

Did I request thee, Maker, from my clay
To mould me man?   Did I solicit thee
From darkness to promote me?

Wherever the Monster went, humanity feared and tormented him.   People shrieked in terror, then cast stones and
other pain-inflicting missiles at the creature.   At last he took
shelter in a hovel near a cottage.   Through a crack in the
wall he watched the inhabitants of the cottage, De Lacey, his
son Felix, and daughter Agatha, and secretly performed manual work for them.   By watching and listening he learned
simple words like "fire," "milk," "bread," and "wood" (as
did Boris Karloff in the movie Bride of Frankenstein).   One
day Safie, a beautiful girl from Arabia, joined the household.
As she was taught to speak their language (and also French)
the Monster learned to use the speech organs given him by
Frankenstein.   With her, the creature also learned history,
science, and the arts.   He learned the story of Paradise
Lost and identified with Adam who was at that point the only
creature of his species in the world.   The Monster, however,
felt that his own being was spawned of Satan and not a benevolent God.   At last the Monster visited personally the eldest
member of the family while the others were out.   He was
blind and unaware of the creature's hideous form.   For a

while the two got along well together.   Then the others returned and, acting decisively human, drove the Monster away.

Next the Monster met little William, a character whose
inclusion in <u>Frankenstein</u> gives another insight into Mary
Shelley's character.   Mary's own son was named William
(nicknamed Willmouse).   She described the character in the
book as follows:

> I wish you could see him;   he is very tall for his age,
> with sweet laughing blue eyes, dark eyelashes, and
> curling hair.   When he smiles, two little dimples ap-
> pear on each cheek, which are rosy with health;

In a letter written by Mary to Percy Shelley, she described
Willmouse: "The blue eyes of your Boy are staring at me
while I write this; he is a dear child, and you love him ten-
derly." It seems impossible that any mother could pattern a
character after her own son, and then dispose of that character in such a lingering fashion as when he met the Monster.

At first the Monster thought he had found a friend in
the innocent child.

> He struggled violently.   'Let me go,' he cried;
> 'Monster! Ugly wretch! You wish to eat me, and
> tear me to pieces--You are an ogre--Let me go, or
> I will tell my papa.'
>   'Boy, you will never see your father again; you
> must come with me.'
>   'Hideous monster! Let me go.   My papa in a
> Syndic--he is M. Frankenstein--he will punish you.
> You dare not keep me.'
>   'Frankenstein! Then you belong to my enemy--to
> him toward whom I swore eternal revenge; you shall
> be my first victim.'
>   The child still struggled and loaded me with epithets
> which carried despair to my heart; I grasped his
> throat to silence him and in a moment he lay dead at
> my feet.
>   I gazed at my victim, and my heart swelled with
> exultation and hellish triumph.

The Monster concluded his narrative with a bizarre yet understandable plea to his creator--as Adam was given Eve to abate
his loneliness.

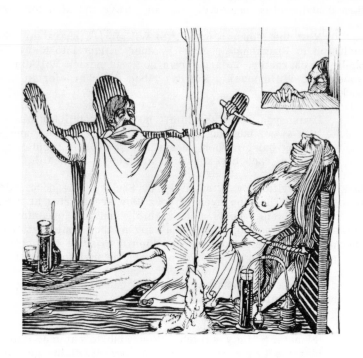

The Monster spies on the creation of his mate; illustration by Nino Carbe from World Publishing Company's 1932 edition of <u>Frankenstein</u>.

We may not part until you have promised to comply with my requisition. I am alone, and miserable; man will not associate with me; but one as deformed and horrible as myself would not deny herself to me. My companion must be of the same species, and have the same defects. This being you must create.

Victor Frankenstein reluctantly gave in to the Monster's demands. He retreated to a secluded area of Scotland, just off the sea. There he set up a laboratory and proceeded to create a horrible female being. The woman was never brought to life. Victor realized the possibilities

in setting another living monstrosity upon the world. Together they might not, as the Monster promised, leave and
never be heard from again; they could propagate a whole
race of murderous horrors. In desperation, Frankenstein,
under the Monster's observation, destroyed the lifeless body
of the would-be mate. Seeing his only chance at happiness
wrecked before his eyes, the Monster crashed into the laboratory and laid on the curse that would affect his creator in
the same way: "I will be with you on your wedding-night."

With the Monster's threat still tormenting him, Frankenstein learned that his best friend Henry Clerval had been
strangled to death by a strong hand leaving black finger
marks around his throat (the same marks found on William's
neck). There were now three murders weighing down Frankenstein's conscience.

There was no doubting the fact that the Monster intended to keep his nuptial date of murder. Nevertheless
Victor married the lovely Elizabeth. He left her for only
a moment in their house in the Alps. Obviously Frankenstein should have known better. The Monster had followed
him before. When Victor returned to the house Elizabeth
was strewn lifeless upon their bed. The Monster roared in
his triumph. Frankenstein attempted to kill the beast with
a pistol, but he escaped into the lake. A crowd of Frankenstein's friends rushed into the room at the sound of the gun-
shot but the killer had already disappeared.

Frankenstein then had but one reason to exist--the
destruction of the Monster whose creation had led to so
much misery. What Victor failed to recognize was (unlike
the popular interpretation of the theme and the later explanation given by Mary in her introduction, written after
the death of her husband and her discovery of religion) that
tragedy did not necessarily result from his emulating God.
In its own right he had performed a successful scientific
experiment. The flaw lay in his refusal to accept the responsibility of the creator as regards his creature.

Frankenstein embarked upon a seemingly endless pursuit of his Monster. The chase took him beyond Russia
toward the frozen wastes of the North (where the Monster
had planned to flee with his mate). There, while the sick-
ened Victor Frankenstein attempted to catch the Monster by
a furious dogsled chase, he was rescued from the biting
cold by Captain Walton.

Thus ended Frankenstein's account. He did not survive
much longer, as the elements had worn through his body's resistance. Aboard Captain Walton's vessel Victor Frankenstein
died, at last free of the Monster.

The gigantic form boarded the ship and learned to
his horror that Frankenstein--the only reason for his dreadful existence--was dead and could no longer assume the guilt
of his crimes. Nor could the Monster now receive forgive-
ness for his actions. The Monster's "God" was dead. Captain Walton listened as the ghastly creation delivered a lengthy
eulogy to his maker, then concluded with utter despair:

> 'But soon,' he cried, with sad and solemn enthusiasm,
> 'I shall die, and what I now feel will be no longer felt.
> Soon these burning miseries will be extinct. I shall as-
> cend my funeral pyre triumphantly, and exult in the
> agony of the torturing flames. The light of that con-
> flagration will fade away; my ashes will be swept into
> the sea by the winds. My spirit will sleep in peace; or,
> if it thinks, it will not surely think thus. Farewell.'

> He sprung from the cabin-window, as he said this,
> upon the ice-raft which lay close to the vessel. He
> was soon borne away by the waves and lost in dark-
> ness and distance.

When Frankenstein was first published, the reviews
were mixed, though mostly unkind. The Monthly Review
had these unfavorable words: "... an uncouth story, setting
probability at defiance, and leading to no conclusion either
moral or philosophical. A serious examination is scarcely
necessary for a vagary of the imagination as this tale presents." Sir Walter Scott wrote in the Edinburgh Review:

> When we have thus admitted that Frankenstein has pas-
> sages which appal the mind and make the flesh creep,
> we have given it all the praise (if praise it can be called)
> which we dare bestow. Our taste and judgement alike
> revolt at this kind of writing, and the greater the ability
> with which it may be executed, the worse it is.

Other reviews at the time were more charitable. The
March 12 issue of Blackwood's Edinburgh Magazine stated:

> Upon the whole, the work impresses us with the high
> idea of the author's original genius and happy power
> of expression. We shall be delighted to hear that

he had aspired to <u>paullo</u> <u>majora</u>; and in the meantime, congratulate our readers upon a novel which
excites new reflections and untried sources of emotion.

<u>The Edinburgh Magazine and Literary Miscellany</u> said:
"There never was a wilder story imagined; yet, like most
of the fiction of this age, it has an air of reality attached
to it, by being connected to the favorite projects and posses-
sions of the times. "

    <u>Frankenstein</u> does seem to have its flaws when read
today.   The writing style is extremely out of date and the
lack of scientific details is often frustrating.   Nevertheless
if one can read through such devices as an uninterrupted
soliloquy in archaic language running in excess of forty
pages, and dwell upon the basic inherent truths, especially
in regard to the relationship between maker and creature,
it can be found undeniably beautiful and meaningful.

    Mary Shelley returned to the theme of seeking eternal
life in a short story entitled "The Transformation. "   It was
published in <u>Keepsake</u> in 1831, the same year <u>Frankenstein</u>
was reprinted with her new introduction.   She was already
a widow.   Percy had drowned in 1822 when Mary was
twenty-four years old.   In 1835 her <u>Ladore</u>, an autobio-
graphical novel, was published.   For the remainder of her
life Mary Shelley did not remarry.   She was given pro-
posals by several eligible men but never accepted.   In the
years before her death in 1851 Mary spent a quiet life,
quite unlike her escapades with Percy, Lord Byron, and
company.   She died in the peaceful role of a loyal housekeeper.

<u>Frankenstein</u> is one of the most often reprinted novels in
the history of literature.   Though written over one hundred
fifty years ago, it is still a big selling item on virtually all
major paperback publishers' lists.   It is as widely read
today as when it was first published.   The book has been
translated into numerous languages and presented in many
formats.   A special "Photoplay" edition with photographs
from the 1931 movie was published that year by Grosset
and Dunlap.   A digest-sized "Armed Forces Edition" was
issued to servicemen during World War II.   Many editions
of <u>Frankenstein</u> have adapted the familiar visage of the
Boris Karloff Monster for their covers.   Others have gone

from original renditions to the purely abstract.

A number of works have been published about Mary
Shelley.   These include Shelley Memorials (1859), by Lady
Jane Shelley;   Shelley and Mary (1882), privately printed
family papers for Sir Percy Florence and Lady Jane Shelley;
Life and Letters of Mary W. Shelley (1886), by Mrs. Julian
Marshall;   La Jeunesse de Shelley (1910), by A. H. Koszul;
Mary Shelley (1928), by R. Church;   Mary Shelley: A
Biography (1938), by R. Glynn Grylls;   Mary Shelley,
Novelist and Dramatist (1938), S. Norman;   The Letters of
Mary W. Shelley (1944), by Frederick L. Jones;   Harriet
and Mary: Relations Between Percy Bysshe Shelley, Harriet
Shelley, and Mary Shelley, and T. J. Hogg (1944), by W. S.
Scott;   Mary Shelley's Journal (1947), edited by Frederick
L. Jones;   My Best, Mary (1953) (letters);   Mary Shelley,
Author of "Frankenstein" (1953), by Elizabeth Nitchie;   and
Mary Shelley (1959), by Eileen Bigland.

In the late 1960s there was an announcement in the
Hollywood film trade papers of a musical to be based on the
affairs of Shelley, Mary, and Lord Byron.   In 1970 Paul
McCartney, the former Beatle, was under consideration for
the role of Percy Shelley.   The film has still not been made.
In 1972, Haunted Summer, the same or possibly another
film about the Shelleys and Byron, was announced.

The Frankenstein Monster passed from Captain
Walton's sight.   But could there be true death for a creature spawned from the grave and partially inspired by
dreams of immortality?   Numerous popularizations in
several media came in the wake of the Monster.   He would
not die.

Notes

1.   Rosenberg, Samuel, "The Horrible Truth about Franken-
     stein," Life, vol. 64, no. 11 (15 March 1968), p. 77.
     Much of the information in this excellent article has
     been incorporated into this chapter on Mary Shelley.

2.   The term "robot" was first used in the Czechoslovakian
     Karel Capek's play R. U. R. --Rossum's Universal Ro-
     bots (1921).

3.   The contemporary French magician Robert-Houdin believed

this automaton chess player to be operated by an amputee inside. Others, however, believed the man-like machine to be an authentic automaton. Facts supporting both views are in the text and notes of the magician's book <u>Memoirs of Robert-Houdin</u>, translated by Milbourne Wraxall and published by Dover Publications in 1964 (with notes by Milbourne Christopher added to the work originally published by T. Werner Laurie, Ltd. in 1942). The book deals with other automata including a brazen living human head created by Roger Bacon and Thomas Bungay and an intelligent man of bronze created by Albertus Magnus.

4. Shelley used the legend as the basis for his lengthy poem <u>Prometheus Unbound</u> (1820).

5. Norton, Haywood P. , "Birth of Frankenstein," <u>Castle of Frankenstein</u>, No. 3 (1903), p. 49.

6. There was a legend about a monster in the Castle of the Frankenstein in Darmstadt, Germany [covered in this book in relation to the announced but never filmed motion picture, <u>Frankenstein's Castle</u>]. According to Mr. Rosenberg in that same <u>Life</u> letter column, it is possible that Mary Shelley had encountered the legend in her readings. But neither she nor her husband had ever visited Germany.

7. An edition of <u>Frankenstein</u> published in 1971 by the Oxford University Press, London, includes in its notes the original passages which Mary Shelley later rewrote.

8. In the Bantam Pathfinder paperback edition of <u>Frankenstein</u>, 1967, which featured a cover painting of Boris Karloff in his test make-up for the 1931 motion picture.

Chapter 2

FRANKENSTEIN HAUNTS THE THEATRE

As early as the first printing of the novel <u>Franken-</u>
<u>stein; or, The Modern Prometheus,</u> the adaptability of the
story to the dramatic stage was recognized. At the time it
was believed that the book had been written by Percy Bysshe
Shelley, since the text contained so many of his atheistic
and radical ideas. As Percy Shelley was too controversial
to have a novel even suspected of being of his authorship
presented on the stage, ideas for dramatizing the story
were abandoned.

By the time of Percy Shelley's death in 1822, Mary
Shelley had already become the acknowledged writer of the
novel. In 1823 the story was finally adapted to the stage in
at least five versions; two serious dramas (with possibly a
third yet to be documented)[1] and three comedies.

The first of the 1823 stage versions of the story was
the three-act "opera," <u>Presumption; or, The Fate of Fran-</u>
<u>kenstein</u> (also known as <u>Frankenstein; or, The Danger of</u>
<u>Presumption</u> and as <u>Frankenstein; A Romantic Drama</u>) writ-
ten for the theatre by Richard Brinsley Peake. Understandable changes were made in adapting the story to the
stage since the novel spanned much of the globe and presented many situations impossible to set or perform on a
stage. (The changes were indicative of future interpretations of the novel that would appear in other media.)
Peake's changes might have seemed drastic, especially to
people living in 1823 familiar with the novel. Elizabeth
was no longer Frankenstein's fiancée; she was his sister.
Frankenstein's love interest was Agatha de Lacey. The
scientist was given a superstitious servant named Fritz
who, unfortunately, was allotted too much time on stage
performing his bits of comedy. James Wallack played
Frankenstein.

Thomas Potter Cooke, the reknowned stage villain
whose portrayals included devils, sinister monks, killers,
and even Lord Ruthven, the bloodthirsty anti-hero of Polidori's The Vampyre, delighted in becoming the first actor
to portray the Frankenstein Monster (or Demon, as the
character was called in Presumption).   Cooke was born a
surgeon's son on 23 April 1786 in Titchfield Street, Maryle-
bone, England.   He spent considerable years in the Royal
Navy until his stage debut as Diego in The Watchword; or,
The Quiet Gate at Drury Lane, 19 October 1816.   "He was
the best representative of the British sailor ever seen on
the stage; was a noble, kind-hearted man, and had the interest of the dramatic profession sincerely at heart."[2]
Cooke's final stage appearance was as William in Black-
Eyed Susan at Covent Garden on 29 March 1860.

But Cooke's most famous role was that of the Frankenstein Monster, which he played 365 times.   As happened
to Boris Karloff over a century later, Cooke became identified with the role.   Cooke's characterization of the Demon
was strong, his make-up bizarre.   His eyes seemed bright
and watery and made a weird contrast against the yellow
and green greasepaint that coated his face.   The black hair
was very long and unkempt.   The lips were black and
usually held in a rigid position.   The arms and legs were
an ugly shade of blue and extended bare from the crude,
shroud-like clothing.

Frankenstein had lost his love, Agatha, and because
of his grief attempted to create a human being.   Fritz had
told Clerval (Elizabeth's intended husband) that his master
was engaged in a diabolical experiment in the laboratory
above the scientist's drawing room.   When Frankenstein was
about to bring the creature to life as a storm raged from
without the house, Fritz spied on him through a window.

Frank[3] - (within) It lives! It lives!
Fritz - (jumps down) There's a hob - a hob-goblin -
and 20 feet high - wrapped in a mantle.   Mercy -
mercy.
    falls down.   Frankenstein rushes in.
Frank - It lives.   It lives.   I saw the dull yellow
eye of the creature open - it breathes hard - and a
convulsive motion agitates its limbs.
he looks with terror to the door - fastens it and
descends the staircase.
What a wretch have I formed! his legs are in

proportion and I had selected his features as beautiful! Oh horror! his cadaverous skin scarcely covers
the work of muscles & arteries beneath - his hair
lustrous black, and flowing - his teeth of pearly
whiteness - but these luxuriances only form more
horrible contrast with the deformities of the Demon.
  Music - he listens.
It is yet quiet - what have I accomplished? The
beauty of my dreams has vanished! and breathless
horror and disgust fill my heart - for this I have
deprived myself of rest and health - and when I
look'd to reap my great reward - a flash break in
upon my darken'd soul, & tells me my attempt was
impious, and its fruition will be fatal to my peace
forever - (he listens again) all is still! - the dreadful spectre of a human form! No mortal could with-
stand the horror of that countenance - a mummy endowed with animation could be so hideous as the
wretch I have endowed with life! Fairest Agatha!
Never more dare I look upon your virtuous faces. -
  Music - Frankenstein on the couch -
Fritz - (looks up once or twice before he speaks)
Oh my nerves! I feel as if I had just come out of
strong fits, and nobody to throw water in my face.
Master sleeps, so I'll, if my legs won't lap up under
me - just - make my escape.
  The door of the Laboratory with a crash falls off
the hinges, as if forced by the Demon.
Fritz - oh -oh - (runs out hastily)
  Music - The Demon appears in the light of the
Laboratory - he looks around cautiously, descends
the staircase rapidly - surveys the apartment -
crosses to Frankenstein, and lays hand upon him.
Frank - (starts up) The Demon corpse to which I
have given life!
  (The Demon retreats, but looks at him intently)
Its unearthly ugliness renders it too horrible for
human eyes!
            (The Demon approaches him)
Fiend do not approach me - avaunt or fear the
fierce vengeance of my arm wreaked on your
miserable head -
  Music - Frankenstein rushes to the table and
  seizes a sword - aims a blow - The Demon
  catches the sword - snaps it - seizes Frankenstein - throws him violently on the floor -
  mounts the large window - loud thunder and

> vivid lightning - The Demon disappears at the
> window.

End of act the first. [3]

The Demon, as portrayed by Cooke, could not speak but only grunted. Cooke enacted the role sympathetically, as when the Demon displayed his sensitivity to light and air while roaming through the woods. When the Demon attempted to perform acts of kindness for Agatha's blind father, his son Felix and Frankenstein tried to destroy him. The brute looked imploringly at his creator but received in return a bullet from Felix's gun. In desperation, the Demon set fire to the blind man's house, ending the second act.

Unable to express himself verbally, the Demon decided to take revenge upon Frankenstein for not accepting him. First the Demon killed William, Frankenstein's little brother. Then during the wedding of Clerval and Elizabeth, the Monster slew Agatha.

The Demon tried to escape by rowing across the lake and to the mountains. But Frankenstein, no longer concerned with his own life, was in pursuit. The climax of the play was quick.

> Demon appears at the base of the
> mountain. Frankenstein follows.
>
> Cler. - Behold our friend - & his mysterious enemy -
> Felix - See - Frankenstein aims his musket at him -
> let us follow and approach him.
> Gyp - Hold masters - If the gun is fired it will bring
> down a mountain of snow on their heads. Many
> an avalanche has fallen there.
> Felix - He fires - Music
> Frankenstein discharges his musket -
> the avalanche falls and annihilates
> the Demon & Frankenstein.

The Curtain falls. [3]

The ending only partially satisfied the moralists who had picketed the theatre because of Percy Shelley's atheistic ideas and the concept of man creating man. To remove the pressure, S. J. Arnold, the producer of the play, stated, "The striking moral exhibited in this story, is the fatal consequence of that presumption attempts to penetrate, beyond prescribed depths, into the mystery of nature."

  Presumption; or, The Fate of Frankenstein premiered
on 28 July 1823 in London complete with its quaint songs
that interrupted the dialogue at various points. The play
was enthusiastically received. Mary Shelley herself attended
a performance of the play and later remarked:

> But lo and behold! I found myself famous. 'Franken-
> stein' had prodigious success as a drama, and was
> about to be repeated, for the twenty-third night, at
> the English Opera House. The playbill amused me
> extremely, for, in the list of dramatis personae,
> came '_____, by Mr. T. Cooke': this nameless
> mode of naming the unnamable is rather good. . . .
> Wallack looked very well as Frankenstein. He is at
> the beginning full of hope and expectation. At the
> end of the first act the stage represents a room with
> a staircase leading to Frankenstein's workshop; he
> goes to it, and you see his light at a small window,
> through which a frightened servant peeps, who runs
> off in terror when Frankenstein exclaims, 'It lives.'
> Presently Frankenstein himself rushes in horror and
> trepidation from room, and, while still expressing
> his agony and terror, ('_____') throws down the
> door of the laboratory, leaps the staircase, and
> presents his unearthly and monstrous person on the
> stage. The story is not well managed, but Cooke
> played _____'s part extremely well; his seeking,
> as it were, for support; his trying to grasp at the
> sounds he heard; all, indeed, he does was well
> imagined and executed. I was much amused and it
> appeared to excite a breathless eagerness in the
> audience."

T. P. Cooke, described as "the beau ideal of that speechless
and enormous excrescence of nature," continued to star in
the play, taking it to the English Opera House-- where Prince
Hermann Pückler-Muskau (1785-1871) had less kind words
than Mary to say about the play (in a letter dated 13 October
1826):

> Fatigued from my tour the day before yesterday, I
> passed the following morning in my own room. In
> the evening I visited the English Opera. The house
> is neither large nor elegant, but the actors very
> good. There was no opera, however, but hideous
> melodrames; first Frankenstein, where a human

being is made by magic,--a manufacture which
answers very ill; and then the Vampire, after the
well-known tale falsely attributed to Lord Byron.
The principle part in both was acted by Mr. Cooke,
who is distinguished for a very handsome person,
skilfull acting, and a remarkably dignified, noble
deportment. The acting was, indeed, admirable
throughout, but the pieces so stupid and monstrous
that it was impossible to sit out the performance.
The heat, the exhalations, and the audience were not
the most agreeable. Besides all this, the performance lasted from seven to half-past twelve,--too
long for the best.

--and to London's New Covent Garden in 1824. Later he
presented the drama for the Paris Grand Guignol. In 1825
the play was performed in New York. A comical version
of the play was presented by the "Senior Wranglers of
Brasenface College" (Brasenose College) in 1824 and showed
the creation of a mechanical man.

Although T. P. Cooke continued to play the Demon
in yet another version of Mary Shelley's story, he revived
Presumption; or, The Fate of Frankenstein in 1826 for the
English Opera House, and later at the Coburg. The play
continued to be revived and finally, in 1830, Cooke tired of
the role and gave the mantle of horror to an actor named
O. Smith. The latter actor also became typecast as the
Frankenstein Monster, so much that the English publication
Punch referred to him as "Lord Frankenstein" in an 1831
issue.

There was another serious theatrical version of Mary
Shelley's novel presented the same year that Presumption
opened. This other 1823 adaptation was simply titled
Frankenstein. The highly melodramatic play was performed
at London's Coburg and Royalty theatres. Finally in 1823
there was a trio of burlesque versions of Frankenstein. A
tailor named Frankenstein, later referred to as "Franken-
stitch" and as the "Needle Prometheus," was the leading
character in the first of these, presented at the Surrey
theatre. This Frankenstein created an artificial man from
the corpses of nine workmen. He skillfully applied his
talents with needle and thread, salvaging the best parts of
the nine bodies. The second comedy was Frank-in-Steam,
in which an ambitious student stole a body and thought he
had brought it back to life. What the student did not know,

however, was that his "corpse" had never actually died but
had been buried in a cataleptic state.   The play was enacted
at the Adelphi theatre.   The third of these comic plays,
presented at the David-Royal Amphitheatre, had a Parisian
sculptor give life to a statue of Aesop, which ran about the
stage in the person of a dwarf actor.

A rather offbeat version of Frankenstein was presented in Paris in 1826 at the Gaîté theatre.   The play was
Le Monstre et le Magicien ("The Monster and the Magician")
by Merle and Anthony and was again an alteration of Mrs.
Shelley's original conception.   Instead of showing science to
be the means of creating life, it was now the powers of
magic.   Furthermore the protagonist of the story was changed
in name from Frankenstein to Zametti.   In Le Monstre et
le Magicien, the Monster given life by Zametti managed to
survive the force of a bolt of lightning, and apparently continued to live through the end of the play, avoiding the traditional spectacular death.   The play was translated into English that same year and was performed at the West-London
Theatre.   In the role of the Monster was, understandably,
the Karloff of his day, T. P. Cooke.   Cooke was receiving
considerable publicity during his days at the first Frankenstein Monster.   During the time in which he was acting the
part he began to confuse the name of the creator Frankenstein with his nameless Monster.   There was more dignity
in referring to oneself as the actor who plays "Frankenstein" than the actor who is always cast as the "Demon" or
worse, "_____."   Mary Shelley was probably quite upset
at the mistake.   She had no way of knowing that the error
would continue for one and a half centuries.

The next opportunity for Cooke to don the guise of
Frankenstein's Monster was in the same year he did the
English-translated version of Le Monstre et le Magicien.
The new play, which opened at the Royal Cobourg Theatre
in London on 3 July 1826, was Frankenstein; or, The Man
and the Monster (also known as Frankenstein, or, The
Demon of Switzerland and The Man and the Monster; or,
The Fate of Frankenstein).   Written in two acts by H. M.
Milner, the drama was based both on Mary Shelley's novel
and Le Monstre et le Magicien.   The character of Frankenstein (a professor of natural philosophy) was played through
the years in this version by a number of actors including
a Mr. Robotham.   A young Henry Irving once played the
Prince del Piombino.

Frankenstein; or, The Man and the Monster took even
more liberties with Mary Shelley's story.   The play was set
in Sicily, where Frankenstein had left his wife Emmeline
and their child, and where he had become attached to the
household of the Prince del Piombino.   The Prince, interested in the arts and in science, found favor with Frankenstein's genius.   Frankenstein's laboratory was located in a
pavilion given to him by the Prince.   It was here that
Frankenstein recited monologues as heavy-handed as those
in the original Mary Shelley novel:

> SCENE SECOND.   (2nd Grooves.)   A nearer view of
> the outside of the Pavilion, appropriated as Fran-
> kenstein's study - practicable door, and trans-
> parent window above (dark).

> Enter FRANKENSTEIN from the Pavilion.

FRANK.   It comes--comes !   'tis nigh--the moment
that shall crown my patient labours, that shall gild
my toilsome studies with the brightest joy that e'er
was yet attained by mortal man.   What monarch's
power, what general's valour, or what hero's fame,
will rank with that of Frankenstein?   What can their
choicest efforts accomplish, but to destroy?   'Tis
mine, mine only, to create, to breathe the breath of
life into a mass of putrifying mortality;   'tis mine to
call into existence a form conceived in my own mo-
tions of perfection!   How vain, how worthless is the
noblest fame compared to mine?   Frankenstein shall
be the first of men!   And this triumph is at hand;
but a few moments and it is accomplished!   Burst
not, high swelling heart, with his o'erwhelming tide
of joy!

While Frankenstein toiled over his lifeless creation,
his servant Strutt continued to try winning the love of
Lisetta, daughter of the Prince's butler, providing some
mild comedy relief for the melodrama.   At last, after the
passage of some time, Frankenstein's project neared completion.

> SCENE THIRD.   -- The interior of the pavilion -
> folding doors in the back - on a long table is
> discovered an indistinct form, covered with black
> cloth - a small side table with bottles, and chem-
> ical apparatus, and a brazier with fire.

FRANKENSTEIN is discovered as if engaged in a
calculation.

FRANK. Now that the final operation is accomplished, my panting heart dares scarcely gaze upon
the object of its labours, dares scarcely contemplate
the grand fulfilment of its wishes. Courage, Frankenstein! glut thy big soul with exultation! enjoy a
triumph never yet attained by mortal man! (music -
he eagerly lays his hand on the bosom of the figure,
as if to discover whether it breathes) The breath of
life now swells its bosom. (music) As the cool
night breeze plays upon its brow it will awake to
sense and motion. (music - he rolls back the black
covering, which discovers a colossal human figure,
of a cadaverous livid complexion; it slowly begins to
rise, gradually attaining an erect posture, FRANKEN-
STEIN observing with intense anxiety. When it has
attained a perpendicular position, and glares its eyes
upon him, he starts back with horror) Merciful
heaven! And has the fondest visions of my fancy
awakened to this terrible reality; a form of horror,
which I scarcely dare to look upon; instead of the
fresh colour of humanity, he wears the livid hue of
the damp grave. Oh, horror! horror! let me fly
this dreadful monster of my own creation! (he hides
his face in his hands; the MONSTER, meantime,
springs from the table, and gradually gains the use
of his limbs; he is surprised at the appearance of
FRANKENSTEIN - advances towards him and touches
him, the latter starts back in disgust and horror,
draws his sword and rushes on the MONSTER, who
with the utmost ease takes the sword from him,
snaps it in two, and throws it down. FRANKENSTEIN
then attempts to seize it by the throat, but by a very
slight exertion of its powers, it throws him off to a
considerable distance - in shame, confusion, and
despair, FRANKENSTEIN rushes out of the apartment,
locking the doors after him. The MONSTER gazes
about it in wonder, traverses the apartment - hearing
the sound of FRANKENSTEIN'S footsteps without,
wishes to follow him, finds the opposition of the door,
with one blow strikes it from its hinges, and rushes
out.)

As Frankenstein moaned about the wretched creature
he had brought to life, Emmeline, carrying her child, and

Ritzberg, her father, were journeying through the storm-
drenched forest in search of the man who had left their
home in Germany. Ritzberg left the two for a moment in
order to discover a path. During his absence the Monster
appeared and became entranced by Emmeline's beauty. As
the thunder and lightning crashed throughout the woods, the
Monster kidnapped the girl. Later the artificially created
man coincidentally carried Emmeline to her father's house
where he warmed her by the fireplace. (The Monster did
not fear flames as he did in the numerous movie versions
of the next century.) Shortly, Ritzberg entered the house
and wounded the Monster with his gun. (Unlike later film
versions, bullets could kill this Frankenstein Monster.) Not
wishing to again feel the pain of a bullet, the Monster retreated from the cabin.

The Monster was unable to gain acceptance by the
human race. Out of revenge for his rejection the Monster
killed Julio, the young son of the Prince who was especially
fond of Frankenstein.

At a feast given by the Prince, Frankenstein learned
of the death by strangulation of Julio. He admitted his guilt
by proxy as Quadro, the Prince's butler, accused him of
murder. The corpse, said Quadro, was found in "Mr.
Frankenstein's" pavilion. Just then the Monster stormed
into the palace, dashing Frankenstein to the floor. The
Prince gave the command to fire, but the Monster's quick
arm snatched one of his officers, who took the bullet. Then
the Monster fled up the steps, roaring triumphantly, and
bringing down the curtain of the first act.

During the second scene of the second act, the
Monster again tried to kidnap Emmeline and also her child.
Bearing a flaming torch (quite unlike the movie version of
the Monster that was seemingly always being pursued by
torch-wielding peasants) the creature set fire to their house,
then braved the flames and carried away his two victims.

The novel Frankenstein was certainly a spectacle with
its grand locations. The play, Frankenstein; or, the Man
and the Monster provided its own, though different, spectacle
in the final scenes. The Monster had fled with his two human victims into the mountains. Pursuing the Monster was
a posse made up of peasants and led by Strutt. The Monster had tied Emmeline, using a rope taken from his waist,
to a pillar of rock. He began to lumber toward her child

as Frankenstein ascended the wall of the mountain. Frankenstein pleaded with the Monster to spare his child, but
the living horror indicated the wound given by mortals. Then
Emmeline's ingenuity provided the solution to Frankenstein's
plight as she managed to take a small flageolet from under
her dress and began to play. The music soothed the savage
beast. The Monster went through a series of deep emotions
until he was forced to lie down from exhaustion.

That was the moment required by Strutt and the
peasants to act. They attacked him as a vengeful unit,
their numbers overpowering and binding him securely. The
creature struggled valiantly, hurling one of the peasants
from the mountaintop. At last he was bound to the moun-
tainside. After the peasants left to celebrate their defeat
of the inhuman killer, the Monster broke his bonds and
lowered himself with the rope down the chasm. As the
peasants celebrated with wine in the cave of a hermit, the
Monster again charged into them. Strutt rushed upon him
with a knife and plunged the blade into his back. Roaring
in agony, the Monster removed the dagger and fled the
chamber.

The final scene of the play brought creator and
created together for a last encounter. The Monster was
climbing up the side of the crater of Mount Etna, an active
volcano seemingly on the verge of eruption. (The impressive prop crater occupied the middle of the stage.) Fatigued
from his wound, the Monster was unable to put up much of
a battle against Frankenstein, who was following him up the
rocky incline. As Frankenstein lunged for him, the Monster
stabbed him with Strutt's dagger. The lifeless body dropped
into the waiting arms of Emmeline. There was no escape
now for the Monster, as soldiers and peasantry were swarm-
ing about him from all sides. In desperation he climbed
toward the apex of the steaming, flashing volcanic crater.
As they began to fire their guns, the Monster leapt into the
boiling inferno. The curtain fell as Emmeline, Strutt, and
the others paid respect to the corpse of Frankenstein.

A third play using the Frankenstein theme in 1826
was first presented on October 9 at the Opera Glass. Titled
The Devil Among the Players, this poetic dramatization featured three characters of horror--Frankenstein (probably the
Monster, as Cooke fostered the mistake in calling the creature by its creator's name), Faust, and the Vampire. (Such
combining of famous characters into one story became a

technique employed in later years by motion picture studios.)
Prometeo Moderno ("Modern Prometheus"), a version of
Frankenstein using the original novel's sub-title, was performed at various theatres including the Adelphi, the Victoria, the Covent Garden, the Surrey, and Sadler's Wells,
and later in theatres in the United States.

Another comic adaptation was presented on Christmas
day in 1849, Frankenstein; or, The Vampire's Victim. The
play not only featured the Frankenstein Monster, but also
Zamiel, another contemporary horror character. The musical called attention to its own divergence from Mary
Shelley's book as one actor sang, "You must excuse a
trifling deviation,/ From Mrs. Shelley's marvelous narra-
tion/ ...." In this drama the Monster was given life in a
halo of blue light. Realizing its own wretchedness, the
creature roared, "I oughtn't suppress/ My raging organ of
destructiveness/ ...." Later the Frankenstein Monster was
defeated by the magical power of music. Again music tamed
the savage beast, as in Frankenstein: or, The Man and the
Monster.

One of the most offbeat of all the stage versions of
the story was a burlesque by "Richard-Henry" (Richard
Butler and H. Chane Newton) titled both The Model Man
and simply Frankenstein, which was presented in 1887 at
London's Gaiety Theatre. The young German medical student Frankenstein seemed to have undergone a primitive sex
change operation for the character was now played by Miss
Nellie (Ellen) Farren. Miss Farren was the Gaiety's top
star. Born in 1846, the daughter of Henry Farren and
granddaughter of William Farren the elder, both important
personages in the history of the theatre, Nellie began her
professional career on the London stage when only eight
years old and pleased even the most difficult audiences.

In the role of the Monster, "Frankenstein's Invention," was the Gaiety's second greatest star, Fred Leslie.
His interpretation of the Monster was hardly terrifying.
Leslie combed his hair straight down and wore an outfit including high boots, a large coat with an enormous flower in
the lapel, a hat, and a monocle in his eye. His own prominent nose and chin completed the bizarre, comic interpretation. In some scenes the Monster paraded about in the costume of a ballerina.

Born Frederick Hobson on 1 April 1855 at 56

Fred Leslie as a hardly monstrous Frankenstein Monster,
Gaiety Theatre, London, 1887

Artillery Place in Woolwich, England, Leslie wanted to be
an actor ever since childhood.   As a youngster Leslie put
on his amateur productions using a makeshift stage.   At
sixteen he quit school to become an actor and began to perform in amateur plays.   Eventually he changed his last name.
In 1878 Leslie received his first professional part, that of
Colonel Hardy in Paul Pry at the Royalty.   Fred Leslie was
not a handsome man.   His features were strong, his chin
large;   he vaguely resembled William Bendix.

When Leslie joined the Gaiety, he made an excellent
teammate for Nellie Farren:

> but for the moment the limelight must switch to
> something more important, to the new star at the
> Gaiety, who was to take it, in an ideal partnership
> with its own Nellie Farren, to even greater heights
> than it had yet achieved.   There must be a 'chord on'
> and a loud and great round of welcoming applause for
> that artist of true genius--Fred Leslie. [4]

Apparently vampires were becoming an established
part of the Frankenstein mythos as this musical comedy
included vampires that plagued the village of Villasuburba in
the Pass of Pizzicato.   There were other new characters
including Spanish bandits, Mary Ann (Emily Cross;   later,
Maria Jones), also called "A Maid of Mystery," and a
goblin (Cyril Maude), a character reportedly so terrifying
that he was cut from the script after only a few performances.

While Mary Ann and the Vampire Visconti (E. J.
Lonnen) visited villainy upon the village, Frankenstein revealed her creation.   "A nameless dread doth in my bosom
lurk," said Frankenstein.   "My scheme is good--but what
if it won't work?"   Frankenstein's invention was a mechanical man.   The Monster gained some humanity by learning
not only to speak but also to sing such numbers as "Love
in the Orchestra" which permitted him to mimmick various
musical instruments.   The Plot became involved as the
Monster discovered love in Spain and eventually became
another victim of the vampire.   All of these incidents were
broken up by songs and ballet numbers performed by the
Gaiety Girls.

In the third and final act of The Model Man, the
Monster attempted to be admitted into the Junior Vampire's

Clubland and kidnapped the heroine. The vampire, and
later Frankenstein, tracked the Monster to the Arctic.
There the ice weakened the vampire. As Frankenstein and
the Monster met, the region was illuminated by "human
stars" through the power of yet another fantastic character,
Tambourina, Goddess of the Sun (Sylvia Grey). The show
ended with the numerous weird characters frolicking about
the stage.

The premiere performance of The Model Man on
Christmas Eve was a real fiasco. The regular group of
theatregoers who sat in the pit claimed that their place had
been transformed into stalls. Before the curtain arose on
the first act, these patrons began to complain until they
had caused a tremendous uproar that sounded throughout the
overture. When the play began no one could hear the songs
or lines for a veritable riot was taking place in the audience.
The appearance of Nellie Farren somewhat brought down the
row, as did her duet of "Five Ages" with Fred Leslie, who
pretended that everything was indeed running without inter-
ference. The patrons in the less expensive seats applauded
when the ballet dancers came on the stage while those in
the pit demanded that they not perform. The theatre was
soon an uproar of shouts and threats and applause, with the
people in the stalls and boxes yelling contrary to those in
the pit. It was a night which left more horror in the memories of the players than the play itself had given to the
audience.

The Last Laugh was another farce using the Frankenstein theme. It played New York in 1915.

In 1927 Frankenstein returned to sobriety as Peggy
Webling wrote her own theatrical adaptation of the Mary
Shelley novel. The play premiered in London that year at
the Preston. It re-opened on 10 February 1930 at London's
Little Theatre, with Henry Hallat as Henry Frankenstein.
Miss Webling had taken the liberty of interchanging the
name of Victor Frankenstein with that of his best friend
Henry. Hallat played the part with melodramatic gusto,
raving how he had created life "no matter by what means. "

Hamilton Deane, whose acting debut was with the
Henry Irving Vacation Company in 1899 and who had adapted
Bram Stoker's Dracula to the stage in 1924, appeared in the
1927 Frankenstein as the Monster, with discolored flesh and
a thick mop of hair. His clothing was covered with a clay-

Hamilton Deane as the Monster, London, Little Theatre,
1930.

like layer making him resemble the Golem of silent films.
(Bela Lugosi also created a Golem-like look for his screen
test as the Monster for the 1931 movie, apparently basing
his make-up on that of Hamilton Deane.)

The Monster as portrayed by Deane was sympathetic.
He was confused by life and death and discovered his humanity through the kindness of a young crippled girl (played
by dark-haired Dora Patrick). At the side of a river, the
pathetic creature, unaware that death can be caused by
drowning, placed the girl's head beneath the water to see
her lovely face through the glassy surface. In other scenes
the Monster was entranced as he beheld the sun for the first
time; he asked why men hated him; and he threw his glass
of wine out of a window and then drank water from a rose
bowl.

The Monster fell in love with Frankenstein's fiancée.
She was captured by him but finally escaped his grasp.
When Frankenstein refused to create a female for him, the
Monster killed his maker. Then pleading to God for mercy,
he waited in the laboratory and allowed a bolt of lightning to
end his artificial life. The reviews of this version of Frankenstein were only fair. Nevertheless the play was a tremendous success. Hamilton Deane traveled with the show
and presented it on alternate nights with Dracula, performing
the lead roles of literature's two greatest monsters. The
Graphic for 22 February 1930 said, "... it would be idle
to pretend that Frankenstein is a very noteworthy play.
Written with romantic confidence and great volubility, there
are times when we wish that the authoress would cut the
cackle and come to the monster." Its review of Hamilton
Deane's portrayal of the Monster was more charitable:

> Mr. Deane, who plays the part of the servant-
> monster Frankenstein, invests his performance with
> even more imaginative power than he invested Dra-
> cula. The elemental pain that streaks across his
> eyes, the inarticulate twistings of his great red
> mouth, would be a credit to Mr. Charles Laughton
> or to Sir Henry Irving. This is a fine piece of
> acting in which the ugliness is far more than skin-
> deep.

The Peggy Webling dramatization of Frankenstein
came under the interest of motion picture director Robert
Florey, and eventually James Whale, when Universal

Pictures decided to film the story. Much of the original
script was retained, with a variation of the scene wherein
the Monster drowned the crippled girl, and with more
changes for the motion picture screen. The script was
adapted for the film by John L. Balderston.

Although Peggy Webling died in 1947, her name continued to haunt Universal Pictures--primarily the legal department. The original agreement made between Universal
and Balderston and Miss Webling stipulated that they would
receive $20,000, plus one per cent of all gross earnings of
Frankenstein. In 1952 Balderston claimed that their original
conception had been used by Universal in all their succeeding Frankenstein movies made over a period of fifteen years.
Balderston and the Webling estate wanted to settle the matter out of court. Their lawyers advised them to the contrary. The case was subsequently taken to court.

An article in the 9 July 1952 issue of Variety stated:

Following two days of arguments in the suit of John
L. Balderston and the estate of Peggy Webling
against Universal Pictures Company, Inc., Superior
Court Judge Arnold Praeger had ordered the plaintiffs to file a new complaint and set Sept. 2 as the
date of the new hearing.

The plaintiffs asked for due payment for Universal's
seven subsequent Frankenstein movies. The studio, however, contended that these films were not based upon the
"dramatic composition" (as stated in the contract) of the
two writers. A settlement was finally reached in May,
1953. Universal was able to get all rights involving their
version of the Frankenstein Monster. In return the studio
gave the plaintiffs a considerable sum believed to exceed
$100,000.

A one-act satirical play titled Frank and Mr. Frankenstein was written by Alfred Kreymborg and performed in
1935. The nature of this play is not known. A serious
version of Frankenstein was performed in 1936. Again, as
with the original novel and the 1927 version, the drama was
written by a woman, Miss Gladys Hastings-Walton. Pre-
miering in Glasgow, this adaptation of Frankenstein at last
remained quite faithful to Mrs. Shelley's concept. Miss
Hastings-Walton tried to show the very real horror of man's
being replaced by the machines that he created.

During the early 1940s a comic play, <u>Goon with the
Wind</u> was presented by the drama department at Fairmont
Public School in Manion, Indiana.   This particular amateur
production is significant in that a very young James Dean
portrayed the Frankenstein Monster with a built-up forehead
and make-up similar to that of Boris Karloff.   Dean's per-
formance got him elected president of the elementary school's
Thespian Society.   Perhaps the role of the Frankenstein
Monster was inevitable.   James Dean's middle name was
Byron, as Lord Byron was his mother's favorite poet.

There were yet other stage versions of <u>Frankenstein.</u>
During the 1950s a play using the Frankenstein Monster and
theme was produced in Bangor, Pennsylvania by Lee Rich-
ards.   The make-up for the Monster was patterned after
that of Karloff.   There was also a stage-play titled <u>The
Maniac</u> in which the actor portraying the Monster, in a
Karloffian mask made by the Universal make-up department,
played a game of cards with a magician and a skeleton.
<u>Get the Picture</u>, a satire about <u>Frankenstein</u> and local poli-
tics, was performed during the mid-1960s at Chicago's
LeShow theatre.   Glenn Howard portrayed Dr. Frankenstein,
while Judy Corrigan played a female Monster with crossed
eyes and a fright wig that stuck out from her head as though
charged with electricity.   In 1967 the San Francisco Mime
Troupe, a member of the Radical Theatre Repertory, presented a street play of <u>Frankenstein</u> in which the Monster's
face was at least part of the time wrapped up in bandages
in the fashion of a mummy.   There were numerous adaptations of <u>Frankenstein</u> on the stage, some quite faithful to
the original concept, some strangley original.   The most
incredible of all theatrical versions was yet to come.

<u>"He Said I Looked like Boris Karloff"</u>

A digression from <u>Frankenstein</u> in the theatre that
bears inclusion here is Joseph Kesselring's "madcap murder
farce," <u>Arsenic and Old Lace</u> which opened on Broadway in
1941.   The three-act play starred Boris Karloff as Jonathan
Brewster, a mad, sadistic killer.   Although other actors including Bela Lugosi have played that role the part was obviously written especially for Karloff.

Originally Kesselring had intended to write a serious
melodrama.   But as the play was rehearsed it became obvious that he had created an ingenius farce where an

incredible number of murders could be used to get laughs from the audience. The Brewster family was unique in that madness was hereditary. The two sisters, Abby and Martha Brewster, seemed harmless enough. In their compassion for lonely old men, they gave them drinks of elderberry wine (spiked with arsenic), then put the bodies in charge of brother Teddy, who in his belief that he was President Roosevelt buried these "fever victims" in the canals he was digging in the cellar. The most bizarre member of the family was Jonathan Brewster whose face seemed familiar to fans of horror movies with its stitched scars. Jonathan, fleeing from the police because of his murders, returned to the Brewster house with his partner Dr. Herman Einstein.

> ABBY. (Stepping down to stage floor.) Have you been in an accident?
> JONATHAN. (His hand goes to side of his face.) No--(He clouds)--my face--Dr. Einstein is responsible for that. He's a plastic surgeon. He changes people's faces.
> MARTHA. (Comes down to ABBY.) But I've seen that face before. (To ABBY.) Abby, remember when we took the little Schultz boy to the movies and I was so frightened? It was that face!
> (JONATHAN grows tense and looks toward EINSTEIN. EINSTEIN addresses AUNTS.)
> EINSTEIN. Easy, Chonny--easy! (To AUNTS.) Don't worry, ladies. The last five years I give Chonny three new faces. I give him another one right away. This last face--well, I saw that picture too--just before I operate. And I was intoxicated.

That picture was obviously Frankenstein. Mentioning to Jonathan who he resembled could arouse him to murder. "He said I looked like Boris Karloff," Jonathan remarked when asked why he killed one of his victims. When Karloff spoke that line on the stage it was one of the high moments in the play.

Jonathan learned that his aunts were also adept at murder and had tied him in the number of victims. The brute attempted to claim one more victim to best his aunts, all while brother Mortimer Brewster tried getting rid of him and placing Teddy in a mental institution. Jonathan was finally apprehended after attacking a policeman who said, "Look at that puss. He looks like Boris Karloff."

The reviews of <u>Arsenic and Old Lace</u> were excellent.
"Maddest and most hilarious comedy of many seasons," said
Richard Watts, Jr. in the <u>Herald-Tribune</u>. "Just about the
maddest, craziest comedy of our time," stated Harold V.
Cohen in the <u>Post-Pittsburgh Gazette</u>.

<u>Arsenic and Old Lace</u> was extremely popular, run-
ning on Broadway alone for 1444 performances. In 1944,
Warner Brothers, which had purchased the screen rights to
the play, released the motion picture version of <u>Arsenic
and Old Lace</u>, brilliantly directed by Frank Capra. The
film boasted as almost impeccable cast, including Cary
Grant as Mortimer and Peter Lorre as Dr. Einstein. An
outstanding mistake was the casting of Raymond Massey in
the Jonathan Brewster role. Massey wore a make-up em-
phasizing deep, stitched cuts, sunken cheeks, and straight
hair to suggest the Karloff Frankenstein Monster. His performance was perfect in its own right. Yet the role
screamed for Karloff himself. Unfortunately, Karloff was
unavailable since he was still doing the play on stage and
had already demanded too much money for starring in the
film.

Karloff was available, however, to star in at least
two radio dramatizations of <u>Arsenic and Old Lace</u>. The
comedy was presented with Karloff on <u>The U. S. Steel Hour
Presents the Theatre Guild on the Air</u> the same year the
play opened on Broadway. On 25 November 1946 Karloff
did the play, drastically edited down to a half hour, on
<u>Screen Guild Theatre</u>. Karloff also did the play twice on
television--on <u>The Best of Broadway</u> (CBS, 5 January 1955)
with Lorre again as Dr. Einstein and on <u>Hallmark Hall of
Fame</u> (NBC, 5 January 1962) in color. In 1969 the play
was updated by Luther Davis as an ABC special. Fred
Gwynne (Herman Munster of <u>The Munsters</u>) was made-up to
resemble a stitched and scarred Karloff and imitated the
British actor's voice. The most famous line in the play,
however, had been changed to "He said I looked like the
Frankenstein Monster." The line seemed pointless, did
not produce any laughs and might have been funny had it
been "He said I looked like Herman Munster." Karloff had
died shortly before this version of <u>Arsenic and Old Lace</u>
was presented. Without Karloff in the role created for him,
the play could never entirely recapture its former charm.

The Living Frankenstein

The strangest stage adaptation of <u>Frankenstein</u> was
created by the Living Theatre, a company of the Radical
Theatre Repertory, a commune of free-thinking performers
directed by Julian Beck and his wife Judith Malina.   The
Living Theatre originated in the mid-1950s in a Manhattan
apartment, the idea of Beck and his wife.   At first the
company performed "avant garde" plays and Greek classics.
While on a European tour, the Living Theatre began to re-
hearse their spectacle <u>Frankenstein</u>.

There was little of Mary Shelley in Julian Beck's
version of <u>Frankenstein</u>.   The play opened with the various
cast members seated around "The Victim" (Mary Mary),
a girl upon whom they concentrated so that she would be
levitated off the stage.   If the levitation proved successful
there would be no play.   If unsuccessful (which was always
the case) the play would go on ... and on, lasting six hours
in the uncut version.   (An abridged version ran three and
one half hours.)

As the girl failed to levitate she was tossed screaming wildly into a coffin.   From that point the stage erupted
into a series of murders and executions in numerous brutal
ways, with the long-haired members of the cast screaming
and howling and running through the audience.   Dr. Frankenstein (played by Beck) entered the scenes of violence and
began to dismember the various corpses so that the dead
could be given new life.   While Dr. Frankenstein labored on
his Monster, Jewish cabbalists imitated him by building a
female Golem (played by Brigit Knabe).   Sigmond Freud
(Steven Ben Israel) assisted in the creation of the Frankenstein Monster.   Blood was pumped into the corpse creation
of Frankenstein.   A mystical third eye was transplanted to
the creature's naval.   The first act ended as twenty acro-
batic members of the cast draped themselves over a huge
scaffold that dominated the stage.   Dr. Frankenstein's
nurse (Pamela Badyk) shouted, "He's opening his eyes !"
Then the actors on the scaffold writhed, the lights dimmed,
and the monstrous composite of twenty human beings peered
out at the audience with red burning orbs, ending the first
of the three acts.

The second act showed Dr. Frankenstein's futile attempt to communicate with the Monster.   Instead the Monster slept and the Living Theatre actors portrayed his

thoughts. When the creature awoke it was in the person of
a single actor, played in various performances by Israel
and by Henry Howard. He told of the perversity of man in
a passage taken directly from Mary Shelley's Frankenstein.
The actors moved about the giant framework to show what
transpired within the Monster's mind. Such diverse legendary stories as those of Icarus, the Minotaur, and the Four
Horsemen of the Apocolypse were incorporated into the plot.
Before the second act's curtain dropped, the Monster killed
Dr. Frankenstein's assistant, who taunted him with a blazing
torch (as in the 1931 movie). When Dr. Frankenstein
learned of the killing he fled. The Monster expressed
anguish at the deed and revealed himself to be a part of
all of us.

In the third act the Monster proceeded to kill his
way through various members of the cast who were reciting
parts of Ibsen's plays. At last the creature again encountered Dr. Frankenstein. They attempted to destroy each
other but resulted in exchanging kisses. The act inspired
the various characters in the play to free their prisoners,
who were being executed for their legal offenses. In the
climax of the play the characters seemed to engage in acts
of love. Then they froze, with the giant version of the
Monster beaming out at the audience and with a voice saying
that the law will not allow them to go on any further.

The Living Theatre did not work from a standard
script. Attempting to share an experience with the audience, the company worked from a basic skeletal script that
had originated as a poem, written in 1965 by Beck in
Velletri, Italy. The piece was titled simply the Frankenstein Poem. An example of the poem, which formed the
basis of the scenario written in Munich and the final synop-
sis composed in Venice, is:

act two

we are inside the monster's head
the eye opens
it's the creation mocked
sight light
a sample from the blue grotto
moths die in coca cola
frying psyches
an ice pick dance
he sees karloff's eye open

the creatures sees all this
and exclaims the exclamations of the monster
has terrible growth odors and instruments
he decomposes as he goes peeling decay
a net dredging the night for victims who are drained
    of blood like ducks and dessicated like mummies

The script itself when eventually put down for the
sake of formality was unbelievably short for such a long
and involved production. It runs some two pages when
printed and gave the actors an opportunity to improvise and
carry on in their own ways. The first act commenced with
the following description of "The Action":

The Doctor Implants the Victim's Heart in the Body
    on the Laboratory Table.
Foot, Brain, and Eye Are Grafted.
The Failure of the Heart.
Paracelsus Appears and Directs the Graft of the
    Third Eye.
Freud Appears and Orders the Sexual Graft.
Norbert Wiener Appears and Advises the Use of
    Electrodes.
The Electrodes are Attached.
The Creature Moves.

The premiere performance of Beck's Frankenstein
was on 26 September 1965 at the Bienalle Festival in Venice,
in the Teatro La Perla. In October the production moved
to Berlin where it was filmed in toto and broadcast over
television in November.

The play eventually came to the United States where
it met mixed reviews. Glenna Syse wrote in the 11 January
Chicago Sun-Times after Frankenstein opened at Mandel Hall:

It is completely unique, often totally theatrical,
funny, devastating and notably ingenius.... Everything that Judith and Julian Beck devise seems to be
so very pleased with its point that it makes it time
and time again with the insistence of a trip hammer.
Length I can take (even shows that finish well after
midnight) but repetition is a childish indulgence that
The Living Theater should have sworn off ages
ago.... As a whole 'Frankenstein' is the perfect
foil for The Living Theater's peculiar talents. I
don't think there is anyone in the cast that really

knows how to speak as an actor.   Given a sentence,
they sound dreadful.   But each and every one of
them know what to do with their body and their
larynx.   Give them a contortion and a howl and they
can really perform.

After the show played for a single night at the University of Southern California on 25 February 1969, critic
Dan Sullivan said in the February 27 Los Angeles Times:

> Scenically, it is spectacular--a three-story jungle-
> gym set with tricky lighting effects and a wonderful
> air of decayed German expressionism. . . .   But the
> Living Theater's tendency to do its own thing no
> matter what makes 'Frankenstein' a much deader
> show than it should be.

> The company's penchant for animal cries, for ex-
> ample, becomes very wearing after a time and too
> many scenes--for instance, when everyone in the
> company gets arrested at the end of the play--go on
> long, long after you have got the point. . . .   I am
> afraid that more than one nap was taken in USC's
> Bovard Auditorium Tuesday night as 'Frankenstein'
> lumbered along to midnight.   In fact, I can testify
> to it.

Life magazine in its 4 April 1969 issue was even
less kind: ". . . despite spells of genuine theatrical excitement, it lapses into undisciplined formlessness that is both
boring and banal. "

Except for the creation of the Monster from parts of
corpses, the Living Theatre's Frankenstein took little from
Mary Shelley.   What the play continuously emphasized was
that our society was conceived in violence and thrived upon
it to survive.   Only by reconstructing society through peaceful revolution can man escape his violent nature.   The creature of Frankenstein was not destroyed at the end of the
production.   As we have all contributed to the creation of
the Monster, it is also our task to contend with it--or destroy it.

A Return to Tradition . . . to an Extent

The Frankenstein theme had become a youth-oriented

property following the Living Theatre version. I'm Sorry,
the Bridge Is Out, You'll Have to Spend the Night, a musical
comedy with a youthful cast, premiered at Hollywood's Cor-
onet Theatre on 28 April 1970.   This satire of the horror
films of the 1930s and 1940s featured Dr. Victor Frankenstein (Stan Zalas, who imitated Karloff most believably) his
Monster (first played by John Ian Jacobs; later by Steve
Dalen) and the stitched results of two previous experiments,
servants Sam and Charlie (Scott Halloran and Lou Claudio);
also, Count Ladislav Dracula (Peter Virgo, Jr. ; later by
the show's original Monster, John Ian Jacobs); Igor, the
hunchback hanged five times, a combination of Quasimodo
and Ygor from Son of Frankenstein (Richard Miller; later
Tony Lane); Prince "Rex" Talbot, the effeminate Wolf
Man; the Mummy and his high priest Dr. Nassar; Count-
ess Natasha Dracula, the insectivorous Renfield, and a
group of vampire girls; and the body snatchers and their
corpse.

The play was written by Sheldon Allman and Bob
Pickett with much affection and included numerous "in" lines
taken from the scripts of old horror films.   The play was
directed by Maurine Dawson who made sure that all the
characterizations had sustained authenticity.   Dr. Frankenstein's main objective was getting a suitable brain for his
nearly brainless Monster for the sole reason of having someone to call him "Daddy."   When the storm brought down the
bridge, John David Welgood and his pretty and innocent
fiancée Mary Helen Herriman were forced to take refuge in
the castle.   The couple, as were most in that situation in
the old films, were naive.   They did not suspect that Dracula, the Mummy, the Wolf Man, Igor and all of the other
fiends in the building wanted them for various reasons.

The Frankenstein Monster was portrayed as a lovable
sort of creature.   Made-up with green Universal Pictures-
type features sans electrodes by artist Pete Colby, and
wearing a heavy white fur vest, he had an innocent liking
for flowers and usually grinned.   Dr. Frankenstein wanted
young Wellgood's brilliant brain for the Monster.   Igor's
brain would go into Wellgood's perfect body.   The Monster's
cranial matter would be dumped into Igor's skull.

One of the play's funnier moments was the confrontation of the Monster and the Mummy.   Neither of the two
creatures could speak and spent considerable time merely
grunting and stiffly waving their arms at each other.   At

last they broke the centuries-old generation gap with a dance
and lumbered through the secret door that led to the laboratory.

The brain-swapping experiment never took place.
The Mummy, learning that the operation would delay or even
prevent the sacrifice of virginal Mary Helen to the Egyptian
god Amon-Ra, dispatched Dr. Frankenstein, Igor, and his
own mentor Dr. Nassar, and freed his new friend, the
Monster. Eventually all of the monsters were destroyed or
cured by various means. They did not stay destroyed. As
each of the various creatures returned to life the villagers
chorused that the monsters always came back because that
was the way the fans wanted it.

Certainly the villagers and singing fiends of that play
were speaking the truth that the classic horrors would always return. The producer of Hair has announced his plan
to do a musical version of Frankenstein. This writer wonders if the proposed play will feature a scene of irate naked
villagers picketing the castle of a pro-establishment Dr.
Frankenstein.

Alive! On Stage! In Person!

The Frankenstein Monster has continued to be featured on the stage, even as a character in puppet shows
like Les Poupées de Paris. During the 1940s a stage actor
acquired the rights to use the name Karloff, doing a comedy
act as "Tony Karloff, the Son of Frankenstein." When the
monster stars of Abbott and Costello Meet Frankenstein did
a personal appearance stage tour in 1948 actor Glenn Strange
wore the first in the line of Don Post rubber Frankenstein
masks. Other shows at the time advertised their Monster
as portrayed by Strange, who along with Universal knew
nothing of the deception. Strange learned of the fraud when
members of his family wanted to see him backstage and
were flatly refused entry.

The Monster was featured in countless live horror
shows that played motion picture houses in the 1940s, 1950s,
and 1960s, oftentimes scheduled at midnight. With names
like House of the Living Dead and Terrors of the Unknown
(the latter with North Carolina television personality Philip
Morris) and posters boasting "Alive!!! On Stage! In Person!
Direct from Hollywood! FRANKENSTEIN MONSTER!" the

Larry M. Byrd in his own Monster make-up, Leavenworth, Halloween 1962.

various monsters appeared after a performance of stage
tricks by Magicians called Dr. Evil (Morris), Dr. Satan,
Dr. Silkini, and others.   The monsters appeared at the end
of the show and were always disappointing.   The Frankenstein Monster was never more than someone in old clothes
and a Post mask.   Sometimes a film strip of lightning
(usually the familiar shot from Bride of Frankenstein) was
projected on the screen.   The lights dimmed to total darkness and eerie music sounded through the public address
system as the monsters stalked toward the audience.   It is
questionable whether or not they ever entered that audience
made up of screaming girls and boyfriends who proved their
courage by throwing whatever was in their hands.   One such
show that played Chicago claimed that its Frankenstein Monster was played by the stuntman who doubled Karloff and
Lugosi in that role.   The claim was never verified nor dis-
proven.

When the Twentieth Century-Fox horror film The Fly
was first released in 1958, actors "flown in from Hollywood"
were made up as various famous creatures including a green-
faced Frankenstein Monster.   The monsters rushed down the
theatre aisles to avoid the usual barrage of flying popcorn
boxes and rubberband-propelled paper clips.   In the 1950s
the Strip City burlesque house in Hollywood did a musical
show titled Frankenstein and His Bride.   In a Halloween
show Larry M. Byrd played the Frankenstein Monster and
did his own Karloffian make-up.   The dormant Monster was
carried on stage in a coffin.   Suddenly the Monster came
to life, broke his bonds, strangled the announcer, and lumbered toward the audience.   A skating Frankenstein Monster
was featured in the 1970 Ice Capades.   And the Monster
was spoofed in a comedy scene presented in 1972 at the
Birdcage Theatre of Knott's Berry Farm, Buena Park,
California.

The story of Frankenstein and his Monster was first
dramatized on the stage.   In that medium the legend became
popular entertainment.   But most of those early versions
would be virtually forgotten by the time Mary Shelley's
classic was adapted to the motion picture screen.

Notes

1.   Sam Moskowitz has stated that there were three serious
     versions done at the time, in "The Sons of Franken-
     stein," the second chapter of his book, Explorers

of the Infinite, Cleveland, World Pub. Co.,
p. 41.
2. Scott, Clement, The Drama of Yesterdy and To-Day (London, 1899), p. 153.
3. Quotations are from the original manuscript of the play, then titled Frankenstein, a Melo-Dramatic Opera, by permission of The Huntington Library, San Marino, California.
4. W. Macqueen-Pope, Gaiety: Theatre of Enchantment (London, 1949), p. 221.

Chapter 3

THE SILENT FRANKENSTEINS

Frankenstein proved to be a commercial film property even in the days of silent movies. Within one ten-year period, three versions of Mary Shelley's novel were filmed, establishing a record for adapting the original story within so short a time.

The first motion picture ever to use the name "Frankenstein" in the title was the misleading Frankenstein's Trestle, made on July 26, 1899 and copyrighted in 1902. For a long while it was naturally assumed that the film, made by the American Mutoscope and Biograph Company, was a Frankenstein film. The production ran only ten feet in 16mm and film historians wondered how much of Mary Shelley's plot could be squeezed into such a short piece. When the film was finally uncovered it proved a disappointment to Frankenstein buffs. Frankenstein's Trestle was but a single shot, photographed by Billy Bitzer in the White Mountains, showing a train crossing a bridge, belonging to a town called Frankenstein.[1] Purists might rationalize that Victor Frankenstein and his Monster were riding on that railroad, but it seems more likely that the footage was taken merely to show off the area's most impressive means of transportation.

The first legitimate motion picture version of Frankenstein was made in 1910 by Thomas A. Edison's film company. According to the script, Frankenstein the film was "A Liberal Adaptation of Mrs. Shelley's Famous Story." The screen's first interpretation of the Frankenstein Monster was apparently created by Charles Ogle, an actor working for the Edison company at the time and who had acquired a reputation for villainous roles. The Monster was hunchbacked and shaggy chested, and wore crude attire like that of Quasimodo. The hands were clawlike and somehow not complete. Most hideous was the face, stark white with

Charles Ogle, the first movie Frankenstein Monster, in
Edison's 1910 <u>Frankenstein</u>.

dark eyes, large forehead, and a mountain of matted hair.

Directed by J. Searle Dawley, Edison's _Frankenstein_ retained little from the original novel, making it more than a "Liberal Adaptation." Frankenstein (no first name revealed) left his "sweetheart" (no name given) and father in order to study at college. There he became engrossed in the artificial creation of a human being. He told of his plan to create life in a letter.

Sweetheart,
Tonight my ambition will be accomplished. I have discovered the secrets of life and death and in a few hours I shall create into life the most perfect human being that the world has yet known. When this marvelous work is accomplished, I shall then return to claim you for my bride.

Your devoted,
Frankenstein

It was two years since Frankenstein left for college. In his laboratory the scientist proceeded to create life. But the life he would create would not be the most perfect human being he had envisioned. According to one of the film's subtitles, "Instead of a perfect human being the evil in Frankenstein's mind creates a monster." The actual formation of the being was quite different from the standard conception of assembling the body from the parts of many corpses. The Monster was formed with blazing chemicals. As _Frankenstein_ is one of the many silent films that has been lost to time (along with the other two versions) it is valuable to relate the creation of the Monster as described in this excerpt from the script, dated 14 February 1910.

4-   The Laboratory Again.
Frankenstein completing his work. Lights the fire in the cauldron--closes the iron doors--bolts same and stands watching the result through small opening in door.

5-   Interior of Cabinet.
Showing the first developing process of creating this human being.

6-   Flash Scene Showing
Frankenstein on the Outside

Realizing That His Experiment Has Been
Successful.

7-   Cabinet Scene.
            Still showing the development.

8-   Flash Scene Outside.
        Frankenstein in Great Excitement.

9-   Interior Scene.
        Flesh begins to creep over the bones.

10-   Flash Scene--
        Frankenstein in Great Joy.

11-   Cabinet Scene.
            The Monster almost completed.

12-   Exterior Flash Scene.
        Frankenstein in horror and fear at the
        result.

13-   Interior Scene.
            Completion of the monster.

14-   Outside Scene.
            Frankenstein realizes that he has created
        a monster and tears himself away from the
        door and stands watching in terror.   The
        iron bars are broken from the doors.   Door
        slowly opens and the hand of the monster
        appears as Frankenstein dashes off.

        Frankenstein was nursed back to health by his father
and sweetheart after becoming sick with the realization of
his deed.   He became a morbid person, as only his evil
and unnatural thoughts allowed the experiment to succeed.
His marriage date was set.   But as Frankenstein sat in his
study he saw the ugly image of the Monster reflected in his
mirror.   Even worse, Frankenstein's sweetheart was approaching the room.   Frankenstein concealed the Monster
behind the curtains, then convinced his sweetheart to only
stay a short while.   She gave him a rose before she left
the room.

        The Monster again confronted Frankenstein whom he

regarded as his God and master.   Jealous over the woman,
the Monster took the rose.   Frankenstein reacted and the
two characters engaged in a struggle, during which the
scientist was cast to the floor.   The Monster then saw his
ghastly reflection in the mirror and fled the room in terror.
"Haunting his creator and jealous of his sweetheart for the
first time the monster sees himself," the title revealed.
Unable to live alone, the Monster returned on Frankenstein's
wedding night.   He realized that the bride separated him
from his creator and lumbered toward her room.   When
Frankenstein entered the room his wife fell at his feet.
"On the bridal night, Frankenstein's better nature asserted
itself," said the film caption.   Again Frankenstein struggled
with his creature and was thrown aside.   The climax of
Frankenstein, introducing some aspects of the Jekyll-Hyde
theme, was described in the 15 March 1910 issue of the
Edison Kinetogram:

> Here comes the point which we have endeavored to
> bring out, namely: That when Frankenstein's love
> for his bride shall have attained full strength and
> freedom from impurity it will have such an effect
> upon his mind that the monster cannot exist.   This
> theory is clearly demonstrated in the next and closing
> scene, which has probably never been surpassed in
> anything shown on the moving picture screen.   The
> monster, broken down by his unsuccessful attempts
> to be with his creator, enters the room, stands be-
> fore a large mirror and holds out his arms entreat-
> ingly.   Gradually the real monster fades away, leav-
> ing only the image in the mirror.   A moment later
> Frankenstein himself enters.   As he stands directly
> before the mirror we are amazed to see the image
> of the monster reflected on Frankenstein's own.
> Gradually, however, under the effect of love and his
> better nature, the monster's image fades and Fran-
> kenstein sees himself in his young manhood in the
> mirror.   His bride joins him, and the film ends
> with their embrace, Frankenstein's mind now being
> relieved of the awful horror and weight it has been
> laboring under for so long.

Then the concluding title: "The creation of an evil mind is
overcome by love and disappears."

Although Frankenstein was a silent movie made in
the days before color, there was music and tint.   The

script suggested that theatre orchestras play "Then You'll
Remember Me" for the opening; selections from "Melody
in F'" as the Monster was created; selections from "Der
Freischütz" as the creature appeared over Frankenstein's
bed; "Annie Laurie" while Frankenstein returned home;
the bridal chorus from "Lohengrin" until the guests left the
wedding; and "Der Freischütz" again until the end.   Various scenes were tinted to convey emotions; the creation
scene showed the heat of the laboratory through yellow and
orange.   Two reviews of Frankenstein stated:

> [1] The formation of the monster in the cauldron of
> blazing chemicals is a piece of photographic work
> which will rank with the best of its kind.   The en-
> tire film is one that will create a new impression
> that the possibilities of the motion picture in re-
> producing these stories are scarcely realized.

> [2] In the course of his research he discovers the
> awful mystery of life & death and immediately deter-
> mines to realize his one consuming ambition--to
> create the most perfect human being that the world
> has ever seen.   The actually repulsive situations in
> the original version have been carefully eliminated
> ... no film has ever been released that can surpass
> it in power to fascinate an audience.   The scene in
> the laboratory in which the monster seemed gradually
> to assume human semblance is probably the most re-
> markable ever committed to a film.

What Edison's Frankenstein Monster had in ugliness,
the second movie version of the creature lacked.   The Monster, or "Brute Man" as he was referred to in the 1915
Ocean Film Corporation Life Without Soul, starred Percy
Darrell Standing without any of the grotesque trappings of
Charles Ogle.   Standing, a husky actor capable of sustaining a brutish scowl, wore no distinguishing make-up as the
creation of Frankenstein.   For reasons known only to script
writer Jesse J. Goldburg, the commerical name of "Frankenstein" did not appear in the title, although the film was
acknowledged as an adaptation from Mary Shelley's novel.
Director Joseph W. Smiley, billed in the film's advertising
as the "Preceptor of Directors," did what no other director
has yet done in filming Frankenstein.   Smiley realized the
potential in location work, as the novel had a global scope.
He took his cast, including William Cohill as Frankenstein,
Lucy Cotton as Elizabeth, George De Carlton as

Lucy Cotton ("Elizabeth") and Percy Darrell Standing in the 1915 Life Without Soul.

Frankenstein's father (doubling behind the cameras as the supervisor of production), Jack Hopkins, Pauline Curley, Violet De Biccari, and David McCauley, to a number of impressive locations. Life Without Soul was shot in Metropolitan New York, the mountain regions of Georgia, Arizona, Florida, and on a steamship on the Atlantic.

A young medical student, Frankenstein, created a Brute Man. The creature had no soul and almost no intelligence. Frankenstein realized that he had created a monstrosity as the Brute Man began to dominate his life. Within the five-reel length of the picture the Brute Man killed Frankenstein's sister, best friend, and wife. Frankenstein, exhausted from all the horror he had inadvertently unleashed upon the world, shot the brute and died. Life Without Soul suffered from a technique so unfortunately common in silent movies dealing with unnatural forces. A frame was provided in which one of the characters read the story of the film from a book. After Frankenstein expired the book was closed and all of the characters were shown to be alive and healthy. This lessened the horror and the impact of the story. Film-makers at the time usually felt that audiences would not accept the depiction of the supernatural or pseudo-science as real and that such stories inevitably had to be revealed as dreams, the tales of madmen, and the like.

The advertising for the movie began with a quotation of Frankenstein: "I Have Challenged the Almighty and am Paying the Penalty!" There were the usual catch-lines: "Transcending anything heretofore attempted in motion pictures, it will live in the minds of the public for years to come." And, "An extraordinary five-part feature of intense dramatics, deep pathos, pulsating heart-interest, and a love theme that brings you back to youthful years."

Life Without Soul premiered for people in the motion picture business on 21 November 1915 at 3:45 P.M. at the Candle Theatre in New York. The projectionist apparently wanted to get through the picture as quickly as possible for he cut each reel short. Consequently the film was somewhat confusing. Additional titles were later inserted into the footage, clearing up much of the story. The reviews of it were favorable. According to the 4 December 1915 edition of The Moving Picture World:

In adapting the story for the screen, Mr. Goldberg

[sic] has troubled neither himself nor his future patrons with the psychological aspect of the theme. If one wishes to read deeper meaning in the fate of man who aspires to grasp the power of omnipotence, he must do so without assistance. The author of 'Life Without Soul' has been guided by but one purpose--to build a photoplay which appeals to the emotions rather than to the intellect, and is at all times good entertainment by reason of its directness and cohesion of plot and the strangeness and attractiveness of its theme. The picture easily fulfills its mission. Supplemented by the resources and excellent judgement of the director Joseph W. Smiley, and the equally efficient acting of the cast, the author of 'Life Without Soul' has wrought a photoplay of distinct merit. Great diversity of incidents and scenes, of views into deep chasms, wild glades, desert sands and the ocean's wide expanse, are intermingled with glimpses of the young scientist bending over his creation in his laboratory and of tranquil home life.

The most valuable member of the cast is Percy Darrell Standing. His embodiment of the man without a soul adequately conveys the author's intent. He is awe-inspiring, but never grotesque, and indicates the gradual unfolding of the creature's senses and understanding, with convincing skill. At times, he actually awakens sympathy for the monster's condition--cut off, as he is, from all human companionship.

And in the 11 December 1915 issue of <u>Motion Picture News</u>:

The story is impossible and the difficulties encountered in its production were great, the main being to make a convincing picture of an entirely imaginative story.

At times the picture refuses to convince, but its interest is always averagely high because of the theme's unusualness.

... On the whole the direction of the picture is in keeping with the story, though there are one or two slips which catch the hypercritical eye.

The photography and locations are two of the picture's pronouncedly strong features.

A third silent version of <u>Frankenstein</u> was made in
Italy. The motion picture went back to the original name
only deleting two letters (more to accommodate the Italian
tongue than any other reason). <u>Il Mostro di Frakestein</u>
(translated as "The Monster of Frakestein") was made in
1920 by Albertini Film--UCI. Scripted by Giovanni Dro-
vetti, directed by Eugenio Testa, and photographed by
De Simone, the film starred Luciano Albertini as Frakestein and Umberto Guarracino as the Monster. Unfortunately
all that is known of the plot of <u>Il Mostro di Frakestein</u> is
that there was a confrontation between creator and creature
in a shadowy cave. The Edison <u>Frankenstein</u>, <u>Life Without
Soul</u>, and <u>Il Mostro di Frakestein</u> unfortunately no longer
exist. No prints survive and the films are known only
through publicity and reviews.

The Jewish Frankenstein

Although there were only three legitimate silent
versions of <u>Frankenstein</u>, the theme--wherein man creates
man artificially--was quite popular. The Golem, the monster of Yiddish mythology, formed from lifeless clay and
given life, was the most enduring of these creatures and a
basis for the conception of Frankenstein's Monster.

In a sense Adam was the first Golem. In the
Jewish <u>Talmud</u> the Bible's first man is thus described:

> How was Adam created? In the first hour, his
> dust was collected; in the second hour, his form
> was fashioned; in the third, he became a shapeless
> mass [<u>golem</u>]; ... in the sixth he received a soul;
> in the seventh hour, he rose and stood on his
> feet. ...

The legendary Golem was first given screen life in 1914.
It was a sustaining life that has kept the creature lumbering
about films through present times.

Tales surrounding various golems may be traced
back to the <u>Talmud</u>. There were numerous legends about
various holy men who gave life to clay through the secret
name of God (or the tetragrammaton [<u>Shem-Hamforesh</u>]).
Consequently there were many golems. Rabbi Raba created
a speechless golem that would otherwise appear human,
according to the <u>Agada</u> of the <u>Talmud</u>. The golem's origin

was discovered by Rabbi Zeira who reduced the creature to dust as Raba had "tampered in God's domain.." The Talmud also relates the creation of a golem-calf by Rabbis Hanina and Oshaga through the Book of Creation. The calf would be consumed on the Sabbath. A golem maid-servant was supposedly given life by Solomon ibn Gabirol of Valencia. Both a poet and philosopher, he was nearly executed by the king for practicing black magic, until he reduced the golem to dust to prove she was not human. A mute golem bodyguard was reputed to be the creation of Rabbi Samuel in France during the Crusades.

Most of these golems were virtually human in appearance. It was, however, the Golem of Chelm which would give the creature a new image, that of a Frankenstein-type monster. This version of the golem legend would provide the basis for all of the motion picture adaptations. Rabbi Elijah created this golem, according to Yiddish folk tales, during the mid-1500s. The Rabbi wrote down the Shem-Hamforesh on a parchment which he placed in the creature's forehead. Like Frankenstein's Monster, this golem became a living horror, destroying much in the city of Chelm, and seemed dangerously able to spread his wrath world-wide. Rabbi Elijah, as did Victor Frankenstein, realized that man must not create man, removed the secret name of God, and returned his golem to dust.

The most famous of the golems was the Golem of Prague, from which the motion picture versions of the legend were in part taken. (Storywise, films were based on the Golem of Prague, while they adapted the image and characterization of the monstrous Golem of Chelm.) The legendary creature dates back to the sixteenth century. The Golem story has been recounted in books such as Phantasmagoriana (one of Mary Shelley's favorites), but most superbly by Chayim Bloch[2] in his book The Golem: Legends of the Ghetto of Prague (Vienna: 1925), translated from the German by Harry Schneiderman: During the sixteenth century in the Jewish ghetto in Czechoslovakia, the Rabbi Loew[3] saw the terrible oppression of his people by the gentiles. Many non-Jews believed that the people in the ghetto used the blood of Christians in their Passover festivals. Oftentimes gentiles, usually the conniving priest Thaddeus who had a fanatical animosity toward the Jews, acquired a child's corpse and placed it where it could be found and linked to Jewish sacrifice. In order to protect his people, Rabbi Loew decided to create a spy and bodyguard from clay to

prowl the ghetto streets.   At times the Golem would even
be made invisible by the Rabbi, making him even more ef-
fective.   The clay form was shaped by Rabbi Loew with the
help of two loyal men.   The creature lay like a corpse
awaiting the infusion of life.

> Then, Rabbi Loew bade the Kohen walk seven times
> around the clay body, from right to left, confiding to
> him the Zirufim (charms) which he was to recite
> while doing this.   When this was done, the clay body
> became red, like fire.

> Then Rabbi Loew bade the Levite walk the same
> number of times, from left to right, and taught him
> also the formulas suitable to his element.   As he
> completed his task, the fire-redness was extinguished,
> and water flowed through the clay body;   hair
> sprouted on its head, and nails appeared on the fin-
> gers and toes.

> Then Rabbi Loew himself walked once around the
> figure, placed in its mouth a piece of parchment in-
> scribed with the Schem (the name of God);   and,
> bowing to the East and the West, the South and the
> North, all three recited together: 'And he breathed
> into his nostrils the breath of life;   and man became
> a living soul' [Genesis ii, 7].

With the combination of the elements Fire, Water,
Air, and Earth, the Golem came to life.   He was a mute
creature of incredible strength.   But he was of such perfection that he was accepted as a man by the populace.
Rabbi Loew realized the value in his deception and named
his creation Joseph Golem.

Rabbi Loew learned many things pertinent to his
people's survival through the Golem.   The Rabbi had stressed,
however, that the Golem must never be used for non-
sacred tasks.   When the Golem was commanded to do mundane jobs trouble resulted.   Once a small flood happened
when the Golem was carrying pails of water with no order
to eventually stop.   When performing the acts for which he
had been created, the Golem fulfilled his missions.   At
times he gave Rabbi Loew information that could only have
come from supernatural sources.   On one occasion Joseph
Golem went wild for lack of anything to do.   The people in
the ghetto panicked as his awesome form threatened to

destroy all life and property.   Only the sudden appearance
of Rabbi Loew brought the Golem under control.

In 1593 Rabbi Loew decided the Golem had become
obsolete, as the threats against the Jews regarding Passover had ceased.   The Golem would be destroyed, reversing
the procedure which gave him life.   Again the Golem was
a lifeless statue.   The creature's clothing was burned and
his cold remains stored in the garret of the Altneu Synagogue in Prague.   (An almost obscure legend followed this,
saying that the Golem's remains were smuggled out of the
synagogue in an attempt to restore it to life.   Although the
ritual of Rabbi Loew was repeated, the Golem did not walk
again.   Almost simultaneously a plague broke out killing
two members of the house into which the Golem had been
smuggled.   There could be little doubt that this was punishment for their sacrilege.   The two people dead from the
epidemic were placed within a single coffin.   The Golem
was put into the second casket, then buried under Gallow
Hill, near Neistaedter Gate on the Vienna state road.   The
most widely accepted story, however, is that the Golem
was left in its lifeless state in the Altneu Synagogue.)   Thus
ends the original legend of the Golem of Prague.

Almost four centuries later the Golem was adapted
to the motion picture screen by the great silent film actor-
director Paul Wegener.   While doing location filming in
Prague for a 1913 supernatural horror film entitled Student
von Prag ("The Student of Prague") made by the German
Bioscop production company, Wegener encountered and became fascinated by the legends of the artificially created
being that predated Frankenstein's Monster by hundreds of
years.   Wegener immediately saw the screen potential in
the traditional story and in 1914 his Bioscop company made
the first movie version of Der Golem (retitled The Monster
of Fate for English audiences by the Hawk Film Company).
Wegener himself played the part of the Golem.   In his interpretation the creature could not possibly have passed as a
human being.   Wegener's Golem was truly a monster, his
face clay-like, his hair seemingly carved from stone, his
boots heavy.   This was indeed a worthy predecessor to the
later Frankenstein Monster of the talkies.

Der Golem was directed by both screenwriter Henrik
Galeen and Wegener himself.   The story was contemporary
and showed how the lifeless Golem was discovered in the
ruins of an old synagogue by workmen and sold to an

antiques dealer. Using the holy texts of the Kabbala the
dealer was able to bring the monster to life. The Golem
was used by the antiquarian as a slave, performing a number of chores. But when the creature of clay met the
dealer's lovely daughter (played by Lyda Salmonova,
Wegener's wife) he fell in love, thus igniting the true spark
of humanity--the soul. Naturally the girl was repulsed by
the awkward, lumbering monstrosity. The Golem went berserk and eventually fell from the summit of a tower to his
death.

For many years Der Golem was considered one of
the many films that would never be screened again, a fate
befallen the silent versions of Frankenstein. A print was
miraculously discovered in 1958 by Paul Sauerlaender, a
European film collector. The owner of a toy store in
Europe was selling old 35mm movie projectors and giving
his customers small lengths (from twelve to fifteen feet)
of silent film which turned out to be this original Golem
feature. Luckily for the sake of film history Sauerlaender
was able to track down the various owners and emerge
from the hunt with a complete print of Der Golem.

The Golem's film career was only beginning. Another version of Der Golem was directed in 1916 by Urban
Gad. Paul Wegener's association with the Golem was also
just beginning. His second film in the series Der Golem
und die Tänzerin ("The Golem and the Dancing Girl") has
presented a mystery to film historians. The Bioscop film
of 1917 may or may not have been made. All that exists
of the film is a set of still photographs. No one reported
ever having seen the finished motion picture. It has been
stated[4] that the film was never screened outside of Germany because of World War I. Whether the picture was
actually made or was only planned by Wegener complete
with publicity stills, still the plot remains intriguing and
offbeat. It was not a horror film but a comedy. Reportedly, Wegener played himself. He attended a motion picture theatre that was showing his original Golem production.
While viewing himself on the screen he noticed that a dancer Olschewska (Salmonova) was so fascinated by his bizarre characterization that she wished to have the Golem
as her own property. Again Wegener put on the heavy
guise of the monster and shipped himself to the dancer's
hotel. After returning to "life" the "Golem's" attempts to
scare the girl resulted in romance with Olschewska. Her
reaction to the creature was quite the opposite of the girl

Paul Wegener as the living creature of clay in the 1920 film
Der Golem. Left is Ernst Deutsch as "Famulus" and right
is Albert Steinruch as "Rabbi Loew."

in Der Golem.   Feminine tastes apparently changed within
a mere three years.

The most important Golem film was made in 1920
by the German company UFA.   Der Golem: Wie er in die
Welt Kam ("The Golem: How He Came into the World") was
the most authentic as far as the actual legend was concerned.
It was set in the fifteenth century and written and directed
again by Wegener and Galeen.   Wegener, who had become
so identified with the role that the mere showing of a picture of himself as the monster freed him during the war
after his capture as a spy, again assumed the coarse disguise of the giant.

Wegener used sets to illustrate the Jewish ghetto.
The film's special effects man Carl Boese suggested to
Wegener that the great German architecht Professor Hans
Poelzig, out of work since the end of World War I, be
given the assignment of designing the sets.   Kurt Richter
had the sets built in a faithful reproduction of the ghetto.
The gothic atmosphere, photographed by Karl Freund, in-
spired the village set recurring in the later Universal
Frankenstein films of the 1930s and 1940s.

In the film story, the Imperator of Prague had de-
creed that all Jews leave Prague as they were practitioners
of black magic.   Rabbi Loew (Albert Steinruck) had the
solution to his people's problems.   With the help of his
assistant Famulus (Ernst Deutsch) the Rabbi carried the
heavy statue of the Golem, which he had fashioned in an
underground crypt, to a closet upstairs.   Later Rabbi Loew
read in an ancient volume on sorcery that the Golem would
live if a certain magic word were placed in the amulet
(shaped like the Star of David) on its massive chest.   Waving his magic wand Loew beckoned: "Astaroth, Astaroth,
appear, appear--speak the word!"   The demon face of the
unnatural entity Astaroth appeared as Loew watched from
a circle of holy flame.   Famulus became terrified at the
strange rite.   The elements raged with hurricane and smoke
as the demon whispered the sacred word to its invoker:
"A-E-M-A-E-R."   Then Astaroth disappeared.   Hastily
Rabbi Loew jotted down the mysterious word and placed the
paper within the amulet.   The Golem lived!

Carl Boese told[5] how the change was effected between statue and man (Wegener).   According to Boese it
was done on screen before the cameras!   Rabbi Loew was

to fumble with the paper upon which the magic word was
written.   His action supposedly attracted the attention of
the viewers who never saw the four men remove the statue
and Wegener take its place.

Famulus became the Golem's guide, giving it commands and explaining its nature to the public.   The function
of Famulus in the film might be compared with the role of
Ygor in the later Son of Frankenstein and Ghost of Frankenstein.   The Golem was taken to the emperor's palace where
it terrified everyone with its superhuman strength.   It sup-
ported the ceiling which had begun to cave in upon the
Rabbi's magical gesture.   The emperor rewarded Loew by
pardoning the Hebrews.

The Golem's work had ended and Rabbi Loew decided
he should again be nothing more than inanimate clay.   But
Famulus had other designs on the Golem.   Famulus restored
the life taken away by the Rabbi and sent the monster to
kidnap Miriam (Lyda Salmonova again) whom he loved but
who preferred another man.   Toward the end of the film
the Golem showed bravery foreign even to the Frankenstein
Monster (shown in many films as being afraid of fire) and
set fire to the home of Rabbi Loew.   Its motive was to
counter the attack of Famulus, who realized that the Golem
had attained a soul by falling in love with Miriam.   Like
the 1931 Frankenstein Monster who discovered his humanity
through a little girl, so did the Golem through Miriam.
And as the Monster was hunted down for his act, so would
the Golem be sought for destruction.

A girl child had an even more direct effect upon the
Golem's downfall.   The giant of dark clay encountered a
number of children playing.   Only one girl refused to flee
in terror from the creature.   Fascinated by the brave
child, the superpowerful Golem let her fingers roam about
its barrel chest and snatch away the mystical amulet.   The
monster was again a useless statue.

We can see this Golem as the great forerunner of
the later Frankenstein films.   An artificially created being
was given the gift of life only to eventually turn upon humanity as a violent horror that must be destroyed.   The
main differences between the Golem and the Frankenstein
Monster were the forces that brought them to life--the
first, magic;   the second, science.   The results were
nevertheless the same.   Der Golem: Wie er in die Welt

Kam established the format for the later Frankenstein films.
Many of the situations depicted in this silent classic were
to become standard Frankensteinian situations.

During the 1920s another Golem feature was reportedly made.   Although many film scholars deny that the picture ever went beyond a publicity poster, the great German
director Fritz Lang has assured that Alraune und der Golem
was filmed.   The poster showed the typical Wegener-type
Golem looming behind the seated demon Mandrake.   Made
by Jupp Wiertz, the film supposedly starred Nils Chrisander
and Guido Seeber and presented not only the Golem but the
infamous Alraune, [6] in a sense a Frankenstein-type creation
of a scientist who artificially inseminated a prostitute with
the sperm of a hanged criminal, producing from this unholy
union a cruel female child.

The Golem remained an inert figure of clay until
1936 when the story was filmed as a talkie, Le Golem, by
the French company Metropolis Pictures, and directed by
Julien Duvivier.   The picture had a flair of authenticity as
it was made on location in Prague.   Rudolph II (Harry
Baur) practiced the black arts and consequently oppressed
the ghetto Jews.   There was a need for Rabbi Loew's Golem, silent for so many years.   This version of the Golem
followed the general mold of Wegener's; but the creature
as portrayed by Ferdinand Hart was almost completely bald,
not sporting the massive wig worn by Wegener, and was
cloaked in a long soiled cape.

Rabbi Jacob (Charles Dorat) located the Golem which
had been in storage for years.   He inscribed God's name
on the Golem's forehead.   The creature returned to life,
broke its chains, and bent its prison bars.   Then the Golem
went on its errand of destruction, destroying armies and
most of Prague.   Rudolph's friend met a most grisly death
under the foot of the lumbering Golem.   The effect was
quite impressive and was achieved by duplicating his face
on a balloon that was squeezed under the Golem's heavy
foot.   With its work completed the Golem was again reduced to lifeless matter as Rabbi Jacob removed the sacred
name.   In a less than convincing effect the Golem's image
was printed on a piece of glass which was then shattered
before the camera.   Unfortunately the background fell apart
with the monster.   One is curious as to why the Golem did
not likewise disintegrate when Rabbi Loew removed the name
from its forehead so many years before. [7]

The Golem was far from remaining dormant.   Like
Frankenstein's Monster, it would be restored to life with
the usual results.   A Czech comedy <u>Cisaruv Pekar a
Pekaruv Cisar</u> (released in the United States as <u>The Emperor and the Golem</u> and also known as <u>Return of the Go-
lem</u> and <u>The Golem and the Emperor's Baker</u>) was made in
color by the State Film Studios in 1951 and directed by
Martin Fric.   This Golem resembled a stone King Kong,
bound at the waist by bolted metal bands, with steam shooting from the mouth.   This was the least human appearing
Golem.   Emperor Rudolph II (Jan Werich) of Prague learned
that the Golem still existed in the ghetto and ordered his
men to find it.   The creature again came to life and was
tamed in the end by the Emperor's baker (also played by
Werich), who promptly put the monster to work in the
bakery.

Four Golem films were planned in 1959 but never
made.   Versions of <u>The Golem</u> were announced by producer
George Pal's Galaxy Company, by the Mirische Company,
and the Frankel-Davis Company, the latter to have been
made in color and stereophonic sound, with a $3,000,000
budget.   <u>The Mask of Melog</u> (Golem spelled backwards) was
to be written by Weaver Wright (pen name for Forrest J
Ackerman).

The monster of clay walked again in <u>Le Golem</u>,
made by ORFT and directed by Jean Kerchbron in 1966.
That same year the British company Goldstar filmed a
Golem story simply called <u>It</u> (released in the United States
by Warner Brothers-Seven Arts), directed by Herbert J.
Leder.   The Golem (Allan Sellers), now a very stone-like
giant with wrinkled face and pointed head, was discovered
in the ruins of a burned warehouse.   Roddy McDowall portrayed the psychotic museum curator who inevitably brought
the Golem back to life to add to his problems (which included pampering the mummified remains of his mother,
who in life had apparently helped drive him psycho).   The
Golem was used to kill the curator's enemies and even
wreck a bridge.   Predictably the army was called upon to
drop the favorite weapon of 1950s science fiction films, the
atomic bomb.   Although the master was destroyed, the
Golem survived.   With no one to command it, the Golem
lumbered into the sea.   The most distinguishing feature of
<u>It</u> was the exuberant performance of McDowall as the mad-
man.   <u>Prague Nights</u>, a trilogy film of 1969, was made in
Czechoslovakia.   The third part is entitled "The Last Golem."

A German film Homo Vampire was listed in 1972 with the
English title The Golem's Daughter.

Notes on the Golem

        The Golem stories have appeared in many forms.
Most famous and literary remains The Golem, a novel by
Gustave Meyrink (translated by Madge Pemberton in 1928),
first published in 1915 by Kurt Verlag, Leipzig. The novel
took Athanasius Pernath, a cutter of precious stones,
through an adventure in which he attempted to learn his
true nature. Haunted by weird visions, premonitions, a
desire to help the needy, and by the legend that the Prague
Golem appears every thirty-eight years, he might actually
be the Golem come to life again. A more recent novel
The Sword of the Golem, by Abraham Rothberg, published
in 1971 by McCall, retold the Prague legend. The Golem
eventually reverted from protector to scourge of the Jews.
Golem, a novel by Myler Eric Ludwid, published in 1969
by Weybright and Talley, was not about the creature of clay,
although it does mention a modern Rabbi Lowe. David
Golem set out to find answers to the questions surrounding
his own life. A book on cybernetics and religion God and
Golem, Inc. , by Norbert Wiener, was published in 1964 by
Massachusetts Institute of Technology Press.

        Isaac Loeb Peretz, the great Yiddish writer of the
century, wrote a very short story titled "The Golem. "
The story (translated by Shlomo Katz) retold the legend of
the Golem and its creation by Rabbi "Loeb. " According
to the story the Golem yet remains waiting for someone to
recall the magic words to restore it to animation. The
modern story "The Golem," by Avram Davidson, which was
published in the Magazine of Fantasy and Science Fiction in
1955, featured a human robot. A Jew, remembering the
legends of the Golem and Rabbi "Löw," inscribed the mystical words on its gray forehead, providing a golem to perform menial tasks about the home.

        H. Leivick (real name Leivick Halper) wrote an
eight-scene play Der Goilem, or simple The Golem, in
1921. The poetic drama, which was presented in both
Europe and the United States, again related the creation
of Joseph Golem by the Maharal or Reb Levi Bezalel. The
man of clay was given life to free the Jews from Thaddeus'
blood accusations (see p. 68). After the creature's real use had

ended, he became haunted by visions (as in Meyrink's novel)
and was unable to function in a world of fearful human beings.
In desperation and longing for the Maharal's eternal company, Joseph Golem took his axe and began cleaving through
the ghetto populace.   At last the Maharal arrived and reduced his confused creation to clay.   In particular, one
speech (translated by Joseph C. Landis) of the Golem re-
calls the laments of the Monster in Mary Shelley's Frankenstein.

> You would be blinded in a single instant
> Were you to look at me against my will;
> For death and dazzling blasts and fiery flames
> And everlasting dying--these are my eyes.
> I live, and do not know myself how long,
> With people and with beasts and with the worms,
> In water and in fire and in stone
> And I can never see the start nor end
> Of me and my everlasting dying.
> I plead: relieve me of my fate of wonder;
> But no one hears my plea.   Just now, as I
> Was flying hither from the field, all at once
> I heard a curious ringing in my ears,
> And in my eyes strange fires began to burn.
> Perhaps--No, what am I saying?--I
> Would enter any house, what matters which,
> For every house would look at me in fear,
> And every house would drive me off in terror.
> (His head sinks as he sits. Thunder and lightning.)

In the early 1960s the New York Opera adapted the play.
The opera The Golem was hardly a success.   A female
golem appeared in the Living Theatre version of Frankenstein.

     The Golem was been featured in comic books and
magazines.   Steve Ditko adapted the Golem legend in issues
7 and 8 of Tales to Astonish, published in 1960 by the
Zenith Publishing Corporation (now the Marvel Comics
Group).   In the first part "I Spent Midnight with the Thing
on Bald Mountain," a sculptor created two statues made
from clay covering human skeletons, one representing good,
the other evil.   The two statues were struck by lightning
and came to life, battling each other until falling from the
top of a crumbling parapet (similar to the ending in the
first movie version of Der Golem).   The concluding story
"I Live Again!" revived the rampaging evil statue who

inadvertently stowed away in an experimental rocket on a
one-way mission to outer space.   T. H. U. N. D. E. R. Agents,
no. 5, published in 1966 by Tower Comics, featured their
lead super-hero against a giant android brute with orange
skin in "Dynamo and the Golem," illustrated by Dan Adkins.
After a rousing battle with the ape-like Golem, Dynamo
kicked the monster into a sizzling volcanic pit.   That same
year, the Golem (patterned after Wegener's conception) appeared in the French comic strip Lone Sloane by Philippe
Druillet and Eric Losfeld, published in Paris.   The Golem
was destroyed by the traditional removal of its magic sign.
The Incredible Hulk (Marvel Comics Group), no. 134, 1970,
had the story "Among Us Walks ... the Golem," written by
Roy Thomas and illustrated by Herb Trimpe.   The Hulk, a
creature patterned after Frankenstein's Monster, was mistaken for the Golem by a child whose father often told the
old legend.   Thus the Hulk became the temporary Golem of
a people oppressed by a dictator.   Vampire Barnabas Collins and werewolf Quentin Collins fought a golem in "The
Thirteenth Star," published in the Dark Shadows (Gold Key)
comic book, no. 11, 1971.   The monster was created to appear every century to destroy any evil member of the Collins family.   The magazine Eerie (Warren Publishing Company), no. 27, 1970, featured a single page item written and
drawn by Tom Sutton titled "The Golem."   The text cap-
sulized the Golem legend and the creature was depicted as
in the film Cisaruv Pekar, a Pekaruv Cisar.   The mighty
Superman encountered the Galactic Golem in Superman
(National Periodical Publications), no. 248, 1972, written by
Len Wein and drawn by Curt Swan.   The criminal scientist
Luthor, in a Frankenstein-type experiment, created the monster in "The Man Who Murdered the Earth" using galactic
energy.   The Galactic Golem was to free Luthor from the
yoke of his oppressor Superman.   But the Man of Steel discovered the weakspot of the Galactic Golem and destroyed it.

The original legend of Rabbi Loew and the Golem appeared in the seventh issue (1967) of Gold Key's Ripley's
Believe It or Not! comic book.   And a pair of giant golems
were commanded by an evil sorcerer in "The Land of Bone,"
written by Buddy Saunders and illustrated by Esteban Maroto,
in Warren's Creepy no. 47 (1972).   A version of The Golem
was presented on French television in 1966.   This Golem,
played by Andre Reybaz, had an angular face that appeared
really to have been carved from solid rock.   He wore a
black hat.   The Golem legend has also influenced other endeavors.   The first large electronic computer made at the

Weizmann Institute in Rehovoth, Israel, was named Golem I.
And to this day there is a Golem Inn at Prague which gives
patrons small souvenir effigies of the creature of clay. More
impressive to tourists to Prague is the ancient humanoid statue
reputed to be the actual Golem, now dormant and waiting to
perhaps someday walk again.

Pseudo-Frankensteins

The concept of scientifically creating human life in
silent films without reference to Frankenstein dates back to
1916. Homunculus[8] was a very long (and boring by today's
standards) serial in six hour-long chapters, made in Germany by Bioscop. Otto Rippert both wrote the script and
directed Homunculus, putting Olaf Fønss, a screen idol in
Denmark, in the role of the manufactured man. Homunculus
was created in a retort by a scientist who, like Frankenstein, desired only to invent a superman of great physical
and mental prowess. The being lived and possessed the intended qualities. But just as the Frankenstein Monster learned
his origin, this soulless creature discovered his own humanity.

And like the Monster, Homunculus degenerated into
an embodiment of horror. Disaster followed him. Eventually the science-spawned creature became a kind of Hitler.
He set himself up as dictator of a country. Not content
with merely oppressing his subjects, he instigated a revolution against himself, then brutally stopped it. As mankind was
powerless to crush the synthetic man, the Nature that had been
violated by the unholy experiment provided a deus ex machina.
Homunculus was dispatched by a celestial bolt of lightning.

Olaf Fønss wore no distinguishing make-up as Homunculus. In his black clothing and Dracula-like cloak he retained his screen image as a hero despite his monstrous
actions in Homunculus. The film, even with its slow pacing
and incredible length, became extremely popular in Germany.[9]

The Master Mystery, a fifteen-chapter serial made
by Octagon and starring the great magician and escape artist Houdini, featured a Frankenstein-type creature in 1919.
A scientist called "Dr. Q," driven mad when he was cheated
out of his own inventions by the combine International Pa-
tents, Inc. , and after the loss of his family, decided to
create an electrical monster (in Madagascar) and get revenge. The monster (Floyd Buckley) was a superpowerful

robot called the Automaton, ludicrous in appearance and in
its jerky movements, which was to possess the brain of an
electrocuted corpse--surely the first movie robot thus endowed.   Houdini played Quentin Locke, a Justice Department
spy who was investigating the combine.   The chapter endings
were overly repititious.   The Automaton and his gang of
criminals, "The Emissaries of the Automaton," appeared at
the end of each episode to capture and bind Locke, usually
submitting him to some horrendous peril.   Naturally Locke
escaped week after week, never once believing that the robot was anything more than a man in a metal suit.   In the
last chapter he unmasked the human villain, proving that
the Frankensteinian experiment had never been completed.

In 1920 Germany created another film featuring a
man-monster of sorts, one that would have a direct influence on the later Frankenstein films.   Das Kabinett des
Dr. Caligari ("The Cabinet of Dr. Caligari") was a Decla-
Bioscop film of 1920, directed by Robert Wiene (whose
screenplay is available from Simon and Schuster).   Although
there was no creation of life motif in Das Kabinett des
Dr. Caligari there was the creature Cesare, played with
style by the great German actor Conrad Veidt.   Cesare
was a somnambulist with an ability to predict the future.
His face stark white like that of a corpse, eyes, lips, and
stringy hair black, his lithe form clothed in black leotards,
the somnambulist was the gimmick of Dr. Caligari (Werner
Krauss), a hypnotist appearing at a town fair.   Dr. Caligari
kept Cesare under his mesmeric control.   When not in use
the sleep-walker rested like a deadman in a coffin-like
cabinet.

Cesare was the henchman of Dr. Caligari.   While
under his power the somnambulist would emerge from his
cabinet and perform acts of murder.   In this way he was
somewhat like the Frankenstein Monster (whom he resembled), who often fell prey to the influences of evil and more
intelligent human beings.   Dr. Caligari had sent the somnambulist to kill a lovely girl named Jane (Lil Dagover).   Silently Cesare stalked in through the girl's bedroom window.
Then the hypnotized creature fell victim to the same force
that had struck the Golem and in later years the Frankenstein Monster.   He fell in love.   Instead of murdering Jane
he carried her through the city.   In pursuit were the townspeople in a sequence to become traditional with the sound
Frankenstein movies.   Exhausted from the chase, Cesare
died.

The film is one of the most important in German cinema. The sets, flat surfaces of cardboard painted in weird designs by Hermann Warm and Walter Röhrig, with their disturbing angles and distorted perspectives (a combination of expressionism and economy), had an immediate effect on film-making. The picture conveyed a sense of sheer madness. Again there was the familiar epilogue of silent films wherein the whole story was revealed to be the tale of a madman in an asylum, with Caligari as the doctor, and the other characters, the inmates.[10] In 1932 Milton Holb contemplated remaking the film as a talkie. He was content, however, in re-releasing the original version with synchronized sound effects and music.

That same year in the United States, Marshall Neilan produced and directed a film with a Frankenstein-type monster. Go and Get It starred Bull Montana as a composite being--a monstrosity with the body of a gorilla and the brain of an executed criminal. The result was a bizarre apeman with a somewhat human face and protruding fangs. Montana lumbered through the picture disposing of those whose accusations got him executed.[11] In the end the ape-monster was destroyed by actor Pat O'Malley. Bull Montana was well cast as the apeman. His height and physique suited him to brawny roles and in 1925 he donned a similar disguise for the part of the prehistoric apeman in the First National production of The Lost World.

Excluding the Golem films, The Magician and Metropolis, both made in 1926, were the most influential on the first talkie Frankenstein and its sequel, Bride of Frankenstein. The Magician was directed by Rex Ingram for Metro-Goldwyn-Mayer. The film was based on Somerset Maugham's novel (1908) which, in turn, was based on the life of the European magician Aleister Crowley, infamously known as "The Great Beast." Paul Wegener, no longer the created Golem, portrayed creator Oliver Haddo, a sorcerer obsessed with an ancient formula. Using the formula Haddo believed he could create life. Just what species of life, the film never revealed. To accomplish the feat he required the heart's blood of a maiden.

Haddo had hypnotized Margaret Dauncey (Alice Terry) and taken her for his bride, despite her real love for young Dr. Burdon (Ivan Petrovich). Their marriage was uneventful, for Haddo merely wanted her for his mad experiment. For the experiment to succeed, Margaret must remain a

virgin. The experiment was to take place in Haddo's tower
laboratory, which reached into the night sky to receive the
life-giving bolts of lightning.   With the aid of his dwarf
assistant, the magician was about to sacrifice his bride,
when Dr. Burdon and a friend burst into the laboratory.
Burdon fought Haddo while his friend destroyed the formula
of life.   Haddo himself was thrown into a blazing fire.   The
two heroes and Margaret escaped precarious seconds before
the tower exploded to crumbling rubble.

The similarities between the towers in The Magician
and in James Whale's 1931 Frankenstein can hardly be coincidence.   Inside and out (a miniature), the tower in Frankenstein is a close copy of that of Oliver Haddo.   Dwight
Frye's characterization as Fritz, Frankenstein's dwarf assistant, was obviously patterned after Haddo's dwarf, including the comic touches later so identifiable with Whale's
production.   In a particular scene in The Magician the
dwarf hobbled down the winding stone staircase to open the
tower door.   The scene was virtually duplicated as Fritz
performed the same action down a similar set of stairs.
There can be no doubt that Whale had seen The Magician
and applied what he viewed to Frankenstein.   Furthermore
in Bride of Frankenstein Whale duplicated the exploding
tower with amazing detail.

Metropolis was Fritz Lang's prediction of the future
world of 2026, with its armies of workers reduced to the
status of efficient zombies and the slaves of machines.   The
UFA film was inspired by Lang's impression of the New
York skyline which he had seen on a visit to the United
States in 1924.   Lang made the film in Germany, working
from a script by his wife Thea von Harbou.   Metropolis
remains an impressive motion picture primarily due to the
futuristic set design and special effects photography.   The
Frankensteinian element in Metropolis arises in the character Rotwang (Rudolph Klein-Rogge), a wild-eyed, wild-
haired mad scientist whose gloved artificial hand showed
what he had sacrificed for his creation.   Rotwang's home
and laboratory was an anachronism, an ancient gothic structure with sinister pentacle amid the architectural splendor
of the twenty-first century.   It was here that the mad
scientist created his female robot--or robotrix--a sleek,
metallic machine of feminine beauty, which he proudly exhibited for Joh Fredersen[12] (Alfred Abel), the mastermind
of Metropolis.   The robot (played by teenager Brigitte
Helm)--called by a variety of names including Ultima,

Futura, and Parody in the book version of Metropolis--was
seated in a metal chair.   "Arise !" Rotwang commanded.
The gleaming machine began to gracefully move until it
confronted the dumbfounded Fredersen.   "Give me another
twenty-four hours," said Rotwang, "and I'll bring you a
machine no one can tell from a human."

The only member of the Metropolis population still
maintaining an individual humanity was a pretty young girl
named Maria (also Brigitte Helm), who preached love and
religion.   In Maria the workers found someone to trust and
follow.   Naturally Rotwang kidnapped the girl to climax his
fiendish experiment.   The words of Klein-Rogge, appearing
in the 1927 Metropolis Magazine souvenir book, related:

> Enthroned on a pedestal was the gruesome and
> mystical 'robot,' covering the imprisoned girl
> Maria whose very heart-throbs are to be trans-
> ferred to it.   When completed, this 'robot' will
> have the appearance of this innocent girl but its
> actions would be evil, according to the will of its
> creator.   Already the 'robot' moves like an 'auto-
> maton.'   The weird incomprehensible smile, the
> slow irresistible movements, the basilisk motion
> of the head, the haunting loveliness of the 'auto-
> maton,' born in the minds of the scenarist and di-
> rector and fashioned by the property man, holds
> us all spellbound.   The stage workers, the elec-
> tricians, otherwise never afraid, ready for a joke,
> never impressed with anything, seemed to feel
> some uneasiness.

Rotwang's final experiment was a symphony of electrical splendor.   Maria was placed on a horizontal platform,
covered with glass tubing and metal bands.   Wired electrodes were placed against her head.   The robot, still sitting before the inverted pentacle, was connected to the unconscious girl by trails of wire.   Great halos of energy
rose above the robot.   Rotwang gloated triumphantly as
synthetic flesh began to form over the robot's metal skin.
He realized total success when the robot stood before him
as a duplicate, and totally evil, Maria.

The creation of the Frankenstein Monster had always
been rather ambiguous, in the novel, on the stage, and in the
silent films.   After James Whale saw Metropolis, the

ambiguity would forever be erased. The creations of Frankenstein would always be associated with wild electrical displays, with the artificial being resting on platforms. Whale recreated the creation scene from <u>Metropolis</u> in the tower laboratory he borrowed from <u>The Magician</u>. In <u>Bride of Frankenstein</u> he would go even further by placing metal bands over the body of the female being and attaching similar electrodes to her head. From what Whale had learned from these two silent films, plus the 1927 stage play <u>Frankenstein</u> by Peggy Webling, he had ample source material to begin shooting his version of the Mary Shelley novel.

Rotwang used the artificial Maria to arouse the workers to revolution. In a climax seemingly incongruous with the world of the future, the false Maria was burned at the stake. As the flesh melted away to reveal the metal underneath, the people of Metropolis realized that they had been duped by yet another machine. [13]

The Golem, Cesare the somnambulist, Oliver Haddo, and the robot creation of Rotwang all contributed to the standard image of <u>Frankenstein</u> of the sound era of motion pictures. Several years were yet to pass. And in 1931 the night's stillness would be broken by the sounds of shovels digging through newly packed soil. The Golem and the others were to live again in the composite being known as the Frankenstein Monster.

Notes

1. "Frankenstein" has not been an unpopular name for various towns. Although the town in <u>Frankenstein's Trestle</u> apparently no longer exists in the United States, there is another American town by that name whose greatest asset is a nunnery (see Ackerman's Introduction to this book). In Germany there exist two towns named Frankenstein, one of which is located near Kaiserslautern. Prussia also had its Frankenstein town, now Frankenstein is Schlesien, Poland.

2. Other books by Bloch involving the Golem are <u>Der Prager Golem</u> and <u>Israel der Gotteskämpfer</u>, both published in 1919. The former told of the creation of the Golem and the deeds performed by the artificial being to save the Jews from their oppression in the medieval ghetto.

3. Rabbi Loew (listed in some texts as Judah Low Ben
    Benzalel or Reb Levi Bar Bezalel) was an histori-
    cal figure; born the son of a rabbi in 1513, legend
    has it that he miraculously foresaw his own death.

4. Gifford, Denis, Movie Monsters, London: Studio Vista;
    New York: Dutton, 1969, p. 41.

5. Eisner, Lotte H. , The Haunted Screen, translated
    from the French (pub. 1952 by Le Terrain Vague)
    by Roger Greaves, Berkeley: Univ. of California
    Press, 1969, pp. 72-4.

6. Alraune was created by H. H. Ewers in his novel.
    The story was presented as a stage play and in two
    motion pictures. The first Alraune (also known by
    the title Unholy Love) starred Paul Wegener as the
    scientist who created the evil woman (played as a
    young woman by Brigitte Helm, the robot of Fritz
    Lang's Metropolis). The film was written and di-
    rected by Henrik Galeen of the 1920 Golem. The
    story was remade in 1930 in sound by Richard Os-
    wald, starring Erich von Stroheim.

7. Scenes from Le Golem along with footage from White
    Zombie, Vampyre, The Return of Chandu, and Un-
    heimliche Geschichten ("Extraordinary Tales") were
    compiled into Dr. Terror's House of Horrors re-
    leased in the early 1940s. A condensed version of
    Le Golem was made available in 8mm as The Man
    of Stone.

8. The idea of creating the homunculus (meaning aritifical or
    miniature man) dates back to around A. D. 300, when an
    Alexandrian Greek, Zosimus, had a vision of creating
    a man with dragon's blood and bones and the transmuta-
    tion of metals. During that time Simon Magus, "arch-
    heretic and sorcerer," supposedly created a being
    in a glass from the soul of a dead boy. Arnold of Villa-
    nova was said to have made an homunculus in the 13th
    or 14th Century in attempting to discover a rejuvenating
    medicine. Paracelsus (1493-1541), however, formu-
    lized the creation of the homunculus--place a man's
    semen in a sealed bottle, bury it in horse manure
    for forty days, and magnetize it. A transparent,
    bodiless human being is to grow from this proce-
    dure. After its birth, the homunculus must be

kept at the temperature of a mare's womb for ten
months and fed human blood. "It may be raised
and educated like any other child, until it grows
older and is able to look after itself." Borel, one
of Louis XIV's physicians, was reported to have
created an homunculus from distilled blood. The
creature emitted red beams of light. Robert Fludd,
a mystical philosopher and physician, admitted to
creating a human head by the same method. As
late as 1775 John Ferdinand, Count of Kufstein in
the Tyrol, was said to have created ten homunculi
in bottles with the help of Abbé Geloni, an Italian
mystic. The story, based on the diary of Ferdinand's butler and some Masonic manuscripts, was
published by Dr. Emil Besetzny in 1873. Goethe
included the homunculus concept in the second part
of his Faust published in 1832. Other adaptations
of the Faust legend have avoided references to the
artifically created man.

9.   The homunculus has appeared in other media. David
     H. Keller, M. D. wrote The Homunculus, a short
     novel published in 1949 by the Prime Press. In
     this delightful fantasy Colonel Horatio Bumble cre-
     ated a living baby in a bottle, using the techniques
     of Paracelsus and a bit of supernatural intervention.
     The Homunculus stressed the power of positive
     thinking. Bumble had complete faith in his project;
     therefore he succeeded. Comic books have also
     used the homunculus theme, particularly Marvel
     Comics' Fantastic Four, #66 and 67, 1967, written
     by Stan Lee and drawn by Jack Kirby. The first
     installment "What Lurks in the Beehive?" related
     how a group of scientists endeavored to create the
     first member of a race of perfect human beings.
     An embryonic being was given life. The creature
     grew to adulthood, emerging in part two "When
     Opens the Cocoon." Known simple as "Him," the
     being proved to be utterly perfect, with golden skin,
     and not the anticipated monster. Knowing that he
     was to be destroyed by his creators, the homuncu-
     lus used his powers to wipe out the group of scien-
     tists and apparently himself. But "Him" survived
     to encounter other super-heroes of the Marvel
     Comics Group, like Thor, God of Thunder. A one-
     eyed Homunculus (Frank Corsentino) was one of the
     many bizarre characters in Moon Child (1972), an

American Media Films production directed by Alan
Gadney.

10. The film was remade in 1962 as <u>Cabinet of Caligari</u> by
     Robert L. Lippert, directed by Roger Kay. The
     remake was weak, focusing on Glynis Johns and her
     nightmares. Cesare was not written into Robert
     Bloch's screenplay. Curtis Harrington, now a suc-
     cessful film director, appeared as Cesare in Ken-
     neth Anger's color experimental film <u>The Inaugura-
     tion of the Pleasure Dome</u>, made in 1954. A more
     recent film <u>The Vengeance of Dr. Caligari</u> was
     made in Berlin by CCC-Film. <u>Dr. Caligari's Black
     Book</u> was a collection of short stories about the
     darker aspects of somnambulism and the carnival.
     Peter Haining edited the anthology. The first edi-
     tion was published in hardcover by W. H. Allen &
     Company in 1968. A paperback edition with some
     story substitutions was published by the New Eng-
     lish Library the following year. One selection was
     "Amber Print" by Basil Copper, in which a special
     print of the original film released Dr. Caligari and
     Cesare to haunt the real world. The book, <u>From
     Caligari to Hitler: A Psychological History of the
     German Film</u>, by Siegfrid Kracauer, published in
     1947 by the Princeton University Press, discussed
     the cinema of Germany.

11. In 1940 Paramount released <u>D. O. A. --Dead on Arrival</u>
     (later re-titled <u>The Monster and the Girl</u>), directed
     by Stuart Heisler. The film's plot was extremely
     similar to that of <u>Go and Get It</u>. A man was un-
     justly executed for a murder commited by someone
     else. George Zucco played a scientist who retrieved
     the deadman's brain and put it into the skull of a
     gorilla (played by Charles Gemora) in order to step
     up evolution a million years. The ape escaped
     from the laboratory and destroyed those responsible
     for his execution one by one. In the climax the
     ape was shot to death by its last victim (played by
     Robert Paige). To an extent, all stories involving
     brain transplants are Frankensteinian. The trans-
     planting of a human brain into the head of an ape
     has always been a favorite pastime of the mad
     scientist. One film <u>The Strange Case of Dr. RX</u>,
     directed by William Nigh for Universal in 1942,
     used not only the threat of brain transplantation

from human to ape skull, but also a generous helping of laboratory apparatus from their Frankenstein
series. The operation was not performed. The
ape (played by Ray Corrigan) and the impending
experiment were only to scare the hero (played by
Patrick Knowles) to death by the sinister Dr. RX.

12. The character was named John Masterman in the British and American versions of the film.

13. In 1927 Thea von Harbou's novel <u>Metropolis</u> was published. The ponderous book underplayed the actual
creation of the humanoid machine and overplayed
the religious implications. The cover of the 1963
paperback edition of the novel, published by Ace
Books, featured not only the female robot but also
a character resembling both Cesare the somnambulist and the Universal Pictures' Frankenstein Monster. <u>Metropolis</u> has never been remade, although
both independent motion picture producer Bert I.
Gordon and American-International Pictures have
expressed interest in a new version. <u>Giant of the
Metropolis</u> was an Italian film, made in color in
1962, taking place in the distant past and handled
with the trappings of the "Hercules" spectacles.
Not connected with the original <u>Metropolis</u>, the
picture did have Frankensteinian overtones. An
evil king attempted to create a perfect human being,
using his son, the brain of his wise father, and the
blood of muscleman Obro (Mitchell Gordon). There
were the usual scenes of the sweaty beefcake hero
tortured almost beyond endurance for fans of this
type of film, before volcanoes, quakes, storms,
and floods destroyed the city of evil. The picture
was directed by Umberto Scarpelli.

Chapter 4

KARLOFF SETS THE STANDARD

Universal Pictures in 1931 announced that it was planning to film Frankenstein. The first talkie version of Mary Shelley's novel would be based on the stage play by Peggy Webling, adapted to the screen by John L. Balderston. Dracula, the first sound version of Bram Stoker's immortal vampire novel, had been made by the studio earlier that same year. The film was so successful that Universal immediately recognized the beginning of a trend toward horror films and again turned to the classics for a follow-up. Frankenstein had been filmed three times during the silent era of movies, three times more than Dracula. There was obviously an audience appeal for the story of the man-made man. Thus Frankenstein seemed to be the logical selection for a horror film intended to be greater than Dracula.

The executives at Universal Pictures, wasting no time, began selecting the tentative cast and list of technicians that would hopefully bring Frankenstein to theatres before the end of the year. Directing was to be assigned to Robert Florey, surely one of the studio's most capable directors. The cast would include such performers as Edward Van Sloan, identifiable to those who had seen Dracula as the elderly Professor Van Helsing and who would be typecast at Universal in this type of role (being considerably younger than these characters), and a youthful, up-coming actress named Bette Davis.[1] Van Sloan was to virtually recreate his Van Helsing portrayal as Professor Waldman in Frankenstein, while Miss Davis was to play Elizabeth, the fiancée of the infamous scientist who created the Monster. The role of Henry Frankenstein[2] was intended for the noted English actor Leslie Howard.

The casting for the Frankenstein Monster was the result of logic. Dracula had made an immediate star of the macabre out of a Hungarian actor, who though a veteran

90

to the European and American stage and a performer in
earlier movies of both continents, was a new face to American horror films. The actor was Bela Lugosi, who was
intrigued with the idea of leaving his vampire role to star
as this entirely different fantasy character. Having just
acted in the Fox Charlie Chan film The Black Camel and
eager to give more variety to his roles, Lugosi heartily
accepted the part of the Monster.

Without first devising the make-up of the creature
and still not entirely sure of the treatment Frankenstein
would be given, Universal's advertising department rushed
out a color, full-page magazine spread which heralded their
up-coming production. The Monster was shown in the advertisement [see illustration] as a green giant of King Kong
proportions, lumbering through a panic-stricken city, walking off with screaming victims in his enormous hands, and
shooting powerful deathrays (in the style of many future
Frankenstein-like robots) from his eyes. The Monster's
face bore no hints as to how the make-up would look. The
countenance of the skyscraping brute was barely more
frightening than a frowning man who growled under a head
of mussed hair. (Many smaller versions of this man walk
the streets today.)

Catchlines such as these accompanied the artwork:
"... no man has ever seen his like ... no woman ever felt
his white-hot kiss .... Surpasses in THRILLS even DRA-
CULA ... world's greatest hold-over picture for 1930 ...
with BELA LUGOSI (Dracula himself) ... as the leading
spine-chiller ... as a story it has thrilled the world for
years. "

Bela Lugosi was quite enthusiastic in his regarding
the part. He was so enthusiatic that he eagerly saved and
pasted all the publicity clippings he could find about Frankenstein in a large scrapbook,[3] in which the film received
two full pages. These were the days of less strict union
regulations. Actors could assist with or do their own make-
up. Lugosi, whose stage career had trained him in the art
of make-up, was still trying to decide on the appearance of
the Monster when the following item appeared in the Hollywood, California News for 20 June 1931: "Bela Lugosi begins work soon on 'Frankenstein,' playing the name role at
Universal. He is now studying makeup for the part. " The
actor finally decided upon a suitable make-up for the test
film that would be made before the actual production of

<u>Frankenstein</u>.   Recalling the silent Golem movies, legitimate
predecessors of the Frankenstein movies, and the Golem-
like make-up Hamilton Deane wore in the play from which
this film was taken, the make-up was designed appropriately.[4]

Press releases, which may or may not be accurate
since such items were written to promote the star at the
moment and not to give scholarly data, further described
the make-up Lugosi would wear as the Monster.   One of
these, appearing in the 7 June 1931 Los Angeles <u>Record</u>
related:

Something has got to be done for Bela Lugosi.   Lugosi has been trying for weeks to make a screen
test for 'Frankenstein.'   He has to wear weird make-
up, with two or three different colors, stripes,
streaks, and striations.   But after a few blasts of
hot air, the makeup all fuses together, making him
a clown instead of a menace.

A later report in the 27 June 1931 edition of another
publication stated:

What probably will be one of the trickiest jobs in
makeup since 'The Hunchback of Notre Dame' will be
seen when the picture 'Frankenstein' is released.
Bela Lugosi, in the starring role, will be built up
with makeup and padding, to resemble the eight foot
superman Mary Shelley, wife of poet Percy Shelley,
wrote about in 1817.

When Lugosi is made up only his chin and eyes will
be visible, greasepaint and putty completely hiding
the rest of his face.   Shoes to which nearly 12 inches
have been added will complete the illusion.

Since actual photographs of Lugosi as the Monster apparently no longer exist, to image the make-up he was to wear
in the feature we can only incorporate these descriptions,
always remembering the appearance of the Golem.

Finally the day arrived to shoot the test scenes of
Lugosi and various members of the proposed cast of <u>Fran-
kenstein</u>.   The Hungarian actor came onto the Universal set
wearing the Monster make-up.   Also on the set were director Robert Florey, cinematographer Paul Ivano, Edward Van
Sloan who was probably photographed in the scene, and

possibly Bette Davis. (It is not known if Miss Davis actually appeared in the test footage. Although she was originally scheduled to play Elizabeth, Carl Laemmle, the head
of Universal Pictures, saw in her a star potential that he
thought would be hampered by her appearing in a horror
film. Therefore he removed her from the cast of Frankenstein. Just when this removal took place is unknown. We
can only say that Bette Davis might have been photographed
in the Frankenstein test.)

Paul Ivano shot the test footage, an entirely different
concept than what finally was accepted by Universal. Unfortunately this short reel of film appears to have been lost
to the decades. Even authorized personnel searching through
the storage vaults at Universal have failed to re-discover the
priceless film. It is hoped that the footage still exists on
some forgotten shelf. Although Ivano followed Florey's direction in shooting the Lugosi-Frankenstein test film, changes
were about to happen, based on several factors, that would
abandon this initial interpretation. The first of these involved Bela Lugosi himself.

Lugosi had been an actor on the European stage
since he graduated from elementary school in his home
town of Lugos, Hungary (where he was born Bela Blasko
on 29 October 1882 and from which he adopted his professional name) and studied drama at Budapest's Academy of
Theatrical Arts. He had gone on to be acclaimed as one
of the country's finest actors, achieving star status in such
distinguished plays as William Shakespeare's Romeo and
Juliet. The actor's motion picture career began in 1914
in an Hungarian silent feature, followed by a number of
starring roles in the German cinema. By the time Lugosi
became an American star in the film Dracula he had already enjoyed the fame and fringe benefits that accompanied
stardom. To the American screen Lugosi was a new--
albeit handsomely terrifying--face, although he had starred
in many American films and stage plays. To Lugosi that
face which cast no reflection in mirrors in his vampire
role was established, and that of a star.

The actor, with the professional conceit understandable to a star of so many years, was told that the Frankenstein Monster would not speak, save for a few growls and
groans in the manner of an animal. Immediately the actor's
pride was shattered. He had made women swoon with his
elegant mannerisms and rich voice. Even his horror role

in Dracula was designed more to make women want his teeth to pierce their jugular veins than, as in the novel by Bram Stoker, to convey total revulsion with a breath that reeked of the grave.   Bela Lugosi's interpretation of Count Dracula was more than of a blood-sucking Rudolph Valentino, a romantic character that his female victims would anticipate rather than flee.   The heavy make-up of the Frankenstein Monster would have been accepted by Lugosi had the creature been played as Mary Shelley had intended--a warm, intelligent, verbose artificial man, going on for long pages with rich monologue.   Such a part would have been welcomed by Lugosi, whose acting style played all the way to the back rows of crowded theatres.   Examination of the test scenes of Lugosi made Universal's executives agree that the whole concept of the Monster, make-up and performance, was not correct for what they really wanted to convey.   They were not too disappointed when Lugosi later responded to the role with a heavily-accented "no. "

The original concept was abandoned in which the following description of the Monster's characterization, related in the 13 June 1931 issue of Television, would have been quite different from what was finally accepted:

> The story deals with a scientist who creates a weird creature resembling a man of the neanderthal age whose mentality is astounding in some respects but whose heart is that of a monster.   Devoid of sentiment, 'Frankenstein' keeps things active wherever and whenever he contacts human beings.

As Lugosi left the production of Frankenstein, so went director Robert Florey.   Together Lugosi and Florey would create new terror in Universal's 1932 adaptation of Edgar Allan Poe's Murders in the Rue Morgue. [5]   Before leaving Frankenstein, Florey had given the plot many of his own ideas, blocking out most of the story.   He conceived the placement of a criminal brain in the Monster's skull, thus giving the brute somewhat of an excuse to kill.   This change from Mary Shelley's conception of a brilliant mind in a grotesque body pleased the Universal executives.   The climax of the eventual film, set in a windmill, came from the imagination of Florey who, staring out of his hotel window, spotted a Van de Kamp's bakery across the street, with its windmill trademark.   The production already had a basic plot when it changed to the directorial hands of James Whale, formerly of the British stage.

At the time he accepted the job of directing Frankenstein, Whale, an extremely talented Englishman with a yen
toward bizarre characterization, had directed few films, including Journey's End and Waterloo Bridge. He was a
genius at presenting the macabre on the screen through characters and settings that could only exist in a parallel nightmare world. Whale began working on Frankenstein with a
cast change. Edward Van Sloan was retained as Henry
Frankenstein's medical school dean, Professor Waldman.
Whale did not favor Leslie Howard as Young Henry. He
substituted Colin Clive, whom he had directed as the star
of Journey's End, and who was adept at protraying the
neurotic creator of soulless life. The selection of a new
actor to play the Monster was another matter altogether.

Since Bela Lugosi was already a horror films star
and unquestionably out of the role, Whale thought it better
to go the opposite route and use an actor with no star status. Then the Monster would be even more mysterious,
with viewers unable to associate him as really a made-up
actor. A number of considerations were made, all unsatis-
factory. (The notable actor John Carradine, whose performances ranged from parts in the worst of the "poverty
row" horror films to distinguished roles in such film classics as The Grapes of Wrath, states that he was considered
for the Monster in 1931, made-up, and tested. Since the
actor has always been extremely thin, the visual strength of
a Carradine version of the Monster is questionable.)

At last Whale remembered a cultured English actor
(he delighted in using English performers) with a particularly
menacing countenance, that he had seen in several films.
The actor, though virtually unknown and lacking any real
name value as far as luring people into theatres was concerned, had already appeared in sixty-five feature length
films and serials. Soon, to the detriment of Bela Lugosi's
career, the star echelon of the horror film would undergo
a significant change.

Creation of a Masterpiece

Boris Karloff was seated in the commissary at the
Universal studios one afternoon in 1931. He was eating
lunch and sipping his traditional cup of tea when he was
summoned by a man who told him that Mr. James Whale,
at a nearby table, would like to speak to him. Karloff was

immediately impressed, since Whale was Universal's most respected director.

The British actor walked to Whale's table and intro-duced himself with his slightly lisping voice. Whale com-mented that he was aware of Karloff's excellent perfor-mances in the Los Angeles stage presentation of The Crim-inal Code (with Karloff portraying Ned Galloway, an im-prisoned murderer), its filmed version made by Columbia (with Karloff in the same role), and in Universal's Graft (with Karloff as a murderous gangster named Terry), all in 1931. The director was impressed by Karloff's six-foot height, his lean, sullen features, and his ability to evoke sympathy through acts of villainy. "We're getting ready to shoot the Mary Shelley classic, Frankenstein," Whale said, probably anticipating the actor's refusal of the part, "and I'd like you to test--for the part of the Monster."[6]

Karloff's sinister features expanded with surprise. "A monster indeed!" he exclaimed. But then he indulged in a bit of recalling of his past. He had already been in a long list of films, acting on the screen for a dozen years. He was forty-four years old. Straight dramatic roles failed to bring stardom to Karloff. Perhaps his luck would change in the portrayal of the Monster. "But I didn't look a gift horse in the mouth," Karloff later told an interviewer. "I needed to eat and I took it."

The actor was not always known as Boris Karloff. He was born on 23 November 1887 with the less menacing name of William Henry Pratt at Forest Hill Road in Dul-wich, a suburb of London. He was the son of James Pratt, an official in the British Indian Civil Service. His seven brothers mostly followed in their father's line of work, ex-cept an elder brother who became a stage actor under the name George Marlowe. William, the youngest of the family that also included a sister, admired George and, to the chagrin of the others whose work took them to such places as China and India, he vowed to become an actor.

William Pratt's acting career suffered through a long beginning. Before appearing on any professional stage he moved to Canada, where he labored digging ditches, selling real estate, driving trucks, chopping trees, and performing various other mundane jobs. Finally his break came in 1910 with an offer to join the Jean Russell Stock Company in Kamloops, British Columbia. Without second thoughts

Boris Karloff as the Monster in a trial make-up not used in the film <u>Frankenstein</u> (Universal).

Pratt left his lumberjack position and took a train bound for
Kamloops.   While anticipating the start of a fabulous career,
he dwelled upon his own name, believing that no one would
pay money to see an actor billed as William Henry Pratt.
He needed a name that rang with individuality.   William's
mother's family name was Karloff.   That name had a certain
sound that would be difficult for people to forget.   The
name Boris was merely snatched from air, sounding Russian, which made it the more sinister.   Together the two
names became Boris Karloff, which sounded right.

Boris Karloff bluffed his way through the stage manager's questioning, supplying a fabricated list of acting credits, and acquired a part in a theatrical presentation of
The Devil.   This was the start for Karloff, who continued
to act on the stage.   In 1919, realizing the potential in the
rising art of motion pictures, the Englishman secured the
part of a Mexican bandit in United Artists' silent film His
Majesty, the American, in which he menaced Douglas Fair-
banks.   More screen roles followed, fluctuating between
featured player and extra, and quite often featuring Karloff
as a French-Canadian, a half-breed Indian, or an Arab
sheik.   This typecasting was premature.

James Whale, impressed with Karloff as both an
actor and a man of presence and culture, was most anxious
to give him a screen test as the Frankenstein Monster.   Unlike Florey's intention to allow Bela Lugosi to decide upon
his own make-up, Whale had the entire task given to a real
genius of greasepaint and nose putty--Jack Pierce, Universal's top artist of disguise.   Pierce, who had previously
worked as a semi-professional baseball shortstop, a theatre
manager for Harry Culver, and an independent film producer, created his first "monster" make-up on Jacques
Lerner in the 1926 Twentieth Century-Fox film The Monkey
Talks.   His knowledge of anatomy made him almost as
capable of creating the Monster as Frankenstein himself.
Completely ignoring the Lugosi concept, Pierce sat down
in deep contemplation, leaving his mind open to the suggestions of Boris Karloff, who displayed an unexpected
ability to assist, and of the boss, James Whale.

It was first decided to keep the Monster's features
as simple as possible, allowing the human to show through
the inhuman.   Horror film characters that are at least
partially human are always more terrifying than a bug-man
from outer space or a lumbering Godzilla smashing its way

through the world's cities.   Lon Chaney's pathetic creature
in The Hunchback of Notre Dame (1923) and his living face
of Death in The Phantom of the Opera (1925) proved that
the distorted human visage can produce true fear, while the
rampagings of a dinosaur through a modern metropolis can
be ludicrous.   Karloff's Frankenstein Monster would be
horrible, yet human allowing for identification by an audience haunted by the feeling that such a face could exist in
real life.

The make-up master regarded the Monster from the
viewpoint of the scientist.   "If the monster looks like something I dreamt after something I ate, don't blame me, blame
science," Pierce told an interviewer for the New York
Times during the filming of Son of Frankenstein eight years
later.   "I made him the way the textbooks said he should
look.   I didn't depend on imagination.   In 1931, before I
did a bit of designing I spent three months of research in
anatomy, surgery, medicine, criminology, ancient and
modern burial customs, and electro-dynamics."

Frankenstein, Pierce said, was a practical scientist
and not an artist.   His artificially-created man would appear as if he were made to function rather than please the
eyes.   The description of the humanoid given by Mary Shelley was vague, allowing Pierce to incorporate his own
theories and knowledge in the Monster's features.

The head was given an overall squareness, flat on
top.   Pierce had read that a surgeon could cut the skull to
get at the brain in six different ways.   The simplest way
would be to saw through the top of the skull, straight across,
leaving it hinged at one side.   The brain would then be
transplanted into the host skull and the "lid" replaced,
joined with metal clamps circumventing the top of the head.
The forehead was high, with a surgical scar running upward
from the right eye; a remnant of the brain operation.   To
give the Monster a primitive, Neanderthal appearance that
would stress his low intellect, Pierce sloped the brow over
the eyes in a pronounced ape-like ridge of bone.   (During
the creation of the make-up other versions, some subtly
different, were tested on Karloff.   One of these, suggested
by Whale, ignored the forehead scar and replaced it with
two tubular masses of malformed flesh, one over each eye
and running up to the hairline, and each fastened by an unsightly ring of metal.)   The high forehead was shaped from
uncomfortable tin and blended with the actor's own features

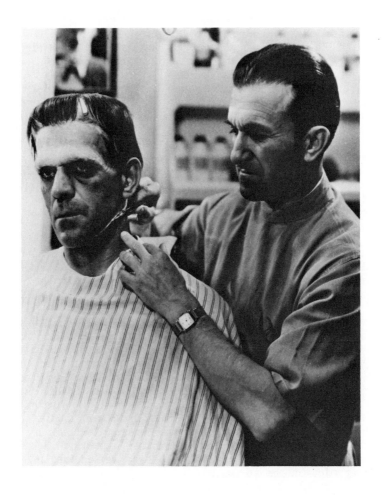

Make-up artist Jack Pierce applies a scar to Karloff's cheek in the final guise of the Monster in the Universal <u>Frankenstein.</u>

with layers of putty.   Covering the top of the head was a
black mass of straight hair, which hung long at the sides
and dropped over the metal clamps in bangs.   Two hollow
metallic caps were placed on Karloff's neck, one on each
side, to simulate the electrodes which Henry Frankenstein
would charge with electricity, the life current that would
spark the spine of the Monster.   The left cheek was given
a long red scar to further attest the workings of a surgeon.
Several of Karloff's teeth in the right side of his mouth
were false.   The actor consented to remove them so that
the side of his face naturally caved in to accentuate the impression of a thin corpse.   Pierce heightened the effect by
darkening the area with shadow.   (In later films, with the
Monster played by different actors, this hollow was indicated
by a black "beauty spot."   In <u>Abbott and Costello Meet
Frankenstein</u>, seventeen years later, the traditional mark
was shown only in the earlier scenes.   Later in the film
the spot was either intentionally omitted--or, more likely,
forgotten.)

The hands of the Monster also told of its unnatural
creation.   The right arm was stitched to show where the
alien hand was attached.   A strip of sewn metal braced the
left arm to reinforce the creature's strength.   The finger-
nails on both hands were discolored with black shoe polish.

The color of the Monster's corpse-like flesh, which
had to photograph on black and white film as close to dead
white as possible, was a bluish gray (a color developed by
Pierce for the cosmetics industry).   Pierce contrasted the
Monster's pallor by darkening the lips with brownish greasepaint.   The make-up was always open for alterations, made
in between scenes, dependent on variations in lighting and
mood.   (When the Monster screamed in terror, subtle
changes were made so that his face seemed to function
naturally and appear different from scenes in which he
smiled with innocent delight.   Such care was lacking in
later films of the series.)

As Pierce finished applying the make-up for the first
time to Karloff's face, the actor looked into the workshop
mirror from his place in the regulation barber chair and
noticed that something still was not right.   There was a
look about his eyes that failed to give the impression of a
newly-awakened being spawned from graves.   Somehow the
Monster looked too aware.   Karloff considered the matter
for a while, then suggested that his eyelids be heavily caked

with putty, giving the creature a look of only partial aware-
ness.   Pierce liked the idea and fashioned two heavy eyelids from mortician's wax and joined them to the rest of the
make-up.   The thoroughly satisfying effect was retained.

The make-up of Frankenstein's Monster was complete
and would be re-applied every morning before shooting in
four-hour sessions including Karloff, Pierce, and one assistant.   The guise, however, was still not finished.   There
was yet the body of the Monster, which would appear as
realistically mismatched as the head and hands.   Jack
Pierce had read that ancient Egyptian criminals were buried
with their hands and feet tightly bound.   When their blood
changed to water and flowed into the limbs, the arms lengthened, and their faces, hands, and feet swelled to hideous
proportions.   The make-up artist thought of applying this
idea to the Monster, since some of the parts used by Henry
Frankenstein would come from criminals.   To get the effect
he desired, Pierce ordered an ill-fitting black suit made by
Universal's costuming department with shortened sleeves to
make the arms seem longer.

Finally Pierce gave Karloff a five-pound brace to
wear on his spine to keep his movements impaired and stiff,
and a pair of raised boots that further hampered his walking, weighing an uncomfortable twelve and one-half pounds
each.   The entire outfit came to forty-eight pounds.   (Wearing the guise proved almost as unbearable to Karloff as
actually being sewn together by Henry Frankenstein.   The
film was shot during the hot California summer.   Sound
stages were not yet convenienced by air conditioning.   To
make the Monster appear larger, Karloff wore a doubly
quilted suit under the black clothes.   After an hour's work
under the hot studio lights, Karloff would be soaking wet
and was forced to change his underclothes or risk catching
pneumonia.   His own perspiration caused the make-up to
crumble.   Minute particles of make-up material fell into
his eyes, causing tremendous pain.   But Karloff endured
the agony aided by Pierce, who was always nearby to remove the particles with eyewash.)

After three weeks had been spent developing the
guise, Karloff was finally given a screen test, wearing the
make-up of the Frankenstein Monster, standing nearly eight
feel tall in the raised boots.   During the test the actor performed his best, trying to emote as realistically as possible
without the use of dialogue.   The make-up photographed

superbly.   There was no doubting that a true masterpiece
of make-up artistry had been created.   It was not, however,
merely the work of Jack Pierce, but the emoting of Boris
Karloff that made it a true masterpiece.

James Whale viewed the test scenes enthusiastically
and immediately knew that Karloff was the right man for the
role.   For Jack Pierce the make-up was the beginning of
many years of creating Universal's most famous creatures.
For Karloff it was the beginning of stardom.   And for both
Pierce and Karloff it was the start of a lasting friendship
and a mutual respect.   In countless interviews Boris Karloff, when asked about the Frankenstein Monster, credited
Jack Pierce as the real genius behind the compelling make-
up.

The sound stage had been set;   the cast selected.
Then one day in August of 1931, Universal Pictures' Frankenstein went before the cameras.

"Frankenstein"--1931

The black screen of the movie theatre faded-in to
reveal a simple stage and curtain.   A man dressed in a
fine suit stepped onto the stage with a personal message to
the audience.

"How do you do," Edward Van Sloan addressed the
people waiting anxiously for Frankenstein to begin.

> Mr. Carl Laemmle feels it would be a little unkind
> to present this picture without a word of warning.
> We are about to unfold the story of Frankenstein, a
> man of science who sought to create life after his
> own image, without reckoning on God.   It is one of
> the strangest tales ever told.   It deals with the two
> great mysteries of creation--life and death.   I think
> it will thrill you.   It may shock you.   It may even
> ... horrify ... you.   So, if any of you feel you'd
> not care to subject your nerves to such a strain,
> now's your chance to ... er ... well, we warned
> you.

Besides the theatrics in the introduction to Frankenstein, Edward Van Sloan's speech served another purpose.
Most horror films of the silent era explained away fantastic

and supernatural occurrences as nightmares or the narratives of madmen.   But like its predecessor <u>Dracula</u>, <u>Frankenstein</u> was, within the context of the plot, a real happening.   This introduction helped attune the viewers' minds to the fact that what they were about to see would be, as far as the characters in the film were concerned, real.

The action in <u>Frankenstein</u> began with a funeral in a bleak graveyard.   The grim ceremony was observed by two sinister figures--one sophisticated, determined, handsome; the other boorish, dwarfed and hunchbacked, with an ugly face locked into a seemingly sadistic mask.   The first man was Henry Frankenstein, a young former medical student, played by Colin Clive.   The hunchback was his assistant Fritz, portrayed by Dwight Frye, who relished such roles. (Frye was best cast as a psychopath.   In <u>Dracula</u> he played Renfield, a wide-eyed lunatic with a particular appetite for flies and spiders.)   Henry Frankenstein and Fritz waited until the funeral procession left the graveyard.   Then hurrying through the shadows, the two ghouls of the night disinterred the newly buried corpse.   The scientist spoke profoundly while patting the casket: "He's just resting ... waiting for new life to come!"

More bodies were needed for the project Henry Frankenstein had been nurturing in his over ambitious mind for so many years.   Another corpse was secured from the gallows.   Henry had hoped to use the brain from the hanging body, but expressed disappointment when he learned that the neck had been broken and the brain was useless.   He needed another;   a perfect brain.

While Henry Frankenstein was the scientific genius, most of the manual work was done by the hunckback.   Managing, surprisingly, to avoid notice, Fritz peered through the window of the Goldstadt Medical College, while the white-haired Professor Waldman lectured to his students about the differences between the normal and criminal brain.   He left specimens of both types for his class to inspect at the end of the period.   After the classroom had been evacuated, Fritz stole his way through the window and toward the two bottled brains.   Uneasy in this room of death with its hanging skeleton, the hunchback was on the verge of collapse. He grabbed the bottle labeled "Normal Brain. "   As he began to leave with his prize he was startled by the sound of a loud gong and dropped the brain with a shattering of glass. (The nature of the gong was never established.   It was

probably a contrived excuse to let Fritz make his blunder.)
There was but one alternative--stealing the other container
marked "Abnormal Brain." (The present writer wonders
how a man of Henry's standing could fail to notice the con-
spicuous label, as Fritz was never shown tearing it off.)

Concern for the young Henry aroused the suspicions
of his lovely fiancée Elizabeth (played by blonde Mae Clarke)
and their mutual friend Victor Moritz (played by handsome
matinee idol John Boles). Knowing the respect Henry always
had for Professor Waldman, they visited the dean at the
university and told him about his former student, who was
now in self exile in an old watchtower. The elderly professor shocked his two visitors, telling them that Henry
dreamt of creating human life from the remnants of the
dead. After listening to the pleas of Elizabeth, Waldman
agreed to accompany them to Henry Frankenstein's tower
laboratory.

Seen from the outside, Henry's watchtower was in
fact a studio miniature. The interior was one of the
cinema's most impressive laboratory sets. Designed by
Herman Rosse, the set was massive, reaching skyward
where a transom would open to receive the lifeless form
Frankenstein had assembled. The walls of the tower were
realistically set in crudely arranged bricks. There were
barred windows and a winding stairway to complete the
illusion. The laboratory apparatus[7] used by Frankenstein
was designed by Kenneth Strickfaden, who created some
weird devices that actually sparked and flashed with believable electric life. In the center of the laboratory was
the horizontal platform which would lift the dormant body
to the transom.

The watchtower was in the middle of a violent electrical storm in an upheaval of nature ideally suited to the
needs of Henry Frankenstein. The scientist looked proudly
at the gigantic human form on the platform, covered with
a white sheet. "There's nothing to fear," Henry assured
Fritz, who was recoiling in terror from the stitched limp
hand. "Look. No blood, no decay. Just a few stitches."
Then Frankenstein pulled the sheet to reveal the top of the
creature's head, with the black bangs and pieces of ad-
joining metal. "And look! Here's the final touch ... the
brain you stole. Fritz. Think of it! The brain of a dead
man, waiting to live again in a body I made! With my
own hands ... my own hands. Let's have one final test.
Throw the switches!"

Henry Frankenstein (Colin Clive) tests his fantastic equipment (built by Kenneth Strickfaden) in Universal's 1931 <u>Frankenstein</u>.

Fritz did as he was told and, aided by Henry who worked the other controls, brought the furies of electricity into the laboratory machines. The test showed that all the equipment was in perfect working order. The storm would be at its peak within fifteen minutes. Frankenstein was thrilled, for the world's greatest scientific experiment was about to begin.

Professor Waldman, Elizabeth, and Victor arrived at the watchtower at precisely the worst time. Forced to give them entrance because of the storm, Henry announced his extraordinary plan to the small gathering:

> Dr. Waldman, I learned a great deal from you at the University ... about the violet ray, the ultra-violet ray, which you said is the highest color in the spectrum. You were wrong. Here in this machinery I have gone beyond that. I have discovered the great ray that first brought life into the world.

The professor was skeptical; demanded proof. "Tonight you shall have your proof," Frankenstein retorted. "At first I experimented only with dead animals. And then a human heart which I kept beating for three weeks. But now, I am going to turn that ray on that body, and endow it with life!"

"And you really believe that you can bring life to the dead?"

"That body is not dead," Henry replied to his former superior. "It has never lived. I created it. I made it with my own hands from the bodies I took from the graves, the gallows, anywhere!"

After Waldman examined the sheeted creation, Henry began the experiment. The platform holding the patchwork corpse was raised to the thundering storm--to the lightning, while the laboratory erupted with the splendors of electricity. No longer was the creation of the Monster left open to speculation as far as procedure was concerned, as Mary had written of it. Electricity had been established as the Mother of the Frankenstein Monster; thus it would remain.

Karloff himself regarded the creation scene in _Frankenstein_ with remembered fear.

The scene where the monster was created, amid
booming thunder and flashing lightning, made me as
uneasy as anyone. For while I lay half-naked and
strapped to Doctor Frankenstein's table, I could see
directly above me the special-effects men brandishing
the white-hot scissorslike carbons that made the
lightning. I hoped that no one up there had butter-
fingers. [8]

At last the electrically-charged body was lowered to
the laboratory floor. Slowly the fingers of the creature
moved. "It's alive! It's alive!" Henry shouted again and
again. He was seized by unholy emotion, so violently that
Waldman and Victor were forced to exert all their combined
strength in restraining him. (The Hayes Office, that seemingly omnipotent board which dictated what could and could
not be publicly screened in those days of movie-making,
was worried about <u>Frankenstein</u>. It dealt with the objection-
able theme of a man trying to play God. James Whale was
careful not to treat the story in an offensive way. The
Hayes Office even allowed actor Colin Clive's next line to
be spoken in 1931. "In the name of God," Henry emoted,
"now I know what it feels like to <u>be</u> God!" The line was,
however, deleted by the censor in a later re-release of
<u>Frankenstein</u> leaving a jump cut where it had been.)

Days later, Henry Frankenstein and Dr. Waldman
were seated in one of the tower rooms. The professor
warned the young scientist, "Here we have a fiend whose
brain. . . . "

"His brain must be given time to develop," said
Henry. "It's a prefectly good brain, doctor. Well ... you
ought to know. It came from your own laboratory. " Waldman's words were grim: "The brain that was stolen from
my laboratory was a criminal brain!"

Frankenstein tried to dismiss the issue, arguing that
the brain would develop normally given ample time. But
Waldman insisted that he had created a monster, one that
would destroy its creator. Then heavy footsteps could be
heard approaching the closed door of the room. It was the
Monster. The two men extinguished their candles, throwing
the room into darkness. The footsteps stopped and the door
began to open. Seen only from behind the Frankenstein
creature lumbered into the room.

The first shots of the Monster's face were expertly directed. It was first seen in a full shot. There was an abrupt cut to a medium close-up, then a quick shift to an extreme close shot. The effect was thoroughly terrifying in 1931 (before the make-up became familiar from overexposure) as if the Monster and the audience were nearing each other. The absence of music in this scene (as well as the rest of the picture) heightened the horror. The Monster and the viewer had met, face to face with the impact their meeting would have had in reality in such a setting as the old tower.

Henry then showed Waldman the effect light had upon the creature that had so recently been "born." He opened the overhead transom, allowing the warm rays of the sun to streak into the chamber. As if recalling the crackling light from the sky and machinery which spawned him, the Monster futilely tried grasping it, unable to touch the intangible. Then light in another form confronted the creature. Fritz rushed into the room holding a blazing torch. This light could burn, eating away the flesh with excrutiating agony (establishing the beast's fear of fire). The hunchback continued torturing the creature. Later he paid for his repeated sadism. Henry and Waldman heard a scream and found Fritz hanging lifelessly from the ceiling, a rope entwined about his neck. Censorship again attacked Franken-stein. The scene in which the Monster actually killed Fritz for his cruelty, understandable for a creature with an imperfect brain, was cut from the final release prints. What remained was a shot revealing only the shadow of the hunchback, his corpse dangling from the rope.

Henry now realized that the Monster had to be destroyed, reversing the process of creation. Leaving Dr. Waldman alone in the laboratory to dissect the pathetic being, Frankenstein returned to his family estate to relax and marry Elizabeth. This made old Baron Frankenstein (played by hefty Frederick Kerr), Henry's stubborn father, happy since he had suspected another woman was taking up his son's time. The villagers had long been preparing for the celebration.

[Facing page: In this scene censored from the 1931 Fran-kenstein, Henry Frankenstein (Colin Clive) and Dr. Waldman (Edward Van Sloan) discover the Monster (Karloff) hanging the sadistic Fritz (Dwight Frye).]

At the watch tower things were not so lax.   Dr.
Waldman was about to end the Monster's unnatural life.
As the creature lay drugged on an operating table, the
professor took notes.   "Increased resistance is necessitating stronger and more frequent injections," Waldman
wrote.   "However, will perform the dissection."   As the
professor prepared to begin taking the Monster apart piece
by piece, the creature moved unnoticed.   The enormous
hand seized the old man's neck and squeezed with fatal
result.

While the wedding feast began getting underway,
Hans (Michael Mark), a woodsman, left his little daughter
Maria (Marylin Harris) to watch their property while he
looked at his animal traps.   During his absence the Monster
lumbered out of the woods and encountered the child.   She
had been tossing flowers into the lake and watching them
float.   Dropping to his knees the creature was delighted.
"Would you like one of my flowers?" she asked, totally unaffected by the creature's bizarre appearance.   He accepted
the flowers with a gutteral vocal sound and smiled for the
first time in his short life.   "I can make a boat," the girl
continued, showing the Monster how nicely the flowers
floated upon the water's surface.   "See how mine floats."

The Monster mimicked her actions with his own
flowers.   When there were no more left he looked inno-
cently at the child, then moved forward ....   Most existing prints of Frankenstein do not have the succeeding action.   It was excised from all American versions of the
picture during the original release but shown in selected
foreign countries.   Since the footage is rarely seen today
(in certain re-release prints and never on television) and
in order to recreate as accurately as possible what happened during that scene, reproduced here is the relevant
portion of the Frankenstein script.

The scene was cut from American prints before the
film was released at Karloff's request (although it did appear in selected prints during a re-release in the Forties).
James Whale had tremendous respect for the actor and
heeded his explanation:

> My conception of the scene was that he would look
> up at the little girl in bewilderment, and, in his
> mind, she would become a flower.   Without moving,
> he would pick her up gently and put her in the

NO. FEET FRAMES   DESCRIPTION   REEL SIX   PAGE 5

29. 16   9   CLOSE UP BESIDE WATER
               The monster throws his last daisy into water -
               he watches it - then looks at his empty hands -
               he holds his hands out -
                              MONSTER
               Grunts -

30. 11   7   VIEW BESIDE WATER
               The monster leans over and picks Maria up -
               she screams - he rises and throws her into water -
               the water splashes up as she lights -
                              MARIA
               No, you're hurting me! Daddy!!

31. 2   0   CLOSE UP OF MONSTER
               Looking off - puzzled -

32. 8   6   VIEW BESIDE WATER
               The child sinking - Monster watching - surprised -
                              MONSTER
               Grunts -

33. 2   15   CLOSE UP OF MONSTER
               Puzzled -

34. 2   1   CLOSE UP OF WATER
               Smooth -

35. 4   1   CLOSE VIEW BESIDE WATER
               The monster rises - goes to f.g. - goes off at
               side and exits -

36. 56   15   VIEW IN BUSHES
               The monster coming thru the bushes - toward f.g. -
               he stops and looks around - walks along - camera
               panning - he stops beside tree and then goes
               on again -

---

water exactly as he had done to the flower--and,
to his horror, she would sink. Well, Jimmy made
me pick her up and do THAT (motioning violently)
over my head which became a brutal and deliberate
act. By no stretch of the imagination could you
make that innocent. The whole pathos of the scene,
to my mind, should have been--and I'm sure that's

the way it was written--completely innocent and
unaware. But the moment you do THAT it's a deliberate thing ... and I insisted on that part being
removed. [9]

An interesting point concerning the scene with little
Maria was made by Ivan Butler in his book The Horror
Film. [10] Butler observed that James Whale's selection of
an "ugly [sic] little girl" with an even uglier manner of
speaking heightened the pathos of the scene. Such touches
were characteristic of Whale. He often attributed offbeat
traits and habits to his characters, giving them true and
yet strange individuality. (When Fritz stopped his hobbling
walk to pull up his sock he demonstrated a true bit of
Whale characterization.)

The omission of the scene accomplished what Karloff
intended, while at the same time bringing a new and more
terrible element into the story. The next time we saw the
little girl she was a bloody corpse, carried by her father
through the streets of the village. [11] Now judging from the
girl's disheveled state, there is the blacker suspicion that
she was raped by the Monster. Hans' entry into town bearing the dead body of his daughter naturally brought the wedding festivities to an end. The pompous burgomaster Herr
Vogel (Lionel Belmore) organized three search parties to
find the murderous fiend. Realizing his own responsibility
for Maria's death, Henry led one of the three groups.

The Monster had already been in Elizabeth's room,
creeping silently through the window, surprising Henry's
bride-to-be while she made ready to appear before the
crowd in her wedding gown, a scene inspired by Mary Shelley's novel. But as the Monster could not speak and demand a mate as in the book, he had no real motivation to
kill Elizabeth. Instead he merely frightened her.

The search of the countryside for the Monster with
irate villagers storming about brandishing clubs and flaming
torches became an established ingredient in the Frankenstein
legend. [12] Finally in the hills (obviously an interior set,
but so atmospheric that it was most acceptable) Henry
Frankenstein encountered his Monster face to unsightly face.
For several moments the living horror looked with hatred
upon his maker. Then braving Henry's torch he lunged out,
knocking down the scientist. The Monster picked up Frankenstein in his mighty arm, then stomped off toward a
deserted windmill, which he then entered and ascended.

Leaving the castle and the dead Dr. Waldman behind, the
Monster (Karloff) fares forth into the countryside. [Over:
In his newly awakened brain, the Monster assumes that the
child Maria (Marylin Harris) is the same as the flower in
his hand and throws her in after the flowers.] Photos from
the 1931 Universal Frankenstein.

Down below, the villagers were using the Monster's
most dreaded enemy.   They were burning down the windmill.
Enraged, screaming with terror and from the pains of the
biting fire, Frankenstein's Monster hurled his creator from
the top of the burning mill.   Henry's wounded and weakened
body smacked hard against one of the windmill vanes, breaking his fall.   The villagers rushed to his assistance, taking him
off the vane and back to his home.

The Monster was trapped.   The flames were in-
creasing and the very structure of the windmill crumbling
all around him.   The creature that had been formed from
the dead was still screaming hideously when the mill collapsed into the remnants of the inferno.

Henry Frankenstein lay in his bedroom recuperating
from one of the most terrifying ordeals ever faced by a
man.   His servants would attend to him and soon there
would be a wedding in the house of Frankenstein. [13]

Frankenstein is undoubtedly the most famous, and
one of the greatest, horror films ever made.   The three
factors which made the film a classic were the direction of
James Whale, whose camera was remarkably fluid for a
film made in 1931 and whose shadowy atmosphere completely
devoid of comedy and music has never been equaled in such
a motion picture;   the make-up masterpiece of Jack Pierce
which remained believable even under the closest scrutiny;
and the performance of Boris Karloff as the Monster.   Karloff's Monster was never a wanton engine of destruction.
It was a pathetic character, begging with speechless lips
and a distorted brain for understanding, receiving only hatred and burning torches from the people.   Without the
genius of Karloff in the role, Frankenstein could have been
just another horror film.

Before the picture was officially released, Karloff
was not regarded by Universal as anything more than a
living prop.   The premiere of the film was in early December of 1931 in Santa Barbara, California.   When the cast
credits flashed on the screen the part of the Monster was
attributed to "?"   Only in the final title after the film had
ended, boasting "A good cast is worth repeating," was Karloff given credit for protraying the Monster.   "I was not
even invited," Karloff remarked about the premiere, "and
had never seen it.   I was just an unimportant free-lance
actor, the animation for the monster costume."

When <u>Frankenstein</u> opened the publicity sometimes was sensational. Registered nurses were stationed in theatre lobbies in case viewers should need their services. Although the picture was terrifying in 1931 it is doubtful that anyone actually required such help. During the picture's initial release in Chicago at the State Lake Theatre there was even more sensationalism. An actor named Jack Kelly wore a Frankenstein Monster costume, his face being sprayed with purple make-up. Kelly's wife stood several feet behind him clutching a string which was connected to a buzzer on his outfit, apparently making him "work." Together they paraded about the streets near the theatre, she guiding him around as if via remote control. As they turned a street corner in downtown Chicago the couple encountered an unsuspecting woman who immediately fainted. When she revived she wasted no time in suing the theatre.

As the reviews hit the trade papers Universal knew that the picture was going to be a success. After <u>Franken-stein</u> opened on December 4th it was praised in the 8 December 1931 issue of <u>Variety</u>:

> Looks like a 'Dracula' plus, touching a new peak in horror plays, and handled in production with supreme craftsmanship. Maximum of stimulating shock in there, but the thing is handled with subtle change of pace and shift of tempo that keeps attention absorbed to a high voltage climax, tricked out with spectacle and dramatic crescendo, after holding the smash shiver of a hair trigger for more than an hour.

> Finish is a change from the first one tried, when the scientist was also destroyed. The climax with the surviving Frankenstein (Frankenstein is the creator, not the monster itself) relieves the tension somewhat, but that may not be the effect most to be desired.

> The figure of the monster is a triumph of effect. It has a face and head of exactly the right distortions to convey a sense of the diabolical, but not enough to destroy the essential touch of monstrous human evil. Playing is perfectly paced.... Boris Karloff enacts the monster and makes a memorable figure of the bizarre figure with its indescribably terrifying face of demoniacal calm, a fascinating acting bit of mesmerism.

Photography is splendid and the lighting the last word
in ingenuity, since much of the footage calls for night
effect and manipulation of shadows to intensify the
ghostly atmosphere.   The audience for this type of
film is probably the detective story readers and the
mystery yarn radio listeners.   Sufficient to insure
success if these pictures are well made.

Indeed Frankenstein was successful.   The film cost
only $250,000 to make, yet it grossed over $12,000,000,
starting a cycle of horror films[14] and a countless list of
imitations.   It has enjoyed numerous re-releases.   As late
as 1969 the motion picture was given considerable distribution on a double bill with the original Dracula.[15]   The picture, like its Monster, seems to be indestructible.   More
remarkable as far as Universal was concerned was the immediate stardom achieved by the actor not "important"
enough to attend the premiere.   Karloff was getting fan
mail in the extreme.   Much of this mail came from children who were able to see through his greasepaint and electrodes to discern the true sincerity inherent in his portrayal
of the Monster.

Finally recognizing that Boris Karloff was a "name
star," the studio rushed him into The Old Dark House, directed by James Whale in 1932.   Karloff played Morgan,
the butler of a weird household.   He was made-up by Jack
Pierce with a heavy beard, scars, and a broken nose.   The
part was again that of a non-speaking brute who groped
around much in the fashion of the Frankenstein Monster.
There was a big difference between The Old Dark House and
Frankenstein.   Despite his lack of dialogue and his mini-
mal scenes, Karloff was given top billing.   A title introducing the film announced that, to dispel all rumors to the
contrary, the actor under the guise of Morgan was indeed
the very same Boris Karloff who played the Monster in
Frankenstein.   Boris Karloff had been transformed into a
star.   Unlike many stars who are manufactured in the studio publicity department--as was the Monster in Frankenstein's laboratory--Karloff was a tremendous acting talent.
A movie actor since 1919, his career was just beginning.

For the Frankenstein Monster, a stitched and burned
creature, was stirring at the base of the old windmill.

Frankenstein Takes a Bride

As early as 1933 Universal Pictures had planned to film a sequel to the extremely successful <u>Frankenstein</u>. The second sound Frankenstein movie was to surpass the original in greatness and feature in the role of a mad doctor the actor who had turned down the part of the Monster in 1931--Bela Lugosi. The Hungarian actor was to emote alongside Boris Karloff, who was signed to recreate his role of Frankenstein's Monster.

A press notice of 1933 reported Lugosi's plans: "His current role is opposite Karloff in <u>The Black Cat</u>.[16] Following this it was planned to co-star the two in Robert Louis Stevenson's <u>The Suicide Club</u> and <u>The Return of Frankenstein</u>."

Neither <u>The Suicide Club</u> nor <u>The Return of Frankenstein</u> saw production that year. Lugosi had again changed his mind by dropping out of the mad doctor part in the Frankenstein movie. <u>The Return</u> remained on the studio's planned production lists until 1935, when James Whale picked up the script and began casting the picture. Karloff was naturally the Monster again. The studio's publicity department had dropped the "Boris," despite its sounding Russian, in the belief that the simple "Karloff" appearing on advertising posters and in a film's credits seemed more foreboding.

Colin Clive was back as Henry Frankenstein. His wife Elizabeth, who had changed her hair color to brunette, was now played by beautiful Valerie Hobson, who years later would be involved in the infamous Profumo (her husband) scandal. The part of Dr. Pretorius, the role rejected by Lugosi, was given to English Ernest Thesiger, whose face was like a human hawk's and whose expression always indicated that he detected a foul odor somewhere. Dwight Frye, Fritz in the first movie, was cast as Karl, a demented killer and body snatcher. Comedy relief, absent from the first film, was given by the beloved English lady Una O'Connor as Minnie, the screeching housekeeper of the Frankenstein estate. Others in the cast included a very young John Carradine as a woodsman, an infant Billy Barty (later to become a famous television and movie personality) tyepcast as a baby, and eternally old Walter Brennan, who in this early phase of his career had a bit part--as noted in the 9 March 1935 "Call Bureau Cast Service" sheet for <u>The Return of Frankenstein</u>--"a Neighbor."

The film was to return to the original novel, picking
up where the 1931 movie had ended, and in many ways be
closer to the Mary Shelley story than its predecessor had
been.   In the novel the real conflict between creator and
creature began when Frankenstein refused to build the Monster a mate.   The mate was never finished in the book but
would come alive on the screen.   This was the premise of
the sequel to Frankenstein.

There was still deliberation about the title.   For a
while it was decided to call the film Bride of Frankenstein.
Again the decision went back to Return, as the Universal
executives feared that confusion would result since the
"Bride" would be that of the Monster.   For a while, according to a 1935 movie fan magazine, the film was going
to be called Frankenstein Lives Again!   After much consideration it was settled on the better title, Bride of
Frankenstein.

In the role of the Bride was the delightful wife of
actor Charles Laughton, the very British Elsa Lanchester.
Whale's own selection of British performers in his casts
made one think that his Frankenstein stories were taking
place in England, although the costumes worn by his actors
were Germanic.   Miss Lanchester also played the part of
Mary Shelley in the film's prologue: "James Whale in his
production of Bride of Frankenstein did deliberately use me
to play both 'Mary Shelley' and the monster's bride," wrote
Elsa Lanchester in a letter to Life magazine for 5 April
1968, "because he wanted to tell that Mary Shelley indeed
had something in common with the dreadful creature of her
imagination. "

Elsa Lanchester was turned over to make-up artist
Jack Pierce for her transformation into a female creature
composed of parts of corpses.   Pierce did not give her the
same trappings as he had given Karloff.   Apparently since
Frankenstein had gained some experience in creating life,
and since he would be aided in assembling the Monster's
mate by sinister Dr. Pretorius, the Bride would not appear
so grotesque.   Miss Lanchester was too short to be a
worthy mate for the gigantic Frankenstein Monster.   Pierce
gave her shoe lifts, then wrapped her hands and arms in
mummy-like bandages and had her wear a floor-length gown
that hid her true height.   This gown was indeed a macabre
article of clothing, for it resembled both a wedding dress
and a burial shroud.

Pierce's own readings in the subject of Egyptology entered into his creating the Bride's make-up. Remembering statues of Queen Nefertiti, Pierce gave the Bride a similar appearance by making her thick mass of hair, streaked with lightning-like silver, stand out from her head. This matched the gauze on her arms for effect. The eyebrows shot up like those of a movie vampire. The Bride's neck showed stitched scars where the head had been attached. The "Bride of Frankenstein" stood seven feet tall in the disguise. She was a veritable monster, a suitable mate for Henry Frankenstein's first attempt at creating a human being. Yet despite her terrible appearance, there was something weirdly attractive about the Bride that made her even more bizarre.

The appearance of the original Monster was changed by Pierce to conform with the incidents in the script by William Hurlbut and again John L. Balderston. One hand and arm, the hair, and right side of the face, had been severely burned by the windmill fire. The head was nearly bald (although a short crop of hair grew back by the end of the picture), and for the first time we could see the stitches and healed wound that ran about the top of the head and down the left side to the ear. (The top wound did in fact lie beneath all of Universal's Frankenstein Monster make-ups--including the later Herman Munster--although it was covered by hair.) The Monster's clothing had also shown damage done by the flames.

Press releases said that the creature's make-up was now a pale green. (Similar statements were printed concerning the Monster's color in Son of Frankenstein in 1939. Green seemed a more suitable color for a being made from dead limbs. It is possible that Pierce changed the color from bluish gray to green for the sake of experimentation. But he later stated that his Frankenstein Monster had always been gray, leaving the inconsistency more credible if conceived by the publicity department. Bride of Frankenstein was filmed in black and white. What photographed best mattered; not what looked best when seen on the live set.

Bride of Frankenstein opened with Mary Shelley in the early nineteenth century speaking about her brainchild Frankenstein to foppish Lord Byron (Garin Gordon) and her husband Percy (Douglas Walton). This was the role credited to Miss Lanchester in the film's titles. Like Karloff in the first film her name became a question mark to

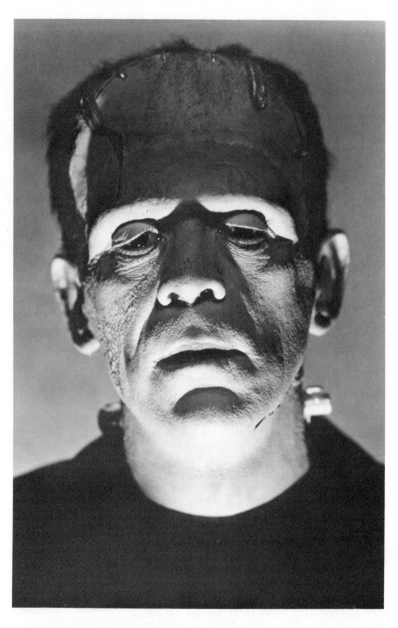

The burned and scarred Monster (Karloff) in the 1935
Universal sequel, <u>Bride of Frankenstein</u>.

identify the actress playing the Bride. Mrs. Shelley explained that the Monster did not die in the flames of the
mill and that the story was just beginning. The scenes of
Mary Shelley presented an almost ludicrous anachronism in
Bride of Frankenstein. The setting for the prologue was
Mary's own era of the 1800s. When her flashback narration dissolved onto the screen with her fading words, the
picture miraculously jumped into the future by almost a
hundred years. [17]

The curious villagers watched until the last burst of
fire sent the wreckage of the windmill into crumbling ashes.
Hans, the father of the poor child drowned by the Monster,
waited after the other spectators had left. He wanted to
see the charred bones of the Monster before he would be
satisfied and return home. Despite the pleas of his wife
(who was not written into the first film) Hans entered the
wreckage. Then the floor collapsed, tossing the man into
the stagnant cistern below the structure. A pale hand
moved out of the shadows. The burned, hate-filled face of
the Frankenstein Monster followed. In another moment
Hans met the same fate as did his Maria. The brutal killing of Hans was witnessed by a passively blinking owl, beginning the story with a decisively James Whale touch of
the macabre.

The set in which the Monster drowned Hans was
only one of many elaborate and often bizarre sets created
for the film by Charles D. Hall. Often his sets included
little absurdities like steps leading nowhere. Some enormous sets representing forests and hillsides were constructed
indoors, with countless naked trees filling the area like staggering prison bars. These were more than obviously manufactured. Yet they were photographed with the sweeping
camera work of John D. Mescall in such a way that the
artificiality was almost welcomed.

When Karloff worked on the scene in which the Monster killed Hans he was subjected to some rather unpleasant
inconveniences. He wore a rubber suit under his regular
clothing to keep out the coldness of the water. Unfortunately
it did not keep out everything. The suit accidentally filled
with air. Karloff then proceeded with the scene, lurching
toward his victim. As he moved, his outfit inflated like a
balloon. To the laughter of the crew he floated. He had
done what the Monster had envisioned for Maria. Karloff
was injured during that scene. His left side was bruised

to the extent that he needed massage and infra-red ray
treatments to relieve the pain and stimulate blood circulation. (A stand-in was spared the hardships of waiting
around under the studio lights in the uncomfortable costume
between takes. Instead of a living double the prop department literally built a stand-in. The prop Frankenstein
Monster was made from a seven-foot high pole of one half
inch piping and moved on rubber tires. The makeshift
double was given a plaster face in the image of Karloff as
the Monster.) The Frankenstein Monster climbed out of
what was believed to be his grave and hurled Hans' wife
into the watery basin. He was free again to obtain mercy
and understanding or deal out a grim revenge.

Young Henry had finally married Elizabeth, making
her the first of the film's two "brides," this one really the
bride of Frankenstein. Henry's father had passed away,
leaving him to be the new Baron Frankenstein. During one
particularly windy night the Frankenstein household was
visited by the spectral Dr. Pretorius who had been expelled
from his teaching position at Henry's former medical school.
Pretorius had his own theories concerning the secrets of
death and the creation of life. Henry did not want to discuss his own experiments with the doctor. But when he
was told that the older scientist had also created humanoid
life, the Frankenstein curiosity made him decide to get
involved.

Henry followed Pretorius to his tiny apartment where
the latter showed him the results of his own experimenting.
From a casket-like chest (purposely designed in that form
by Whale) Dr. Pretorius removed six glass jars, each containing a tiny, living homunculus. Henry gasped at this
"black magic," seeing the miniature archbishop, ballet
dancer, king (in the likeness of Henry VIII), queen, mermaid (from an experiment involving seaweed), and devil
who, Pretorius boasted, resembled himself. The king's
habit was to climb from his jar to get to the queen. [18]
Frankenstein was startled to learn that the doctor did not
work from the scraps of the dead but literally grew his
homunculi from seeds.

Pretorius approached Henry with the idea of collabor-
ating on a new living being, combining their techniques.
Frankenstein, recalling the ecstacy of his last excursion at
usurping the rights of God, accepted the weird invitation.
Together they would create a woman. "That," said

Pretorius, "should be really interesting."

(The following scenes were cut from the final release prints of <u>Bride of Frankenstein</u>: Dr. Pretorius had
introduced Henry to Karl, a homicidal maniac working as
a resurrection man--one who dug up bodies for dissection
by doctors and medical students. Karl had once brought
Pretorius the body of a woman known to suffer from cata-
lepsy. Observing that the "corpse" was still warm he proceeded to dissect her. The doctor had cut up much of the
woman before she screamed and he killed her out of mercy.
Pretorius finished his story telling Henry that Karl feared
him. As long as that fear existed Karl would be the perfect servant. Meanwhile in the village, the burgomaster
tried to convince the townspeople that there never was a
Monster made from the parts of deadmen; that he was just
a large but otherwise normal human being.)

The Frankenstein Monster was roaming the countryside. His hulking form was seen by a young shepherdess
who, terrified, lost her balance and toppled into a lake.
Reversing what he did to Maria, the Monster rescued the
girl from the water. She began to scream repeatedly.
Two hunters, thinking the Monster was attacking the girl,
shot and wounded him.

Prowling through the forest, his arm aching from
the pain of the bullets, the man-made man entered the hut
of a blind hermit (played by bearded O. P. Heggie). The
hermit immediately convinced the Monster that he was a
friend. In a truly beautiful and moving scene, the blind
man soothed him with a sentimental number played on his
violin--Ave Maria. Hearing the sightless man thank God
for his new-found friend, the Monster, for the first time
in his artificially given life, shed tears.

In the days that followed the hermit taught the Monster to speak simple sentences. "Bread ... good," is
a classic example of the creature's dialogue. Karloff disliked the idea of letting the Monster speak since he claimed
it broke the illusion established in the first film. However,
the speaking Monster gave new insights to his character
and closer approached Mary Shelley's concept.

The Monster had finally found a true friend. But
his happiness was not to last. Two hunters (one played by
gaunt John Carradine) entered the hut and tried to shoot

the giant, who retaliated and in the confusion and congestion, accidentally started the hut on fire. The Monster rushed out of the burning structure.

The villagers declared that the Monster was a vampire and had to be disposed of in the traditional ways. Bearing their torches they pursued the creature through the forest, descending upon him en masse, and binding him to a crude cross (symbolically identifying him with the crucified Christ). The trapped Monster was dumped into a wagon and imprisoned, chained to a throne-like seat in another macabre contrast. Chains could not hold the Frankenstein Monster. After a few tugs at his metal bonds and after overpowering his guards, he tore off the jail door and escaped. Panic seized the town as the Monster attacked all who stood in his way. (There were scenes filmed of Karl at the same time creeping through windows of homes robbing and wantonly killing his own victims, taking advantage of the confusion. These scenes were excised from the film, probably for the sake of better pacing.) As the Monster rampaged through the village to freedom, pursued by torch-wielding townsmen, the vibrant march composed for the picture by Franz Waxman[19] sounded over the action.

The Monster was chased to a graveyard, where he disappeared through a hidden entrance to an underground crypt. In that subterranean vault Dr. Pretorius had just disinterred the skeleton of a young girl. Alone, he was confronted by the Monster, who was delighted to learn that he would soon have a wife.

Later Henry Frankenstein began regretting his decision to make a second living creature. When he refused to go on with the experiment Dr. Pretorius revealed the card he had up his surgical smock--the living, demanding Monster. To insure that Baron Frankenstein would not desert him in this great work of mad science, Pretorius told the Monster to kidnap Elizabeth and take her to a secluded cave.

Forced to go on with the project Henry Frankenstein took Dr. Pretorius to the tower laboratory in which the original beast had been brought to life. There the two scientists began assembling the female body. The brain was grown by Pretorius' own process. But Frankenstein required a new female heart--a relatively <u>fresh</u> one. Dr. Pretorius squinted menacingly and told Karl to get him a

new heart.   In the original conception of the story, mad
Karl apparently crept into the cave, killed Elizabeth, and
sliced out her heart, presumably offscreen, for the Monster's mate.   This was later considered too gruesome for
the picture.   Instead Karl killed an unidentified woman on
the street and returned with his trophy which, he told
Henry, had come from a recent accident victim now lying
heartless in the morgue.

The sequence in which the Bride was given her artificial life was even more spectacular than that of the original Monster.   Huge bolts of lightning zigzagged across the
dark, stormy heavens. [20]   The top of the watch tower was
bombarded with sprays of white-hot sparks.   Great kites
rose into the sky to attract the natural electricity.   Then
the Bride, secured to a horizontal platform, was charged
by a vibrant, phallic electrical device which descended from
the ceiling to instill the beginnings of life into her on this
bizarre wedding night.   The form was raised to the ceiling
to receive the full power of the electrical storm, while in
a series of quick editorial cuts the weird devices of Frankenstein were shown to spark, hum, light up, and spin.
Over all this turbulence blared the climactic music of
Franz Waxman.

After the female body was lowered, Baron Frankenstein and Dr. Pretorius heard a low gasp from beneath the
bandages which completely wrapped the body.   The eyes
were staring wide open.   Again Henry spoke the lines of
power: "She's alive! Alive!"   The living woman, created
by two mortals, was unwrapped.   The head of the being,
with its upstanding electrified hair, snapped unnaturally from
side to side.   Dr. Pretorius, with his own brand of James
Whale humor, stepped back and said with the poise of an
ordained minister, "The Bride of Frankenstein!"   The scene
was even more bizarre as reverant music, accompanied by
wedding bells, came over the soundtrack of the film.   This
was James Whale at his best.

When the Monster was called in to meet the woman
with whom he was to spend the rest of his life, she did not
rush to his titanic arms so that he could carry her over
the threshold of their bridal crypt.   Instead she recoiled
in horror from her "husband's" monstrous appearance (not
taking the time to first see herself in a mirror) and moved
toward Henry.   Her motivation was really the result of
Elizabeth's heart, which had almost found its way into the

Bride's body before script changes were made.   Again the
Monster tried to attain the lanky woman's love.   With a
wide grin contorting his pathetic face, Frankenstein's original creature stroked her hands with delight.   The Bride
screeched again with a voice that reverberated through the
laboratory.   "She hate me," the Monster said, "like others!"
Unable to endure more pain in his heart, the Monster lumbered forward.   Pretorius looked in horror as the beast's
gigantic hand reached for a lever protruding from the wall.
"The lever!" Pretorius shouted, holding out his hands.
"Look out for that lever!   You'll blow us all to atoms!"

       The Monster told his creator to leave with Elizabeth,
who was now standing in the doorway of the laboratory.
The creature forced Pretorius to stay.   "We belong dead!"
he growled.   Then with a tear streaking his cheek the Monster pulled down the lever, which (like so many levers installed in laboratories in horror films to inevitably get rid
of incriminating evidence) ignited a chain reaction of ex-
plosives that erupted in a violent cataclysm of flames, falling bricks, and searing death, destroying himself, Pretorius, and the Bride of Frankenstein.

       The master scene in which the laboratory exploded
showed not only the Monster, the Bride, and Dr. Pretorius,
but also Henry Frankenstein.   The scene was quick, ex-
pansive, barely giving the viewer time to see both Frankenstein and the older scientist.   Nevertheless both scientists
were present, indicating that the scene was filmed prior to
that showing Henry's escape with Elizabeth.   (One version
of the script had Elizabeth die in the explosion.)   The final
shooting script, still titled The Return of Frankenstein,
gave Henry the suspicion that Elizabeth's heart was in the
Bride.   At the last moment Elizabeth, alive and well,
banged on the door of the laboratory, but was inadvertently
killed with the others in the explosion.   Had Elizabeth's
heart been stolen, Henry would have had even more reason
to perish with his two creations.   The storyline was changed
to that of the typical Hollywood happy ending.   Since the
costly scene had already been filmed, wrecking the set, it
was retained with the hope that no one would notice the inconsistency.   Hardly anyone did as their eyes naturally
watched the explosions.

[Facing page: The Monster (Karloff) was happy only on
rare occasions as when he first beheld his monstrous Bride
(Elsa Lanchester) in the 1935 Bride of Frankenstein.]

The reviews of <u>Bride of Frankenstein</u> were favorable, as in the following clipping from the 15 May 1935 issue of <u>Variety</u>:

> Perhaps a bit too much time is taken up by the monster and too little by the woman created to be his bride. Karloff (the Boris is shelved) is, of course, at top form as the monster using the same bizarre makeup as in the first Frankie film. He nevertheless manages to invest the character with some subtleties of emotion that are surprisingly real and touching. Especially is this true in the scene where he meets a blind man who, not knowing he's talking to a monster, makes a friend of him.
>
> When the film was previewed in Hollywood it ran 90 minutes, but seems to have been clipped 17 minutes since, oke since the footage is not missed.

<u>Bride of Frankenstein</u>,[21] surprisingly unlike most sequels to great films, was even better than its predecessor. With its more impressive sets and photography, its excellent music score, its humorous flavor and caricatures of human beings, and the performances of a superb cast headed by Karloff, the film was James Whale's masterpiece and the best of its type ever produced. For Whale there would be no more horror films. Universal executives tended to shy away from his new version of the Monster which, they contended, made him more human and less monstrous. (The Monster was actually one of the most "human" characters in the movie.) A controversial character himself, Whale was found mysteriously drowned in his own swimming pool in 1957.

The Frankenstein Monster had survived a burning windmill. An exploding watchtower should not be much worse for a creature infused with artificial life. Perhaps in the rubble of charred brick and crumbling ash a son could be born with the name of Frankenstein.

A Son to the Household

Boris Karloff had become identified with the Frankenstein Monster. He was a star, having received top billing in many films, most of which featured the Englishman as a horror or mystery character. People would stop him on the street, point, and say in astonishment, "Look, that's Frankenstein!" The image had become a part of him. Boris Karloff was grateful for his new popularity. As a personal in-joke he did the growl of the Frankenstein Monster in his next film in 1935, The Raven. In this Universal motion picture he played an escaped criminal named Bateman who roared and shook his fist like the Monster when he saw that he had been hideously disfigured through the surgery of Bela Lugosi.

In 1936 Karloff gladly accepted a role offered by Warner Brothers which was definitely an imitation of his Frankenstein movies. The picture was his first of that year, The Walking Dead, directed by Michael Curtiz. Karloff played John Ellmann in the film, a man wrongly convicted of murder and executed. Ellmann's corpse was taken to the super-laboratory of a scientist (played by Edmund Gwenn) who, like Frankenstein, subjected the body to his remarkable electrical equipment because he knew of the man's innocence. The result was that Ellmann returned to life in a manner quite similar to the numerous re-charge scenes of Frankenstein's Monster.

Karloff's make-up in The Walking Dead was an imitation of his Frankenstein Monster. He was given a short haircut streaked with electrically charged gray, which made his forehead look high and his head somewhat flat on top. His face had the deathly pallor and sunken cheeks that reminded viewers of his original Monster. The way he looked and the manner in which he silently stalked through the picture were very reminiscent of Frankenstein's creature.

Ellmann, in a state of life-in-death, lumbered after those who were responsible for framing him. Although he did not kill his enemies directly his appearance was enough to send them screaming into such agents of destruction as a speeding locomotive. Finally Ellmann died himself, but not before giving the chilling warning, "Let the dead . . . stay . . . dead."

Warner Brothers used scenes from The Walking Dead in the comedy film Ensign Pulver, released in 1964. Husky Burl Ives played a ship captain who only had this one film to screen repeatedly for his crew. (New footage had been added to the old scenes of the laboratory resurrection of Ellmann and the film was re-titled Young Dr. Jekyll Meets Frankenstein.)

The same year of <u>The Walking Dead</u>, Twentieth Century-Fox made <u>One in a Million</u>, directed by Sidney Lanfield.
The picture, which introduced Sonja Henie to the screen
and boasted an all-star cast, included a short ice-skating
spoof of horror films featuring the zany Ritz Brothers. Al
Ritz was made up with a face and padded suit patterned
after Karloff's in the original <u>Frankenstein</u>. The Ritz
Frankenstein Monster also remained together aided by an
enormous safety pin stuck to his chest. In 1939 a small
semi-professional company called Pixilated Pictures filmed
a version of <u>Frankenstein</u>. [22] It was significant in that the
film was the first amateur Frankenstein movie of any consequence, considered important enough to receive some
magazine coverage at the time.

However, that year the most elaborate, expensive, and
lengthy Frankenstein movie was made by Universal. <u>Son of</u>
<u>Frankenstein</u> was the most superbly mounted film in the
series and may even have been filmed (though not released)
in color. Gone are the stark blacks and whites of the typical Universal black and white film. The images are in
variations of rich grays reminiscent of a color film printed
on black and white stock. Many of the sets are simple and
uncluttered as were those of many early color films. Unfortunately there are not records in the Universal files to
confirm whether or no <u>Son of Frankenstein</u> was originally
intended for color release. The matter is a speculative
one.

James Whale was no longer associated with the series.
With his absence <u>Son of Frankenstein</u> was to be handled in
a different style. Boris Karloff (his name fully restored)
would still appear as the Monster. The film was scripted
by Willis Cooper, who placed the story twenty-five years
after the death of Henry Frankenstein, who had reportedly
died of shame over his past deeds. For the first time the
story had a defined contemporary setting. [23]

One of Cooper's first changes from Whale's concept
was the locations. Though supposedly in the same locale
as the previous films the town in which the Monster was
created was now simply called "Frankenstein." Since members of the family were of that town, a "von" was placed
before their last name to mean "... <u>of</u> Frankenstein."
Cooper also rearranged a bit of local geography. Originally Henry Frankenstein created the Monster in a watchtower located in the mountains and a considerable distance

away from the family estate. In the second film the tower
was completely reduced to a clump of ashes and a few
pieces of brick. In Son of Frankenstein the tower appeared
differently, was located on the family property, and was in-
tact except for the roof which had been blown off. The
tower now had a family crypt and a pit of bubbling sulphur,
which was not seen before, and which was reported as
dating back to the time of the Roman Empire. These were
inconsistencies. But Universal wanted the film to stand on
its own merits with basic threads of continuity, hoping that
people would have forgotten a few details over four years.

The Monster himself was changed for the third film
in the series. Despite all of his fervent learning in the
last movie to speak and attain some humanity, in Son of
Frankenstein he lost his ability to talk and, except for a
few touching scenes, had become more like a silently stalking robot. This was the beginning of the downfall of the
Monster's characterization. Within the next few films he
would become hardly more than an animated prop, appearing near the end of the picture to grope around a while
before the villagers set fire to the castle. In Son of
Frankenstein the Monster spent most of his time in a dormant state. When he finally did come to "life" he seemed
more like a human machine, almost totally devoid of emotion.

The appearance of the Monster was altered for the
film. All traces of burn scars had vanished over the years.
His forehead was strangely higher now, the top of his head
sloping back slightly. Less care was taken with the make-
up so that it appeared unfinished under the revealing close-
up lens of the camera. Karloff had put on weight over the
years and the Monster seemed less cadaverous than before.
Finally, the Monster was given a cumbersome fur vest to
cover his clothing. Karloff disliked the vest since it
changed the image even more, but primarily because it was
extremely hot and uncomfortable. Wearing that make-up
for a full day's shooting was enough of a discomfort for
someone already in his fifties. The added burden of the
vest made performing even more difficult, especially since
half of Karloff's scenes had him lying motionless on his
back for long intervals. Universal finally realized that the
fur vest was not right for the Monster and discarded the
idea for later films in the series.

Boris Karloff received only second billing in Son of

Boris Karloff put less humanity into his third portrayal of
the Monster in Universal's 1939 <u>Son of Frankenstein</u>.

<u>Frankenstein</u>, a demotion since the last film where his name
headed the credits.   The prestige name of Basil Rathbone
appeared above his in the cast titles.   Rathbone, who would
go on at Universal to make the Sherlock Holmes movie
series, played Wolf von Frankenstein, the son of the infamous scientist who created the Monster.   The actor disliked being considered a star of horror films though he
acted in a number of them, even during his last years.
(He died of a heart attack in 1967 at a spry seventy-five
years of age.) Rathbone was a perfect choice as the son
of Frankenstein, but was guilty of some embarrassing over-
acting in a number of scenes, especially when he tried to
remain calm during a dart game and attempted concealing
his knowledge that the Monster walked again.   Bela Lugosi
was finally definitely cast in a Frankenstein film.   Given
third billing, he played Ygor, a gross, heavily bearded
shepherd who had been hanged for grave-robbing.   Ygor
miraculously survived the hangman's noose, emerging from
the attempted execution with a broken neck, but very much
alive.   Officially dead, Ygor was free to do as he pleased.
He took refuge in the vacant Frankenstein laboratory structure, where he could be heard playing eerie strains on his
recorder.   Sometimes he would knock on the hardened pro-
trusion of his broken neck, feeling no pain.

Ygor was Lugosi's greatest role, lacking the hammy-
ness that had characterized his Count Dracula and other portrayals which were usually just variations of his vampire
performance.   Speaking with a gruff voice to indicate his
damaged vocal cords and through the impairment of a set
of large false teeth, Lugosi was almost unrecognizable due
to his make-up and excellent performance.

There was also Police Inspector Krogh, played by
English actor Lionel Atwill.   For Atwill it was the start of
a long series of Frankenstein films.   He would appear in
every succeeding serious entry in the Universal series,
playing either an inspector or village official.   Inspector
Krogh had boyhood ambitions to become a great general.
Those dreams were shattered when he was visited by the
Monster in an episode never shown in the earlier films
and which changed the Monster's innocence to sheer brutality.   The inspector's words made up one of the most vivid
speeches in any film of the series.   He addressed the new
Baron von Frankenstein, who had asked if Krogh ever
actually saw the so-called Monster.

"The most vivid recollection of my life," said Inspector Krogh.

> I was but a child at the time, about the age of your own son, Herr Baron. The Monster had escaped and was ravaging the countryside, killing, maiming, terrorizing. One night he burst into our house. My father took a gun and fired at him and the savage brute sent him crashing to a corner. Then the brute grabbed me by the arm! One doesn't easily forget, Herr Baron, an arm torn out by the roots.

Inspector Krogh now wore a wooden arm, which he manipulated with military precision with his good hand.

Son of Frankenstein was produced and directed by Rowland V. Lee, who, unlike Whale, handled the subject with total sobriety. The characters were real and developing, not the exaggerated caricatures that populated the first two films. They were shown in ordinary situations not related to building monsters in the laboratory. The Frankenstein legend was made believable. For the first time in the series, audiences could identify and sympathize with the characters. Frank Skinner, as had Franz Waxman, wrote a superb musical score which inevitably found its way into many later features and serials. The music actually seemed to say "Frank--en--stein" with its ascending notes of three written in four-four time.

Baron von Frankenstein, his wife Elsa (also a bride of Frankenstein, played by Josephine Hutchinson), and their cute but obnoxious little son Peter (blond, curly-haired Donnie Dunagan), traveled by train to the family estate. During the journey Wolf told his wife that people were now calling the Monster by his family name. This reflected the popular mistake. At the station they were given the coldest reception by the townspeople who still recalled the horrors of the Monster and saw in Wolf another potential mad scientist.

The von Frankensteins moved into the family mansion. The interiors of the house were designed by set decorator Russel A. Gausman and art director Jack Otterson. The latter was also responsible for some of the designs used in the Empire State Building. The interiors in Son of Frankenstein were less extravagant than those in the

preceding film, but they were more impressionistic, resembling those of some of the German silent fantasy pictures.   There were jutting angles and stark, barren walls
with strong straight-line shadows.   Photographed superbly
by George Robinson, the sets in the third Frankenstein entry added to the eerie mood of the film.

After the family had gotten reasonably settled in their
new home, Wolf von Frankenstein visited the ruins of his
father's laboratory, where the Monster was said to have
been created and destroyed.   There he met the half-crazed
Ygor, who revealed an ominous sight--the Monster, stretched
on a slab in the family crypt, dormant yet alive.   Apparently he was not even scratched by the last film's explosion.
Ygor snickered and told the Baron that the Monster can
never die and that he should make the brute well again.
The Baron, with the help of Ygor and Benson the butler
(played by Edgar Norton), attempted to bring the creature
back to healthy life, using his late father's laboratory equipment.   (Actually much new prop apparatus had been built
for the third movie.)   After charging the Monster with electricity and finding little movement in the large form, Wolf
gave up the project thinking that nothing could ever re-
animate him.   This established the familiar laboratory
scenes of future Frankenstein movies in that the platform
holding the Monster worked on a swivel and was not raised
to a storm.

Later things began to happen that chilled the marrow
of Wolf von Frankenstein.   Peter described a giant dressed
in a fur coat, who stiffly walked with large steps and
visited him through a secret wall panel.   Benson had mysteriously vanished.   Baron von Frankenstein rushed to the laboratory, where he met the walking Monster, now undeniably
alive and well.   Friendship existed between Ygor and the
Monster.   The broken-necked shepherd was the only person
for which the beast had any fondness.   And so the Monster
did what the officially dead man asked, mainly killing off
one by one the jurors responsible for sending him to the
gallows.   Von Frankenstein himself fell under the suspicious
monocled glance of Inspector Krogh.

The Baron confronted Ygor in the laboratory.   The
shepherd tried killing the scientist with a hammer, but as
he swung Wolf shot him fatally with his revolver.   When
the Monster discovered that his only friend had been killed
he let out an unearthly scream.   With a fiendish grimace

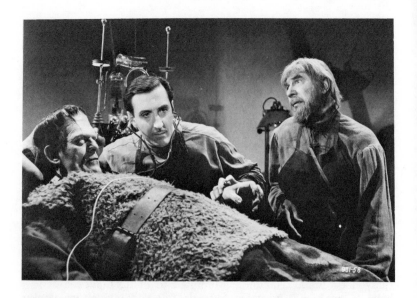

[Top:] Wolf von Frankenstein (Rathbone) attempts to revive his father's creation (Karloff) as Ygor (Lugosi) watches; [Bottom:] stuntman Bud Wolfe doubles for Karloff as the Monster is kicked into a sizzling pit of sulphur: both scenes from Universal's <u>Son of Frankenstein</u> (1939).

twisting his features he stomped off toward young Peter's bedroom. The little boy, glad to see that his giant friend had returned, did not resist his enormous, grasping hands.

The Monster led the boy through the catacomb-like passageways of the estate that led toward the sizzling pit of sulphur. He raised the boy over his squarish head and was about to release him to scalding death when some latent humanity clicked within his transplanted brain. Despite Wolf's having shot Ygor, the Monster could not murder the boy, especially in so gruesome a manner. Instead of tossing him into the brimstone the Monster placed the boy on a ladder. Peter ascended to the upper room and helped his titanic friend to the top.

But Inspector Krogh had arrived, his gun blazing at the hateful creature he met so many years ago. As if recognizing the policeman and enjoying a bit of ironic sadism, the Monster yanked off his wooden arm. With little Peter trapped beneath one gigantic boot the creature swung the artificial limb over his head like a club. The man and the boy seemed hopelessly doomed when suddenly Wolf von Frankenstein arrived and, exhibiting athletic prowess that would have made Tarzan of the Apes envious, swung down on a chain and kicked the Monster (actually stuntman Bud Wolfe) with the full push of his feet, sending him down into the sulphuric cauldron. Like a smoldering pebble in an erupting volcano the screaming Monster sank beneath the vat of molten sulphur. For a third--and most spectacular--time, Frankenstein's Monster had been destroyed.

Son of Frankenstein was the biggest Frankenstein effort of the Karloff trilogy. It certainly looked the most expensive. Unfortunately its ninety-five minutes made the story too long (the Canadian version being considerably longer). The film dragged in spots. Nevertheless it was the last of the classic Frankenstein movies.

Again the reviews were favorable. According to the review in the 14 January 1939 Weekly Variety:

> For offering of its type, picture is well mounted, nicely directed, and includes cast of capable artists .... Universal had given 'A' production layout for the thriller in all departments. Story is slow and draggy in getting underway prior to first appearance of Karloff, but from that point on, sustains interest at high peak.

Boris Karloff[24] never again played the Frankenstein Monster in a feature length motion picture. He later appeared in other Frankenstein films, but not as the Monster. After making Frankenstein--1970 in 1958, Karloff stated, "I'll never play the Monster again because I have sentimental affection for the character. I owe him so much that I owe him a little respect, a little rest." Although the Englishman never played the Monster in another full-length movie, he donned the guise on two other occasions. The first of these was during an all-star baseball game played in 1940 at Gilmore Stadium in Los Angeles. The game was between the leading men and the comedians of Hollywood. Karloff, in the Universal Frankenstein Monster make-up and clothing, stalked out of the dugout and lumbered up to home plate. Catcher Buster Keaton did a backward somersault and feigned unconsciousness. The Monster swung his bat at the ball and hardly tapped it due to the restraining clothing. Then he stalked toward first base. The first baseman fainted on the spot. At second base all Three Stooges fainted. The same happened at third base, allowing the Frankenstein Monster awkwardly to make a home run. The event was recorded by Ken Murray who incorporated it into his nostalgic Hollywood, My Home Town special first run on television in the early 1960s. The other instance in which Karloff again wore the make-up of the Frankenstein Monster was for an episode of Route 66 [see the chapter on television] in 1966.

Boris Karloff, unlike many other actors, enjoyed being typecast as a horror movie star. "The Monster was the best friend I ever had," the actor said. "Certainly I was typed. But what is typing? It is a trademark, a means by which the public recognizes you. Actors work all their lives to achieve that.... I got mine with just one picture. It was a blessing." Working for three decades after wearing the make-up of the Monster in Son of Frankenstein, Boris Karloff went on to star in over seventy-five movies, most of which were called, despite his dislike of the term, horror films. He was already scheduled to do a film in Europe called The Dark (eventually made without him in 1969 as Horror House for American-International Pictures) when on 2 February 1969 at the age of eighty-one Boris Karloff died in a hospital in Sussex, England, from a respiratory illness.

Tributes to Karloff mentioning his career as the Frankenstein Monster appeared in newspapers, on television,

Buster Keaton faints at the sight of the Frankenstein Monster
(Boris Karloff) coming up to bat at the 1940 all-star baseball game in Los Angeles.   Photo courtesy of UPI.

and on radio.   Motion picture director Ross Hunter announced
in 1970 plans to film a biography of Karloff which would undoubtedly feature the movie Frankenstein Monster.   A number of books about the actor were published during the first
few years after his death.   One of these <u>The Frankenscience
Monster</u>, a paperback edited by Forrest J Ackerman, published by Ace Books in 1969, was a collection of articles,
interviews, and personal impressions of the actor.   <u>Franken-
stein and Me</u>, a book written by Karloff and announced for
publication by Don Marlowe in 1969, has still not been issued.

Karloff received one of the greatest of Hollywood
tributes in 1957 when he appeared on Ralph Edwards' television show <u>This Is Your Life</u>.   In addition to seeing a number of photographs from his Frankenstein Monster role, Karloff was given the doorknobs from his old Universal dressing
room, which he dramatically put to his neck, plus the actual
electrodes handed him on television by Jack Pierce.

The only truly great Frankenstein Monster of the
films was Boris Karloff.   He left behind the giant boots
and heavy make-up after the film in 1939.   Still, beneath
the property of the von Frankensteins, that bubbling pit was
doing what it had not done, surprisingly, through all those
long years following the glory of the Roman Empire.   The
molten sulphur was cooling ... hardening....

Notes

1.   The fact that Bette Davis might have been tested for
     <u>Frankenstein</u> was related by William G. Obbagy,
     President of the American Bela Lugosi Fan Club.
     He has made a ten-year study of the life of Lugosi
     and related matters.

2.   The 1931 movie was based on the Peggy Webling play,
     which interchanged the first names of Victor and
     his best friend Henry.

3.   The scrapbook is now among the fantasy film archives
     of Forrest J Ackerman.   The quotations concerning
     Lugosi's <u>Frankenstein</u> are from that scrapbook
     through the courtesy of Mr. Ackerman.

4.   Edward Van Sloan, in an exclusive interview with
     editor Ackerman in the 31st issue, December 1964,

of <u>Famous Monsters of Filmland</u>, revealed: "Lugosi was made up to look like ... <u>the Golem</u>! His head was about 4 times normal size, with a broad wig on it. He had a polished, claylike skin."

5. A still photograph of the Monster from <u>Frankenstein</u> was used in the coming attractions trailer of <u>Murders in the Rue Morgue</u>.

6. Reported in "Memoirs of a Monster," by Boris Karloff as told to Arlene and Howard Eisenberg, in <u>The Saturday Evening Post</u>, (3 Nov. 1962), p. 79.

7. This apparatus continued appearing in humerous feature-length films and serials made by Universal. Curiously the sound effects used over some of the laboratory machines were used as the rocket ship sounds in that studio's Flash Gordon serials. The machines themselves were demonstrated at a special effects exhibit held in 1966 at Hollywood's famous Lytton Center of the Visual Arts. "Special Effects", an 8mm home movie of the exhibit, was made available by this writer.

8. Karloff, as told to Arlene and Howard Eisenberg, in <u>The Saturday Evening Post</u> (3 Nov. 1962), p. 79.

9. Interview by Mike Parry, "CoF Interviews Boris Karloff," in <u>Castle of Frankenstein</u>, no. 9 (November 1966), p. 12. This scene was satirized in the 1972 film <u>Schlock</u>, made by First Leisure films. The prehistoric, ape-like "Schlockthropus" similarly threw a girl feeding ducks into the lake.

10. London, A. Zwemmer; New York, A. S. Barnes, 1967; p. 42.

11. The "Frankenstein Village" was originally built for Universal's anti-war film <u>All Quiet on the Western Front</u> (1930). This quaint village set with its old-style houses and archways not only appeared in subsequent Frankenstein movies, but also in non-horror films made by that and other studios. Both Universal's <u>My Pal, the King</u> (1933), starring Tom Mix and Mickey Rooney, and its <u>Sherlock Holmes Faces Death</u> (1943), starring Basil Rathbone and Nigel Bruce as Holmes and Dr. Watson, used the

set. The village, built on the lot of Universal Pictures, still remains and is in use. It can (along with actors parading around dressed as the Frankenstein Monster) be seen on the tour given of the studio.

12.   Stock footage of the angry townspeople in Frankenstein was later used in the films Bride of Frankenstein (1935), The Mummy's Tomb (1942), and House of Dracula (1945). Scenes of the creation of the Monster later appeared in Bride and The Ghost of Frankenstein (1942). Shots of the Frankenstein laboratory apparatus in operation were clipped into later entries in the series like Frankenstein Meets the Wolf Man (1943) and House of Frankenstein (1944), the Flash Gordon serials and television's Munsters in the 1960s. All were made by Universal. Astor's Missile to the Moon (1959) used a clip of the Frankenstein equipment to represent the interior workings of a space ship! Way ... Way Out (1966), made by Paramount, used scenes from the ending of Frankenstein. "Wayne and Shuster Take an Affectionate Look at the Monsters" was an hour-long documentary made in the United States in 1966 for Canadian television. The show used clips from virtually all of the Universal Frankenstein movies, starting with the original.

13.   When Frankenstein was re-released years later on a double bill with its sequel Bride of Frankenstein this epilogue was removed so that the two films would flow together. The second Frankenstein movie picked up at the burning windmill, ignoring the convalescing Henry. Still later the scene was replaced in Frankenstein.

14.   Karloff always disliked the term "horror film." It was coined, he said, by Universal when they needed some term to describe Frankenstein. The word "horror," Karloff contended, conveyed revulsion; "terror film" would have been more appropriate. The term stuck, however, and has been used ever since. "The original monster and my later roles are tales of mystery and adventure," Karloff said. "Our stories were nearer to Grimm's fairy tales or Edgar Allan Poe."

15. A special press party, which was televised, invited
    various members of the Count Dracula Society of
    Los Angeles to Universal Pictures to celebrate the
    re-release of <u>Frankenstein</u> and <u>Dracula</u>. Society
    members came dressed as various Universal mon-
    sters, including Frankenstein's creature. One of
    the made-up Frankenstein Monsters was Anthony
    Brzezinski, whose amateur film <u>Horrors of Fran-
    kenstein</u> (1964), with Kenneth Carrol as the creation,
    received some magazine coverage.

16. A special bit of film was shot on the set of <u>The Black
    Cat</u> for publicity reasons. In this short scene Kar-
    loff and Lugosi were playing chess. Staring with
    menace they called each other "Dracula" and "Fran-
    kenstein," then broke into a joke and started laugh-
    ing. The clip was shown on "Monsters We've
    Known and Loved," a segment of <u>Hollywood and the
    Stars</u> (6 January 1964), the David A. Wolper tele-
    vision documentary series for NBC. Among the
    other items shown were still photographs of Karloff
    as the Frankenstein Monster, scenes from <u>Der
    Golem</u> and <u>Das Kabinett des Dr. Caligari</u>, etc.

17. The time period in which Universal's Frankenstein
    movies were set has frequently been a matter of
    confusion. Some of the clothing worn in <u>Franken-
    stein</u> implies a contemporary setting. The sets sug-
    gest an earlier period. A body was shown removed
    from a public gibbot. The practice of hanging bodies
    on gibbots for all to see was abandoned in Europe
    before the advent of the twentieth century. <u>Bride</u>
    seems to have been placed during the early 1900s,
    with actors in old-fashioned clothing. There were
    no automobiles, just horses and carriages used for
    transportation. In one scene Karl opened a coffin
    containing a skeleton from which all the flesh had
    long since rotted. The casket bore the inscription
    "1899." The film could not have pre-dated that
    year. A telephone was used but called an "elec-
    trical device." The telephone was patented as such
    in 1876. <u>Son of Frankenstein</u> was set in the pre-
    sent of 1939. The Frankenstein movies made during
    the 1940s still gave impressions of an earlier time.
    People rode on horseback or in old style carriages.
    Occasionally a character turned up with a flintlock
    pistol. Since the locale of these films was definitely

in the vicinity of Germany--with people given the
title "Herr"--where were the Nazis? The logical
assumption is that the Frankenstein movies were
set in a nebulous place and time to which viewers
could retreat from the real life terrors of World
War II, in an area of Europe existing in some
parallel realm untouched by the madness of Hitler.
If the Nazis were incorporated into the plots the
Frankenstein Monster would not have been so terrible.

18. Dennis Wheatley, in his novel <u>To the Devil--A Daughter</u>,
     London, Hutchinson & Co., 1953, retold an old le-
     gend upon which this scene was taken. Count von
     Kuffstein had created a set of homunculi living in
     bottles containing rain water, chemicals, and human
     blood; "... one of the males was said to have es-
     caped from his jar and died from exhaustion while
     attempting to get into the jar that imprisoned the
     prettiest of the females."

19. Waxman's score for <u>Bride of Frankenstein</u> became a
     popular piece of Universal music, becoming es-
     pecially identified with the studio's Flash Gordon
     serials.

20. One famous shot of real lightning, optically prolonged
     on the screen in <u>Bride of Frankenstein</u>, has become
     a common stock shot.

21. Scenes from <u>Bride of Frankenstein</u> were used in <u>House
     of Dracula</u> (1945) and in the "World Premiere" fea-
     ture-length movie made for television <u>Silent Night,
     Lonely Night</u> (1969), both from Universal. <u>Cry
     Uncle</u>! (1971) directed by John G. Avildsen and dis-
     tributed by Crest Films, was a murder mystery in
     which the television viewing of <u>Bride of Frankenstein</u>
     was significant in the solving of the murder.

22. Listed by Walter W. Lee in his summer, 1958 <u>Science-
     Fiction and Fantasy Film Checklist</u>.

23. Cooper's first draft of the script was a more direct sequel
     to <u>Bride of Frankenstein</u>. Wolf, the son of Henry
     Frankenstein, drove to his father's estate and there
     found not only the body of the Monster, but also the
     skeletons of Henry, the Bride, Pretorius, and his

homunculi. Scenes from <u>Bride</u> were to be incorporated
into the new film. The Monster, brought to life by a
bolt of lightning, demanded that Wolf create for him a
"friend." Wolf, however, planned to give the Monster
a good brain. Toward the end of the film, the army
was called upon to destroy the Monster. Meanwhile,
the Monster was about to operate on Wolf's young son,
transferring his brain to the skull of the corpse that
would eventually become his "friend." Wolf entered
the laboratory and, seeing his son about to die beneath
the Monster's scalpel, stabbed the giant with a knife.
Then the militia rushed in and fired upon the Monster,
driving him into a seemingly bottomless pit. A hand
grenade dropped into the pit apparently destroyed the
Monster. This plot was rejected, perhaps because the
Monster appeared too intelligent or because it relied too
heavily on <u>Bride</u>.

24.   Karloff's fifty-first birthday coincided with the filming
      of <u>Son of Frankenstein</u>. On 23 November 1938,
      with Karloff and the other members of the produc-
      tion--including Bela Lugosi, Basil Rathbone, Lionel
      Atwill, Donnie Dunagan, Josephine Hutchinson, Ed-
      gar Norton, Willis Cooper, Rowland V. Lee, and
      George Robinson--on the set, the actor was treated
      to a surprise party. All the actors were still in
      make-up. It was strange to see a grinning Fran-
      kenstein Monster, with the Baron, Ygor, and the
      others, read the inscription on the whipped cream
      cake: "Happy Birthday, Boris."

Chapter 5

A CHANGE OF IMAGE

Boris Karloff was out of the Monster's boots and make-up. Yet the list of Frankenstein movies was only beginning.

The Frankenstein Monster's next appearance was in 1940, in a Pete Smith novelty short "Third Dimensional Murder," made in the stereo process and directed by George Sidney. Ed Payson played the Monster in make-up (by Jack Kevan) surprisingly close to that created by Jack Pierce. The make-up seems to have been made of strips of cloth covering Payson's cheeks and chin. Blood dripped from the bangs and stitched scars surrounded the wrists, neck, and went up each side of the high forehead. Inspired by the Monster in Son of Frankenstein, Payson wore a fur vest. "Third Dimensional Murder" was a murder mystery set in an old mansion. The killer turned out to be the Frankenstein Monster, who mixed a cauldron of molten lead, then emptied it on his victims (and the audience) in 3D. Technicolor provided the film's green tint.

In 1941, Universal again resurrected their own Frankenstein Monster for Helzapoppin, directed by H. S. Potter and adapted from Ole Olson and Chic Johnson's vaudeville mayhem. A potpourri of visual gags almost buried the thin plot. One of these gags involved the Frankenstein Monster (played by stuntman Dale Van Sickel, who also appeared in the film without the Pierce make-up as a normal human being). Martha Raye had fallen into the orchestra pit at a party rigged so that anything could happen. A pale hand touched her shoulder and a deep voice offered her assistance. Miss Raye looked up to see the Frankenstein Monster, who promptly lifted her off the floor and tossed her back upon the stage with one mighty thrust.

Universal did not take another serious venture into the world of Frankenstein until 1942. The title of their

[Left:] Monster Ed Payson hurling a telephone into the audience in Third Dimensional Murder (1940); [right:] stuntman Dale van Sickel appeared briefly as the Monster in Universal's 1941 comedy Helzapoppin.

fourth production in the series was to be The Ghost of
Frankenstein. With Karloff out of the role he had created,
someone else who had box office potential with the horror
films audience had to be hired for the part of the Monster.
In 1940 the studio had made a film titled Man-Made Monster
(later re-released as The Atomic Monster), directed by
George Waggner. The film was originally intended for Karloff and Lugosi, and based on the story The Electric Man.
Kenneth Strickfaden, who designed Henry Frankenstein's
apparatus, created a new set of weird electrical devices
for the film, including a new metal platform. Dr. Regas
(Lionel Atwill) used the machinery to transform "Dynamo"
Dan McCormick into a glowing and stiffly walking creature
of electricity (with the special effects of John P. Fulton),
completely subservient to his will. McCormick stalked
about obediently, Dr. Regas' "creation" in a variation on
the Frankenstein theme. Inevitably the Man-Made Monster
electrocuted his creator and perished as barbed wire cut
through his insulated rubber suit, allowing his artificial
life to drain off.

        Dan McCormick was played by youthful Lon Chaney,
Jr., a husky actor whose finest performance was as the
slow-witted brute "Lennie" in the 1940 film adaptation of
John Steinbeck's Of Mice and Men. In 1941 Chaney would
become an immortal in horror films history as the star of
The Wolf Man, also made by Universal. Bits of the Lennie
characterization would affect Chaney's Wolf Man and other
fantastic roles, providing not only a youthful image to off-
set the older Karloff and Lugosi, but also to create characters with whom the audiences could sympathize. Viewers
welcomed the new image, Chaney's popularity grew with incredible rapidity, and Universal had their latest Frankenstein Monster.

        The actor was born Creighton Tull Chaney in 1906
in Oklahoma City, son of the legendary "Man of a Thousand
Faces." Creighton had no plans to become an actor during
his high school days, while Lon Chaney, Sr., was creating
his memorable screen characterizations. The elder Chaney
died in 1930; Creighton secured his first movie role two
years later, a bit part in Bird of Paradise. Creighton's
career was slow until he finally acquiesced to adopting the
name "Lon Chaney, Jr." in 1937. That year he signed a
contract with Twentieth Century-Fox. Beginning with his
Frankenstein performance he dropped the "Jr."

Jack Pierce again did the make-up for the Monster.
Chaney was stockier than Karloff, without the latter's gaunt
appearance. The new Frankenstein creature, though possessing the familiar electrodes and scars, took on a new
image that seemed to fit Chaney's more brutal and unsym-
pathetic performance. This was the beginning of the change
in the Monster, where he stomped about killing wantonly.
It also signaled the degeneration of the series in which the
Monster, with hardly any real characterization, would eventually become an undistinguished prop.

The rubber forehead piece worn by Chaney in The
Ghost of Frankenstein provided the actor with considerable
trouble. Molded by Ellis Burman (who also assisted with
assembling the laboratory set and fashioned the prop brain
used in the film), the forehead irritated Chaney's skin so
that he spent a week off the picture. During one especially
tedious day's shooting Chaney kept complaining that the forehead was causing him terrible pain and asked that the make-
up be removed. When no one complied with his demands
Chaney finally tore off the forehead piece, finding that his
own forehead had burst open and was covered with blood.

Ygor had been shot to death in Son of Frankenstein.
But Universal's characters seemed to be possessed of super-
energy. In The Ghost of Frankenstein Ygor returned (again
played by Bela Lugosi) complete with haircut and trimmed
beard. Apparently the time between films was utilized in
learning good grooming. Eric Taylor's original screenplay
for The Ghost of Frankenstein differed considerably from
what finally emerged on film. Wolf von Frankenstein had
moved to the miniature town of Vasaria and began running
an asylum for the insane. The Monster and Ygor became
separated as the brute was put into jail. Ygor went to visit
Dr. Frankenstein, where he met his hunchbacked assistant,
Theodor (movie scientists somehow had penchants for hiring
the handicapped). The two twisted men recognized a common bond and became friends. Meanwhile, Wolf demonstrated his newly developed ray, by which the dead tissue could
be revived, to a pair of university scientists. After learning of the giant that had been imprisoned, Wolf left his laboratory and met the bearded killer he thought dead. Meanwhile the Monster had escaped jail and burst into Frankenstein's sanitarium, where he killed Martha, Wolf's nurse
and sister-in-law, and freed one of the mad inmates of the
asylum against Ygor's wishes. Wolf and his wife "Elayne"
discovered Martha's body. In desperation, Frankenstein

A new Monster (Lon Chaney, Jr.) lumbers across the rooftops with Cloestine (Janet Ann Gallow) in Universal's 1942 <u>The Ghost of Frankenstein</u>.

gassed the threesome along with Elayne, then vowed, "There is only one thing I can do to rid the world once and for all of my father's monster--dissect it! The monster must be unmade, limb by limb, organ by organ."

Ygor revived and was told by Theodor how he had once been a medical student but his misshapen appearance had forced his expulsion from the university.

Wolf never dissected the Monster. Inspired by the ghost of his father he decided to implant a new brain in the Monster's skull. The brain of a recently deceased scientist named Gutterman was the likely choice. But Theodor substituted the brain of Ygor. While Wolf operated on the Monster, the hunchback aroused the inmates to poison the water and drive the people from the town. With the brain of Ygor, the Monster, now sporting a series of metal clips over the scar on his brow, joined the madmen in a raid on the town, killing the entire police force. As the Monster broke into a store, he lost both his eyesight and hearing. Wolf told Theodor that he had not yet fully revived Gutterman's brain and proceeded to restore the Monster's lost senses. At last Wolf learned the true identity of the Monster's brain. But in trying to stop the beast Frankenstein was flung into one of his own machines, which caused the laboratory to explode destroying all inside.

The story was substantially changed by W. Scott Darling. Wolf von Frankenstein, his family, and Theodor were all written out of the script. In the place of Wolf was Ludwig (played by the distinguished British actor Sir Cedric Hardwicke), "the second son of Frankenstein" and Doctor of the Mind. In the place of Theodor was the less disturbing (at least physically) Dr. Bohmer, played with sinister relish by Lionel Atwill.

The sulphur pit into which the Frankenstein Monster had plunged was now a hardened mass. Why the sulphur had waited since the time of the Roman Empire to harden within the space of three years was not explained. The villagers, believing their hamlet cursed by the very existence of the Frankenstein castle, decided to blow it up, including Ygor who had somehow survived all the bullets taken in the last picture. When the castle fell to the townspeople's dynamite, Ygor found that the Monster was not dead. The sulphur had preserved the artificial being. Outside the castle the weakened Frankenstein being was at

The Monster (Chaney), appearing ghostly from his covering of hardened sulphur, is led from the castle by Ygor (Lugosi) in <u>The Ghost of Frankenstein</u>.

least partially rejuvenated as a bolt of lightning leapt from the sky to strike his sulphur-covered form (which for advertising posters resembled a ghost).   "The lightning--it is good for you," chuckled Ygor.   "Your father was 'Frankshstein' ... but your mother was the lightning!   She has come down to you!"   Together the two horrors strode off to Vasaria where Ludwig Frankenstein would be forced to give the Monster its full electrical strength.

In Vasaria the Monster (with a clean set of black clothes) was intrigued by a young girl, Cloestine (Janet Ann Gallow) who did not fear him (ala the Golem).   When he took her to the top of a roof to recover her lost balloon, the villagers attacked.   The Monster was chained and put into prison.   Surprisingly no one in Vasaria knew the identity of the strange giant man with gray face and inhuman features.   The towns of Frankenstein and Vasaria were traversed on foot by Ygor and the slow-walking Monster. Surely such spectacular news could have gotten around within three years.

Ludwig went to the courtroom where the Monster was restrained.   When he denied knowing the identity of the beast, his father's creation broke the chains, then fled to Ygor, who waited outside with a haywagon and played haunting strains on his recorder.   Later the Monster entered the sanitarium and killed Ludwig's other assistant, Dr. Kettering (Barton Yarbrough).   When the Monster menaced Frankenstein's pretty daughter Elsa (Evelyn Ankers, a popular Universal horror films heroine), Ludwig filled the corridor with gas.   The Monster dropped unconscious.

Frankenstein transported the gassed Monster to the giant platform in his electrical laboratory, where the creature was restrained with straps.   (It has always remained a mystery why Universal scientists, regardless of their field, maintained such laboratories with platforms capable of supporting giants.   Perhaps this time the excuse was in the person of Lionel Atwill--Dr. Regis incognito--for the new Frankenstein equipment was the apparatus built for Man-Made Monster.)   The Monster revived amid the usual spectacle of electricity and tore aside his chest band.   Frankenstein, aware of the creature's strength, vowed to dissect him. Dr. Bohmer, once Frankenstein's superior but now unwillingly subservient due to a brain operation that failed, called the proposed project murder and refused to help.   Before Ludwig could begin to disassemble the Monster he was visited by his father's ghost--giving authenticity to the film's title--who talked him out of destroying the beast and replacing the criminal brain with a good one.   The ghost (also played by Hardwicke in an image superimposed on the wall) vanished and Ludwig decided to give the Monster Kettering's brilliant brain.   But Ygor played upon Bohmer's resentments of Ludwig and convinced the scientist to use his crafty brain instead.   Together they could rule the country.   The Monster had still other plans.   He kidnapped little Cloestine with designs on her innocent brain.

The Monster, learning that Ygor wanted to donate his brain, crushed him behind a metal door.   Dr. Bohmer salvaged his brain and substituted it for Kettering's.   After the operation Ludwig showed the "reformed" Monster to Eric Ernst (Ralph Bellamy), Elsa's fiance and Vasaria's prosecutor investigating the disappearance of Kettering.   To Ludwig's horror the Monster smiled, then spoke in the gutteral voice of Ygor (dubbed into Chaney's mouth by Lugosi): "I am not Dr. Kettering.   I am Ygor!"   No longer would the Monster be a pathetic creature, for Ygor's corrupt brain had made him undeniably evil.

Again the villagers stormed the castle.   The Monster fought them with poison gas.   He tossed Ludwig aside, then suddenly stopped aghast, totally blind.   Dying, Frankenstein explained that Kettering's blood was the correct type for the Monster's optic nerves but Ygor's blood was not.   In a sightless rage the Monster hurled Bohmer into a machine, electrocuting him.   Then the beast lumbered about the laboratory, stumbling into machinery which burned and exploded.   His pale face began to melt and peel.   Eric led Elsa away from the castle as the burning walls fell in to apparently see the last of Frankenstein's ghost and his Monster.

The 3 February 1942 issue of the Hollywood Reporter published the following review:

> [The film] inevitably stands on an imaginative par with all of its interest-gripping, quasi-scientific predecessors.   No exhibitor needs be told what they have done at the box office.
>
> George Waggner, more than ordinarily skilled in manufacturing screen thrills, guided the artful production.   Erle C. Kenton's direction makes

The Monster (Chaney) meets his deadliest enemy, fire, in the climax to Universal's <u>The Ghost of Frankenstein</u>.

magnificent use of every element of suspense, and
Lon Chaney, having dropped the Jr. , comes into his
traditional own as the giant monster. The cast is
definitely above average.

The Frankenstein Monster had a new image. No
longer did he motion pathetically for an explanation of his
humanity; nor did his face show the torment of a creature
existing in a world of aliens. He walked stiffly with but
one purpose--to kill. Universal's writers knew that the
possibilities in plotting the adventures of such a shallow
character were limited. The name of "Frankenstein" was
still potent at the box office, but the stories needed more
than a lumbering killer. That boost in the Monster's muscular arm would happen the following year on a particular
night "when the wolfbane blooms and the moon is full and
bright. "

Frankenstein Meets the Others

Universal felt that the Frankenstein Monster, though
physically stronger due to the electrical recharges given by
the two sons of Frankenstein, was no longer powerful enough
to sustain an entire film. What was needed was the inclusion of a second monster and a new type of horror film.
While the Frankenstein films of the Thirties were intended
to terrify an adult the new audience production with the
stress on action would thrill a younger audience.

During the early 1940s Universal's second most popular monster was the Wolf Man. When Chaney assumed
the role of the Monster in The Ghost of Frankenstein the
advertising boldly stated that the picture starred the "creator
of the Wolf Man. " There was little debate at the studio over
the title of the second Wolf Man feature. What could be
more commercial than Frankenstein Meets the Wolf Man?

The Frankenstein Monster was last shown as a blind
creature speaking in the voice of Ygor. Although Chaney
preferred playing the Monster to the Wolf Man, he was
naturally cast as the man doomed to become a werewolf on
the night of every full moon. As Lawrence Talbot was
doomed as the Wolf Man so Chaney was to appear as the
character in all succeeding Universal Frankenstein movies.
The most logical choice as the Monster, since he was to
speak in Frankenstein Meets the Wolf Man, was Bela

Lugosi. Ygor's voice would not require dubbing. Lugosi's career was already suffering. He had turned down the part of the Monster in 1931 and had ever since regretted his decision. The actor was willing to accept most any role. He accepted the part of the Monster for <u>Frankenstein Meets the Wolf Man</u> in 1943.

Lugosi's health degenerated as did his career in the films following <u>Dracula</u>. During the early 1930s bodily pains forced the use of morphine and Lugosi became addicted. The actor was finally cured after a stay in a hospital but died shortly thereafter, on 18 August 1956. His request that he be buried in the black cloak of Count Dracula was fulfilled.

Jack Pierce again applied the Frankenstein Monster's make-up, this time with a slightly smaller forehead piece. Unfortunately even in make-up Lugosi was miscast in the role. His familiar Dracula-like features were not concealed despite the heavy disguise. The actor's health was poor and reflected in the portrayal of the Monster. For reasons known only to Universal the Monster's dialogue was cut from Curt Siodmak's script and all references to his blindness deleted. The result was an already weak appearing Frankenstein Monster groping about stupidly with arms extended forward. Regrettably it was <u>this</u> image of the staggering Monster with outstretched arms that stuck with the public.

Since Lugosi's health kept him from anything strenuous in <u>Frankenstein Meets the Wolf Man</u>, he did little in the film except lumber around, grimace in some close-ups, and occasionally growl. "That yell," said the film's director Roy Neill, "is the worst thing about the part. You feel like a big jerk every time you do it."[1] Lugosi needed some assistance. Eddie (also known as Edwin) Parker was a stuntman who would eventually double many of Universal's monsters. His work as the Monster began in <u>The Ghost of Frankenstein</u>. The six-four Parker was primarily known for serials and Westerns in which he both stunted and acted (usually an indistinguished "heavy"). His size and muscular build made him ideal to perform the more dangerous feats of the Frankenstein Monster. It was the unbilled Eddie Parker who did most of Lugosi's work, especially in the climax, in <u>Frankenstein Meets the Wolf Man</u>. Parker died of a heart attack after stunting on the "Jack Benny Show" in 1957.

The picture opened with two graverobbers breaking into the tomb of Lawrence Talbot.[2]   Coincidentally, the full moon restored to animation the werewolf believed killed by the blows of a silver cane in the earlier film.   The next time the human Talbot was conscious he was in the Queen's Hospital in England.   That night Talbot again became the Wolf Man, escaped and killed a constable, then returned to the hospital.   He confessed, but the English Dr. Mannering (Patrick Knowles) refused to believe in werewolves.   Talbot was confined in a straightjacket but made the transformation, gnawed his way free, and went out desperately to locate the old gypsy woman Maleva (Madame Maria Ouspenskaya), mother of the werewolf whose bite had made him inherit the lycanthropic curse in The Wolf Man.   Maleva said that only one man could possibly give him the privilege of true death.   That man lived in Vasaria;   he was Dr. Ludwig Frankenstein.

In Vasaria the odd pair were received more than coldly when Talbot and Maleva expressed a desire to meet Dr. Frankenstein, who had died in the fire.   Time had passed since the Wolf Man chewed through his straightjacket and again the moon rose full.   A child was killed by the bloodthirsty werewolf, arousing the villagers to hunt down the beast.   A rifle slug sent the Wolf Man crashing through the burnt timbers of the Frankenstein castle and into an underground ice cavern.   In the morning, Talbot discovered the Frankenstein Monster in the ice.   For the first shot of the creature, a full screen close-up, director Neill chose not to use Lugosi but Parker.   The stuntman's face showed a much stronger Monster, with bulging neck muscles.   It was somewhat disappointing after the Monster eyes opened and in long shot Lugosi stomped through the cavern.

After the Monster was freed from the ice by Talbot, the two of them sat before a warming fire in the following scene cut from the release prints because the Monster spoke.   "I can't see you," the Monster said.   "I'm blind, I'm sick.   Once I had the strength of a hundred men.   If Dr. Frankenstein were alive, he'd give it back to me ... so I could live forever."

[Facing Page: (top) stuntman Eddie Parker, doubling for Lugosi, bears Baroness Elsa Frankenstein (Ilona Massey); (bottom) the Monster (Lugosi) and Lawrence Talbot (Chaney) chat by the fireside in a deleted scene; both from Universal's 1943 Frankenstein Meets the Wolf Man.]

"Do you know what happened?" asked Talbot.

"I fell into the stream when the village people burned the house down. I lost consciousness. When I woke, I was frozen into the ice."

"Buried alive," said Talbot with a shudder, recalling his own premature burial. "I know! I know!"

Then the Monster cried, "Dr. Frankenstein created my body to be immortal. His son gave me a new brain, a clever brain. I will rule the world forever if we can find the formula that can give me back my strength. I will never die. I will never die."

"But I want to die," Talbot replied. "If you wanted to die what would you do?"

The Monster grinned. "I would look in Dr. Frankenstein's diary. He knew the secret of immortality. And he knew the secret of death."[3]

Here the completed film resumes with the Monster, mouthing deleted lines, attempting to find the Frankenstein diary. All of value that they uncovered was a photo of Baroness Elsa Frankenstein. On the pretext of purchasing the Frankenstein estate, Talbot (using the name Taylor) met the beautiful Elsa (played by Ilona Massey), who managed to acquire a European accent since The Ghost of Frankenstein and who "could" be considered the "Frankenstein" who met the Wolf Man. That night the two of them attended a street festival when Dr. Mannering, who had been following Talbot's trail of animalistic killings, arrived. To further complicate matters the Monster walked into town and in a ludicrous scene frightened off most of the population. Talbot grasped his arm and assured the beast that he was his friend (a meaningless scene if you are unaware of the Monster's blindness). Then the two of them fled in a horse-drawn wagon.

The scene was deleted in which Talbot again spoke with the Monster in the ruins of the laboratory. "What made you come out?" Talbot asked angrily. "You gave us away! You spoiled our last chance! I was working on the doctor, on Elsa. I almost pursuaded them to help. Then I had to run and save you from the people of Vasaria. And now I daren't come out!"

"I was afraid," the Monster said, "you had left me."

Meanwhile the villagers were restless.   The mayor
(Lionel Atwill reformed) tried calming them down.   Elsa,
Mannering, and Maleva, who had been held prisoner, ventured to the Frankenstein ruins.   There they encountered
the Monster who would have attacked them if not for Talbot's intervention.   If the lines had not been omitted the
Monster would have been heard saying, "This man will give
me back the strength of a hundred men?   Then I won't hurt
him."   Elsa produced the Secrets of Life and Death by
Dr. Frankenstein from a secret compartment in the wall.
Reading the diary Dr. Mannering learned that the Monster
could be destroyed by draining off his artifical energy.   The
almost immortal Talbot could find death if his real energy
were transmitted elsewhere.   The Frankenstein machinery
was repaired and Talbot and the Monster were strapped to
platforms in wait of the experiment.   Unknown to the Monster he too was to find eternal death.   New machinery had
passed through Vasaria and was delivered the laboratory.
Once more the villagers moaned, with Vazec the innkeeper
suggesting to the others (including "Rudi," played by former
"Fritz" Dwight Frye) that they blow up the dam which turned
the Frankenstein generators, drowning them all.

Although Dr. Mannering was the hero of the film, he
did exhibit some of the traits of Universal's stock mad
scientists.   Inspired by the machinery, Mannering spoke to
himself: "I can't destroy Frankenstein's creation.   I've got
to see it at its full power."   Hurriedly he readjusted the
machinery and the laboratory erupted with power.   Elsa
entered as the Monster vibrated with electricity.   The camera came nearer to the character in a progression of cuts,
culminating in an extreme close-up of his eyes.   The heavy
lids opened.   Frankenstein's Monster looked about and in a
less extreme shot he smiled.   The creature was at its peak
strength and no longer blind.   (Again the scene lost its
meaning as there was never any mention of the Monster's
blindness.)

The Frankenstein Monster burst its bonds and, for no
reason other than dramatic license, attacked Dr. Mannering
and lumbered up the stairs bearing Elsa in his arms.   Talbot, who had been neglected, fell under the influence of the
full moon.   His face sprouted hair and fangs (with the varied
make-ups of Pierce and the perfect lapse dissolves of special effects expert John P. Fulton) and the Wolf Man tore

through his bonds. In a flash of movement the Wolf Man
leapt upon the Monster from behind and caused him to
stumble down the stairs. The moment that the audience
had waited for had arrived. The battle between the "Frankenstein" and the Wolf Man was on!

Dr. Mannering and Elsa escaped and Vazec proceeded to light the dynamite at the dam while the two horrors fought. The Monster tossed machinery about with
superhuman strength as the snarling Wolf Man leaped from
high places, fangs aimed at the creature's throat. The dam
exploded sending water down the hillside toward the ruins.
At last the river crashed in through the wall, engulfing
both monsters in crumbling walls and an uncontrollable tor-
rent. Soon every bit of the Frankenstein ruins, along with
the Monster and the Wolf Man, passed from view. Again
Vasaria was safe from the horrors of Frankenstein.

The 19 February 1943 issue of the Hollywood Reporter reviewed:

Roosevelt meets Churchill at Casablanca, Yanks meet
Japs at Guadalcanal--and yet these events will fade
into insignificance to those seemingly inexhaustible
legions of horror fans when they hear that Frankenstein meets the Wolf Man. Yay, brother! This is
the picture they've been waiting for and it's a nightmare, a symphony on the organ of doom with all stops
out, with Moussorgksy's 'Night on Bald Mountain'
for a chaser. The business it is going to do will be
limited only by the seating capacity of the theatres in
which it will play.

Universal had provided fans with two infamous monsters. The Frankenstein films of the 1940s were aimed at
a substantially younger audience than the adult Karloff films
of the 1930s. Younger fans demanded more if there were
to be additional films in the series. The studio decided to
go into the multi-monster business full force and star five
fiendish horrors in their upcoming film of 1944 The Devil's
Brood.

The Wolf Man naturally would return along with the
Frankenstein Monster. For the other three monsters Universal tapped both the past and other studios. The original
Count Dracula, not on the screen since 1931, was resurrected in the person of John Carradine. Daniel the

hunchback was an attempt to at least suggest Victor Hugo's
Quasimodo of Notre Dame and was portrayed by J. Carrol
Naish, who gave the best performance in the film.   The
fifth so-called "monster" was Dr. Gustav Niemann, a mad
scientist played by Boris Karloff, who had been making a
series of "mad doctor" films at Columbia.   For fans who
did not pay attention to studio trademarks it would seem
that the film was a crossover between the Frankenstein and
"mad doctor" series.   Karloff refused to portray the Monster, but accepted this other role, keeping his tongue in his
cheek.   Nevertheless it looked good after the film was released under the title House of Frankenstein, starring Boris
Karloff.   Many viewers entered the theatre expecting to see
Karloff again wearing the make-up of the Monster.   Some
left the theatre utterly confused, believing the English actor
had somehow played both parts.

Again there was a new Frankenstein Monster.   By
now the character had been so reduced in prestige that
Universal no longer found it necessary to cast a famous
horror star in the role.   Instead they turned to the Westerns and a six-three, ex-wrestler, ex-rodeo performer,
whose real name was ideally Glenn Strange (Sam the bar-
tender on television's Gunsmoke in later years).   Strange
told the present writer how he acquired the role of Frankenstein's Monster:

It's kind of a funny thing in a way.   Jack Pierce
was making me up for a show with Yvonne DeCarlo
and I had to wear a big scar.   I was lying in the
chair.   Now I didn't know this, but they had been
testing guys for the Monster.   Guys like Lane
Chandler.   But I didn't know it.   I didn't know Jack.
This was the first time I ever met him.   He said,
'Just a minute,' and went over to the phone and
called Paul Malvern.   Well, I knew Paul very well.
I'd made a lot of Westerns for him.   Paul was on
the lot and was going to produce House of Frankenstein.   He came down and Jack said, 'Here's the
contour we've been looking for.   Right here.'   And
Paul said, 'That's fine with me.   Do you want to
put it on him and try it out?'   So when I was through
with the DeCarlo show they put it on me.   I went
out and did a few little walk-throughs in the Monster
get-up and they said 'Okay.'   And that was it.   That's
the way I became the Frankenstein Monster.

Luckily for Glenn Strange, the mad doctor was played by Karloff who created the role of the Monster.

> Nobody ever helped anybody as much as Boris Karloff helped me. I never forgot that. I asked him for advice because I wanted to do this thing as near as he did. He was very kind about it. He would stay on the set and coach me. I knew when I was on tour with the Abbott and Costello thing he was in New York doing Arsenic and Old Lace. A lot of people came backstage and congratulated him on the Abbott and Costello thing. And in the Sunday paper in New York he had given them the story of not he doing it, but me doing it. The whole thing. So right after I read that story, when I'd finished the act, I'd always come out for two or three minutes and talk to the audience. I would always say, 'If you folks liked me as the Monster in Abbott and Costello Meet Frankenstein, then I want to give most of the credit to the man who created it, and the man who helped me in the show that I did with him where he did the doctor. And he coached me on the walk and the movements and so forth. And if I made a good Monster, the credit goes to one of the nicest guys I know, Boris Karloff.' Later on somebody told him what I was doing. But it was the only thing to do. He was getting all the write-ups for the thing and naturally, even though the younger generation knows better today, would. But even today you say to the older generation, 'Who's the Frankenstein Monster?' and they'll say 'Karloff.'

The actor's first encounter with the Frankenstein Monster was years before.

> Like my brother and I, when we saw the Frankenstein Monster in El Paso, Texas. Neither of us knew a thing about make-up, but we know that people couldn't just dig somebody up out of a grave, a piece here and there, and make a man out of it. And he said, 'You know they can't build a guy up like that and make him breathe again. But where the hell did they ever find a guy that looked like that?' This was the first Karloff Frankenstein. I never dreamed I'd be playing the part myself someday.

With Glenn Strange in the role, the Monster took on
a new glory despite the fact that he would walk only in the
final minutes of House of Frankenstein and its inevitable sequel.   Since virtually no one in the audience knew what the
actor looked like beneath the gray make-up there existed a
sense of mystery about the character.   As with Karloff in
1931, viewers saw only the Monster without seeing the rec-
ognizable faces of a Chaney or Lugosi.   Strange's features
were ideal for the Monster, with high cheekbones and just
the right amount of wrinkles and large hands.   The Frankenstein Monster looked super-powerful, even though Strange
accidentally hinted at the domestic by forgetting to remove
his wedding ring during some of the filming.   (Perhaps the
Monster still fondly remembered the Bride.)

House of Frankenstein, directed by Erle C. Kenton,
opened as Professor Lampini's traveling Chamber of Horrors
passed the Neustadt Prison.   Two of the bearded inmates
were the hunchbacked Daniel and Dr. Niemann, a mad
scientist obsessed with Frankenstein's transplantation of
brains.   A violent thunder storm raged and lightning struck
the prison, providing an escape route for Niemann and
Daniel.   They were given shelter by Professor Bruno Lampini (played by George Zucco, star of many minor horror
films), whose main exhibit was the actual skeleton of Count
Dracula.   Dr. Niemann commanded Daniel to kill Lampini
and his driver.   Then they shaved, assumed the others'
identities and drove the show toward "Visaria" for Niemann's
mad revenge on those responsible for sending him to prison.

The town Vasaria not only emerged in the new film
with a slightly altered spelling;   it was also moved to a different location.   Script writer Edward E. Lowe had apparently neglected to consult Siodmak's original treatment or
the previous Frankenstein movie.   For the old Ludwig Frankenstein estate would be in the town of Frankenstein and
Niemann's laboratory would be situated in Visaria.

Niemann had promised to make Daniel "like other
men," tall and straight.   He also had other plans to use
Frankenstein's records.   Before going to Visaria he first
wanted to search the Frankenstein ruins (the House of
Frankenstein of the title) for the coveted notes.   And before
that he would finish business in the town of Reigelberg with
his old enemy Herr Hussmann (German actor Sig Ruman)
the burgomaster.   Dr. Niemann, as Professor Lampini,
exhibited the horror show and later removed the stake from

Dracula's ribs to restore the vampire to life.   In return
for watching Dracula's coffin by day the doctor demanded
he kill Hussmann.   Count Dracula in bat form killed Hussmann, then kidnapped Rita (Anne Gwynne), the wife of his
grandson.   After a wild horseback chase, the police led by
Inspector Arnz (Lionel Atwill again in a role similar to his
Krogh in Son of Frankenstein but with two good arms)
watched the Count's coach overturn.   Dracula attempted
reaching the coffin dropped by Daniel.   But as the sun arose
he was reduced to a skeleton.   Thus climaxed the Dracula
sequence of the film, ending a story in itself.

The second part of the film centered upon the Frankenstein Monster and the Wolf Man.   In the village of Frankenstein, Daniel rescued a pretty gypsy girl named Ilonka
(Elena Verdugo, now the nurse of television's Marcus Welby)
from a sadistic member of their band, and promptly fell in
love with her.   The Frankenstein ruins were still on the
hilltop, damaged by the flood of the previous movie.   (Perhaps the villagers rebuilt part of the structure which was
shown totally destroyed in Frankenstein Meets the Wolf Man.)
Dr. Niemann and Daniel explored the ruins that night finding
the underground ice cavern.   Again the Frankenstein Monster was found in a frozen state along with the Wolf Man.
Thawed out, the Wolf Man became Lawrence Talbot and
agreed to find the Frankenstein records.   In return Niemann
promised to lift his werewolf curse.   Apparently Talbot's
resistance to cold was better than that of the Monster, who
was taken dormant from the ice this time.

Dr. Niemann and his strange brood journeyed to his
estate where he naturally had a fully equipped Frankenstein-
type laboratory.   The Monster was placed in a glass chamber where steam was to combat the tissue deterioration
caused by the ice.   Glenn Strange breathed by the use of
air tubes affixed to his nostrils by the prop men.   The
hoses were too long.   Strange was unable to exhale the bad
air.   He nearly suffocated before someone noticed that he
was pushing the panic button installed in the chamber if anything went wrong.

Dr. Niemann revealed his true plans when he kid-
napped two more of his former enemies, Ullmann (Frank
Reicher) and Strauss (Michael Mark).   To Ullmann the doc-
tor said, "I'm going to give that brain of yours a new home.
In the skull of the Frankenstein Monster!   As for you,
Strauss, I'm going to give you the brain of the Wolf Man,

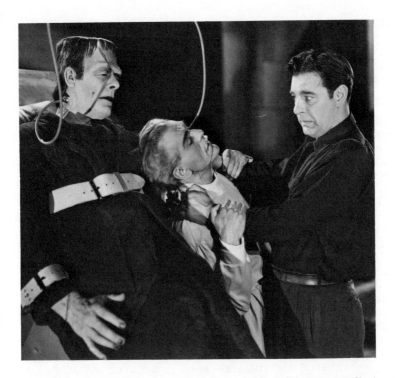

The Monster (now Glenn Strange) watches Lawrence Talbot (Chaney) try to force Dr. Niemann (Karloff) to perform operation to cure Talbot of being a werewolf, in <u>House of Frankenstein</u>, Universal 1944.

so that all your waking hours will be spent in untold agony, awaiting the full of the moon, which will change you ... into a werewolf!"[4] Perhaps Niemann's work had been too much of a strain, unless he believed that the entire make-up of a person and not the brain constituted his personality. Giving Strauss the Wolf Man's brain should kill the former and merely give the werewolf a new body. Later Daniel requested that his brain be transplanted into Talbot's body. But Niemann wanted Talbot's body for the Monster's brain to "add to and subtract from." There was a brain for everyone and every brain in its place.

Meanwhile the Wolf Man had been killing under the influence of the full moon. Jealous of Ilonka's love for Talbot, Daniel told her that he was a werewolf. When she learned the truth she made a silver bullet. As the

lycanthrope attacked her she fired it, putting the man she
loved at peace. Wounded fatally, Ilonka fell upon Talbot's
body and died.

Dr. Niemann was more concerned with the Monster
than with the fate of Talbot. The brains of Ullmann and
Strauss had already been removed. The Frankenstein Monster was strapped to the familiar platform and was receiving the great charges of dancing electricity. (One particular shot in the regeneration sequence showed a dummy
of the Monster actually electrified. Although Strange did
all his own scenes as the Monster the dummy's face was
in the image of Eddie Parker. It is reasonable to suspect
that the prop Monster was left over from some previous
Frankenstein epic in which Parker did wear make-up.)
Daniel brought the corpse of the woman he loved into the
laboratory. If Niemann had operated on Talbot Ilonka would
still be alive. That was the straw that broke the hunchback's back. Savagely he attacked his former master,
choking him to death, when the fully charged Frankenstein
Monster broke his restraining straps and hurled Daniel out
the skylight window.

As usual the villagers were in the area with their
fiery torches. They had been looking for the werewolf that
was preying upon their people. It would be an understate-
ment to say they were surprised in finding the Frankenstein
Monster instead. Luckily they knew the Monster feared fire.
Bearing Dr. Niemann in his arms the brute stomped out of
the castle, followed by the mob of townsmen. "I had to
come out of the castle where Karloff had brought me back
to life," Strange reminisced.

> I had a big strap that went underneath my coat, with
> a ring or snap on it. Karloff's double wore a belt
> around himself and I'd snap into the ring and then
> put mine around him. Because nobody can walk
> around with a guy hanging under your arm, and com-
> ing down those steep steps besides. There must
> have been about thirty or forty of those steps. They
> were chasing me with these torches. Somebody
> whizzed one of these torches--they were big with a
> long club, and all that burlap on them--and hit me
> right between the shoulders and almost knocked me
> off one of those steps.

With the shouting villagers in pursuit, the Monster was

Glenn Strange carries Karloff's double down castle steps, in <u>House of Frankenstein</u>.

driven with his burden into the swamp. Niemann pleaded
not to go that way because of the quicksand. But the Monster would rather go anywhere than face those torches.
With the marshland ablaze the Monster began to sink into
the quicksand. Shortly the Frankenstein Monster's head
dipped beneath the surface of the bog, followed by the gasp-
ing Dr. Niemann. Glenn Strange said:

> Then we went down into the swamp where we went
> into the quicksand. "That's where they lined up this
> big ring of tumble weeds, then a little clear spot,
> and then another ring. They were dousing this with
> some sort of chemical; I don't know what it was,
> I said to the special effects man that I couldn't move
> very fast with these boots on, and carrying this guy
> besides. And now he's really just out and I had to
> carry his whole weight. He said I had plenty of
> time to get across there. But actually I didn't.
> That was just one flash and burning all around there.
> I went straight through it, kicking the stuff out of
> my way as I went. It singed his hair. I almost
> lost that camera, I got in that water so fast, carry-
> ing him with me.

The review in the New York Herald Tribune of 16
December 1944 was not entirely favorable:

> You will have to be extraordinarily squeamish to
> get even a passing chill out of 'House of Franken-
> stein,' which came to the Rialto yesterday. The
> Universal offering would appear to have all the
> ghoulish ingredients of an effective horror film,
> but they manage to be about as frightening as win-
> dow models in broad daylight.
>
> The plot stumbles along endlessly in its top-heavy
> attempt to carry on its shoulders too many of yes-
> terday's nightmares.
>
> Despite the combined efforts of such expert menaces
> as Boris Karloff, Lon Chaney, John Carradine,
> J. Carrol Naish and Glenn Strange, the 'House of
> Frankenstein' is only a little more terrifying than
> the house that Jack built.

House of Frankenstein was a good action film, as
was its predecessor, with slick direction by Kenton, a

powerful musical score by Hans J. Salter, good make-ups and special effects, and an all-star cast of villains. Unfortunately none of the monsters--especially the Wolf Man-- were shown to any real advantage, the main characters being Dr. Niemann and Daniel. It almost seemed a waste having the actors endure the uncomfortable make-ups only to appear with them in a few scenes.

The scenes of the monsters were even fewer in the next and final serious entry in the Universal series, House of Dracula in 1945. The picture was inferior to its predecessors and such an obvious attempt to capitalize on House of Frankenstein that perhaps it should never have been made. Universal must have considered the series culminated in 1944, for Count Dracula and the Wolf Man seemed dead beyond any hopes of revival. Nevertheless both of them turned up in House of Dracula with no attempts made to explain their survivals. Again there had to be an impressive total of five monsters. New versions of the mad doctor and hunchback were created by writer Edward T. Lowe. The "mad" doctor was Dr. Edelmann (Onslow Stevens), who began in the film as a respectable scientist who just happened to live in a gothic castle complete with Frankenstein laboratory. (He could have gotten them from former neighbor Dr. Niemann.) The hunchback was now an otherwise attractive young woman named Nina (Jane Adams). Dr. Edelmann had been experimenting with molds that softened human bone and had promised eventually to mend the girl's twisted body.

Count Dracula (Carradine) came to the house (actually the house of Edelmann and not the vampire) seeking a cure for his vampiric condition. The scientist agreed to help him, suspecting that the causes of undeath were more medical than supernatural. That same night the doctor had a second unearthly visitor, Lawrence Talbot (Chaney). As the doctor was too busy to see him, Talbot quickly left the building. Edelmann was later summoned to the Visaria jail by Inspector Holtz (once again Lionel Atwill). Talbot had been put behind bars to await the rising of the full moon. When Edelmann witnessed the transformation from man to animal he agreed to help cure Talbot.

Edelmann theorized that Talbot's affliction was, again, attributable to his physiology rather than Gypsy curses. The mold that would help Nina and Dracula could also relieve the pressure of the cranium on Talbot's brain which,

added to self-hypnosis at the sight of the moon, caused the
physical metamorphosis. So far there was not enough mold
to perform the operation. Out of desperation Talbot hurried
to the edge of the cliff and leaped into the sea. Dr. Edelmann later followed him down where the water rushed into
the subterranean caves. There, after nearly being killed
by the Wolf Man before the moon set, Dr. Edelmann looked
about the cave. He noticed that the cave was ideal for
growing the mold. The scientist also possessed the luck
of the typical Universal scientist. Also in the cave was
the skeleton of Dr. Niemann and the preserved body of the
Frankenstein Monster (Strange), where they had been swept
by the quicksand years before. Strange recounted:

> Remember when I was lying in the quicksand in
> House of Dracula and the opening scene had me with
> the skeleton of Karloff? Well, I was in there all
> day long and that stuff was cold! They poured it
> down a chute and into this cave-like thing. And
> Chaney came down with a fifth and I think I got
> most of it. He poured it down me and it warmed
> me up some. They finished shooting and I went up
> to the dressing room. Of course they had a nice
> fire up there. They took the make-up off and by
> the time I got about half undressed I was so looped
> I could hardly get up. I got warm. And then I got
> tight. But I think he just about saved my life that
> day.

Later in his laboratory, Dr. Edelmann began to re-
charge the Monster (in the first of three relatively below
par regeneration sequences) for the sake of science, but
was talked out of it by Talbot and Nina. Dracula, however,
had begun to retreat to old ideas and placed his spell upon
Miliza. When Edelmann interrupted his meeting with her
on the pretext of giving him another transfusion, Dracula
mesmerized him and reversed the blood flow. Edelmann's
blood was contaminated by the blood of Dracula. The scientist revived with the aid of Nina; then she summoned Talbot.
Dracula was flying to Miliza's bedroom. The vampire bat
regained human shape as Edelmann drove off Dracula with
a crucifix and Talbot and Nina rushed in to attend to Miliza
(thus far the first meeting of Dracula and Talbot on the
screen). Dawn was nearing and Dracula had only one place
to hide--his casket in the basement of Edelmann's castle.
The doctor saw the coffin lid close. Then he opened it so
that the dawning sunlight bathed the undead creature,

reducing Count Dracula once again to bones.

There was much of the picture left to go. In es-
sence this <u>was</u> a Dracula film and the title fiend had already
been destroyed. But Count Dracula survived in Dr. Edelmann whose contaminated blood transformed him into a
Jekyll-Hyde type of living vampire (with a subtle Jack
Pierce make-up), with no reflection and who periodically
would delight in attacking jugular veins with his teeth. During a typically Universal montage dream sequence, Edelmann saw Dracula, envisioned himself the master of the
Frankenstein Monster who ravaged the countryside (incor-
porating footage of Strange with scenes from The Bride of
Frankenstein), and confronted by a cured Nina. In one mad
spell Edelmann again began to energize the Frankenstein
Monster but was stopped by a blown circuit. After regain-
ing his sanity the doctor used the mold to free the pressure
on Talbot's brain. When the full moon next arose Talbot
stood beneath its light. There was no transformation (nor
would there be unless he were subjected to exertion, an
escape provided by Universal if the character should ever
be revived). When Nina turned to thank Dr. Edelmann he
was gone. The electrical sounds issuing from the laboratory
told her what he was doing.

The villagers were already on their way with clubs
and torches, after being incited to riot by Steinmuhl (Skelton
Knaggs) whose brother Siegfried (Ludwig Stossel, television's
"Little Old Wine Maker") had been killed by Edelmann.
Edelmann had turned on all the power and was helping the
Frankenstein Monster off the platform when Nina entered the
laboratory. The mad human vampire stalked toward her,
and in a scene utilizing shadows with artistic effect, he
strangled her. Before she died Nina's screams summoned
Talbot, Miliza, Holtz, and the mob. The group burst into
the laboratory. The Monster killed one policeman with a
single blow. In a wild frenzy Edelmann thrust Holtz into a
machine, electrocuting him (the same death Atwill had in
The Ghost of Frankenstein). Then he turned toward the
others with death on his transformed face.

Talbot snatched up Holtz's luger. Though he dreaded
it, he fired at the advancing Edelmann until his face returned to normal and his body fell to the floor. There was
yet the Frankenstein Monster, again possessing his so-called
"strength of a hundred men," with which to reckon. Talbot
sent the mob away, then found himself battling the Monster.

The former werewolf pushed a great cabinet, filled with
chemicals, onto the Monster, who found himself in another
familiar fire.   Perhaps there was more reason this time
for familiarity.   For as Talbot and Miliza escaped the
building the remaining footage of the Monster stumbling
through electrical explosions, crackling flames, and falling
timbers was all footage from The Ghost of Frankenstein.
In a way Chaney was fleeing from himself.

Despite good performances, direction, make-ups,
and special effects, House of Dracula was vastly inferior to
House of Frankenstein.   While the first of the "house" pictures featured numerous locations and a particularly exciting
chase sequence (involving the police, Dracula, and the traveling show) in league with the high budget Westerns and action films, the sequel took place almost entirely within the
castle.   As for the plot, it was difficult to believe that two
monsters as famous as Count Dracula and the Wolf Man
could go so long living in the same building without their
knowing of each other's existence.   Nor did Dracula suspect
that the Frankenstein Monster was in the next room.   With
the exception of Dracula the monsters were wasted.   Frankenstein's Monster appeared in so little film it hardly
seemed worth the effort to make-up Glenn Strange.   And
the Wolf Man only appeared briefly in the Visaria jail and
in the cave.   Nevertheless the review in Variety, 29 November 1945, was quite good:

> 'House of Dracula' is Universal's horror special for
> the year and upholds traditions of company's past
> offerings in this field.   In point of eerie effects,
> fantastic characters and a plot in keeping with the
> mood early established, 'Dracula' has been well
> turned out by Paul Malvern, on production end, and
> Erle C. Kenton directing.   Edward T. Lowe's origi-
> nal screenplay lends credence to the actions of a
> cast identified with characters they play, and while
> there are the usual discrepencies in plot in stories
> of this nature, picture as a whole shall please hor-
> ror addicts.

The Universal Frankenstein Monster had met his
assortment of horrors.   As he perished for the second time
beneath the burning castle we sensed that he would never
lumber again. [5]   But there were two more characters to
meet who could, in their own way, cause as much trouble
as Dracula and the Wolf Man.

Frankenstein for Laughs

Bud Abbott and Lou Costello made up Universal's top
comedy team even when the studio became Universal-International in November of 1946.   The slapstick team's films
were declining as were the Frankenstein movies of the 1940s.
Universal-International decided to boost the thin Abbott and
pudgy Costello and capitalize on the former successful multi-
monster films by combining them in a blend of comedy and
horror titled The Brain of Frankenstein in 1948.   In its
original conception the movie would feature not only the
"Big Three" of Frankenstein's Monster (Glenn Strange),
Dracula (Bela Lugosi in his only other screen portrayal of
the vampire Count), and the Wolf Man (Lon Chaney), but
also Kharis the Mummy, Count Alucard (the Son of Dracula),
and the Invisible Man.   In the final screenplay by Robert
Lees, Frederic Rinaldo, and John Grant, the number of
monsters was reduced, omitting the Mummy and Alucard.
Perhaps the reasons were practical ones.   Chaney had been
starring as Kharis in the Mummy series and had worn the
noble garb of Alucard in 1943's Son of Dracula.   To his
fans he was Lawrence Talbot and there was little chance
that he would play three major roles.

The title, "The Brain of Frankenstein," was retained
even in the final shooting script.   However the film was essentially designed to arouse laughter instead of terror and
since that title sounded very much like a straight horror
film, the film was released under the less ominous name
of Abbott and Costello Meet Frankenstein.

When the studio was sold to become Universal-
International, both John P. Fulton and Jack Pierce were
replaced by younger men.   Doing the special visual effects
in Abbott and Costello Meet Frankenstein were David S.
Horsely and Jerome H. Ash.   The team duplicated many of
the Fulton tricks but failed somewhat in reducing Lugosi
to a slow-moving animated cartoon in the man-bat transformations. Bud Westmore, of the family of famous Hollywood make-up experts, replaced Pierce and made some
changes in both design and application of the established
monster guises.   Westmore made subtle alterations in the
Frankenstein Monster.   The forehead scar was more jagged
and the electrodes placed higher on the neck.   The hair
was longer and combed back at the sides.   Even the color
was changed from blue gray to silvery gray.   Portions of
the make-ups in both the Monster and the Wolf Man were

[Top:] Mad Dr. Edelman (Onslow Stevens) prepares to unleash Frankenstein's Monster (Strange) against the townspeople in Universal's <u>House of Dracula</u> (1945); [bottom:] the weakened Monster (Strange) is examined by Sandra (Lenore Aubert) and the evil Count Dracula (Lugosi) in Universal's <u>Abbott and Costello Meet Frankenstein</u> (1948).

molded from sponge rubber. These pieces were relatively
comfortable to wear as opposed to the make-ups created by
Pierce. "We had Jack Kevan and Emil Levine," said Glenn
Strange, "and of course Buddy Westmore in the Abbott and
Costello thing. They did some things I liked very much.
That is they made the scars in pieces and kept them that
way and put them on. Jack Pierce built them with cotton
and dried it. He'd set you in there for four hours and that
was it. I think by making the scars and putting them on it
saved quite a bit of time."

Glenn Strange enjoyed himself in Abbott and Costello
Meet Frankenstein. The studio was simultaneously making
Mr. Peabody and the Mermaid on nearby sets and the Frankenstein Monster and Ann Blyth in her fish tail having lunch
together surprised many tourists. Both Strange and Chaney
in their make-ups were later invited to the special Mr. Peabody and the Mermaid party where they hammed up some
villainy on the stage. Abbott and Costello Meet Frankenstein opened with Florida railroad baggage clerks Chick
Young (Abbott) and Wilbur Brown (Costello) receiving crates
containing the supposed dead body of the Frankenstein Monster and the skeleton of Count Dracula. These were exhibits for McDougal's (Frank Ferguson) House of Horrors.
Despite a warning telephone call from Europe from Lawrence Talbot, the two zanies delivered the crates. In the
House of Horrors, Dracula rose from his coffin and used
a small flasher to temporarily energize the Monster, who
vocally acknowledged the vampire as "Master." The two
living horrors fled the museum, leaving an infuriated
McDougal to demand their return or else the insurance
money. Wilbur knew the monsters were alive, but naturally
no one would believe him.

Dracula's plan was to give the Monster a new brain,
one "so simple, so pliable, that he would never oppose his
master." Sandra Mornay (Lenore Aubert) informed the
Count that she had the perfect brain for him--that of Wilbur,
her date for the following night's masquerade ball. The
Count, incognito as "Dr. Lahos," attended the masquerade
ball in his usual tuxedo and cape. Wilbur found himself
admired by Dracula and also by a second date, Joan Raymond (Jane Randolph), actually an insurance investigator
hunting down the missing exhibits. At the ball Dracula
hypnotized both Joan and Wilbur, while Lawrence Talbot,
having arrived in America, nearly killed McDougal as the
Wolf Man. Dawn arrived and Talbot in his normal state

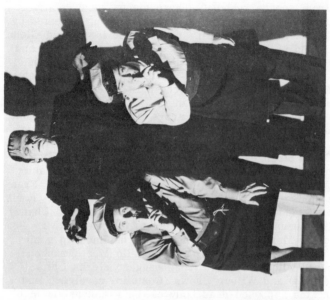

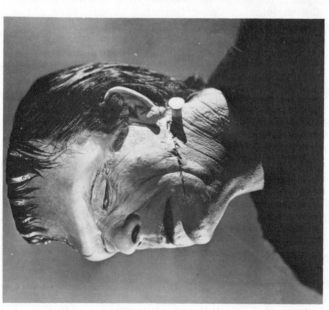

[Left:] the Frankenstein Monster (Glenn Strange); [right:] Bud Abbott and Lou Costello unaware of the Monster (Strange) lurking behind (publicity still); both from <u>Abbott and Costello Meet Frankenstein</u> (Universal 1948).

joined Chick to rescue Joan and their rotund friend.

The Frankenstein Monster had been in a weakened state, awaiting the brain operation to be performed by the vampirized Sandra and Dr. Frank Stevens (Charles Bradstreet), who eventually opposed Dracula and rescued Joan. Actor Glenn Strange broke into laughter numerous times as Costello continued to ad lib jokes and call him "Junior" and "Frankie." Costello's motive might have been the lengthy reel of outtakes showing the Frankenstein Monster laughing and cursing at him for ruining the scenes. The Monster had faced many hazards in the past but none like Lou Costello.

When the operation was about to begin, Wilbur was strapped to an operating table. Next to him was the dormant Frankenstein Monster, strapped to a horizontal platform. The laboratory sparked with the Strickfaden machines and a collection of new gadgets. Dracula observed as Sandra placed her scalpel against Wilbur's head without giving him ether. Suddenly Chick and Talbot entered the laboratory and hurried to Wilbur's rescue. Chick accidentally knocked Sandra out with a chair, then vacated the laboratory with Dracula in pursuit. It was left for Talbot to rescue Wilbur. But as Talbot began to unbuckle Wilbur's restraining straps, he gaped out the window in horror. Wilbur's body shook as he saw Talbot now as the snarling Wolf Man. Desperately Wilbur kicked and sent his platform cruising across the laboratory, only to be intercepted by Dracula. The two horrors struggled against the operating table. Then the Wolf Man sprang after the vampire, both of them leaving the shrieking Wilbur.

The laboratory apparatus had been working all this time. Although Dracula and the Wolf Man were no longer in the room, the worst was yet to come. Frankenstein's Monster snapped his bonds and stalked toward the helpless Wilbur. Before the Monster could reach him Sandra revived and tried commanding him. For a moment the spell worked; but then the Monster picked her up in his arms and tossed her through the skylight. Surprisingly the Monster seemed to take on a different facial contour and style of walking as he turned again to reach for Wilbur. To perceptive viewers the Monster in that one shot was reminiscent of The Ghost of Frankenstein. The Monster was not Strange in that brief appearance, but Chaney. Strange told this writer,

Lon doubled for me once when I broke the bones in
my foot. I was walking along in <u>Abbott and Costello
Meet Frankenstein</u> with a girl to throw her through
the window. I stepped on a camera cable. And
those boots, [6] you know, don't have any counter in
them. And it flopped over. We thought we'd lose
about three days shooting. But when they put the
walker on, what they did was--you know the soles
of these boots were four inches thick. You don't
see them, but they're built up inside. It's cork or
something like it. And they cut a section out in
there so this walker would sit down in it. Then
they slit the boot so I could get it on, and then
laced it, and then taped it, so you couldn't see it.
I don't know how much they weighed but they were
heavy. In the meantime Lon wasn't working that
day, so he came down. They put the Monster's
make-up on him and he did the scene for me.

Before the Monster could get him Wilbur was saved
by Chick. The two fled the laboratory and what followed
was sheer mayhem. Every door opened by Chick and Wilbur unleashed either the Frankenstein Monster or the battling
werewolf and vampire. In one particular comedy bit Costello purposefully disregarded the suggestion of Strange in
order to get another laugh. The Monster was to slam his
fist through a door and barely miss Wilbur's nose on the
other side. Repeatedly Strange told the comedian where to
stand so that he would not be hurt. Naturally Costello took
a step forward. When the powerful silver-gray fist crashed
through the balsa wood door Costello was solidly clipped on
the nose.

Count Dracula managed to reach a balcony of his
castle. In a final attempt to escape the savage lycanthrope
Dracula transformed himself into a bat. Before he could
escape the Wolf Man leapt upon the winged animal. Count
Dracula and the Wolf Man plunged from the balcony into the
turbulent waters below. Meanwhile the Frankenstein Monster was chasing Wilbur and Chick to the far end of a pier.
The two baggage clerks tried to get away in a rowboat as
the Monster hurled barrels at them, but the small craft
was still tied to the pier. Dr. Stevens quickly splashed
gas along the pier and set it ablaze. In a scene proving
that even the Frankenstein Monster could overcome his
fears after making seven serious motion pictures, the giant
bravely walked into the flames as the pier collapsed sending

him (in the form of a mechanical dummy) into the water.

Everything seemed all right now to Chick and Wilbur until a cigarette was lit by an unseen hand and the disembodied voice of Vincent Price[7] cackled that the Invisible Man had arrived too late "to get in on the excitement." As the film was geared to a primarily young audience, extreme caution was taken in presenting the monsters on the screen. While Frankenstein's Monster, Count Dracula, and the Wolf Man were each responsible for a list of corpses in the preceeding films, only the villains were killed in the Abbott and Costello film. Count Dracula only took Sandra's blood. And the Wolf Man did not complete his attack on McDougal. Despite the villainies, the monsters acted their antiseptic best.

Abbott and Costello Meet Frankenstein has long been considered the absolute blasphemy by purist horror film devotees. What greater sin could there be than to take such revered monsters and put them into a film with Abbott and Costello? Actually the monsters were portrayed, for the most part, entirely straight, due to the direction of Charles T. Barton and actors who still took their roles seriously. Take out Abbott and Costello and a straight horror story remains with Dracula seeking a new brain for the Monster, a theme familiar to the Frankenstein movies. The motion picture showed what would have happened if Abbott and Costello (with their screen images remaining consistent) were unfortunate to meet those infamous fiends.

Technically the film was superior to most of the serious Frankenstein films. The film was mostly action, making good use of the actors while in their weird make-ups, unlike their brief appearances in House of Frankenstein and House of Dracula. Certainly it was the best of the Abbott and Costello films. For what it was the motion picture was a total success. As a spoof of the horror genre nothing has ever equaled Abbott and Costello Meet Frankenstein. [8]

The 28 June 1948 issue of the Hollywood Reporter stated: "Charles Van Enger's camera work helps establish the eerie mood, and the art direction of Bernard Herzburn and Hiland Brown is excellent. Frank Skinner supplies a good musical score, and the editing is a credit to Frank Gross." The corresponding issue of Variety stated:

Combination of horror and slapstick should pay off

brilliantly for 'Abbott and Costello Meet Frankenstein'
in situations where the customers like their humor
wild and whacky.   The comics are at their nerve-
wracking best.   The added assist of Bela Lugosi as
Dracula, Lon Chaney as the Wolf Man, and Glenn
Strange as Frankenstein's Monster is so much more
gravy.

Glenn Strange later played the Frankenstein Monster
on various occasions on television.   His only other screen
portrayal of the Monster was in an amateur movie serial
The Adventures of the Spirit, Chapter Four, "Frankenstein's
Fury."   The serial was made in color in 1963 by this
writer.   His most unusual portrayal of the Frankenstein
Monster was in the late 1950s in Hollywood.   From twelve
noon till midnight for ten days, Strange, disguised in a
clown costume and black mask, was perched atop the 150-
foot-tall radio mast of station KTLA.   The object was for
listeners to decipher the clues given on the air and identify
the mystery man.   Both Karloff and Chaney received the
majority of votes.   The unmasking was televised.   A clerk
climbed the radio mast as the clown revealed himself to be
the Frankenstein Monster.   There was a struggle between
the two of them.   During the commotion a dummy was substituted for the clerk and was thrown from the mast by the
Monster.

Abbott and Costello's encounter with the Frankenstein
Monster sparked a long list of films in which they met other
classic horrors.   In 1953 Universal-International released
Abbott and Costello Meet Dr. Jekyll and Mr. Hyde, directed
by Charles Lamont and starring Boris Karloff as the scientist with the dual identity.   In one particular sequence Costello, as a turn of the century detective named Tubby, pursued the shaggy Mr. Hyde into a wax museum.   Among the
exhibits were wax dummies of the movies' Count Dracula
and the Frankenstein Monster (both actors standing rigid).
The Monster looked basically the same as in the earlier
Abbott and Costello film, except that the cheek scar was
raised and more severe.   The identities of the two actors
is not known.   They were probably bit players or extras,
Glenn Strange suggested, denying the publicity given out on
some of the still photographs that it was he under the make-
up.   When a live electrical wire came loose and brushed
against the Monster's electrodes the creature began to move
stiffly toward Tubby.   Luckily he evaded the Monster's
grasp.

Universal abandoned the Frankenstein Monster until he became a happy family man on the television program "The Munsters" and in the feature length movie adaptation <u>Munster, Go Home</u> (both covered in the chapter on television). But while the familiar Frankenstein Monster with squarish head and electrodes remained dormant, other studios began to use the character. The most significant list of new Frankenstein movies would prove that what Universal sought to hide for purposes of good taste could be shown in gruesome colorful close-up.

Notes

1. Obbagy, William H., "Bela Lugosi," Part II, <u>Horrors of the Screen</u> (Number 3, 1964), p. 42.

2. The scene of the two ghouls approaching the crypt was later used on the <u>Munsters</u> television show and identified as the infamous Burke and Hare. Other scenes from the film were used in the 1969 TV special <u>The Wolf Men</u>.

3. <u>Movie Story</u> magazine (March, 1943) fictionalized the story of <u>Frankenstein Meets the Wolf Man</u> including the Monster's dialogue. This magazine and <u>Screen Romances</u> did similar adaptations of the <u>The Bride of Frankenstein</u>, <u>House of Dracula</u>, and <u>Abbott and Costello Meet Frankenstein</u>.

4. This was the first film in the series to specifically refer to the creatures as "The Frankenstein Monster" and "The Wolf Man."

5. The Frankenstein Monster was imitated in 1946 in a color Paramount musical <u>Blue Skies</u>, directed by Stuart Heisler. Billy DeWolfe stalked across a restaurant floor mimicking the Frankenstein Monster, but wore no horror costume or make-up.

6. These boots were worn by Buddy Baer as the giant in Warner Brothers' <u>Jack and the Beanstalk</u> (1952), also starring Abbott and Costello.

7. Vincent Price began his career in horror films in Universal's <u>Invisible Man Returns</u> (1940).

8. Stock footage from <u>Abbott and Costello Meet Franken-
    stein</u> appeared in <u>The World of Abbott and Costello</u>
    (1965) and <u>Sweet Charity</u> (1968), both Universal, and
    on the Bill Cosby television special "Hey, Hey, Hey--
    It's Fat Albert" (1969).

Chapter 6

THE HAMMER OF FRANKENSTEIN

As Universal had given up its claim of being the
world's foremost factory of horror films, a new production
company in Great Britain would unearth the old classic monsters for new motion pictures series.   Hammer Films was
the creation of James Carreras in the late 1940s.   Eventually Hammer Films became situated on the banks of the
Thames River, where his Bray Studios were enlarged to
four sound stages.   When Hammer decided to revive the
monsters abandoned by Universal, its first such venture
was The Curse of Frankenstein, released in the U. S. by
Warner Brothers in 1957.   Hammer took on an entirely new
approach.   Unlike Universal's attempts to imply rather than
show physical representations of horror (i. e. , blood, isolated organs), Hammer dwelled on them in the most detailed
close-ups--always shown in vivid, bloody color--along with
a generous roster of well-endowed servant girls and bar-
maids who usually spilled out of their low-cut dresses.
There was a new audience to be satisfied--an audience that
required gore and sex to be horrified and to be lured to the
box office.

Jimmy Sangster avoided the plot of the 1931 Frankenstein for his scripting of The Curse of Frankenstein.   Using
some elements from the original novel, he wrote a new
story to be directed by Hammer's most competent director
of horror films, Terence Fisher.   Curse was set in Vic-
torian Switzerland.   Following Universal to an extent, Fisher
decided to create a new set of horror film stars--good actors, more youthful than the aging performers who populated
the films of the 1930s and 1940s.   Emphasis in Curse, unlike Universal, would be placed upon Baron Victor Frankenstein instead of his creation.   Distinguished actor Peter
Cushing was selected to portray Baron Frankenstein not only
as a dedicated scientist, but a pleasure-seeking man who
committed murder when it suited him.

Peter Cushing, born on 26 May 1913 in Kenley, Surrey in England, left his job as a surveyor's assistant for an acting career. His first appearance was a walk-on in J. B. Priestley's Cornelius performed by the Worthington Repertory Company. In 1940, Cushing began his film career in Hollywood. Ironically, his first role was assigned him by James Whale, the director of the Karloff Frankenstein, for The Man in the Iron Mask (1939). Continuing his career in films and on the stage, Cushing yearned to return to his native England and sailed into Liverpool in March 1942. There he settled and eventually became the new Victor Frankenstein.

For the role of the Creature (the term Monster had been abandoned) Fisher found a virtually unknown actor named Christopher Lee, whom he directed in Song for Tomorrow (1948). Christopher Frank Carandini Lee was born in London on 27 May 1922, his mother's family being one of the oldest in Italy, having intermarried with the Borgias. After World War II, Count Niccolò, an Italian ambassador to England and Lee's cousin, enflamed his interest in acting. The Count introduced Lee to an executive of Two Cities Films, who said that his six foot six inch height made him too tall for acting. Three weeks later, however, he acquired a small part in a film Corridor of Mirrors. Approximately thirty films later, and still no name actor, Lee's height was to be of advantage in The Curse of Frankenstein.

> [T]he idea of Frankenstein came up with Hammer. They were looking for someone to play the Creature.... They obviously wanted a very tall man, a man who had some knowledge and experience of movement and mime and who was able to act without speaking if necessary. My agent suggested me. I went up to see them, and they said yes. It was as simple as that. [1]

Hammer make-up artist Phil Leakey totally ignored the classic and over-familiar Universal mold for his version of the Creature. The Creature's face was a grisly arrangement of yellow and white putty, with a stitched gash running the width of the forehead, and black hair in a type of early Beatle cut. Both eyes were different colors, making one suspicious of Baron Frankenstein who surely could have gotten a matched set. Publicity for the film stated that different make-ups were created for the various

foreign versions of the film--a cyclopean version for Great
Britain, a four-eyed Creature in Japan.   However, Lee has
informed this writer,

> There is no truth whatsoever in the rumour that I
> wore a different make-up in The Curse of Franken-
> stein for supposedly different versions of the film.
> At no time did the Creature have three eyes.   Only
> two, one of which was diseased and ultimately be-
> came an eye-socket alone, because of receiving a
> bullet in the face.

> [Elsewhere, Lee added]   The make-up I wore took
> 3-1/2 hours to get on.   I could hardly move my
> head, or eat, or do anything.   I had all sorts of
> things glued to my face--undertaker's wax, plastic,
> all sorts of horrid things.   I felt enbalmed.   It was
> most unpleasant.   But I just took refuge behind my
> face and tried to forget it all. [2]

Lee was dissatisfied with the make-up, describing it
as "looking like a circus clown" in an issue of Britain's
Picturegoer.   Nevertheless the actor made the best of the
part of, as he put it, "a creation that lacked reality," portraying the Creature both as a savage fiend and tormented
beast, stiffly moving about and uncertain of its own human
capabilities.

> In The Curse of Frankenstein the depth of charac-
> terization was inevitably limited by the fact that I
> didn't speak.   But, on the other hand, a certain
> walk, a certain reaction, a certain thought going
> through my mind, was very important to the inter-
> pretation of the character.   I had a damaged brain,
> so therefore I walked slightly lop-sidedly;   and
> everything I did I did as if it was forced out of me,
> as if I was rather unwilling to do it, controlled by
> somebody else's brain--not my own. [3]

When Hammer first considered doing a new Frankenstein film, there were temptations on the part of the actors
to play it tongue-in-cheek.   Fischer, however, believed that
the old school monsters could still be terrifying, especially
with the added realism and color.   "In Curse," said Fisher,
"which started out as a bit of a giggle almost, the great
temptation was for the actors to send it up, to overdo things.
That's always the danger with these films.   But once I'd

told them to take it straight, they knew exactly what I was after. "[4]

   The Curse of Frankenstein opened with Baron Victor Frankenstein awaiting execution by guillotine for murder. The priest in his cell became a listener to whom the Baron narrated an incredible story.   Victor and his tutor Paul Krempe (Robert Urquhart) experimented in the Frankenstein castle for years until they successfully brought a dead dog back to life.   Together they considered more important experiments and decided to create a living man.   Krempe, however, was reluctant as Victor took the hanged body of a killer from the gallows and later acquired such necessary organs as the hands of a dead sculptor and a pair of eyeballs.   Victor took more initiative in securing the brain by murdering a famous scientist.   Inadvertently the brain was damaged by Krempe.

   The completed Creature lay wrapped in bandages like a mummy and suspended in a tank of chemicals.   Krempe, fearing the consequences involving Elizabeth (Hazel Court, who would appear in many horror films), Victor's fiancée, refused to help with the experiment.   Since the equipment was made to be operated by both men, the Baron failed in his attempt to give the Creature life.   That night a bolt of lightning activated the advanced (for its day) equipment, setting the laboratory alive with flashing colored lights. The Baron raced into his laboratory where the Creature stood awkwardly, then ripped off its facial bandages.   The being attempted to strangle its creator until Krempe knocked it unconscious from behind.   After the Creature escaped and killed a blind man, Krempe shot it through the head.   Promising to bury it, Victor again gave it life.   When Justine (Valarie Gaunt) the servant girl told the Baron that she was to have his child, he sent her to the room where, unknown to her, the Creature was chained.   Frankenstein locked the door and left her to the furies of the creation.

   On the night of his wedding to Elizabeth, Victor showed Krempe the chained Creature, now possessing a repaired brain and able to follow the Baron's simple commands.   Krempe, unable to convince Victor to destroy the Creature, knocked him aside and headed for the town to

[Facing page: Baron Victor Frankenstein (Peter Cushing) examines the Creature (Christopher Lee) assembled from corpses as assistant Paul Krempe (Robert Urquhart) observes.   From Hammer Films' The Curse of Frankenstein, 1957.]

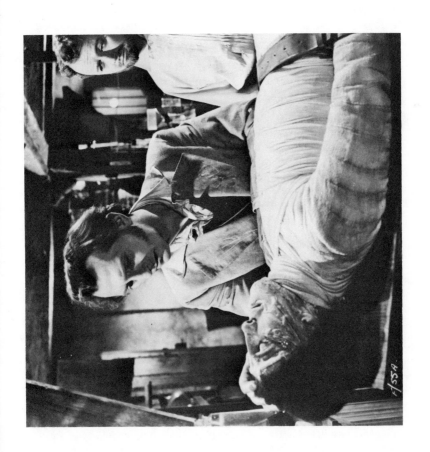

inform the authorities. But Victor bolted after and intercepted
him.   Meanwhile the Creature ripped his chains from the
wall and eventually grabbed Elizabeth.   Arriving with a flint-
lock, the Baron fired at his creation but killed Elizabeth
instead.   The Creature then stalked toward Frankenstein,
who hurled a lamp against its body and set it ablaze.   The
inhuman torch (stuntman Captain Jock Eason) fell through
a skylight and into a tank of acid below, where it dissolved.
After completing his story to the priest, Victor was visited
by Paul Krempe, his only hope for salvation by admitting to
the existence of the murderous Creature.   Krempe, however, denied the Baron's claim and left him to die under
the blade of the guillotine.

        The Curse of Frankenstein provided an entirely new
concept of the famous story and had to compete against the
established image that had been with the public since 1931.
The Creature lacked the strength and appeal of the Universal Monster.   Still, making the best of a modest budget
(£60,000) and recreating a feel of the era with its emphasis
on details, the film stood on its own merits.   Here is the
review in the 19 June 1957 Hollywood Reporter:

> What Anthony Hinds, the producer, and Jimmy
> Sangster, the writer, have tried to do in retelling
> this almost straight rendition of the original Fran-
> kenstein story is to make it human.   They have
> succeeded to the extent of making it almost un-
> bearably pathetic and real.   The gathering together
> of the various bodily parts of the monster, played
> by Christopher Lee, is shown in careful detail.
> The result of humanizing the story and its charac-
> ters is to make the creature less a monster than a
> pitiful and degrading half-human.   You are left
> feeling not so much frightened as nauseated.

        Hammer's gamble that new audiences would delight
in being horrified with gore rather than being terrified by
atmosphere, plot, and performances proved successful. [5]
Suddenly a new series had been born, while two names had
been added to the agenda of famous horror films stars.
Christopher Lee refused ever again to portray the Creature,
but became identified with the part of the vampire Count in
Hammer's Dracula series.   Cushing, on the other hand,
realized the financial security in becoming identified with a
continuing part, especially one with the scope of the dynamic
Baron Frankenstein.   The actor molded the role to fit his

personality and emerged as the single most satisfying element of the entire series.   To new audiences Peter Cushing
was Baron Victor Frankenstein just as Karloff was the Monster.

Hammer Films also recognized the potential in
Cushing, and in continuing the Frankenstein series avoided
the familiar plots of Universal.   Instead of reviving the
Monster in each succeeding film, the Baron himself would
return as the central figure, each time to create a new
monster or perform some otherwise questionable experiment.   The formula worked beginning with the first sequel.
Terence Fisher directed Jimmy Sangster's second Frankenstein script, The Revenge of Frankenstein (released by
Columbia), in 1958.   Baron Victor Frankenstein (Cushing)
was led to the guillotine, where a twisted dwarf prison
guard named Karl Werner (Oscar Quitek) rushed in and
shoved the priest under the terrible blade.   The scientist
had rescued himself by bribing Karl with a perfect body of
his own creation.   A free man, Frankenstein now only lived
for revenge against the humanity that sentenced him to die.

Posing as a Dr. Stein, the Baron became established
at the Workhouse Hospital in the village of Carlsbruck.
There he took care of the worst of the population, whom he
usually diagnosed as needing various amputations.   Not even
the Medical Council suspected what he did with those severed
organs.   When Hans Kleve (Francis Matthews) recognized
Dr. Stein as Victor Frankenstein, the Baron showed him his
latest creation.   It was a perfect body suspended in a glass
case, lacking only the brain which the misshapen Karl was
to gladly donate.   Dr. Stein did not consider the fact that a
chimpanzee he had also done brain transplant experiments
with had become a monstrous cannibal;   he proceeded with
the transplantation.

Recreating the visual splendor in The Curse of
Frankenstein, Dr. Stein turned on his colorful apparatus
and the newly created being came convulsively to life.   He
could speak right from the start and seemed perfect in every
way, save for a stitched cut along the forehead.   Karl
(Michael Gwynn) in his new form threw his old body into a
furnace and encountered a sadistic janitor who beat him over
the head and produced the dreaded damage.   From that moment on, Karl gradually assumed his former twisted form
and experienced cravings for human flesh.   The monstrous
Karl finally crashed into a society party attended by Dr.

Stein and Hans and before falling in a dead heap identified
Baron Frankenstein.   When the patients at the Workhouse
Hospital learned of the Baron's true identity, they brutally
beat him.   Victor Frankenstein died on Hans' operating
table, but not before telling him what to do with his brain
and the artificially created body hanging in a glass case.
Shortly after, a mustachioed "Dr. Frank" set up practice
in London.   Baron Victor Frankenstein had become his
creation.

The Revenge of Frankenstein was the only legitimate
sequel to The Curse of Frankenstein.   By the time Hammer
made The Evil of Frankenstein (1964), directed by Freddie
Francis, virtually none of the story of the original was retained.   The main reason for the new approach (which was
actually an old approach) was the fact that Universal would
release The Evil of Frankenstein.   Many of the old familiar
trappings of the Universal series were incorporated into the
story along with elements reminiscent of the 1950s Dick
Briefer Frankenstein comic books.   Since Universal was
involved, Hammer was able to at least attempt a make-up
similar to that worn by Karloff.

The new Frankenstein Monster make-up was created
by Roy Ashton, who stated that with "... this assembly of
hands and fingers and bits and ... a sewn-up cranium with
the brain thrown in[, t]he producer really wanted it to look
as if it had been made up of corpses from the graveyard."[6]
The make-up was worn by Kiwi Kingston and was anything
but convincing.   Resembling a young amateur's attempt to
imitate Jack Pierce, the square-headed creature was a
sloppy pasted together affair, with clear lines separating
the putty from Kingston's real face.   The hair was stringy
and sparse.   And the actor lumbered about on raised boots.
The image had none of the impact of Lee's make-up and
aroused many giggles from young members of the audience
who could have done better.

After being discovered while removing a heart from
a corpse, Baron Frankenstein (Cushing) and his assistant
Hans (Sandor Eles) returned to the Frankenstein chateau in
Karlstaad.   The chateau had been thoroughly looted and was
a shambles.   Victor then told Hans how he created the Monster many years ago, the film going into a flashback.   The
flashback was totally unlike Curse and made Evil seem to
be a sequel to a film that was never made.   In a laboratory
more advanced than the ones in Curse and Revenge, the

Baron alone brought life to the Monster.   The hideous being
lived until driven off a cliffside by a mob of angry villagers.

In the village during a carnival, the Baron noticed
that the Burgomaster was wearing his own ring.   After a
violent outburst, Frankenstein and Hans were forced to make
a swift exit.   First they hid in the tent of a hypnotist called
the Great Zoltan; and later in a cave where a deaf and
dumb beggar girl lived.   Inside the cave, frozen as he was
in two Universal movies, was the Frankenstein Monster.
At the chateau the Baron brought the creature to life but
only the hypnotic power of Zoltan could make it respond.
Frankenstein became enraged when he learned that Zoltan
was using the Monster to rob and kill (including the thief
Burgomaster who had ordered the charlatan out of town).
After the Baron expelled him from the chateau, Zoltan ordered the Monster to kill his maker.   Both Frankenstein
and Zoltan commanded the beast until the Baron won.   The
Monster (as did Briefer's Monster in 1954) impaled the
hypnotist with an iron spear.   The Monster eventually drank
some liquor and chloroform and smashed his way through
the laboratory in an intoxicated rage.   The inevitable fire
started with the inevitable villagers nearby, leaving Baron
Frankenstein and his Monster to a flaming destruction.

The Evil of Frankenstein[7] established a precedent
with the Hammer Frankenstein series.   Continuity was no
longer necessary.   Baron Frankenstein would turn up anywhere in order to perform some new and unorthodox experiment.   For a while the Baron lost interest in creating life
from piecing together corpses.   In the fourth Hammer Frankenstein film, the Baron ventured into a realm hardly expected of the infamous scientist.

Frankenstein Created Woman, (considered in 1958 as
And Frankenstein ..., a take-off on Brigitte Bardot's And
God Created Woman) a Hammer/Seven Arts production, was
directed by Terence Fisher and released in 1966 by Twentieth Century-Fox.   Baron Victor Frankenstein's (Cushing)
frozen body was revived by Dr. Hertz (Thorley Walters).
The period he spent in suspended animation apparently gave
him time to think, for now he was obsessed with the transference of human souls into different bodies.   Again the
Baron was assisted by a man named Hans.   (Either this
was an attempt at continuity, or else the Hammer writers
were at a loss for Germanic names.) Hans (Robert Morris)
was in love with Christina, the disfigured, crippled daughter

of the innkeeper. Christina was portrayed by twenty-one-
year-old Susan Denberg, whose physical attributes were
made famous in Playboy magazine. The blue-eyed blonde
from Austria was forced to hide her beauty in the earlier
scenes of Frankenstein Created Woman. Christina's face
was hideously scarred, due to the make-up created by
George Partleton, and her hair was black. It would take
the scientific genius of Baron Frankenstein to bring out her
Playmate beauty.

Hans came to Christina's rescue when three rowdies
taunted the girl. In revenge against Hans, they killed
Christina's father and made it appear as if he were guilty.
Hans was beheaded for the patricide of which he was innocent. Unable to live without Hans, Christina leaped into the
river but was rescued by Frankenstein and Hertz. After an
operation by the Baron, Christina emerged in all her blonde
beauty. Frankenstein then stole the corpse of Hans from
its grave and, using his laboratory devices, transferred its
soul to the body of the girl. Apparently scenes were
filmed (or at least posed for publicity purposes) of the Baron
becoming so attracted by his creation's beauty that he raped
her on the operating table. At any rate she was the most
beautiful creature ever created by Frankenstein in the history of motion pictures.

Christina became a killer possessed by Hans' spirit,
hunting down the three men who caused her lover's death
and disposing of them with typical Hammer brutality. In
the climax of Frankenstein Created Woman, Christina
jumped from a high cliff to her death, carrying out the
suicide from which Frankenstein had originally rescued her.
And Baron Frankenstein walked away to contemplate his
next gruesome experiment.

Frankenstein Must Be Destroyed was Hammer's fifth
Frankenstein movie, directed by Terence Fisher and released by Warner Brothers in 1969. Considering his past
experiments, Baron Frankenstein (Cushing) seemed quite con-
ventional (interested in brain transplants, making the film
relevant to the heart transplants of the Twentieth Century).
His methods, however, were more brutal and despicable
than ever. A masked killer stalked the streets and savagely
sliced off the head of a passerby. A burglar, meanwhile,
sneaked into a basement laboratory, where he encountered
a frozen corpse and then the man with a hideous mask.
After a fight with the monstrous killer, the burglar fled.

By this time audiences had grown to associate Peter Cushing with Baron Frankenstein, so that when he tore off the
mask there was no further need for identification.   Hastily
Frankenstein disposed of the evidence and fled.

Taking residence in Anna Spengler's (Veronica Carlson) boarding house, he endeavored to carry on his experiments in brain transplants.   Anna and her boyfriend, Dr.
Karl Holst (Simon Ward), had been selling drugs stolen
from the asylum where Holst worked (another attempt at
relevancy).   Seizing upon this information, Frankenstein
blackmailed them into assisting in a kidnapping plot.   To
carry on his work, Frankenstein needed the help of Dr.
Frederick Brandt (George Pravda), an inmate at the asylum.
During the abduction, Brandt was killed.   Back at Frankenstein's new laboratory, the Baron decided to salvage the
brain and, in some disturbingly realistic scenes, transplanted
it into another man's skull.   When Brandt saw the stitched
gash around his bald head and realized that he now possessed a new body (Freddie Jones), he reacted with horror.
Anna encountered the monster as he staggered across the
cellar laboratory and stabbed him with a scalpel.   The
monster crept into his former house where his wife Ella
(Maxine Audley) treated him with revulsion.   Only one
thought tortured his mind--destroy Baron Frankenstein.   The
Baron, believing Anna guilty of the monster's escape, stabbed
her to death without compassion, then hurried after him.
Entering the house, Baron Frankenstein saw it go up in
flames at the hand of his latest creation.   Managing to salvage Brandt's notes, Frankenstein hurried outside, only to
be caught by the monster and carried back into the inferno.

For Peter Cushing, it was virtually a final death.
He did a cameo shot as Baron Frankenstein (along with
Christopher Lee as Dracula) in the United Artists color
comedy One More Time, directed by Jerry Lewis in 1969.
A bald version of the Universal Frankenstein Monster rose
off the Baron's operating table as Sammy Davis, Jr. entered the laboratory through a secret door.   But Frankenstein Must be Destroyed threatened to be Cushing's last
performance as the Baron in a Hammer film.

Hammer wanted a new and more youthful image for
Baron Frankenstein, with the start of a series more than
ever imitating the old Universal films.   The new Baron
Victor Frankenstein was portrayed by Ralph Bates, a long-
haired English actor with some resemblance to Colin Clive.

Since this was to truly be the beginning of a new series, the
first entry The Horror of Frankenstein (1970) was a thinly
disguised remake of The Curse of Frankenstein.

The Horror of Frankenstein, directed by Jimmy
Sangster and released by Associated British Picture Corporation, followed young and somewhat perverse Baron Victor Frankenstein through school until his desire to create
life became an obsession.   Setting up his laboratory in his
castle in Ingoldstadt, young Victor began to experiment.
The film was an intentional spoof on the genre, with attempts to capture the offbeat humor and characterizations
of James Whale.   Frankenstein's early experiments, for
example, included the animating of a severed hand which
flexed its middle finger in the direction of his assistant.
The most humorous moments in the film involved Dennis
Price as a body snatcher who would sit and instruct while
his wife (Joan Rice) did the grave digging.   After Frankenstein began to assemble his Monster, he murdered the
father (Bernard Archer) of Elizabeth (Veronica Carlson) in
order to snatch his brain.   Elizabeth, who had been Frankenstein's sweetheart since childhood, was besieged by
creditors and finally came pleading for Frankenstein's help.
He took her in as a cook.

When Frankenstein's assistant Wilhelm (Graham
James) tried to stop him from bringing his creature to life,
the fanatical scientist electrocuted him and completed the
experiment by himself.   The Monster snapped his bonds
and confronted Frankenstein, who calmly replied, "Hello,
my name is Victor Frankenstein."   Not understanding, the
Monster thrust Frankenstein aside and stomped out of the
castle.   The Monster, as portrayed by musclebound Dave
Prowse, was Hammer's third attempt at creating an original
Frankenstein Monster.   This version was the least inspired
of the three.   Its bald head, covered with deep gashes held
together by metal clips, retained the basic Universal shape.
Stitched scars ran across its bare, herculean chest.   A
metal collar encircled the neck like that of a bulldog.   The
interpretation had physical strength but little else.

Baron Frankenstein went after his Monster and captured him in the woods.   Thereafter he began to use the
Monster to eliminate those of his choosing, including the
wife of the body-snatcher whom Victor had already killed
because he knew and demanded too much.   The Monster
eventually menaced Elizabeth.   The police entered the

Frankenstein castle and hurried to the laboratory where the Monster was hiding in a large container into which acid could be dropped. A little girl wandered into the laboratory and inadvertently released the acid as the police entered; they found nothing. The film ended with Baron Frankenstein emptying the container and finding only the Monster's shoe.

But Hammer was not going to end the new series so prematurely. In 1972 they announced the filming of Frankenstein and the Monster from Hell, their first to boast such a title. The Hammer Frankenstein series was the only enduring Frankenstein series since the days of Universal. Afficionados of the genre have criticized the films for their overuse of gore. But the Hammer films have endeavored to take a fresh approach to the subject and were the first of their kind to be made in color. Not all of them have been classics but they were generally entertaining and competently made. And even while Hammer Films was producing the various curses and revenges of the Baron, other studios were using the popular name of Frankenstein in films usually of inferior quality.

Notes

1. This interview by Mike Parry appeared as "CoF Interviews Christopher Lee," Castle of Frankenstein, no. 10 (February 1966), pp. 14 & 16.

2. Fellner, Chris, "The Intriguing World of Hammer Films," Monster Mania, no. 2 (January 1967), p. 21.

3. "The Loneliness of Evil," Shriek, no. 3 (Summer 1966), p. 8.

4. "Interview: Terence Fisher; Horror is my Business," Monster Mania, op. cit., p. 10.

5. Scenes from The Curse of Frankenstein were used in the black and white film Lolita (MGM, 1962).

6. "Michel Parry Interviews Roy Ashton, Monster Makeup Master of Hammer Films," Castle of Frankenstein, no. 8 (1966), p. 28.

7. When The Evil of Frankenstein was shown on U.S.

television, additional scenes involving the mute girl's childhood encounter with the Monster were filmed to give the picture added length.   Stock shots from _Evil_ were incorporated into Hammer's _Kiss of the Vampire_ (1963) when it was shown on network television as _Kiss of Evil_.

Chapter 7

FRANKENSTEIN LUMBERS ONWARD

After Universal Pictures had ceased production of
their Frankenstein films, and before Hammer Films had
returned to the genre with their own series, other motion
picture companies realized that the creature assembled
from cadavers was still a major box office draw. Torticola
contre Frankensberg (translated as "Twisted Neck vs.
Frankensberg") was a thirty-six minute long satire of horror films, made in France by Paul Paviot in 1952. Torticola (Michel Piccoli) was a monster created from parts of
corpses by the strange Dr. Frankensberg. He resembled
the Universal Monster, the mask being designed by make-up
artist Hagop Arakélian, with a very high forehead and flowing black hair that reached beyond the shoulders. Wearing
sackcloth, gloves, black pants, and raised boots, Torticola
haunted the countryside of Pomerania.

A pretty girl named Lorelei (Vera Norman) was
forced to discontinue her studies because of poverty and
take up residence with her uncle and guardian, Dr. Frankensberg (Roger Blin). In Todenvald, Frankensberg's castle,
Lorelei not only met the hideous Torticola, but also a talking cat and a man with the brain of a cat, all the products
of her uncle's mad genius. Unknown to the girl, Frankensberg and his sinister assistant Furrespiegel, planned to
drain her blood into the veins of the Frankensteinian Torticola. But in the end, the artificially created monster
proved that he was human after all and saved the hapless
Lorelei. Torticola contre Frankensberg was divided into
three parts, each approximately ten minutes long. The
segments were entitled "The Laboratory of Horror," "The
Prey of the Damned," and "The Monster Has a Heart."
That same year, one of the short "Fearless Fosdick Adventures" made with puppets used the Frankenstein theme. It
was entitled Frank N. Stein. Fearless Fosdick was created

203

by Al Capp in the "Li'l Abner" newspaper comic strip as a
satire of Dick Tracy.

In 1957, American-International Pictures, in order
to capitalize on the success of I Was a Teenage Werewolf,
made earlier that year, continued their series of movies
starring juvenile monsters with I Was a Teenage Frankenstein. Herman Cohen produced and Herbert L. Strock directed this first in the line of the worst Frankenstein
movies ever made. I Was a Teenage Frankenstein was set
in the present where Professor Frankenstein (Whit Bissell),
a descendant of the original creator of monsters, was also
obsessed with the artificial creation of human life. He had
a secret basement laboratory equipped with the latest (and
seemingly least expensive) apparatus for bringing the dead
to life, including the standard Jacob's ladder. When an
automobile crashed outside of Frankenstein's laboratory,
the scientist and his assistant salvaged one of the mutilated
corpses and smuggled it into the laboratory. There they
replaced a useless hand and leg, then brought the creature
to life with all the power of their meager equipment.

Gary Conway, a young actor with the body of a
Hercules, portrayed the Teenage Frankenstein Monster,
wearing a form-fitting T-shirt and a pair of the ivy league
slacks that were so popular in 1957. Since Universal owned
the familiar Frankenstein Monster make-up, American-
International invented a new face. The Teenage Frankenstein had a battered face that resembled a blob of flesh-
colored putty. The enormous right eye bulged out and the
small left eye peered from a black socket. The face was
hardly a good make-up job, not to mention the result of a
scientist who could otherwise make the body perfect. The
Teenage Frankenstein walked stiffly out of the laboratory
and into the street. Peering into a window, he saw a beautiful girl preparing for bed. Attracted by her beauty, the
monster crashed through the window and, as she screamed,
killed her. As he lumbered out into the night, a number
of witnesses saw his ghastly face.

Frankenstein realized that he would have to give his
creature a new visage. He and the monster roamed through
lover's lane until the brute found a teenager (also played by
Conway) whose face he liked. Then he killed the boy and,
after an operation by Frankenstein, was soon wearing his
face. The Teenage Frankenstein was admiring his new face,
marred only by a few stitches, when Professor Frankenstein

revealed his plan to dismantle him and ship the parts to
Europe where he would be reassembled.   Not wanting to be
taken apart, the Teenage Frankenstein snapped the metal
wrist bands with which his creator was strapping him to the
operating table.   The monster was killing Frankenstein as
the police rushed into the laboratory.   Stepping away from
them, the Teenage Frankenstein stumbled into the laboratory
machinery, the wrist bands making contact with the apparatus and electrocuting the brute as the screen suddenly burst
into full color.

American-International never made a real sequel to
I Was a Teenage Frankenstein despite the popularity of the
teenage monster film.   However, in 1958 the studio did use
the character in the satiric horror film How to Make a
Monster, again produced by Cohen and directed by Strock.
How to Make a Monster took place behind the scenes at
American-International.   Pete Crummond (Robert H. Harris)
was fired after doing horror make-ups for the studio for
the past twenty-five years (an in-joke, as American-International had only been in existence for a few years at the
time How to Make a Monster was made).   The studio intended to abandon horror films in favor of musicals.   Drum-
mond was permitted, however, to finish working on the
studio's final horror film, Werewolf Meets Frankenstein.

To have revenge for his dismissal, the mad make-up
artist mixed a secret ingredient into the make-ups of Larry
Drake (Gary Clarke) who was portraying the Teenage Werewolf and Tony Mantell (Gary Conway) who was playing the
Teenage Frankenstein (described in the film as the "last of
the Frankensteins").   Under Pete's spell, the Teenage
Werewolf killed John Nixon (Eddie Marr) in the screening
room as he watched the two monsters about to fight in the
bit of footage already filmed;   and the Teenage Frankenstein choked Jeffrey Clayton (Paul Maxwell) to death in his
garage.   Both victims had made the decision to cease
American-International's production of monster films.

Unaware of what had happened, Tony and Larry attended a special farewell party at Pete's home (with the
screen again going from black and white to color).   All the
heads of Pete's former monsters adorned the walls and in
an exhibition of madness, the make-up artist revealed his
plan to add the actual heads of Tony and Larry to the collection.   In attempting to escape, Larry knocked over a
candelabra, setting the place ablaze and allowing the heads

to melt from the real skulls beneath.   Tony and Larry
managed to escape as Pete died in the flames trying to save
his "children."   How to Make a Monster was better than
I Was a Teenage Frankenstein and was an amusing effort
to make the little American-International seem to be a major
studio.   Gary Conway never again portrayed the Teenage
Frankenstein and later spent much of his time trying to live
down the role.   Eventually he became the co-star of television's Burke's Law and later starred in his own series
Land of the Giants.

　　　　　Allied Artists produced their own Frankenstein entry
that same year.   The "Shock" package of Universal horror
films was in current television circulation and the name of
Frankenstein had again become commercial at theatre box
offices.   This latest film was given the futuristic title of
Frankenstein--1970 and had the distinction of starring Boris
Karloff as the new Baron von Frankenstein, another in the
long line of last living descendants of the original scientist.
As Baron Victor von Frankenstein, Karloff wore face make-
up to show how the scientist had been tortured and disfigured
by the Nazis during World War II.   In prison, Frankenstein
became embittered and possessed by a mad plan.

　　　　　Frankenstein--1970 opened at night with a creature
seemingly the Frankenstein Monster pursuing a girl (Jana
Lund) through the woods.   The creature, whose face was
out of camera range, limped along on raised boots.   The
shoulders were enormous, the hands stitched, the fingers
ending in sharp claws.   Seen from behind, the giant chased
the girl into the river where it proceeded to strangle her.
Suddenly a voice yelled "Cut!" and the audience learned that
this was the cliché plot device of revealing a piece of opening action to actually be a movie in production.   The Frankenstein Monster in this case was merely a German actor
named Hans (Mike Lane, best remembered for his role two
years earlier as a boxer in The Harder They Fall).[1]

　　　　　These opening scenes were extremely atmospheric,
with their barren trees and steaming waters.   Unfortunately
the rest of the film did not compare with the beginning.
What followed was a shoddy production directed by Howard
W. Koch.   There was hardly anything futuristic about the
film even when seen in 1958.   With the exception of the
atomic reactor, the story could have been set earlier in
time.   Karloff himself seemed to express a contempt for
the role he was playing (especially considering his 1930s

performances as the Monster) and in one of the only in-
stances of his career, overacted.

The film company was on location at the Frankenstein castle in Germany to make an authentic Frankenstein
movie for American television.   Baron Victor von Frankenstein detested the idea but allowed his privacy to be invaded
for a substantial fee, to be used for an atomic reactor.
Reluctantly the Baron agreed to appear in the introduction
of the film, shot in the family vault of the Frankensteins.
There he described how his ancestor Richard Freiherr von
Frankenstein I created a Monster.   He further explained
that his ancestor had removed the vital organs from the
Monster and sealed it away in a large coffin in the vault.

After being left alone in the vault, the Baron opened
the coffin which actually concealed a staircase leading to
the basement laboratory where wrapped like a mummy with
only a skull for a head, there lay what remained of the
original Frankenstein Monster.   Baron von Frankenstein
reported into a tape recorder that the skull had been frozen
to a state of brittleness by which it could be reshaped.
Then he removed a sheet from a clay bust of himself the
way he looked as a younger man before being tortured by
the Nazis.

When Frankenstein's loyal servant Schuter (Norbert
Schiller) discovered the scientist with the skull-headed
creature, the Baron was forced to kill him.   But Schuter
would live again, for his vital organs were immediately
transplanted into the body of the Monster.   With a clumsy
move, the Baron dropped the jar containing Schuter's eyes,
ruining the organs.   (These prop eyes were so realistic
that, it is reported, some members of the crew became
sick at the sight of them.)   Frankenstein disposed of the
eyes in a garbage disposal that sounded suspiciously like
a toilet flushing.   With the arrival of the atomic reactor,
Victor von Frankenstein brought the Monster (again played
by Mike Lane) to life.   Wilhelm Gotfried (Rudolph Anders),
Frankenstein's friend, began to suspect that the scientist
was continuing his ancestor's work.   Frankenstein finally
decided to show Gotfried what he had been doing and within
a short time the Monster had a pair of eyes.

In the climax of the film the police were hurrying to
the laboratory.   Frankenstein knew that his only salvation
was in destroying all evidence of his work.   He began to

work the reactor when the Monster snapped out of the
scientist's hypnotic power and began to stalk toward him
for revenge.   As the Monster strode toward his creator,
the laboratory exploded.   Later the face of the Monster
beneath the bandages was revealed as that of Victor von
Frankenstein as he once looked.   He had modeled the Monster's face in his own image, apparently to one day have
his own brain exchanged with that of Shuter, making creator
and creature one.

Frankenstein's Daughter, also made in 1958, was
Astor pictures' contribution to the list of worst horror
films of all time.   Directed by Richard Cunha, the film
was another attempt to capitalize on the teenage movie
craze.   Oliver Frankenstein (Donald Murphy), incognito as
Oliver Frank, had used a drug to turn teenaged Trudy Morton (Susan Knight) into a type of female Jekyll and Hyde
with shaggy eyebrows and buck teeth.   But this was not his
main endeavor.   In a laboratory set up in a former wine
cellar, Frank was attempting to create life as had his
father and grandfather.   But they had only created male
monsters.   Oliver, a true male chauvinist, believed that
only a female would obey his commands without question.
When a young girl named Suzy (Sally Todd) refused his
romantic advances on Mulholland Drive, Frank ran her
down in his convertible, then took her mangled corpse back
to the laboratory.   Using her head, Frank completed his
female creation, which came to life amid the furies of what
laboratory equipment Astor's meager budget would allow.

Frankenstein's Daughter (played by an unknown male
actor) stalked from the shadows and into the light.   Her
face, as made-up by Harry Thomas, was even worse than
that of the Teenage Frankenstein.   The left half of the face
was a mass of twisted tissue.   An open, stitched wound
ran down the center of the forehead to the tip of the nose.
Enormous metal rods protruded from the neck.   The back
and sides of the head were enclosed in bandages.

The female horror escaped from the house and
roamed through the streets, where she violently killed a
garage mechanic.   Weakened, she returned to her creator

[Facing page: Baron Victor Frankenstein (Karloff) stands
before his ancestor's creation, now restored again to life
in Frankenstein--1970 (Allied Artists, 1958).]

to receive more power. Later, Frankenstein's Daughter
was chained to a chair. She snapped the chains and pursued Trudy and her boyfriend Johnny Bruder (John Ashley)
to the laboratory. Frankenstein gave her the order to kill
the teenagers. As the monster came toward Johnny with
its clutching, gloved hands, he grabbed a bottle of acid and
hurled it, somehow missing the creature but striking her
creator in the face. The monster turned to watch her
creator slump to the floor with his face sizzling from the
acid. Her arm passed by a Bunsen burner which set her
clothing ablaze, destroying yet another inferior monster of
Frankenstein. The advertising for Frankenstein's Daughter
was misleading. Posters depicted an obviously male monster (presumably the original Monster) with a bare, hairy
chest, carrying off a girl. Some newspapers ran advertisements featuring the Boris Karloff or Glenn Strange versions
of the Monster carrying away the same girl. Anyone unfortunate enough to have paid money to see Frankenstein's
Daughter in a theatre soon realized they had been deceived.

At least as poor as Frankenstein's Daughter was
Frankenstein Meets the Space Monster made in 1964 by
Futurama Entertainment Corporation and directed by Robert
Gaffney. Much of the film consisted of newsreel footage of
astronauts, rockets, and the army. The rest of the film
was a travesty of the name of Frankenstein. Frank Saunders (Robert Reilly) was a United States astronaut, the
product of unorthodox technology. In order to send a completely programmed and perfect human being into space,
Saunders was created from parts of corpses, given an artificial skin, and a remote-controlled brain. There was the
danger, however, that if anything damaged that artificial
brain, Frank would become a veritable Frankenstein. (The
creators of the robot were clever enough to give him so
adaptable a name.)

A group of aliens had landed on Earth to kidnap girls
to repopulate their own world, which had been left barren
by war. Leader of the aliens was Princess Marcuzan
(Marilyn Handold) who with her bald, pointy-eared accom-
plice Nadir (Lou Cutell) planned the abduction. The artificial astronaut was fired into space and later parachuted
back to Earth. Frank met up with one of Marcuzan's henchmen (wearing a dime store space helmet) who blasted his
face with a laser gun. The left half of Frank's face was
burned. The artificial brain showed through the skin as
did the internal wiring and circuits. He had become the
expected "Frankenstein. "

Tracing the whereabouts of Frank, his creator Dr.
Adam Steele (James Karen) began to repair the astronaut.
Steele's assistant Karen Grant (Nancy Marshall) was captured by the aliens and taken to their spaceship.   Frank
lumbered off to her rescue.   After saving Karen and the
other women, Frank encountered Mull, the hideous space
monster released from its cage by the alien guards.   After
a tremendous battle, "Frankenstein" overcame Mull and
used a laser gun to destroy the aliens and himself.   R. H.
W. Dillard, one of the writers of the Frankenstein Meets
the Space Monster screenplay, later claimed that the film
was a comedy intended to mock the cheap, thoughtless horror films like I Was a Teenage Frankenstein.   "My approach and that of my colleagues to Frankenstein Meets the
Space Monster is one that I advise everyone who cares for
serious art to take in regard to the contemporary cheap
horror film," Dillard writes.   "Laugh, mock, and enjoy,
and all the while rejoice that the great ones were made and
are still there for us to seek out and experience to the
full. "[2]

El Testamento del Frankenstein (translated as The
Testament of Frankenstein) was also made in 1964.   Filmed
in Spain, the picture was directed by Jose Luis Madrid and
starred Gerard Landry and George Vallis.   One of the most
offbeat of all Frankenstein movie titles appeared in 1965.
Jesse James Meets Frankenstein's Daughter had been announced for filming as early as 1962 but the film was
hardly three years in the making.   It was finished in a
matter of weeks.   The movie, directed by veteran William
Beaudine for Embassy Pictures, had nothing to do with
Astor's Frankenstein's Daughter.   The daughter of the title
was actually Maria Frankenstein, the granddaughter of
Count Frankenstein, who had created the original Monster
and also invented an artificial brain.   Maria (Narda Onyx)
and her brother Rudolph (Steven Geray) had come to an
abandoned mission near a little Mexican village in Arizona,
where they began to set up their monster shop.   Children
began to disappear mysteriously, causing the superstitious
villagers to leave.   The last such family was that of
Mañuel (Felipe Turich), his wife Nina (Rosa Turich), and
their daughter Juanita (Estelita).

Jesse James (John Lupton) and the muscleman Hank
Tracy (Cal Bolder), the last remaining members of the
notorious James gang, were fleeing from a posse.   Hank
was wounded by a bullet during the chase.   Encountering

Juanita, Jesse and Hank were told where they could find a
doctor.   Naturally the doctor happened to be Maria Frankenstein.   Immediately, Maria was attracted to Jesse, but when
he rejected her love in favor of Juanita, the evil female
scientist resolved to have vengeance against the outlaw.

Forcing her brother to help, Maria transplanted the
artificial brain into Hank's skull, transforming him into an
obedient robot and cleverly renaming him Igor.   Hank had
become a monster, with a stitched wound encircling the top
of his shaved head to reveal where the top of the skull had
been removed.   For attempting to stop the operation, Rudolph was strangled by the monster at Maria's command.
Returning in time to witness the murder, Juanita found
Jesse.   The outlaw returned to the mission to encounter the
monstrous Igor.   No longer knowing his former partner,
Igor knocked him unconscious.   Maria prepared to perform
the same operation on Jesse's brain when Juanita and Mar-
shal McFee (Jim Davis) arrived.   Seeing Juanita, Igor began
to recall his past (although his artificial brain should have
had no such memories) and turned upon Maria, killing her
brutally.   Then Igor moved toward Jesse with violent intent when Juanita, seizing the outlaw's gun, shot the monster to death.

Toho, the production company in Japan that special-
izes in science fantasy films of giant monsters smashing
Tokyo, announced several Frankenstein films in 1965.   The
first two were Frankenstein vs. the Giant Moth, in which
the Monster was supposed to fight resident Toho creature
Mothra, and Frankenstein vs. King Kong (not to be confused
with the proposed Willis O'Brien film described later in
this chapter).   But that same year, Toho did make a Frankenstein film.   Originally it was to be titled Frankenstein
vs. the Giant Devilfish and feature a sixty foot tall Frankenstein Monster in a struggle to the death with an enormous
octopus.   The battle scenes between the two monsters were
shot but never included in the final product.   What was released that year was a film made by Toho in cooperation
with the American producer Henry G. Saperstein entitled
Furankenshutain tai Baragon (translated as "Frankenstein vs.
Baragon" and also known in Japan as simply "Frankenstein
tai Baragon") and released in color by American-International in the United States as Frankenstein Conquers the
World.   Toward the end of World War II, the immortal
heart of the Frankenstein Monster was removed by force
from Germany and brought to Japan where it was lost in

Japanese "Frankenstein" battles giant Octopus in a scene never used in Frankenstein Conquers the World, copyright 1966 by American International Pictures, Inc.

the atomic horror of Hiroshima.   The heart somehow possessed the property of regenerating itself into a complete
organism.

A strange looking boy was discovered in Hiroshima
twenty years later.   The boy had a strange face, with a
high forehead like that of the Frankenstein Monster.   Although he was explained as being definitely European he was
obviously Oriental.   Dr. James Bowen (Nick Adams), a
scientist experimenting with the regeneration of dead cells,
examined the boy in the Hiroshima Garrison Hospital.
Quite alarmingly, the boy (now played by an older actor)
was growing at an incredible rate.   His teeth were becoming
large and uneven.   Unsightly veins protruded from the forehead.   It was believed that the giant was the result of the
undying Frankenstein heart. [3]   A German scientist stated
that "Frankenstein" came back to life no matter how many
times he was destroyed (referring to other studios' films).
If the giant could grow another limb, it was indeed Frankenstein.   Chained in a warehouse, the giant, angered by the
press, broke free, leaving a crawling hand behind to establish his identity.   Hungry and confused, Frankenstein fled
to the hills where he began to terrify people and devour
livestock.   Believing that Frankenstein would not harm a
human being, Bowen pursued the creature, now ten times
taller than a man.

During an earthquake, a prehistoric reptile called
Baragon (in the Japanese version) crawled from underground to ravage the area, causing the world to believe
that Frankenstein was responsible.   Bowen and his party
were attacked by Baragon until Frankenstein arrived and
engaged the fire-breathing reptile in a long battle.   Frankenstein seemed to have lost any past fears of fire for it
was he that fought his adversary with a burning torch.
Recognizing Bowen, brave and noble Frankenstein killed
Baragon, and standing triumphantly over the scaly carcass,
was swallowed up by another earthquake.

Furankenshutain tai Baragon was directed by Inoshiro
Honda, who was famous for his many giant Japanese monster films made at Toho.   Honda aimed his monster epics
at a younger audience and created a veritable genre which
other Japanese film companies soon imitated.   The strong-
point of this movie was the special visual effects created
by Eiji Tsuburaya, with whom Honda had been working in
all of his giant monster productions.   Tsuburaya was a

master at creating miniature buildings and props through
which the actors portraying Frankenstein and Baragon could
stomp. By this film, Tsuburaya's once carefully made
miniatures were showing sloppiness but still gave visual
excitement to an otherwise non-traditional and mostly ridiculous Frankenstein effort. [4]

Furankenshutain tai Baragon ended begging a sequel
and Toho and Saperstein soon joined forces again to make
their second Frankenstein movie, in color and again utilizing
the talents of Honda and Tsuburaya. Furankenshutain no
Kaiju--Sanda tai Gailah (meaning "Frankenstein Monsters--
Sanda vs. Gailah") was the original title for the film which
featured two enormous Frankenstein creatures named Sanda
and Gailah. Sanda was the final growth of the Frankenstein
from the previous film, now covered with long brown hair
and with an even uglier face. Gailah was more hideous
than Sanda and covered with green hair. If there was a
resemblance between the two, it was only natural since
Gailah was the result of Frankenstein's severed hand which
had been washed into the sea. There the hand had continued to regenerate, combining with plankton. The reason-
ing was simple enough. Thus two monsters, one still
benevolent, the other vicious and destructive, could be
incorporated into one film. Upon completion of the film
Saperstein decided that the creatures looked more like King
Kong than Frankenstein monsters. All references to Frankenstein were eliminated, new footage was added to present
different premise and the title was changed to simply Sanda
tai Gailah and, in American prints, to The War of the Gargantuas. The film was released in Japan in 1966 and in
the United States the following year by UPA.

In the waters off southern Japan, a gigantic octopus
(the same one originally scheduled to appear in Frankenstein
vs. the Giant Devilfish) attacked a ship. Suddenly a green
monster covered with scales and long hair emerged from
the water and destroyed the cephalopod. The Green Gargantua devoured the ship's captain, then went on a spree of
destruction that even the military could not halt. A group
of scientists including Dr. Stewart (Russ Tamblyn) and his
assistant (played by Kumi Mizuno, recreating her role from
Furankenshutain tai Baragon) theorized that this Green Gargantua was spawned from the baby Brown Gargantua that
one day disappeared from their laboratory. (A flashback
showing the juvenile Brown Gargantua was filmed after it
was decided to remove any references to Furankenshutain

tai Baragon.) References were also made to a living, disembodied hand. The scientists believed that the two creatures were brothers since one was born from the other and
that the gentle Brown Gargantua still lived.

Dr. Stewart warned the authorities not to fire weapons at the Green Gargantua because every one of its scat-
tered cells could grow into a new monster. Setting a trap
with electrified water and laser beams, the military ignored
the scientist's pleas and nearly destroyed the brute. Suddenly the Brown Gargantua appeared and rescued his brother.
Later, after realizing the true evil nature of the Green Gargantua, the brown one attacked him. The battle raged in
the streets of Tokyo, buildings toppling as the monsters
lashed into each other. The gargantuas continued to battle
their way into the sea, where the military began to drop
bombs on them. The explosions caused a fortuitous volcanic eruption, presumably destroying the gargantuas until
another film might be made.

Perhaps there was a sequel planned for Sanda tai
Gailah. In 1966 Toho announced an upcoming movie as The
Frankenstein Brothers starring Tab Hunter. The film could
merely be a proposed title for Sanda tai Gailah with Hunter
originally intended for the Tamblyn role, as both gargantuas
were referred to as brothers. On the other hand The Frankenstein Brothers could be a third film in the series which
was never made.

In 1966 Arthur Rankin, Jr., made a multi-monster
film for children entitled Mad Monster Party? The picture
featured Baron Boris von Frankenstein, the Monster and
his nagging Mate, Count Dracula, the Werewolf, the Creature, the Mummy, the Invisible Man, Dr. Jekyll and Mr.
Hyde, the Hunchback of Notre Dame, and other assorted
creatures. All of them were puppets which came to life
through single frame animation. The picture was made in
color, directed by Miles Bass, and released by Embassy
Pictures. The monsters were designed by Jack Davis, a
cartoonist best known for his work in the EC horror and
satire comic books of the 1950s. The Frankenstein Monster resembled the Universal version but was different
enough to avoid any copyright violations. It had greenish
skin, a bald head with a stitched gash circumventing the
crown, electrodes on the neck, a fur jacket, and bare feet.
The Monster's Mate resembled comedienne Phyllis Diller
who did the voice. Baron Boris von Frankenstein was

made in the image of Karloff who spoke for his own animated figure.

Len Korokbin and Harvey Kurtzman (the creator of
EC's Mad comic book) wrote the script. (Some of the
writing was also done by the uncredited Forrest J Ackerman.) They were fans of the old monsters and spoofed the
genre with love. Baron von Frankenstein had invented a
new explosive which he raised to the lightning amid the
crackling apparatus of his laboratory. In order to celebrate
his latest discovery, Frankenstein decided to invite all the
famous horror characters to a party at his island castle.
During the party, Dracula tried to make an alliance with
Francesca, the Baron's secretary. When Dracula caught
the Monster's Mate spying on them, he tried to put her
under his spell. But the grunting Monster appeared and
hurled the Count across the room.

A late arrival was Felix Flanken, the Baron's
nephew. Frankenstein had announced that he was retiring
and was to give his position as head of all the monsters to
someone else. All of the creatures desired that coveted
position, but the Baron gave it to Felix. Dracula made an
alliance with the Monster and his Mate, then organized all
of the creatures to eliminate Felix. They would have succeeded if a giant gorilla called "It" had not come to the
island and scooped them all up in his mammoth hands.
Felix and Francesca escaped in a speedboat as Baron von
Frankenstein dropped the explosive and destroyed the monsters, himself, and the island. Free of the horrors of
Frankenstein's island, Felix and Francesca both learned
that they were robots created by the Baron. Mad Monster
Party? was more than just a children's film. The spoofing
was in good taste and older viewers could sit back and enjoy seeing the old monsters that might have scared them in
their youth doing essentially the same things, only in humorous situations.

Another multi-monster film was made in Spain by
Omnia in 1970. El Hombre Que Vino de Ummo (translated
as "The Man Who Came from Ummo"), also known both as
Los Monstruos del Terror (translated as "The Monsters of
Terror") and as Dracula Hunts Frankenstein, and released
to English speaking countries as Dracula vs. Frankenstein,
was a color feature boasting not only Frankenstein's Monster and Count Dracula, but also the Mummy and the Werewolf. A scientist (Michael Rennie) from the planet Ummo

intended to conquer the universe. His first step was to
revive the bodies of the four most terrible monsters in
Earth's history. With these creatures doing his bidding,
the alien could destroy the Earth. (It seems unlikely that
the military forces of the world could not cope with the
Frankenstein Monster, Dracula, the Mummy, and the Werewolf. Certainly they could produce some improved blazing
torches, wooden stakes, and silver bullets.) Frankenstein's
Monster (Paul Naschy) and Dracula never got the chance to
fight each other before a secret agent (Craig Hill) discovered
and destroyed the plot of world conquest.

Flick (seen in the United States as Dr. Frankenstein
on Campus) was made in Canada and released in 1970 by
Astral Films. Directed by Gil Taylor, the color film followed the career of young Viktor Frankenstein (Robin Ward)
from his expulsion from a European university through his
days spent at a North American university. Upon his arrival, Frankenstein was derided for his name, with jokes
about his being a ghoul or having bolts in his neck. He
made a lover of a blonde coed (Kathleen Sawyer) but refused ever to remove his clothing when they made love.
A professor (Sean Sullivan) in charge of the university's
new computer made Viktor his assistant to develop a method of brain control. Staff members of the student newspaper disliked the youthful scientist and trapped him into
being photographed holding a marijuana roach. Out of revenge, Frankenstein injected his brain control pellets into
three students. He directed one of them to kill the other
two and then the student photographer and reporter. The
film climaxed with Viktor Frankenstein, pursued through a
museum by students aware of his crimes, plunging off a
high bannister. As he struck the floor his back revealed
stitches that tore open, exposing him as an artificially
created man. In this case Frankenstein and the Monster
were synonymous. Apparently Frankenstein was the creation of the professor, who seemed hardly disturbed over
his loss, as if the being would someday rise again. Flick
was a slick production with good performances, especially
by Robin Ward. The film catered to a youthful audience
and contained all the cliché protest and drug scenes expected to take place on a modern campus.

Dracula vs. Frankenstein (not the same film as El
Hombre Que Vino de Ummo), made in color by Independent-
International Pictures and released in 1971, did not begin as
a Frankenstein or Dracula movie. It was originally shot

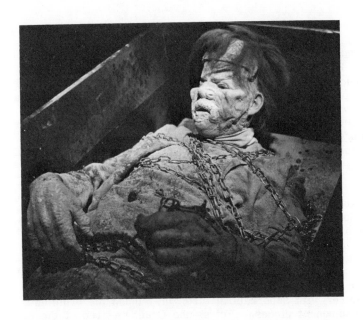

John Bloom's 7'4" made him the tallest actor ever to portray the Monster. From <u>Dracula vs. Frankenstein</u> (Indepentent-International, 1971).

---

as <u>The Blood Seekers</u> starring J. Carrol Naish as Dr. Durea, Lon Chaney as the "Lennie"-type Groton, the Mad Zombie, and Angelo Rossito as the evil dwarf, Grazbo. The film, however, was too short and incoherent. To salvage the footage Independent-International's Sam Sherman rewrote the script, introducing Frankenstein's Monster and Count Dracula. The production title of the lengthened version was <u>Blood of Frankenstein</u> and was eventually changed to <u>Dracula vs. Frankenstein</u>. Playing the Frankenstein Monster was John Bloom, a seven-foot, four-inch tall actor, wearing a make-up designed by George Barr and executed by Tony Tierney. The new Monster had a lumpy, dark-colored, clay-like face not unlike that of the Golem, with a metal band around the top of the head.

Count Dracula (Zandor Vorkov) removed the chained body of the Frankenstein Monster from its ancient grave in Oakmoor Cemetery. Learning that Dr. Durea, proprietor of an amusement park "House of Horrors," was really Dr. Frankenstein (the usual only remaining member of that family), Dracula brought the Monster's body to him. In

the laboratory behind the "House of Horrors," Dr. Frankenstein had been trying to create a blood serum using the
corpses of girls axed to death by Groton and Grazbo.   Dracula persuaded Dr. Frankenstein to revive the original Monster with his laboratory apparatus.   (The equipment, built
by Kenneth Strickfaden, was first used in the 1931 Frankenstein.) Dr. Beaumont (Forrest J Ackerman) was the first
to feel the wrath of the monsters.   He died in the powerful
grip of the Frankenstein creature.

   Later in the "Horror Chamber" exhibit room of his
concession, Dr. Frankenstein was pursued to his death as
he blundered through the darkness into the descending blade
of his guillotine.   Shortly after, Groton was shot from the
roof of the building by the police.   When Dracula tried to
attack a girl for whom the Monster had developed an affection, the expected battle began.   In a clearing near the old
graveyard, Dracula and the Monster struggled until the
vampire, with supernatural strength, ripped the brute into
its component pieces.   But as the Count sneered at the decapitated head of the Frankenstein Monster, he was trapped
by the fatal rays of the sun and reduced to a decomposed
corpse.   The original script of the film included a scene
in which the Monster was bitten by Dracula and became a
towering, blood-sucking vampire.   The idea was abandoned,
however, when Bloom, because of his heavy make-up, could
not keep the fangs in his mouth.

   A film with a similar title, Dracula contra el Dr.
Frankenstein (translated as "Dracula vs. Dr. Frankenstein")
in Spain and Dracula, Prisonnier du Docteur Frankenstein
("Dracula, Prisoner of Dr. Frankenstein") in France, was
released in 1971.   The film was a French/Spanish co-
production made by Comtoir Français de Film and Fenix
and directed by Jesus Franco.   With the return of Dracula
(Howard Vernon) there came a new wave of vampirism in
the Carpathian Mountains.   Dr. Frankenstein (Dennis Price),
with his assistant Morpho (Luis Barboo), set up a laboratory in that part of the world and created a monster (Fer-
nando Bilbao), resembling the Universal Pictures character,
who, unlike mortal men, could battle and destroy Dracula.
Another scientist, Dr. Seward (Alberto Dalbes), sought
Count Dracula to cure him of his vampiric condition.   The
two scientists, then, vied to be the first to reach the King
of Vampires, each with his own purpose.

   In 1972, Lee International Films began filming

Byron's Evil, directed by Andrew Sinclair. The film
starred Oliver Reed both as Byron and the Frankenstein Monster. The production was temporarily stopped due to lack
of finances. No other information about the film is available at this writing but the title character may be Lord
Byron.

Two versions of the Frankenstein Monster were
featured in the Italian color film La Figlia di Frankenstein
(translated as "The Daughter of Frankenstein" and released
in the United States in 1971 by New World Pictures as Lady
Frankenstein, which had been announced prematurely as
Madame Frankenstein), directed by Mel Wells. The film
received an "R" rating and stressed sexual perversion in
the advertising. Lady Tanya Frankenstein (Sarah Bay) returned from medical school to the chateau of her father
Baron Frankenstein (Joseph Cotten). The Baron was
crushed to death by the Monster he had created, a beast
with a large, bald cranium covered with scar tissue and
stitches, with the right eye bulging from its socket. The
Monster then left the chateau to terrorize the countryside.
Tanya vowed to create her own superhuman being which
would destory the original Monster. Marrying Charles
Marshall (Paul Muller) for his brain and not his crippled
body, Tanya found sexual satisfaction only in her lover, the
muscular idiot shepherd of the Frankensteins.

When Charles found them in the act of love, he
smothered the young man. Charles knew that he could only
be the recipient of Tanya's love in one way. Willfully, he
submitted his brain to Tanya, who transplanted it into the
shepherd's body and brought her perfect lover to life. Returning to the chateau to destroy anyone with the name
Frankenstein, the original Monster engaged the second in
a furious battle and perished. At last Charles, with the
shepherd's body, was able to make love to Tanya. But
realizing that she could never be truly satisfied, he
strangled his beautiful creator. La Figlia di Frankenstein
proved so successful that producer Roger Corman, who
purchased the film for American release, the same year
announced his plans for a sequel.

In 1972, eight Frankenstein films were announced,
none of which have been made at the date of this writing.
The first three are to be low budget productions. Brain of
Frankenstein was announced by Kirt Film International while
Marlene Films reported Frankenstein: Curse from the Grave.

An independent producer announced <u>Frankenstein--Demon of</u> <u>Dracula</u>, based on an original story by this writer. I have attempted to write a story in the flavor of the horror films of the 1940s. Dr. Gustav Frankenstein, in attempting to reassemble his ancestor's Monster and give it a new brain, hopes to revive the perfect guinea pig to use in his environmental experiments and also clear the family name. Count Dracula, however, forces Frankenstein to give the Monster the brain of his obedient but dead servant, thereby obtaining an immortal and indestructible slave. In the climax of the film, the Monster and a werewolf, Frankenstein's former assistant cursed by Dracula's wolves of hell, fight to the death as dynamite brings the caverns down on all three monsters.

Two more ambitious projects, both adapted from the original novel, were also announced in 1972. The first was a three million dollar version of <u>Frankenstein</u> with a sympathetic Monster to be directed by Francis Ford Coppola with a possible Paramount release. For years Coppola has been contemplating a definitive film version of the story. Another literal adaptation of <u>Frankenstein</u> was announced by Metro-Goldwyn-Mayer with Sir Laurence Olivier intended to play Frankenstein.

... and Featuring Frankenstein's Monster

Not all motion pictures featuring the Frankenstein Monster have been exclusively Frankenstein films. In some films the Monster's role has been minor, or even only a walk-on. <u>Haram Alek</u> (translated as "Shame on You") was made by Studio Guizan in Egypt in 1953. Directed by Issa Karama, this comedy was one of a series starring Egyptian comedian Ismail Yassine. Frankenstein's Monster, a mummy and a werewolf made guest appearances.

The Frankenstein Monster and Count Dracula appeared in the 1955 <u>La Fantasma de la Opereta</u> (translated as "The Phantom of the Operetta"). The film, directed by Enrique Carreras for Gral Belgrams in Argentina, was a satire of horror films and starred Amelita Vargas, Alfredo Barbieri, Tono Andreu, Gogo Andreu, and Inez Fernandez. The Frankenstein Monster was portrayed by a lean actor, wearing make-up patterned after the Universal Monster, who was struck over the head with a vase in one scene by the vampire Dracula.

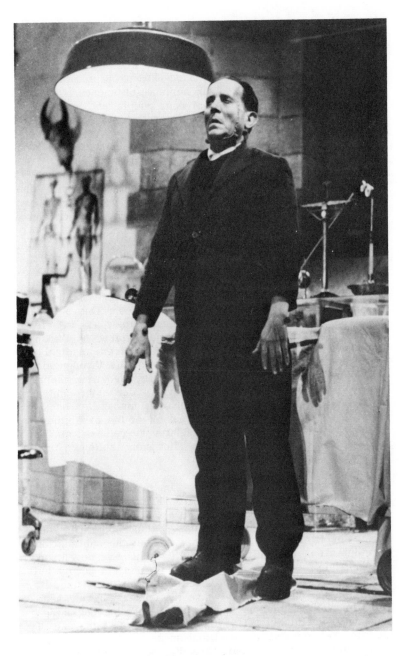

Manuel Arbó as the Frankenstein Monster in the 1954
Spanish film, <u>Tres Eran Tres</u>.

Tres Eran Tres (translated as "Three Were Three")
was made in Spain in 1954 and released by Victory Films.
The picture was directed by Eduard G. Maroto and photographed in black and white with some color scenes. Tres
Eran Tres concerned a group of poor people who formed a
film company called Tiacapa and determined to make three
inexpensive movies. Their three films--a Western, a
Gypsy story, and a parody of horror films--constituted the
rest of the picture. "Una de Miedo" (translated as "A
Horror Story") was the first of the three. Dr. Salsamendi
(Antonio Riquelme) was a scientist who wanted to create his
own Frankenstein Monster. The creature (Mañuel Arbó)
came to life with a stitched face and bolts on the neck and
wrists.

Dr. Terror's Gallery of Horrors (1967) was another
film fitting into the category of "worst films ever made."
The American General color production, directed by David
L. Hewitt, was an incredibly shoddy assemblage of short
horror stories based on plots by Russ Jones. One of these
was "The Spark of Life," starring Lon Chaney as Dr. Mendel. Dr. Mendel explained that he was inspired by Baron
Eric von Frankenstein, who was dismissed from medical
school for trying to bring the dead back to life through electricity. With the help of his students Dr. Sedgwick (Jerry
Benson) and Dr. "Cushing" (Ron Boyle), Mendel brought
Amos Duncan (Vic McGee), an executed, mad killer back to
life with a machine or two. The result of the experiment
should be obvious. The film was later re-released as The
Blood Suckers and finally sold to television as Return from
the Past.

Necropolis (1970), a color film made by Cosmo-
seion/Q Productions and directed by Franco Brocani, consisted of storyless episodes starring such characters as the
Frankenstein Monster, Heliogabalus, Satan, and Attila the
Hun. The film attempted to revolt against the sublimation
by which all of our culture and civilization have developed.
Frankenstein's Monster delighted in his inherent beauty but
found that he could not happily exist in today's civilized
world, saying dolorously, "I have the universe in my head."
The film was fragmented and confusing with the beginning
and ending seemingly reflecting each other. At the end of
the film Heliogabalus dressed and spoke as the Monster had
at the start. The two characters had become identical.

Frankenstein's Monster has made even briefer

appearances in some motion pictures. In Federico Fellini's
I Vitelloni (translated as "The Young Men") a man appeared
at a festival wearing an enormous head mask of the Monster.
In Goof on the Loose (1962), a comedy short subject made
by Ray Dennis Steckler, the Monster (Rich Dennis wearing a
Don Post mask) carried off a girl. Escape from Zahrain,
made that same year, was an adventure story about a group
of escaped prisoners being pursued across the desert. The
color film did not have a Frankenstein Monster. But it did
feature Anthony Caruso as a burly character referred to
throughout the film as "Frankenstein."

In Good Neighbor Sam (1964), made in color by
Columbia, Jack Lemmon disguised his face which was pic-
tured on a billboard, by painting it over with the features
of the Frankenstein Monster. The Candidate, made that
same year by the English company Altantic-Cosnat, featured
a party in which someone came dressed as the Frankenstein
Monster, wearing an Ellis Berman mask. Someone wearing
a Berman Frankenstein mask also appeared at a costume
ball in the Elvis Presley feature Double Trouble (MGM,
1967). The British film Catch Us if You Can (formerly
titled The Dave Clark Five Runs Wild and seen in the
United States as Having a Wild Weekend), made by Warner
Brothers in 1965, featured Richard Bailey as Guy, a middle-
aged husband who escaped from this world via his collection of movie memorabilia. During a masquerade ball, Guy
dressed up as the Universal Frankenstein Monster in a
simplified make-up and helped the Dave Clark Five escape
from a gang of crooks. In one scene he grabbed one of
the pursuers in an imitation of Boris Karloff.

Ghost in the Invisible Bikini (originally announced as
Pajama Party in the Haunted House), a color film made in
1966 by American-International, guest-starred Karloff as a
restless spirit and featured two dummies of the Frankenstein Monster. The first was an original conception with
bulging eyes and a pimply face. The second, wearing a
Post mask and fright wig, moved out from behind a secret
wall panel. The Frankenstein Monster, in the Universal
image, clumsily walked through the underground complex of
the enemy in Columbia's color extravanganza Casino Royale
(1967). David Niven as Sir James Bond, an aging secret
agent, tried to find his way out of the complex before it
exploded. Bond asked directions of a tall man whom he
discovered to be the Monster.

Frankenstein's Monster, Dracula, and the Mummy (actors wearing Don Post masks) made cameo appearances in a dream sequence of Isabell, a Dream (about 1968), apparently a semi-professional film made by Luigi Cozzi in Italy. Both the Monster and Dracula (actors again in Post masks) made guest appearances in another Cozzi film Tunnel Beneath the World (1970), based on a story by Frederik Pohl. In Adalen '31, a film about the riots in Sweden made about 1970, a group of young people went to a theatre running a non-existent film entitled Frankenstein in London.

Every Home Should Have One (1971), a British film made in color, directed by Jim Clark, and released through Lion International, starred comedian Marty Feldman (who wrote the script) as a frozen porridge salesman trying to write a television commercial for the product. In one sequence he watched an old Frankenstein movie (made especially for Every Home Should Have One tinted to appear as an old black and white film) on television. While watching the film, he fantasized himself to be Dracula and fought the Monster before he and the heroine settled down to a bowl of porridge. The image of the Frankenstein Monster has also been seen in films like Earth vs. the Spider (American-International Pictures, 1958).

Frankenstein South of the Border

There have been so many Frankenstein motion pictures made in Mexico that they deserve a chapter to themselves. In general, the Mexican horror films of the 1950s through the 1970s present a nostalgic look backwards, for they imitate the pictures made by American studios in the 1930s and 1940s. The films are packed with action and "old style" monsters and are often extremely atmospheric. They are, however, usually unsophisticated and regarded as a lower form of entertainment by serious film aficionadoes.

Mexican Frankenstein Monsters have tended to be patterned after the copyrighted Universal character. But the name of the creature has often been strangely spelled, perhaps in an attempt to avoid any copyright infringements when the films are released in the United States by either Azteca or Columbia Pictures.

El Castillo de los Monstruos (translated as "The Castle of the Monsters"), made by Producciones Sotomayor

in 1957, was a satire on horror films.   Mexican comedian
Clavillazo starred with Evangelina Elizondo as a newly-wed
couple on their honeymoon.   When their car ran out of gas-
oline in front of a sinister looking castle, and with a thunderstorm raging down on them, the couple took refuge in
the building.   There they met inferior versions of such
American monsters as Count Dracula (German Robles), the
Mummy, Wolf Man, Creature from the Black Lagoon, and
the Frankenstein Monster, now called "Frentestein."   Patterned after the Universal Monster, Frentestein had a
stitched gash running horizontally across the high forehead
and electrodes on the neck.   But the white shirt and sport
jacket were hardly the thing for a Frankenstein Monster,
regardless of his name, to wear.   After all of the monsters
chased the newlyweds about the castle, the human beings
fled for their lives.

     The Monster underwent a less drastic name change
for Frankestein, [also, Frankestain], el Vampiro y Com-
pañia (translated as "Frankestein, the Vampire and Company"), made in 1961 by Cinematografica Calderón, and
directed by Benito Alazraki.   Frankestein somewhat resembled Frentestein from El Castillo des los Monstruos in
this unauthorized Mexican "remake" of Abbott and Costello
Meet Frankenstein.   Paco and Agapito, working for an express agency, were assigned to deliver the wax figures of
Frankestein and the Vampire to an old mansion.   It was
soon evident that the bodies were not made of wax but were
the authentic monsters.   All the while the Wolf Man in his
human form was trying to track down and destroy the bodies.
The Vampire came to life and determined to transplant the
brain of the stupid Agapito into the skull of Frankestein and
use the obedient creature to conquer America.   (At least
his plan was less extravagant than most world-conquering
fiends.)   During a fiesta, Agapito was captured while the
hapless Wolf Man transformed into a beast under the influence of the moon.   At the laboratory, the transplantation
of Agapito's brain was about to take place when the Wolf
Man leaped into the room.   The Vampire and the Wolf Man
battled savagely as a fire started, destroying them.   Frankestein, attempting to flee the crackling flames, sank into the
bogs.

     The following year, Filmadora Independiente made
Orlak, el Infierno de Frankenstein (translated as "Orlak, the
Hell of Frankenstein"), directed by Rafael Baledon.   Orlak
was the super-powerful creation of the evil Dr. Frankenstein,

but unlike most Frankenstein creatures, Orlak was controlled
by a metal robot head, over which was a device in the shape
of a box.   Later, Dr. Frankenstein gave his creation a rubber face in the image of another man, complete with electrodes on the neck.   The true nature of the creature was
revealed when he stood too near a fire, which melted his
mask, exposing Orlak to be an inhuman monster.

Masked wrestlers who occasionally leave the arena to
star as movie superheroes are extremely popular in Mexico.
The real life wrestler Santo (meaning "The Saint"), the hero of
"the silver mask," has encountered the Frankenstein Monster
in a number of action films patterned after the American serials.
Santo en el Museo de Cera (translated as "The Saint in the
Museum of Wax" and seen on American television as Sam-
son in the Wax Museum to avoid confusion with the "Saint"
created by Leslie Charteris) was made in 1963 by Filma-
dora Panamericana.   A mad scientist, the proprietor of a
wax museum, was turning human beings into monsters with
a drug that altered cells.   One of the exhibits Santo found
in the wax museum was a figure in the exact image of the
Universal Frankenstein Monster.   The same dummy, and a
wrestler named "Frankestein," appeared in La Señora
Muerte (translated as "Madame Death"), a 1968 color film
by Filmica Vergara (Cinecomisiones) about a disfigured
woman trying to regain her lost beauty through face transplants.   Blue Demon, another masked wrestler and second
to Santo in popularity, fought "Frankestein" in the ring in
Arañas Infernales (translated as "Infernal Spiders"), made
by the same studio in 1966 and directed by Federico Curiel.
The film involved the transformation of the hands of living
human beings into spiders.

Both Santo and Blue Demon teamed up to battle a
legion of horrors in 1969.   Santo y Blue Demon contra los
Monstruos ("Santo and Blue Demon vs. the Monsters"),
made in color by Cinematografica and directed by Gilberto
Martinez Solares, featured the Vampire and his bride, the
Wolf Man, the Mummy, the Cyclops, an alien creature,
and--with his newest name--"Franquestain" (called "Franque-
stein" in the end credits and on the posters advertising the
film), played by Mañuel Leal.   For the first time in history, a Universal-type Frankenstein Monster sported a mus-
tache and beard.   This might have been to coincide with the
French sounding name, but was more likely to help disguise
the Don Post/Glenn Strange custom mask worn by Leal.

The corpse of Bruno Halder (Carlos Ancira), a mad

scientist, was brought back to life by his hunchbacked,
dwarfed assistant in the former's castle laboratory. Blue
Demon, who had sneaked into the castle, was rendered unconscious by Halder's zombie henchmen and subjected to a
duplicating machine that created his evil double. Halder
then proceeded to revive Franquestain and the other monsters, causing them to do his bidding. The monsters went
on a killing spree, with Franquestain murdering a young
couple in the woods. Led by the false Blue Demon, the
monsters attempted to kidnap Halder's brother and his
daughter, and kill her boyfriend Santo, all out of revenge
over some previous encounter.

   The monsters, throwing punches like American movie
stuntmen, made several attacks on Santo and his friends,
but the silver masked hero was always victorious. In a
particularly amusing sequence, the Vampire (David Alvizu)
was disguised as a wrestler to battle Santo in the arena.
Once Santo exposed the Vampire, the other monsters entered the ring, causing pandemonium in the stadium. Finally, on the rooftop of a nightclub, Franquestain snagged
the girl while the other monsters apparently killed Santo.
In a scene that was certainly unique, Franquestain, with
Santo's homing device stuck to his neck, drove the monsters and their two prisoners back to the castle in a car.
Santo followed as Halder was about to begin his diabolical
experiment on his brother and niece. After a furious battle, Santo defeated the false Blue Demon and revived the
original. The two of them fought off the band of monsters
with fire, then destroyed the laboratory apparatus which,
in turn, blew up the castle.

   Santo's next battle with a Frankenstein creation was
in the 1971 film Santo contra la Hija de Frankenstein
("Santo vs. the Daughter of Frankenstein"), made by Guillermo Calderón and directed by Miguel M. Delgado. Perhaps Mexican screen writers have exhausted their variations
on the name "Frankenstein." The monster created by the
daughter of Frankenstein was given the name of Ursus. The
film opened with a battle between Ursus and Santo. During
the fight, the monster fell upon a sword and was impaled.
With Ursus out of the way, the Frankenstein girl could go
on with her experiments in finding an elixir that would restore her youth. To work properly, the elixir required the
blood of young women. Even then the effect was only temporary. Frankenstein's daughter knew that she could discover the secret of eternal youth with the help of Santo.

In order to force Santo to work with her, she kidnapped
the hero's girlfriend. But after Santo performed his daring
heroics, he defeated the daughter of Frankenstein and saved
the girl.

The later Santo films, like Santo y Blue Demon contra los Monstruos and Santo contra la Hija de Frankenstein,
are a puzzling example of Mexican cinema. The earlier
Santo films were obviously made for a young audience with
their comic book plots and action. Now, however, sex is
prevalent with nudity throughout and Santo himself going to
bed with his leading ladies, leaving on only his silver mask.
The effect is strange indeed with this marriage of both juvenile and adult film fare.

An unverified title Conde Frankenstein (translated as
Count Frankenstein) probably does not exist. The film is
almost certainly no more than a typographical error actually
referring to one of the Mexican movies about the vampire
Count Frankenhausen.

The Frankenstein theme was used numerous times in
other Mexican horror films. El Monstruo Resucitado (translated as "The Revived Monster"), made in 1952 by International Cinematografica and directed by Chano Urueta, was
described as follows: "A la Mary Shelley ... scientist
brings dead body back to life, gives his 'zombie' new brain."
A mad doctor disinterred the corpse of a genius and took it
to his laboratory, gave it the savage brain of a wild man,
and then brought the dull witted creature to life as a slave.
Ladrón de Cadaveres (translated as "Thieves of Bodies"),
made in 1957 by the same company and directed by Fer-
nando Mendez, was another film centering around masked
wrestlers. A wrestler named Guillermo Santa (Wolf Rubinskis) was killed by a mysterious murderer. The killer
gave the corpse the brain of a gorilla, then brought it back
to life. Guillermo had become a monster with a stitched
cranium, and ape-like fangs, possessing the strength of a
beast. The monster eventually toppled off a roof to its
death.

Even more Frankensteinian was La Momia contra el
Robot Humano ("The Mummy vs. the Human Robot--seen in
America as The Robot vs. the Aztec Mummy), made in
1960 by Cinematografica Calderón and directed by Alfred
Salazar. In this entry to the Aztec Mummy series, the
Bat, a criminal mastermind, created a remote controlled

human robot to destroy the ancient horror.   The robot was
fashioned from the parts of corpses and covered with a
metal armor-like shell. [5]   The human machine was given
animation in a typical Frankenstein laboratory, with the
Bat raving that he had created life.   The two monsters
came together in the awaited battle, with the Aztec Mummy
ripping the Human Robot into scrap.   Gomar, a human
animal created by transplanting organs, and with the brain
of a beast, menaced the heroines of <u>Las Luchadoras contra</u>
<u>el Medico Asesino</u> (translated as "The Wrestling Women vs.
the Murdering Doctor" and seen on American television as
<u>Doctor of Doom</u>), a 1962 film about a masked scientist kid-
napping girls for brain transplants.   The doctor later took
parts of Gomar, a new brain, and a female corpse to produce Vendetta, telepathically-controlled female wrestler.
In the climax of the film, Vendetta was shot down from a
tower.   Neutron (played by Wolf Rubinskis), the black
masked superhero, encountered Frankensteinian science in
<u>Los Automatas de la Muerte</u> ("The Robots of Death"), made
in 1962.   The evil Dr. Caronte with his human robots (all
from the first film in the series, <u>Neutron, el Enmascarado</u>
<u>Negro</u>, translated as "Neutron, the Black Mask") created a
Frankenstein-type brain from the brains of three dead
scientists, nourished with human blood.

The Sexy Frankensteins

        The Frankenstein theme was not applied to films
made for an "adults only" audience until the early 1960s.
From then on the Monster created by Victor Frankenstein
could engage in more activities than terrifying the countryside and being pursued by torchlight.   The first sex film--
or "nudie" as such productions were called in those more
innocent days of exploitation films--featuring the Frankenstein Monster was <u>House on Bare Mountain</u>, made in color
in 1962 by Olympic International Films and directed by R.
Lee Frost.   Granny Good (Bob Cresse) had a nude party
in an old mansion.   Among the uninvited guests were the
Frankenstein Monster (Warren Ames wearing a Berman
mask) and Dracula (Jeffrey Smithers).   One of the many
naked girls at the party did the "twist" with the Monster
before the police, suspecting that an orgy was going on,
raided the place.   The Monster and Dracula were unmasked
as party crashers but the werewolf who was also at the
party was real.

Frankie Stein (played by Frank Coe made-up in the image of the Universal Monster), Dracula, and the Mummy were all the creations of a mad scientist in the science fiction satire <u>Kiss Me Quick</u> (also known as <u>Dr. Breedlove</u>), made in color by Russ Meyer's Fantasy Films in 1963. Frank Coe also played an alien named Sterilox, who came to Earth since his own planet was barren of women. Sterilox visited the scientist Dr. Breedlove (modeled after Dr. Strangelove) who had developed a method of creating living women. The three familiar monsters were the results of earlier experiments. Sterilox first fell in love with a vending machine. Eventually he discovered that girls were much better and rocketed back to his own world with one of Dr. Breedlove's pretty creations. A behind-the-scenes shot from <u>Kiss Me Quick</u> of Coe wearing the Frankenstein Monster make-up later appeared in part two of <u>Highlights of Hollywood Nudist Life</u>.

<u>Sexy Proibitissimo</u> (translated at "The Most Prohibited Sex"--and known to the French as <u>Sexy Super Interdit</u>) was a fictionalized history of the striptease made by M. Martinelli. The film had sequences involving both Count Dracula and the Frankenstein Monster. Dr. Frankenstein (played by an actor resembling Peter Cushing) brought his Monster to life. The creature was somewhat in the Universal mold, with scraggy hair at the back of the head, wounds with large metal clamps along the sides and crown of the head, and large electrodes on the neck just behind the ears. With the Monster strapped to a table, Frankenstein left him in the care of his shapely assistant. The assistant thought she would arouse the Monster by doing a striptease. The Monster, seeing the naked woman, snapped his bonds and went after her.

<u>Angelic Frankenstein</u> (1964), made by the Athletic Models Guild, was the first homosexual Frankenstein film. The picture concerned the creation of a monster that looked barely fourteen years old. The cast and crew remained anonymous but all films from the Athletic Models Guild were apparently made by Bob Mizer.

The Frankenstein Monster, looking like the Universal character and wearing a fur coat as in <u>Son of Frankenstein</u>, appeared in <u>Fanny Hill Meets Dr. Erotico</u> (about 1965). A sequel to <u>Fanny Hill Meets Lady Chatterley</u>, this film was made in color by Barry Mahon. Fanny Hill returned to the castle of Lady Chatterley, hoping to find the latter but

instead meeting Dr. Erotico. The mad scientist, who had
been working on his own version of the Frankenstein Monster, hired Fanny Hill as a charwoman. When Fanny Hill
was cleaning the laboratory, she accidentally turned on the
switch which brought the Monster to life. The creature
promptly fell in love with the beauty. But when the doctor's lesbian maid also fell in love with Fanny Hill, the
Monster thought she was trying to harm the object of his
affection. And so he killed the maid. The film ended with
the villagers setting fire to a shack and burning the Monster who was hiding inside.

Mondo Sexo (1966), made by Trans-Continental Artists Pictures, was a series of stripteases. One of the
strippers was named Fanny Frankenstein. A very short
silent movie featuring the Frankenstein Monster was Frankenstein Cherie ("Darling Frankenstein"). The 1967 color
film featured Harrison Marks (wearing a rubber mask) as
the Frankenstein Monster, chained to a wall to watch the
nude Wendy Lunt walk by him. Pour Messieurs Seuls
(translated as "For Gentlemen Only") was made in Germany
by Ralph Habib. Released by Allemagne in 1967, the film
featured a room filled with giant ashtrays in the image of
the Frankenstein Monster. Nude girls posed before photos
of the monsters from Bride of Frankenstein in Bien Faire
et les Seduire, also known as Sexyrella, made about 1968.

Harrison Marks returned, not as the Monster, but
as Frankenstein Marks in the British film The Nine Ages
of Nakedness (1969). The picture was made in color by
Token Films and written and directed by Marks. A photographer went to a psychiatrist to learn the reason for his
irresistibility to women. The doctor learned of the man's
ancestors buried deep within his memory. One of the ancestors was Frankenstein Marks.

Hollow-My-Weanie, Dr. Frankenstein (also known as
Frankenstein De Sade) was another homosexual film, made
in color in 1969. The film did little more than show Dr.
Frankenstein and his shaggy hunchbacked assistant putting
together a poorly made-up Monster in a laboratory that
was probably the director's basement. Mercifully, Mary
Shelley died over a century before her brainchild sank to
such depths. The Sexual Life of Frankenstein was a film
made in 1970 by Harry Novak. Although there is no data
on the film at this moment, some reports say it was very
poorly made. Both sexes appeared in the nude in

<u>Frankenstein of Sunnybrook Farm</u>, made in 1971 by William
Rotsler.   The film involved a group of nudists who went to
a friend's home to watch a psychedelic film with the above
misleading title.

The "Underground" Frankensteins

The Frankenstein Monster has also appeared in a
number of so-called "underground" films.   These are in-
dependently produced films, usually the work of a single film-
maker, which are released to selected theatres through a co-
operative network.   Most underground films are made in 16mm.

<u>Frankenstein's Experiment</u> (also spelled "Xperiment")
was a color short subject made in 1963 in England by the Delta
SF Group.   The 8mm film featured Aub Marks as a grotesque
Ygor, with bushy sideburns and eyebrows and deformed eyes
and nose.

<u>Lurk</u> (1964) was a satire of James Whale's <u>Franken-</u>
<u>stein</u>.   The film, made in color by Rudy Burckhardt, was
scripted by dance critic Edwin Denby.   Red Groons portrayed the Frankenstein Monster.   That same year, Robert
Breer made a semi-animated cartoon entitled <u>Fist Fight</u>.
Among the images in the film were photographs from <u>Bride</u>
<u>of Frankenstein</u>.   <u>Memento</u> (1968) an underground film made
by Philipe Brodier in France, commented on life by combining such diverse images as Julian Beck, General West-
moreland, North Vietnamese children, Ché, and the Aurora
model of the Frankenstein Monster.

There was nothing about Frankenstein in Robert
Greenberg's film of 1969, <u>I Was a Teenage Frankenstein</u>
<u>End Part 2</u>.   The film, made in color, was a seven-minute
commentary on contemporary youth.   Originally the picture
had no title and was spliced at the end of the second reel
of a 16mm print of <u>I Was a Teenage Frankenstein</u>.   When
the two films were separated, the bit of film imprinted
with "I Was a Teenage Frankenstein End Part 2" remained
at the beginning of Greenberg's picture.   The short subject
had a title.   <u>The Eye of Count Flickenstein</u> (1969) by Tony
Conrad was actually a parody of Dracula.   The short film
merely had the camera pan to the Count's eye and then cut
to a television screen showing only static.   Various pictures and masks of the Frankenstein Monster also added to
the backgrounds of <u>Lions Love</u> (color) and Tom Baker's
<u>Bongo Wolf's Revenge</u>, both made in 1971.

Frankenstein Misrepresented

To add to the confusion in attempting to catalogue all
motion pictures featuring the Frankenstein theme, some
films have used the name without having anything to do with
the subject. Frankenstein's Bloody Terror (released in the
United States in 1971) confused mostly everyone who saw it.
The picture had nothing to do with Frankenstein or his
bloody terror. The film was made in Spain in 1968 and
originally titled La Marca del Hombre Lobo ("The Mark of
the Wolfman"), shot in 70mm, color, and in the 3D process.
Independent-International changed the title to Frankenstein's
Bloody Terror in hopes of capitalizing on the famous name.
The original story concerned werewolves and vampires,
necessitating some changes if the picture were to be accepted by the public as a Frankenstein movie.

Anyone missing the opening titles of Frankenstein's
Bloody Terror might have thought they had walked into the
wrong theatre. A painting by Gray Morrow of the Frankenstein Monster, somewhat resembling the Universal character, filled the screen. In a series of dissolves, the Monster's image transformed into that of a man, and then into
a werewolf. While all this was going on, the announcer
roared that the infamous family of monster makers had
been struck by the curse of the werewolf. The family
name was consequently changed to Wolfstein. After the
last of the credits had flashed on the screen, no further
mention was ever made of Frankenstein. La Marca del
Hombre Lobo was the first in the series of werewolf movies
starring Paul Naschy. The corpse of Wolfstein lay in a
crypt with a silver dagger through its heart until freed by
Gypsies who stole the weapon. Valdemar (Naschy) killed
the revived werewolf, but was bitten. Having inherited the
curse of Wolfstein, Valdemar became the pawn of a vampire (Dracula in the German versions) and his wife. The
climax of the film was an elaborate battle between all the
monsters. [6]

Frankenstein cum Cannibis was a Dutch social drama
of 1970 dealing with drugs. There was nothing Frankensteinian about the 1971 color film Frankenstein in a Fish-
bowl. The film was a short documentary shot in 16mm
and blown up to 35mm. The film vividly followed two
women through the ordeals of plastic surgery.

To further complicate the listing of Frankenstein films, a number of motion pictures having nothing to do with the subject have been released in Germany with the name Frankenstein added to the titles. Madigan's Millions, an Italian film directed by Stanley Prager and released in the United States in 1969 by American-International, was released in Germany as Ich Wollt'ich wäre Frankenstein (translated as "I Wish I Were Frankenstein"). Dustin Hoffman made his screen debut in this film. El Vampiro de la Autopista ("The Vampire of the Highway") was a Spanish film made in 1970. This vampire film was released in Germany as Der Vampir von Schloss Frankenstein (translated as "The Vampire of Castle Frankenstein").

Apparently the name "Frankenstein" is becoming a synonym with "monster" in Germany. Many of the Japanese science fantasy films made in color by Toho, directed by Inoshiro Honda and with special effects by Eji Tsuburaya, have been given Frankenstein titles in that country. Nankai no Dai Ketto (translated as "Big Duel in the North Sea" and seen in the United States as Godzilla vs. the Sea Monster) was a 1966 film released in Germany as Frankenstein und die Ungeheuer ("Frankenstein and the Monster from the Sea"). Gojira no Musko (seen in the United States as Son of Godzilla), made in 1967, was retitled Frankensteins Monster jagens Godzillas ("Frankenstein Pursues Godzilla"). Kingu Kongu no Gyakushu ("King Kong's Counterattack," released in America as King Kong Escapes), made the same year, was the only such film that can be rationalized as a Frankenstein movie. Based on a short cartoon from the King Kong television series, the film involved the mad villain Dr. Who and his creation, the giant ape-like robot called Mechani-Kong. When the robot failed to mine a new element for Dr. Who, the fiend captured King Kong and placed him under an hypnotic spell to do the work. Inevitably King Kong escaped and battled the giant robot with Mechani-Kong meeting destruction. The film was shown in Germany as King Kong--Frankenstein's Son. [7]

Toho's were not the only Japanese films whose titles were changed in Germany. Daikyaju Gappa (translated as "Giant Monster Gappa" and seen in the United States as Monster from a Prehistoric Planet) was made in 1967 by the Nikkatsu Corporation. But the film was given the new title Gappa, Frankenstein Fliegend Monster ("Gappa, the Flying Frankenstein Monster"). All of these Japanese films were about enormous monsters battling each other, the world, or both.

The Animated Frankensteins

　　　The first appearances of the Frankenstein Monster
in animated cartoons were in 1933.   The Monster, in the
image of the Karloff trial make-up, sat with Dracula and
Quasimodo in a theatre in Mickey's Gala Premiere, [8] made
by Walt Disney Productions.   The characters appeared in
a dream with caricatures of other movie personalities, all
watching Mickey Mouse on the screen.   That same year, a
Frankenstein type monster with a bald, skull-like head was
created when a chemical dripped out of a retort in Betty
Boop's Penthouse, made by Dave Fleischer.   The monster
stalked across a tight wire-like clothesline to reach the
sexy Betty in her penthouse when she sprayed him with her
potent perfume, transforming him into an effeminate,
dancing flower.

　　　In Porky's Road Race (1937), one of the Looney
Tunes made in color by Warner Brothers and directed by
Frank Tashlin, an early version of Porky Pig entered a
celebrity road race.   Borax Karoff, in the image of the
Frankenstein Monster, tried to win the race through sabotage but eventually lost to Porky.   The Frankenstein Monster continued haunting Warner Brothers cartoons.   He had
a scene as a shivering coward in Porky's Movie Mystery
(1939), directed by Robert Clampett.   Sniffles and the Book-
worm, directed that same year by Chuck Jones, featured
a Frankenstein Monster who appeared to have been carved
out of wood.   The Monster emerged from the book Frankenstein and then fell from a shelf to his destruction.   A
creature in the shape of the Frankenstein Monster called
Neon Noodle menaced Daffy Duck in The Great Piggybank
Mystery (1946), directed by Clampett.   Bugs Bunny assumed
the form of the Karloff Monster in What's Cookin', Doc
(1944).   In Hair Raising Hare (1945), directed by Jones,
Bugs fought a shaggy monster created by a mad scientist
inspired by Peter Lorre.   The creature fled when he
realized an audience of people were watching him.   The
same monster returned in Water, Water, Every Hare (1952),
a cartoon in which a Karloff-type scientist tried to put
Bugs' brain into the head of his giant robot.   The monster
shrank down to miniature size due to a certain chemical.
In Hare Conditioned (1945), directed by Jones, Bugs did an
imitation of a terrible fire-breathing "Frankincense monster."   Bugs created a Frankenstein Monster to fight the
Tasmanian Devil in Dr. Devil and Mr. Hare (1964).

　　　Paul Terry's Terry-Toons, released by Twentieth

Century-Fox, also utilized the Frankenstein Monster. In
Frankenstein's Cat (1942), directed by Mannie Davis, a
monster with a mechanical body and the head of a Frankensteinian cat, terrorized the peaceful animals that lived near
his castle. When he devoured a baby bird, the superhero
Mighty Mouse fought the beast. Obedient bats carried Frankenstein's Cat away from the castle, but the world's might-
iest mouse flew after him, knocked off his head, freed the
bird, and sent the robot-like body crashing to the earth.
Picking up his head, Frankenstein's Cat ran away never to
return. In The Jailbreak (1946), another Mighty Mouse cartoon, the Monster and Dracula were prisoners at Alcatraz.
The Frankenstein Monster was the servant of Dracula in a
nightmare sequence of The Ghost Town (1944), directed by
Davis, and lumbered about in Fortune Hunters (1946), directed by Connie Rasinski, both starring Gandy Goose.
And in King Tut's Tomb (1950), Heckle and Jeckle, the
talking Magpies, encountered an Egyptian dancer who magi-
cally transformed into the Frankenstein Monster.

Magoo Meets Frankenstein (UPA, 1960), directed by
Gil Turner, pitted the near-sighted Mr. Magoo against Professor Frankenstein, who had transferred the intelligence of
a chicken to the head of the Monster. But he wanted to
give the creature a man's brain power. Mr. Magoo uncon-
sciously wandered into the castle, never once realizing that
he was anywhere but a European hotel. The professor tried
to put the metal brain transference cap over Magoo's head.
Magoo, thinking he was getting a bowl haircut, yanked off
the cap and placed it over the professor's head. Magoo
left the castle with Professor Frankenstein, the Monster,
and the alligators from the moat all saying "Cockle-doodle-
doo. "

Woody Woodpecker, created by Walter Lantz in a
series of cartoons released by Universal, met the Frankenstein Monster in the 1934 animated short Toyland Premiere.
The Monster was one of many toys, made in the images of
celebrities, that came to life in a department store before
Christmas. The 1961 cartoon Franken-Stymied was about
an inventor trying to get Woody for the subject of his
mechanical chicken plucker. Monster of Ceremonies (1966)
was about a mad scientist who wanted to make a creature
like the Frankenstein Monster. Using Woody in his experiment, the scientist transformed him into a type of Frankenstein Woodpecker, lumbering about like a robot.

During the late 1960s, a theatrical commercial featuring cartoon drawings of the Frankenstein Monster propagandized theatre patrons against the "monster" Pay Television. Yellow Submarine (United Artists, 1968), the Beatles' full length animated cartoon, showed Ringo Starr enter a laboratory where, lying on a platform, was the Frankenstein Monster. Ringo started the electrical apparatus and the Monster came to life, gradually metamorphosing into another Beatle, John Lennon. This was the first appearance of the Monster in a cartoon feature length film.

The Frankenstein Monster was in a crowd scene in The Yolk, a cartoon made in color by John Lange in 1971. From Lou with Love, an animated short cartoon featuring the Monster, was begun in 1972 by Robert Konikow and Milton Gray for release by Pterodactyl Productions, but was never completed.

The Intended Frankensteins

Producers have a knack for announcing films which, for various reasons, are never made. Occasionally a film will reach the scripting stage. But more often a treatment is the end result of these proposed motion pictures. Sometimes a producer will register a title and never pursue it. Quite a few Frankenstein motion pictures have been announced in the trade magazines but never went before the cameras. Four Frankenstein titles were reported in 1958. These include Blood of Frankenstein (no connection with the film that eventually became Independent-International's Dracula vs. Frankenstein), Martian Frankenstein which was supposed to be made in England, Frankenstein from Space, and Frankenstein's Castle.

Frankenstein from Space was a partial script by Weaver Wright (Forrest J Ackerman) and Budd Bankson. The story, published in Famous Monsters of Filmland #3 (1959), was set in the (then) futuristic time of 1975, when rockets had replaced airliners but scientists were still involved in familiar, unorthodox experiments. A passenger rocket crashed in the snow near the laboratory lodge of Dr. Thomas Frenken and his wife Marlene. They rushed to the scene of the crash and found two corpses in the wreckage. The first was a crushed body with an undamaged head. The second was a huge body with a smashed skull. Assuming the good head to be that of a scientist, Dr.

Frenken joined it to the giant body and brought the composite
being to life with his special serum rhodomoline. Later it
was learned that the head belonged to Gaston Garou, a Blue-
beard killer. The monster attempted strangling Marlene as
Dr. Frenken rushed into the room and uselessly fired six
bullets into the powerful body. Then the creature escaped
to the snows, performing acts of violence, until he was
chased carrying a young girl to a ski slide. The monster
flashed down the slide with the girl and flew through the
air, impaling himself on an upright pole. (A later idea
was to have the monster become a werewolf.)

     Reno-International films thought about making Fran-
kenstein from Space for a while, with actor Vincent Price
and science fiction writer Fritz Leiber both considered for
the part of Dr. Frenken. The part of the monster was to
either go to Jon Lackey or Tor Johnson, an enormous performer who had played in a number of horror films. The
prospect came up of possibly doing the film in 3D, but
Frankenstein from Space remained an unfinished script.

     Frankenstein's Castle was supposed to have been
made in the actual Castle of the Frankenstein in Darmstadt,
Germany. But that project was also abandoned. The Castle
of the Frankenstein was constructed shortly before 1252 and
still exists to the west of the village of Niederbeerbach.
The Frankenstein was a stronghold with high walls and a
deep moat offering protection. Among the legends about
the castle is the story of a ghastly monster.

> Legend which so often glorifies noble deeds took
> hold of one of the barons: 'Knight George.' Once
> upon a time there was a terrible man-eating mon-
> ster in the neighbourhood of the Katzenborn (Cat's
> Well) which frightened the whole valley of Nieder-
> beerbach. It would only retire for good if the most
> beautiful [girl] that was to be found in the valley were
> sacrificed. This was Annmary, the forester's daugh-
> ter. 'Knight George' confronted the ogre and in the
> furious struggle that followed he struck it a mortal
> blow, but he, too, died of a poisoned wound he had
> received in the hollow of the knee. The tomb of the
> hero stands in the choir of the church of Nieder-
> beerbach. [9]

The Frankenstein has undergone restoration and is currently
being offered as a hotel to tourists.

The one-page filler story, "The Castle of the Frankenstein" by Tom Sutton, in Eerie no. 19 (Warren Publishing
Company, 1968), retold the legend in illustrated form.   The
monster was depicted as a dragon with the Universal Pictures creature symbolically in the background.   Another
comic strip telling of the origin was "The Monster of the
Frankenstein," written by the present author and illustrated
by Jesse Santos.   The story featured a manlike monster and
appeared as a Ripley's Believe It or Not entry of Mystery
Comics Digest no. 10 (Western Publishing Company, 1973).

About 1960, a Chicago drive-in theatre with a pro-
pensity for altering the titles of their films, advertised a
movie called The Wild Witch of Frankenstein.   But this is
surely some other motion picture, probably Frankenstein's
Daughter.   The Scarab (originally entitled Fantastique) was
a film announced in 1961 by producer Jack H. Harris.
Writer Jim Harmon wrote the treatment of the proposed
film based on an original idea by Harris.   The Scarab took
place in London about the turn of the century.   An unknown
killer was at large and there were enough "red herrings"
or deliberate but innocent suspects to keep everyone in the
film (and the audience) guessing.   The would-be villains
and the intended actors portraying them were Dr. Frankenstein (Boris Karloff), Dr. Jekyll (Lon Chaney), and Jack
the Ripper (Claude Raines).   There were even more heroes--
Sherlock Holmes (Basil Rathbone), Dr. Watson (Herbert
Marshall), Inspector Lestrade (Sir Cedric Hardwicke),
Jules Verne (Paul Henreid), Mark Twain (Franchot Tone),
Buffalo Bill Cody (Tim McCoy), Annie Oakley (Nan Leslie),
and John L. Sullivan.

In The Scarab, the current Dr. Victor Frankenstein,
Dr. Jekyll, and others had attended a medical conference
in London.   Frankenstein returned to his ancestral castle
in the town of Frankenstein, Germany.   In the catacombs
beneath the castle was the lifeless form of the Frankenstein
Monster, decomposing after so many generations of true
death.   In order to atone for the horrors set upon the world
by his ancestor, Frankenstein, a suspect due to his mysterious experiments with glands, returned to England in order
to help track down the mysterious killer.   With the aid of
Dr. Jekyll, who was beginning his own experiments that
would someday transform him into Mr. Hyde, Frankenstein
attempted to utilize clues to create a form in the only
possible image of the killer.   The killer was eventually
exposed as an enormous insect that had emerged from an

Egyptian sarcophagus in a wax museum. The creature was destroyed as the museum was burned to the ground. The Scarab was an ambitious project, abandoned because of lack of financing. With such a proposed cast it is not difficult to see one reason that the film was not financed.

Willis O'Brien, who created the special visual effects for the 1933 masterpiece King Kong, had planned on doing a version of Frankenstein as early as 1928. O'Brien's Frankenstein was to utilize models brought to life by single frame animation. Set costs could be cut and the Monster could perform unbelievable stunts if the film were to be animated in miniature. First National, for which O'Brien had done the effects in The Lost World (1925), liked the test footage for Frankenstein that O'Brien had shot. But the film was never made.

In 1961, O'Brien wrote a treatment and partial script for a proposed tongue-in-cheek, animated film in full color titled King Kong vs. Frankenstein which was later changed to King Kong vs. the Ginko. The film presented the problem of how the giant gorilla Kong could ever engage the smaller Frankenstein Monster in a fair fight. O'Brien had the answer. Carl Denham, who had originally captured the monstrous ape in King Kong, speculated on the possibilities of staging a boxing match in San Francisco between Kong and some other monster. Kong, he explained, was not dead but had been smuggled back to Skull Island after his fall from the Empire State Building. The grandson of the infamous Dr. Frankenstein was in town and was bribed to create a monster worthy of battling the giant simian. In a laboratory in Africa, Dr. Frankenstein created a towering monster called the Ginko, made from parts of animals like elephants and rhinoceroses. O'Brien described the Ginko:

> He is about twenty feet tall with long arms which
> almost touch the floor. His legs are short and
> heavy with wrinkled skin, like those of an elephant.
> The head resembles that of a gorilla but more on
> the human side. The skin, overall, is thick and
> warty, like a rhino. He apparently has a good dis-
> position and mimicks things he sees humans do.

O'Brien designed at least thirteen different faces for the enormous creature. Some of the faces were quite human in appearance, or even demonic. Others resembled

such animals as hogs, dogs, or apes, with sharp teeth,
horny protrusions, and pointed ears.   The final version
seemed to be some giant combination of man and gorilla
with the tough skin of a pachyderm.

Carl Denham brought King Kong from Skull Island to
San Francisco where he and the Ginko boxed to a packed
auditorium.   The Ginko provided further entertainment by
lifting an elephant and by letting the story's heroine walk
across a rope in his hands held over his head.   When the
rope broke, the otherwise tamed Kong thought the Ginko
was harming the girl.   Breaking out of his cage, Kong
attacked the Ginko fiercely.   The battle of the monsters
raged over San Francisco, utilizing cable cars and all the
other things characteristic of the city.   The two creatures
eventually fought atop the Golden Gate Bridge, then plunged
into the bay to be swept toward the open sea.

Willis O'Brien took his treatment to film producer
John Beck who, in turn, gave the project to George Worthing
Yates and forgot O'Brien altogether.   A new treatment was
written by Yates in 1961 with the title Prometheus vs. King
Kong (also announced as King Kong vs. Prometheus).   Carl
Denham was written out of the plot.   "Prometheus," the
new name for the former "Ginko," was created by a scientist referred to as Kurt.   When Prometheus was rampaging
along a beach, clutching the heroine in his enormous hands,
Kurt tried to lasso him.   Kurt pulled the rope, causing the
monster to topple over and crush him.   After Kurt was
buried, his gravestone revealed him to be Kurt Frankenstein.   The grandson of the scientist who built the original
Monster, Kurt had created this "Prometheus V" as a type
of giant slave, with a brain controlled by anyone speaking
into his radio microphone.   By creating this fifth in the
line of Frankenstein monsters, Kurt had dreamed of freeing
man of labor, permitting him to devote his time to better
things.   Unknown to everyone, Prometheus was only feigning
submission and indeed possessed a crafty brain.

King Kong and Prometheus were to fight it out in
San Francisco's Candlestick Park.   At first Prometheus
obediently demonstrated his strength to the press by winning a tug of war with four giant diesel earthmovers.   Both
Prometheus and Kong were unshackled in the park.   Then
the creature made by Frankenstein revealed his true thinking ability and killed the man who had been controlling him
via microphone.   The two monsters battled in Candlestick

Park, then fought their way through the city and finally to
the same climax conceived by O'Brien.

John Beck did not make <u>Prometheus vs. King Kong</u>.
But he took the project to Toho in Japan where it became
the 1962 movie <u>Gojira tai Kingu Kongu</u> (translated as "Godzilla vs. King Kong" and seen in the Unites States as <u>King
Kong vs. Godzilla</u>).   Model animation was abandoned in
favor of actors wearing unconvincing monster suits.   Willis
O'Brien had died that year.   His widow was invited to the
preview of the film but she stayed home and wept.

In 1965 three Frankenstein films were announced but
mercifully never made: <u>Hercules Meets Frankenstein</u>, <u>The
Cool Ghoul Meets Frankenstein</u>, and most inane of all,
<u>Jayne Mansfield Meets Frankenstein</u>.   A Belgian magazine
in 1967 published the plots of four imaginary Frankenstein
films which one hopes were never intended for filming.
<u>Frankenstein Meets the Black Woman</u> took place after the
Third World War.   The Monster, attempting to find a living
companion, met the only other survivor on Earth, a pygmy,
whom he married.   <u>I Was a Little Frankenstein</u> was the
story of a small boy who assembled a plastic model of
Frankenstein's Monster.   The model came to life and
strangled the boy.   <u>Horror of Frankenstein</u> (no connection
with the Hammer film) was about a large man who had a
peculiar horror of the film <u>Frankenstein</u>.   When he met a
little girl named Maria at the lake, he promptly raped her.
Finally, <u>House of All Monsters</u> had the most ridiculous plot
of all.   Robert Hirsch and not the Monster had been burned
to death in the blazing windmill of the 1931 film.   Years
later, the super-criminal Fantomas was terrorizing the
world.   Baron Frankenstein, later to be revealed as Wolf
Man Lawrence Talbot, learned that Fantomas was really
the Monster.   Dracula, jealous of Fantomas' power and
stature, attacked the Monster with his fangs, turning him
into a vampire.

The first issue of <u>Live Naked</u> (1968), a nudist's
magazine from Phenix Publishers, contained a photo story
for a supposed film <u>The Naked Horror of Frankenstein</u> that
was apparently never made.   The plot concerned a group
of college nudists who went to an old mansion in hopes that
it could be used for communal living.   The Frankenstein
Monster (Chuck Gallo) was discovered lying under a sheet
and he and the Wolfman (Rance Farraday) soon caused
havoc among the students.   When the nudists made-up as

the creatures and attempted to enact their weird experiences
on a stage, the real monsters returned.   A remake of Frankenstein was announced for filming in England in 1970.   As
there is no other information concerning this title, it is
most likely that Frankenstein actually referred to Hammer's
Horror of Frankenstein or to the NBC four-hour television
film.   A title mentioned in 1971 was Frankenstein Meets
the Hell's Angels.   There is no documentation for this supposed film.   (Possibly the title is a misnomer and actually
referred to an exploitation picture called Werewolves on
Wheels.)

Old Theme, New Name

        While the many descendants of Frankenstein were
busy attempting to create life, other scientists were creating
monsters of their own.   Since they had not acquired Frankenstein's blueprints they had no reason to give him due
credit.   But the results of their mad experiments were
usually the same.   The Brain That Wouldn't Die (given the
title "The Head that Wouldn't Die" in the end credits) went
into production for Sterling/Carlton in 1959 but was not
released by American-International Pictures until 1962.
The picture, directed by Rex Carlton, surely was not three
years in the making, since it ranks along such quickly made
efforts as Frankenstein's Daughter.

        When Dr. Bill Cortner's (Jason Evers) girlfriend
was decapitated in an automobile wreck, he salvaged the
head and took it to his laboratory.   A scientist experimenting with organ transplants, Cortner kept the head alive in
the hopes of finding a perfect body to attach to it.   Behind
a locked door in the laboratory was a poor man's Frankenstein Monster--a creature made up of transplants and given
life by the doctor's own drugs.   Cortner found the body he
desired in a disfigured photographer's model.   Before he
could perform the operation to make his former love whole
and entire, the monster, with whom the head had been
communicating telepathically, smashed out of its prison,
revealing its pointed head, ugly flesh, and bulging, mis-
placed orbs, and destroyed its creator.   The film ended
with the creature lumbering out of the burning laboratory
bearing the model in its arms.   A sequel was planned but
thankfully never made.

        A Frankenstein type motion picture was made in

England in 1966 as part of the famous "Carry On" comedy
series. Carry on Screaming, directed by Gerald Thomas
for Anglo-Amalgated, featured the monstrous Odbodd (Tom
Clegg), a creature resembling the Frankenstein Monster but
with pointed ears and hairy face and hands. Outside the
house where he lived with a whole troupe of monsters,
Odbodd captured a girl but, in the struggle, left one of his
fingers behind. From this severed finger grew a full sized
version of the monster called Odbodd, Jr. (Billy Cornelius).

Frank's Greatest Adventure, written and directed by
Philip Kaufman, was made in color by Jeriko Film in 1967.
Two years later American-International released it under
the title Fearless Frank. A young man named Frank (John
Voight) was killed in the film's prologue. The scene dissolved to a picture of the Frankenstein Monster. After the
credits of the film, Frank was brought to life as a type of
superhero. Claude, the evil brother of the good doctor
that brought Frank to life, created "False Frank" (Voight),
whose stitched face and questionable origin made him seem
the monster he was intended to be. Affected by society,
Frank gradually became evil while False Frank strived to
be good. Eventually the two Franks exchanged roles and
fought until the evil one was destroyed.

Scream and Scream Again (very closely adapted
from the novel The Disorientated Man[10] by Peter Saxon)
was directed by Gordon Hessler and released in color in
1968 by American-International. An unknown fiend was at
large, killing in the fashion of a vampire by draining his
victims' blood. And a kidnapped athlete was being robbed
of his limbs every time he went to sleep in the bed of a
strange hospital. When Keith (Michael Gothard), the "vampire," was finally apprehended, he tore his own hand off,
leaving it in the handcuff clamped to a police automobile,
and fled to the house of Dr. Browning (Vincent Price).
Then he comitted suicide in a vat of acid. Later, Browning
revealed his laboratory to a police detective, showing an
assembly line of creation, whereby he built perfect and
emotionless human beings, or "composites," from stolen
organs. Browning too had been so assembled in this scheme
by a secret organization to conquer the world. In the climax, Browning, as punishment for his error in arousing
the interest of the police, was hurled into his own acid vat.
The film was fast paced and extremely entertaining. But
Christopher Lee's role as the secret organization's top
executive was small and Peter Cushing's part was barely
more than a cameo.

John Carradine played a mad scientist creating living
beings from transplanted organs, and then controlling them
via robot heads, in The Astro-Zombies, made in 1968 by
Row, Ltd. , and released the following year by Geneni. Ted
V. Mikels directed this combination of spy and horror film
in which the Astro-Zombies were created in an old mansion
and then became the object of foreign spies.   During a gun
battle between the government and the spies, the mad doctor was mortally wounded.   Before dying, he destroyed the
device which controlled the zombies.

Ido Zero Dai Sakusn (translated as "Monster from
Latitude Zero" and known in the United States as Latitude
Zero) was a Japanese science fiction film made in color in
1969 by Toho and Don Sharp Productions, directed by Honda,
and released by National General.   Based on Ted Sherde-
man's radio serial of about 1940 involving such fantastic
elements as atomic submarines and an invasion of zombies,
the film starred Cesar Romero as Captain Craig McKenzie
who created a Frankenstein Monster of sorts to destroy the
undersea citadel of science called Latitude Zero as a step
in conquering the world.   Taking the body of a lion, the
wings of a condor, and the brain of his former lover, he
created a griffin (through the special effects of Tsuburaya).
But the brain of the woman scorned caused the griffin to
destroy McKenzie's submarine as an avalanche rained down
on them.

Other creatures created from parts of corpses were
less elaborate.   The British Dr. Blood's Coffin (1961) was
a Caralan film released in the United States by United
Artists and directed by Sidney J. Furie.   It was released
to theatres in black and white and to television in color.
Dr. Peter Blood (Kieron Moore) was a scientist who brought
a corpse (Paul Stockman) back to life by first giving him
another heart.   When Dr. Blood tried to force his love on
the creature's wife, it attacked the scientist.   The two of
them fought as chemicals were knocked over and the laboratory was engulfed by fire.

In Man Without a Body, a British film released in
1968 by Film Plays and in the United States by Budd
Rogers, and directed by W. Lee Wilder and Charles Saunders, a well-meaning scientist (Robert Hutton) took the
ancient yet living head of the prophet Nostradamus and
joined it to a headless corpse.   In the final scenes of the
picture, the monster, stalking about with a white casing

over the head, fell from a staircase, leaving the head
caught on a clanging bell.   In Beast of Blood (which was
shot under the title Return to the Horrors of Blood Island),
a color film made in the Philippines by Hemisphere, directed by Eddie Romero, and released in 1970, the insidious
Dr. Lorka (Eddie Garcia) tried to graft heads onto other
bodies in a prelude to restoring his decapitated chlorophyl
monster.   But in the end the headless monstrosity rose
from the operating table, killed him, and destroyed the
laboratory.

La Residencia (translated as "The Boarding House"
and released in the United States in 1970 as The House
that Screamed) was another variation on the Frankenstein
theme.   In order to create a woman as perfect as his
dominating mother, a boy murdered the girls in her boarding school and assembled the selected pieces.   He never
considered bringing his creation to life in this Spanish
film. [11]

Yet another variation on the Frankenstein theme was
released in 1971, Mutual General's color film entitled The
Incredible Two-Headed Transplant, directed by Anthony
Lanza and released by American-International.   The dead
head of a homicidal killer was grafted onto the body of a
retarded giant (John Bloom, who played the Monster in
Dracula vs. Frankenstein) and brought back to life.   The
result was a two-headed monstrosity, the giant body forced
to kill upon the whims of the evil brain.   The picture did
not pretend to be serious.   Lionel Atwill as Dr. von Niemann created a simpler form of life in The Vampire Bat,
a Majestic film of 1933, directed by Frank Strayer.   Villagers
believed that it was a vampire that attacked people and
drained their blood.   Actually, von Niemann had created a
blob of living tissue that pulsated in a tank in his laboratory.   The organism required food of human blood which
the mad doctor supplied through the victims kidnapped by
his hypnotized, black-cloaked servant.

Many mad doctors of the films have avoided most of
the disgusting work of disinterring corpses and stitching
them together in favor of securing only the brain and using
metal, wires, and circuits for the torsos of their artificial
men.   Many such scientists have gone to great lengths to
create Frankensteins of steel that have the power to do all
that a man can do--except think.   Luckily there have been
enough human brains available to inventors who prefer their

monsters to have nearly invulnerable bodies.

Moe Howard, Shemp Howard, and Larry Fine, the
Three Stooges, nearly lost their heads in the Columbia
short subject Dopey Dicks (1950), directed by Hugh McCol-
lum. A pair of mad doctors (played by Stanley Price and
Philip Van Zandt) had created a tall, manlike robot. On
its trial walk the robot's head was accidentally knocked off.
Determined to attach a human head to their creation, the
scientists pursued the Stooges through their mansion. After
a long chase through the building, with the doctors and the
headless robot after them, the Stooges escaped in a car only
to find that the artificial man was their driver.

The Colossus of New York (Paramount 1968), directed by Eugene Lourie, was more faithful to the Frankenstein theme. When young genius Jeremy Spenser (Ross
Martin) was killed in an automobile accident, his scientist
father (Otto Kruger) could not endure such a waste to the
world and instructed his other son, an electronics wizard,
to construct an enormous robot body. Then the preserved
brain of Jeremy was placed within the creature's head.
The robot (Ed Wolff) vaguely resembled the Frankenstein
Monster with its high forehead and large cranium. A long
cloak draped the robot's massive shoulders. The creature
was brought to life in a typically Frankensteinian laboratory,
lumbered awkwardly about, and begged for death rather than
remain in that horrid form. To increase Jeremy's re-
morse he could no longer see his wife. Only his young
son (Charles Herbert) looked with sympathy upon the awesome electronic giant. Eventually Jeremy became a monster and crashed into the United Nations building, destroying
anyone that happened to get in the way of the death ray he
somehow acquired. When his son rushed up to him, the
confused Jeremy begged him to pull the switch, inaccessible
to himself, thus ending his unnatural existence.

In the 1968 color film Torture Garden, scripted by
Robert Bloch for Amicus Films in England and directed by
Freddie Francis, a select group of forever youthful Hollywood stars maintained their immortality by having their
brains transferred to robot bodies. A number of androids
formed in molds and possessing transplanted human brains
were featured in the Czechoslovakian film, released in
1972, Pane, Vy Jste Vdova ("Mister, You Are a Widower").
In 1943, a "Colonel Stoopnagle and Budd" comedy short
entitled "The Inventor" featured an even less gruesome

variation on the Frankenstein theme involving a robot.   A
man created a Frankenstein robot from the parts of many
"dead" automobiles.   "The Inventor" was made by Educa-
tional Pictures. [12]

The concept of Man's inventions dominating or even
destroying him is a theme prevalent in science fiction literature and motion pictures.   This theme obviously suggests
Victor Frankenstein creating a Monster which he cannot
control and which eventually drives him to his own destruction.   To cover all such films in this text would be pointless.   More recently, science fiction films such as 2001:
A Space Odyssey (MGM, 1968) and Colossus: The Forbin
Project (Universal, 1970) have taken the theme of invention
dominating inventor to the ultimate extremes with highly advanced computers willingly setting themselves up as masters
of mankind.   This theme is more frightening than that of
the Monster created piecemeal from cadavers, because of
the proximity of the threat of mankind's being manipulated
by thinking machines.   In Colossus, Forbin, the inventor
of a computer that linked with a similar Russian device to
take over the world, said that all inventors like himself
should read the novel Frankenstein.

The resuscitation of the dead, an obvious Frankensteinian theme, has been so prominent in motion pictures
that it would be virtually impossible and hardly necessary
to list every such instance.   There have been, however,
films in which the revival of corpses through science has
been so based on the public image of Frankenstein and his
laboratory that they bear mentioning.   Face of Marble
(Monogram, 1946), directed by William Beaudine, starred
John Carradine and Robert Shayne as scientists attempting
to bring the dead back to life.   Their laboratory was another
fantastic display of electrical apparatus, with a platform
upon which dead bodies were charged with power a la Frankenstein.   When the scientists finally succeeded, their walking dead had the power to walk through solid walls.

Robert Shayne was back reviving the dead in The
Indestructible Man (1956), made by the same studio under
its new name Allied Artists and directed by Jack Pollexfen.
When the film was released to television an opening title
made references to the experiments of Dr. Frankenstein.
Butcher Benson (Lon Chaney), an executed killer, swore to
somehow get revenge upon members of his gang who turned
state's evidence against him.   Two scientists attempting to

find a cure for cancer experimented on his corpse, charging it with electricity, and inadvertently bringing him back to life.   Unable to speak due to his burnt out vocal cords and possessing a body made invulnerable by the experiment, Benson killed the scientists in the fashion of a stiffly walking Frankenstein Monster, then proceeded to hunt down his former gang members.   Toward the end of the film his face was disfigured by fire.   In the climax he was destroyed by the power that gave him life--electricity.

Other films have taken the Universal Frankenstein Monster make-up and adapted it to creatures appearing in films having nothing to do with the Frankenstein theme.   In The Thing (also known as The Thing from Another World), made in 1951 by RKO, and in The Three Stooges in Orbit, made in 1962 by Columbia Pictures, the make-ups designed for the aliens were all seemingly patterned after the Frankenstein Monster.

Frankenstein's Monster has been seen in a plethora of forms since his screen debut in 1910.   But in the 1930s there was a new audience craving entertainment within their homes.   This was not visual entertainment, except as could be created in the mind;   the new medium required no payment at the box office;   the only admission was the dials on that wonderful old radio console occupying a place of honor in the living room.

Notes

1.   This sequence was incorporated into the Allied Artists film Daughter of Dr. Jekyll (1957) when it was released to television and required more footage to give it added length.

2.   Dillard, R. H. W.   "Even a Man Who is Pure at Heart: Poetry and Danger in the Horror Film," Man and the Movies, ed. by W. R. Robinson. Baltimore: Penguin Books, 1967, p. 72.

3.   Two conflicting plot summaries were released by Toho. In one, the boy ate the heart, which transformed him into Frankenstein.   When the boy in the American version was described as eating everything he thought edible there seemed to exist the possibility of another version of the story.

4. Scenes from <u>Furankenshutain tai Baragon</u> later appeared in Toho's <u>Kaiju Soshingeki</u> (translated as "Operation Monsterland" and seen in the United States as <u>Destroy All Monsters</u>), released in 1967, and <u>Godzilla's Revenge</u> (1971).

5. This robot costume was first used in <u>La Nave de los Monstruos</u> ("The Ship of the Monsters"), made by Producciones Sotomayor in 1959.

6. The West Coast premiere of <u>Frankenstein's Bloody Terror</u> was covered on television. Several people dressed in Frankenstein costumes were present at the affair.

7. Scenes from <u>Nankai no Dai Ketto</u>, <u>Gojira no Musko</u>, and <u>Kingu Kongu no Gyakushu</u> were incorporated into the Toho film <u>Godzilla's Revenge</u> (1971), directed by Honda and the last to feature the work of Tsuburaya who died that year.

8. <u>Mickey's Gala Premiere</u> was retitled <u>Movie Star Mickey</u> for home movie distribution by Hollywood Film Enterprises.

9. From the souvenir pamphlet given to visitors of the Castle of the Frankenstein.

10. <u>The Disorientated Man</u> was published in 1967 by Paperback Library and reprinted in 1970 under the title <u>Scream and Scream Again</u>. The major difference in the novel was the inclusion of a group of aliens responsible for the Frankensteinian science shown in the film.

11. A satire <u>La Otre Residencia</u> ("The Other Boarding House") was made that same year in Spain.

12. "The Inventor" was included in <u>The Sound of Laughter</u>, a 1963 Union film which also featured other comedy shorts.

Chapter 8

FRANKENSTEIN ON THE AIR

When Frankenstein was dramatized on radio it had
the potential of being even more horrifying than on the
screen.   There were no pictures with radio.   The only
images were those conveyed in the inner sanctum of the
human being--the imagination.   What can be imagined can
be far more gruesome and terrifying than anything actually
seen.   On the radio Frankenstein's Monster could fit the
qualifications set by the listener.   He could be mildly horrible so as not to arouse too much fear, or his appearance
could correspond exactly to the creature that haunted Universal Pictures.   The beast could even be so ghastly that
the program had to be listened to in a fully lighted room.

The first radio dramatization of Frankenstein was
presented in 1932, partially to capitalize on the popularity
of the Boris Karloff movie.   Unlike most classics that were
dramatized on radio in thirty-minute or hour-long versions,
this adaptation of Mary Shelley's novel was stretched into a
thirteen-chapter radio serial.   It starred George Edwards
as Baron Victor Frankenstein.   The radio serial followed
the novel very closely, but rearranged various incidents.
Some elements were borrowed from the 1931 movie to give
listeners who had not read the novel some familiarity with
the tale.   The Baron was given a superstitious servant
named Julio, inspired by the film's hunchback Fritz.   But
the radio version did not follow the established pattern of
the film with its grunting Monster.   The radio creature
spoke fluently, often going on with lengthy orations, which
read well but sounded overly melodramatic when heard aloud.

Captain Walton's ship Voyager was sailing toward
England from the frozen reaches of the North Pole.   A
man, sick and raving, who identified himself as Baron
Frankenstein was picked up and taken to a cabin.

There he confessed his great "sin" of creating "a Monster
... a creature who delights in taking human life." With
the Monster lurking nearby, Frankenstein told his story to
Walton, thus making a frame for each episode. Every
installment opened with Frankenstein talking to the captain.
The conversation would then segue to a flashback. The
endings of the chapters were repetitious. The Baron's
narrative would reach a climactic point or "cliffhanger."
When Walton eagerly asked what happened next, Victor
would give a reply like, "I can tell you no more today,
Captain. I am weary now. And the memory of the past
upsets me. Please be patient." Captain Walton remained
patient--for nine such installments. He, like the listening
audience, had to come back the following day--same time,
same station--to hear the next chapter. Despite its naiveté,
Frankenstein was remarkably sophisticated when compared
with some of the radio drama of the very early 1930s.

Elizabeth, Victor's fiancée, and his friend Ernst
Clerval (Henry in the novel) saw the bandaged, lifeless
form on the bench in Victor's laboratory. The creature
was intended to be strong, handsome, intelligent, and noble.
The storm was nearing its apex when Frankenstein addressed the spectators.

> BARON: [sounds of wind] Before you, you see a
> great inanimate figure, entirely covered with
> bandages. By means of pulleys, Julio and I will
> raise that figure to the top of the tower, where
> it will remain for an hour. Then we will lower
> it and I think the figure will have life.
> ELIZABETH: No, you cannot do it, Victor. You
> must not. I'm afraid.

After the experiment was completed, the Baron unwrapped the face and for the first time realized it was
hideous. Then the impossible happened. The being actually grew in size as the aftereffect of the electricity.
Later the Monster smashed Julio to pieces and escaped.
Frankenstein and Elizabeth eventually married, and
took in William, Elizabeth's nephew (her cousin in the
book). When next Frankenstein and his Monster met,
the creature could speak (but could not apparently
remember if his maker's name was pronounced
"Frankenstein" or "Frankenstyne").

> MONSTER: I do not wish to die. I wish to live.

I wish to be happy as other men are.
BARON: Why ... what do you ask of me?
MONSTER: You made me. You gave life to me.
Now make a mate for me ... a woman who may
share my life with me.
BARON: What you ask ... is impossible. It shall
be my mission in life to destroy you.

The Baron refused to create a female. But his artificial
creature was not about to lumber off without leaving a grim
threat.

MONSTER: So be it, Frankenstein. You and yours
shall suffer for this.
BARON: What do you mean by that?
MONSTER: I killed one man ... and I can kill
others. And unless you heed my demand, unless
you fashion for me a mate, then you and all your
family will suffer. I will kill all who stand in
my path. I will leave a trail of death and destruction wherever I go. But I will not kill you.
You will live until I bend you to my will. The
creature shall rule the master!

The homicidal Monster made good his threat, first
by murdering William and placing the blame on Justine,
then by slaying a complete stranger. Elizabeth would be
next unless Victor fashioned his mate. When Victor destroyed the incomplete female body, the Monster threatened
to return "on the day that you are reunited with your wife!"
Ernst Clerval was killed by the Monster while on board
ship. Then, despite Victor's precautions, the Monster,
who had been hiding on the roof of his house, came in and
squeezed the life out of Elizabeth. After this, Victor pursued the Monster across the world to the North Pole.
Aboard the Voyager, the Baron feared he would die from
the cold before killing his creation. Inevitably Baron Frankenstein succumbed to the elements.

MONSTER: My master ... my creator.... What
ails him? Let me speak with him.
WALTON: Foul Monster! Baron Frankenstein is
dead! Destroyed by your hatred and vice. Now
you shall die! Fire, men! (sounds of gunshots)
MONSTER: (yells in agony) You would destroy me.
The blood pours from my wounds. But I still
have life! Let me look on the body of Frankenstein!

SAILOR: Shall we fire again, Captain?
WALTON: No, wait.
MONSTER: Frankenstein, you are dead. Victim of
    my hatred. Victim of your own selfishness. Oh,
    Frankenstein, I am filled with remorse. And yet,
    soon I am about to die. They have dealt me mor-
    tal wounds, Frankenstein. My creator, I mourn
    for you.

After consigning Frankenstein's corpse to the sea, with a
scream the Monster leapt overboard to his death amid the
floating chunks of ice, never to be seen again.

    The 1932 radio drama of Frankenstein, despite its
overplayed acting (which was the norm in the majority of
radio plays) and superfluous dialogue, remains as the only
dramatic adaptation of Mary Shelley's novel to recreate the
geographical splendor of the original. The drama spanned
Switzerland, England, the Black Sea, and Russia. Naturally
on a medium requiring only voices and sound effects this
was economically possible. The drama's most severe draw-
back was the choice of George Edwards as Baron Frankenstein. People who had seen the Universal movie were ac-
customed to a young British Frankenstein. But Edwards
portrayed the scientist with a mature, heavily accented
voice sounding more like his own father, the toplofty burgomaster, or even Jean Hersholt's revered characterization
as radio's kindly Dr. Christian. However, Frankenstein
remained surprisingly faithful to Mary Shelley.

    Radio drama was still an infant and there were many
versions of Frankenstein yet to come. Mary Shelley's Monster was heard next on the radio in 1935. To help publi-
cize the film Bride of Frankenstein, Universal prepared
a fifteen-minute script of some of the picture's more dramatic scenes and sent it free upon request to exhibitors all
over the country. The intention was to dramatize the scenes
using performers from acting schools or little theatre groups.

    Frankenstein was dramatized during the 1940s on the
Columbia Broadcasting System anthology series Suspense.
This half-hour version was virtually a different story alto-
gether. In the Suspense adaptation of Frankenstein, Victor
(Stacy Harris) was a licensed and practicing physician.
One day while strolling through the farmlands near his
laboratory and while Elizabeth was away on a short vaca-
tion, Dr. Frankenstein was speaking with his friend James,

a minister. Victor told James that he was involved in an
experiment that terrified him. When the minister requested
an explanation, the doctor made an attempt to reveal all.

> VICTOR: (sounds of birds, cattle) I've made some-
> thing. It's tremendous. It's impossible, but I
> think I've done it. And it goes against everything
> you believe, James.
> JAMES: Wh-what have you done?
> VICTOR: I've put it together. Heart, brain, nerves,
> muscles, everything. I ... I've done it. Do you
> understand? A complete body.
> JAMES: And you're upset because of that? You
> think you've done something wrong?
> VICTOR: Last night I made it move. I'm not cer-
> tain, but I think I can give it life. (Pause.)
> Don't you see why I'm afraid, James? I've
> created a man.

Reverend James accompanied Victor Frankenstein to
his laboratory. There the doctor told how his desire to
create life began when he accidentally restored a dead dog
to life by injecting it with a new compound with which he
had been experimenting. The fluid contained the secret of
life. The Suspense version ignored the established electrical laboratories of the movies and went to the original
novel which mentioned injections causing galvanic actions
in a dead body. Frankenstein unveiled his assembled
creation. When James gasped at the hideous form Victor
said that the face was not yet finished. That would come
later. (Naturally the face never was finished.) The scientist injected the lifeless form with his special fluid. Suddenly the creature moved. The head jerked, the eyes
blinked, the ears moved slightly to pick up sound. Frankenstein's creation was alive.

Later Victor spoke to Elizabeth after her return,
giving him an opportunity to get away from his work. When
he returned to his workshop he learned to his horror that
the Monster had broken its confining straps, gotten off the
table, and was standing before him, looking with a curious
stare. Victor wondered how the creature could have broken
its straps, since unlike most versions this Monster was no
taller than an average man. The Monster made a low
vocal noise and commenced breathing heavily. Victor addressed the thing.

VICTOR: (sounds of Monster breathing) Do you
understand what I say? Do you feel any pain?
Are you hungry? I'm a man ... like you. You
are a man. Do you understand? (Sound of footsteps.) This is a mirror. You can see yourself.
Look. (Monster growls.) It's all right. It's all
right.

The Monster saw his own ugliness and reacted with
staring eyes. Victor tried to get the creature back on the
table where he could replace the straps. But the Monster
lashed out, wrecking some of the equipment and escaping
from the laboratory by breaking open the locked door. Together, armed with rifles, Victor and James hunted the
Monster. Frankenstein also carried a hypodermic needle,
hoping to drug the creature and spare taking back its unnatural life. They tracked the Monster to a barn. Victor
beckoned the minister to let him enter the barn alone. Inside he faced the ghastly handiwork of his own ambition.
The creature waited for his creator in a corner of the
building. But as Victor attempted speaking to the Monster
the brute attacked him fatally. James rushed into the barn
and fired his rifle. The Monster was not killed, however,
and fled from the barn.

JAMES: He never recovered consciousness again.
Outside, I looked for the thing I'd shot at, but
there was no sign of it. I returned to the lab and
burned every paper, destroyed every single evidence of Victor Frankenstein's terrible experiment. But the result of that experiment has
never been found; nor have I been able yet to
convince the authorities that such a thing ever
existed.

The Suspense version of the story did not suffer from
the heavy-handedness of the serial. By the 1940s radio
drama had reached its peak. The actors in this thirty-
minute Frankenstein even underplayed their lines, which
was a rarity on radio melodrama.

During the 1940s Frankenstein was done on a CBS
program Let's Pretend, a show catering to a younger audience. The show excelled in children's classics and fairy
tales. The scheduling of a story in which a man creates
another man was extraordinary for Let's Pretend. Basil
Rathbone, who had been regularly playing Sherlock Holmes

on the air, switched from deduction to induction by assuming
the role of Victor in an adaptation of Frankenstein presented
around 1946 on CBS' Stars Over Hollywood.   Rathbone, whose
voice was perfectly suited for radio, was an ideal choice to
play Frankenstein.   He had already portrayed an offspring of
the infamous scientist in the film Son of Frankenstein.

Mary Shelley's story received an updated treatment
on 25 September 1947 on the American Broadcasting Company's horror series Quiet Please.   The title of the half-
hour play was "Is This Murder?"   Quiet Please always
starred Ernest Chapel as the protagonist, who would relate
his story in retrospect either to someone in the story or
directly to the radio listener.   His voice was always sympathetic and listeners could excuse some of the horrors he
related.   The play was written and directed by Willis Cooper,
who had written the screenplay for Son of Frankenstein.   "Is
This Murder?" was not a true adaptation of Frankenstein.
The play was an original story based on the Frankenstein
theme--the manufacturing of an artificial man.   The drama
opened with Chapel playing a character appropriately named
Ernest addressing both a lawyer and the audience.

> ERNEST: Thank you very much for coming to see
> me.   I would have come to your office but, uh
> ... I'm sorry.   Infirmities prevent my going out.
> That's why I have to have it so dark in here, too.
> Would you care for a drink?   There's some ex-
> cellent sherry there on the sideboard.   At least
> I've been told it's excellent.   Amontillado, I think.
> Oh, I don't indulge myself.   But help yourself.
> Please do.   I asked you to come here because I
> think I need some legal advice, about murder,
> I'm afraid.

Ernest was quite hazy about this question of murder
and began to relate his tale.   He had been involved in the
manufacture of artificial limbs--hands, arms, legs--that
functioned as if real.   Dan, his assistant, was in love with
a pretty girl named Joyce.

> ERNEST: Have you ever read the works of Mary
> Wollstonecraft Shelley?   Never heard of them?
> Well, she was the wife of the poet Percy Bysshe
> Shelley.   She was a novelist.   She died in 1890
> which was about sixty years ago.   But I'm afraid
> one of her novels was more or less ... er,

responsible for what I'm going to ask you about.
You don't ... I mean, you aren't familiar with
her works. Why, the best known novel she wrote
... was <u>Frankenstein</u>. (Music reaches crescendo.)
Oh, it's nothing at all like the <u>Frankenstein</u> you've
seen in pictures. No Boris Karloff, no Bela Lugosi with a flasher, no weird castles. But it's a
powerful book, with a very important message.

Ernest mused about creating a Frankenstein Monster
from the various mechanical devices that served to replace
real arms and legs. But such a creature would be composed of man-made materials and not pieces of corpses.
Willis Cooper's script showed his esteem for the original
novel. It also revealed his fondness for the Universal films
with his references to Lionel Atwill's wooden arm (from
<u>Son of Frankenstein</u>) and Lugosi's flasher (<u>Abbott and Cos-
tello Meet Frankenstein</u>).

> DAN: (Sound of electric saw) This new arm almost
> has its own brain.
> ERNEST: (sawing stops) Not much like the one, er,
> Lionel Atwill? Was that his name?
> DAN: Yes, Lionel Atwill.
> ERNEST: ... Wore in the picture. The one he had
> to manipulate with his other hand.

Cooper made yet another comment on the Universal
movies when Ernest and Dan talked about placing a human
brain in a creature made of their artificial parts. The
creature would have steel fingers, plastic muscles, a
chromium-plated skull with wide-angle lenses for eyes and
microphones for ears.

> ERNEST: And what for a brain?
> DAN: You know what Frankenstein used. (Sound
> of electric saw.) A brain. The wrong kind of
> brain.
> ERNEST: That was in the picture. (Sound of ham-
> mering.) He got a criminal brain by mistake.
> Remember?
> DAN: I wonder what would have happened if he got
> a good brain. (Sound of hammering.)
> ERNEST: You've got the book and the picture mixed
> up.
> DAN: But what would happen if you could make a
> synthetic man and put a real good brain in it?
> (Sound of hand saw.)

The idea seemed plausible although to Ernest it was impractical. Meanwhile the workshop duties had been keeping Dan away from Joyce. She told Ernest that she would kill Dan if he were really seeing another woman. Ernest questioned his assistant, asking what he had been doing in the workshop for so many nights. Dan's explanation was more than a speech. He showed Ernest what he had been working on for such a long time. It was a humanoid, totally functional, and requiring only a human brain to make it live. Soon Dan had his brain, when conflicts developing between him, Joyce, and Ernest reached a terrible peak.

Finally Ernest turned on the lights to ask his lawyer if a murder had been committed. Seated across from the lawyer was an automaton, its hide made of gleaming metal. Ernest's body had been killed but his brain lived in the robot. He had become the creature of whom he knew so much.

An authentic adaptation of _Frankenstein_ was performed about 1950 on the half-hour syndicated anthology series _Favorite Story_.[1] Ronald Colman introduced the favorite stories. The show's gimmick was that a famous personality would write in a letter requesting to hear the story that was his favorite. _Frankenstein_ was requested by someone identified with howls of laughter instead of growls of terror. He was Fred Allen, one of radio's greatest humorists. There were the usual changes from the novel in the _Favorite Story_ version of _Frankenstein_. Dr. Victor Frankenstein had been telling his friend Clerval how, using both ancient and modern methods, he had formed a human body from dead organs and tissues. The creature lay awaiting life in his secluded mountain laboratory. Victor had retired for the night, planning to charge the creature in the morning with electricity. A violent storm arose during the night and the eight-foot tall body was struck by lightning. Then Dr. Frankenstein awoke.

> VICTOR: (sounds of wind and thunder) As the very next stroke of lightning seemed to electrify the very air in my sleeping chamber, I thought I heard ... a sound? From my laboratory? Did I dream this? Or did it really happen! The curtains around my bed were parted and I saw the Monster! Its yellow skin! Its unblinking eyes! The dried, papery lips ... moved! (sound of Monster grunting)

Victor fled to the safety of sleep, praying that his
experience would be only a nightmare upon his waking. In
the morning he found that the living Monster was no longer
in the laboratory. Later Dr. Frankenstein received the
terrible news that his own brother, young William, had
been strangled by a creature of enormous strength. When
the Monster returned to his creator he could speak. His
gutteral voice seemed to issue from a grave. Frankenstein
fired the gun at the giant killer but it had no fatal effect.
The Monster demanded a mate. If Frankenstein refused to
create one all his friends would die including his wife on
their wedding day. Victor could not complete his second
creation and destroyed it. The Monster's threat again
echoed through his mind: "I ... will ... be ... with ...
you ... on ... your ... wedding ... day."

On his wedding day Victor heard a scream. Elizabeth had been killed by his creation.

Dr. Frankenstein was finishing his story to Clerval,
who said the creature was only a figment of his tortured
brain. Clerval soon learned how real the figment was.
Loud footsteps clumped from behind him. Clerval turned
to see for the first time the grisly face of the Monster.

> CLERVAL: Good God!
> MONSTER: You ... are a friend ... of Dr. Fran-
>   kenstein?
> VICTOR: No! No! Clerval is no friend of mine!
> MONSTER: (sound of heavy footsteps) You ... lie!
> VICTOR: I don't know him! He's not a friend!
> MONSTER: I ... kill ... all who are friends of ...
>   Frankenstein (Monster growls)
> CLERVAL: Get away from me! No! Get away!
>   Stay back! Stay back! Ahhhh! Ahhhhhhhhhh ....
> MONSTER: (pause) He ... is ... dead!

The Monster would not kill his creator. Instead he promised to be with him for all his days. The Favorite Story
adaptation ended with Victor warning the audience to beware
and not to mention his name, for the Monster still lurked
in the shadows, waiting to kill all friends of Dr. Frankenstein.

There were other versions of Frankenstein done on
the radio. One of them starred the notable British actor
James Mason as Victor Frankenstein. Orson Welles

probably did a sixty-minute version on his highly imaginative CBS anthology <u>Mercury Theatre on the Air</u> in the late
1930s, both producing and starring.   Most of these programs left the story open for sequels, with the Monster
escaping or left in a predicament from which he could
readily save himself.   But the radio dramas did not imitate
the movies in that respect.   When the Frankenstein Monster
vanished at the end of each show, that particular version
was never heard from again.

More Horrors Ahead

<u>The Avenger</u> began in the pages of the Street and
Smith pulp magazine as a crime-fighter with a pliable face.
When the character was adapted to the radio the format became a carbon copy of the popular show <u>The Shadow</u> (also
owned by Street and Smith), right down to plot construction
and acting styles.   The radio Avenger was really Jim Brendon, whose remarkable anti-crime inventions included a
"diffusion capsule" which rendered him invisible via black
light and gave him a sinister laugh and filtered microphone
voice like the one The Shadow used to chill the evil hearts
of criminals.

In 1942 the Avenger met a Frankenstein-like scientist
in "The Mystery of the Giant Brain."   Professor Rodano, a
typical mad scientist, had been experimenting with the brains
of animals stolen from the zoo.   He created three iron robots that stomped about doing his bidding.   One day his
automatons would do things men feared, commanded by a
living brain of his own creation which would eliminate the
need for control batteries.   Miss Sinclair, his assistant,
reprimanded him for his mad scheme but was taken into
the basement laboratory by an obedient robot.

One of Jim Brendon's marvelous inventions picked up
impressions of evil thoughts and suffering animals which came
from the vicinity of Rodano's mansion in the town of Midvale.
Brendon and his girlfriend Fern (like The Shadow's girlfriend,
Margo Lane, only she knew the hero's true identity) went to
Midvale to solve the mystery.   The bio-chemist met a man
who told of a "big man" stealing foxes and killing their
owner and taking four bullets without harmful effect.   Fern,
with all the bad luck of Margo Lane, went to an old mansion to use a phone to contact the police.   She was greeted
at the door by a giant robot and the grinning Professor

Rodano. The scientist was delighted for now he had another human brain to add to the monstrosity, along with the brains of Miss Sinclair and Giles, his former assistant, both locked in the basement.

> RODANO: Now listen, all of you. Tonight the
> mighty Rodano will perform the greatest opera-
> tion in the history of surgery. I will add three
> human brains to the living animal brains I have
> already preserved.

The scientist commanded one of his robots to pull the curtain to show the spectators the composite Frankenstein-brain throbbing in a glass case.

> RODANO: Well, what do you think of it?
> FERN: What is that horrible thing? It's moving!
> RODANO: Of course, it's moving. It's alive!
>   It's the composite living brain of fourteen animals.
> SINCLAIR: It's the most horrible thing I've ever
> seen!

The madman gloated over how he would add the human brains that night to the monstrous creation and then place it into the metal head of a special new robot he had built. But the unseen Avenger, using his diffusion capsules, and with a <u>pop</u> and <u>whoosh</u> courtesy of the sound effects man, stopped the madman from throwing the switch that would begin this final experiment. In the confusion, one of the robots accidentally smashed the glass case holding the Frankenstein brain. The freed brain seized the professor like some hideous octopus. Rodano screamed for help but his robots were incapable of movement, as Giles wrecked their control batteries. Professor Rodano, like Frankenstein, was defeated by his own terrible creation. Exposed to the air, the giant brain soon deteriorated. The Avenger had brought the severe and unseen hand of justice to another mad fiend.

In 1935, Boris Karloff, just before acting in <u>Bride of Frankenstein</u>, was interviewed on <u>Hollywood on the Air</u>. With appropriate electrical sound effects, Karloff said: "I shall create a Monster like Frankenstein's. No brain--just a huge creature which shall guard against reporters and interviewers. Connect the electrodes! Throw the switches! It lives! It moves! It lives! Karloff's Monster lives!" When the "Monster" finally spoke it was with the

interviewer's voice.   "Alas," Karloff continued, "I have
created a Frankenstein Monster.   It's a fan magazine
writer."

   A take-off on the old radio program You Are There
was broadcast from Champaign, Illinois in 1956.   Ron Haydock (editor of Fantastic Monsters of the Films in later
years) wrote the script in which an interviewer spoke with
Dr. Frankenstein while he worked on his Monster.   The
short play was performed by student actors.   A radio version of Frankenstein featuring student actors was also presented by Columbia University in New York, with Henry
Mazzo as the Monster.

   Radio commercials have used Frankenstein and the
Monster to advertise Turtle Wax and Baskin Robbins ice
cream in the middle 1960s, Remington electric shavers in
1969, and the Movieland Wax Museum of Buena Park,
California, in 1972 with actors imitating Karloff's voice.
"Frankenzyme," a mad scientist with a Peter Lorre voice,
invented an enzyme detergent containing arsenic in a satire
involving the pollution problem on the "Credibility Gap"
news from KRLA Pasadena on 20 March 1970.   In 1972,
Castle of Frankenstein magazine's editor Calvin T. Beck
began a radio program that discussed horror, science fiction, and fantasy films.   The series, originating at WHBI-
FM in New York City, was scheduled every Tuesday at
three o'clock in the morning.   Frankenstein and his awesome creation had haunted the radio waves as early as
1932.   In the early 1950s, television, the "monster" that
destroyed radio drama, would find a new niche of horror
for the Monster of Frankenstein.

Note

1.   An edited version of this broadcast has been made avail-
     able on a record album Ghost Stories, released by
     Ball Records.

Chapter 9

FRANKENSTEIN TELEVISED

As television replaced radio as the most popular
medium of entertainment, the Frankenstein Monster also
made the transition to the small screen. Television was
in its so-called "Golden Age" when the Monster first
sneered into the living rooms of viewers. Lon Chaney
starred as the Monster in Frankenstein, presented in 1952
on the ABC anthology program Tales of Tomorrow. The
actor wore a make-up created by Vincent Kehoe, who gave
the Monster a bald head, stitched gashes on the cheeks,
chin, and cranium, and a deep cut held together by small
metal clamps running across the forehead and around the
back of the head. These were the days of "live" television,
before video tape permitted the correction of mistakes.
Chaney, thinking that he was going through the final dress
rehearsal, was careful not to destroy the breakaway props.
In one scene the Monster raised a chair over his head,
growled, then, instead of slamming it to the floor, gently
set it down. Actually the cameras were on and viewers
could not understand the peculiar behavior of the creature.
Certainly some of his off-color mutterances had never been
spoken by any other Frankenstein Monster.

In 1957, the hour-long anthology show Matinee
Theatre (NBC) did the first color presentation of Frankenstein. Primo Carnero, former boxing and wrestling champion, portrayed the Monster. Carnero's size gave this
version of the Monster real strength. Like Chaney, Carnero was made-up with a bald head and with a face and
head covered with unsightly scars and stitches. Apparently
the producers of the show considered the story too gruesome for television, especially since it was presented in
the afternoon when some children may have been home from
school. An announcement was made at the opening of the
show that Frankenstein was adult entertainment and that any

266

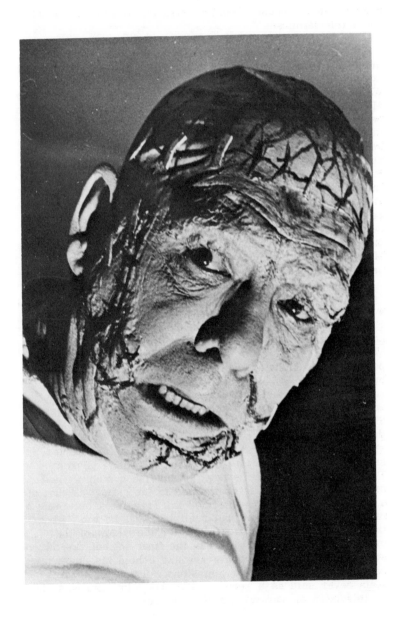

Lon Chaney returned to the role of the Monster for ABC-TV's 1952 <u>Tales of Tomorrow</u>.

children in the house should be sent off to some room without a television set.

The Monster was given life by the electrical equipment of Victor Frankenstein.   But Frankenstein was injured
by the giant, temporarily blinded, and sent to a hospital.
While the scientist was recuperating in his hospital bed, the
Monster roamed the countryside, being persecuted by human
beings and killing them out of revenge.   Frankenstein refused to believe his creature still lived and preferred to
believe the rumors circulating among the villagers that the
culprit was a werewolf.   The giant visited the blindfolded
Frankenstein and let him feel his enormous hands.   Speaking in a gutteral voice, the Monster told Frankenstein that
unless he created a mate for him, he would not stop his
reign of horror.   Frankenstein concluded with the Monster
being driven by Frankenstein off the castle wall to his apparent death.   The final shot of the presentation was of the
Monster's slowly moving hand protruding from the rocks
below, hinting at a sequel that was never made.

Hammer Films attempted to make a television series
with the American company Screen Gems in 1958.   Tales of
Frankenstein was a deviation from their own Curse of Frankenstein in that it went back to the Universal image of the
Monster.   Don Megowan, a strong, powerful looking actor,
portrayed the Monster in make-up resembling that created
by Jack Pierce but without any scars or electrodes.   In the
role of Baron Frankenstein was Anton Diffring, a European
actor who had starred in numerous horror films.   Curt
Siodmak, who wrote the screenplay of Frankenstein Meets
the Wolf Man and the original story of House of Frankenstein, directed the first episode of the television series,
entitled "The Face in the Tombstone Mirror."   Baron
Frankenstein wrapped his creation up like a mummy and
brought it to life.   The brain used in the giant was that of
a sick man, which accounted for the creature's becoming a
monster.   The Monster, not realizing what he was, attacked the Baron, then went off after the widow of the
original owner of his brain.   In the final scenes, the Monster stumbled into an open grave and beheld his unearthly
visage in the mirror of a tombstone.   Tales of Frankenstein never sold as a series.   But this pilot film was shown
on television on various anthology series.

In 1968, Frankenstein was presented on England's
Thames Television.   Writer Robert Muller attempted to

Unnamed actor as the Monster and Sarah Bodel as Elizabeth
in the Thames Television 1968 Frankenstein.

present the story as originally intended. "We decided,
rightly I think, not even to attempt to compete with the
film," said Muller, "but to go right back to the book--the
original images that must have raged in Mary Shelley's
mind as she was writing it." Frankenstein (Ian Holm) was
a student from Switzerland attending a university in Germany, as he was in the novel Frankenstein. Elizabeth
(Sarah Bodel) was his fiancée. The Monster, stalking about
partially bandaged and wearing a flowing cloak, did not show
his face at first. He was eventually revealed with scar
tissue on the cheeks and stitches across the forehead.
Frankenstein was generally faithful to the book, the major
changes being its nineteenth-century setting and the fewer
locations.

In 1971, Universal Pictures and NBC announced plans
for a four-hour Frankenstein film to be run in two parts as
a "World Premiere" television feature. Frankenstein was
to be based on the novel and not on the other Universal
Frankenstein movies. Set in nineteenth-century England,
the film, produced by Hunt Stormberg, was to present the
Monster as a rational being, turned into a living horror
only after his exposure to the civilized world. In 1972 the
proposed film was announced with the new title Dr. Frankenstein. But as of this writing the film has not gone into
production.

Frankenstein Settles Down

In 1964, Universal took their Frankenstein property
to television. Monsters were enjoying new popularity, but
in a different way. The same creatures that once had
caused spines to shiver were suddenly the objects for comedy. The Munsters, a CBS situation comedy series featuring the old Universal monsters in the roles of a "typical"
American family, proved that horror and humor could be
blended with the gruesome characters themselves providing
the laughs.

The origins of The Munsters seem to go back further
than 1964. The 1940s comic book series by Dick Briefer
(see Index) was very similar to the show. In 1943, Bob
Clampett, whose Time for Beany had been one of early
television's most popular shows, conceived a television
series called The Monster Family, and developed it by
September, 1945. Head of the family was Frankie Monster,

whose name was to suggest Frank Sinatra, the most popular
singing star at the time.   Women seeing the Frankensteinian
creature would swoon "Frankie!" and fall into a dead faint,
but not for the same reason Sinatra's fans toppled off their
feet.   Frankie had a lovely vampire for a wife and a little
monster son.   The Monsters thought they were normal
everyday people and could never understand why people reacted strangely to them.   Clampett made preliminary sketches
of the first episode, wherein the Monster Family went to the
beach and caused pandemonium.   Years later, the drawings
were taken to Universal, Clampett never heard from them
again, and The Munsters eventually became a hit on television.

Fred Gwynne, a cartoonist, writer, and the former
star of the television series Car 54, Where Are You? played
Herman Munster, the head of the weird household.   (The
role of Herman was originally offered to John Carradine,
who refused because of a motion picture he was doing that
occupied his time.)   Herman was the Frankenstein Monster,
now settled down as a typical (to situation comedies, anyway) bumbling husband and really no more than a seven-foot
three-inch tall kid.   Gwynne's narrow face and lantern jaw
made him the ideal choice for wearing Bud Westmore's gray
(with green highlights) make-up.   There were a few changes
made from the original Pierce make-up in order to make
Herman a bit less monstrous and more munstrous.   The
scar on the cheek was removed and Herman usually had a
wide grin on his long face.   "There was some talk of taking
the scar off my forehead," said Gwynne, but they decided to
leave it.   And I think they were right.   You should stick
with the character."

Other members of the family included Lily Munster
(Yvonne de Carlo), a vampire, Eddie Munster (Butch Patrick), their ten-year-old son and a future werewolf, Grandpa (Al Lewis), Lily's father, a retired Count Dracula, and
the only "unattractive" member of the family, blonde and
beautiful Marilyn (Beverly Owen; later, Pat Priest).   The
Munsters lived together in a gloomy old mansion in Mockingbird Heights.   Occasionally the Munsters were visited by
more distantly related family members, such as a werewolf, the Creature from the Black Lagoon and a couple of
beings also created by Dr. Frankenstein.

Herman Munster usually got himself into monstrous
trouble, some of which even Gwynne might not survive.

Doubling Gwynne in the more strenuous scenes was stuntman
Jefferson County (real name Bill Foster), who very closely
resembled Gwynne while made-up as the Frankensteinian
Herman.   The Munsters originally starred in a special
fifteen-minute pilot film in which Herman's make-up was
more on the gruesome side and in which his character was
not quite as "typically American" as on the actual show.
After the pilot film sold and The Munsters went into production as one of television's last black and white shows,
Herman's appearance and characterization gradually became
less and less monstrous.   In some of the early episodes
Herman even sported hairy hands.   By the second season of
The Munsters, Herman's make-up had become more of a
caricature, perhaps to be less a monster and more of a
good-natured imbecile.

     In the first episode of The Munsters, entitled "Mun-
ster Masquerade" and directed by Lawrence Dobkin, the
photography was extremely atmospheric and could almost
be mistaken for a horror film of an earlier era.   Marilyn
and her family were invited to a masquerade party to be
held at the mansion of her current boyfriend.   Unknown to
the Munsters, the host of the party (played by Frank Wilcox)
had made himself up as the Frankenstein Monster.   Herman,
naturally, thought his host was not wearing a mask and felt
insulted when he was accused of wearing a mask.   Charlie
Munster (Gwynne), Herman's twin brother, visited the
family in the episode "Knock Wood, Here Comes Charlie."
He was an Englishman with blond, wavy, combed back hair,
who always wore flashy clothes.   Charlie was a confidence
man whose current scheme was selling a machine which supposedly extracted uranium from sea water.

     Johann (Gwynne), yet another Herman lookalike, was
brought to Mockingbird Heights by Victor Frankenstein IV
(John Abbott).   Discovered roaming the woods near the
ancestral Frankenstein castle in Germany, Johann was an
exact double for Herman.   The only differences were in
his scowling face, his fur vest, his inability to do much
more than stiffly walk about and snarl, and his fear of fire.
Holding Johann at bay with a blazing torch, Dr. Frankenstein introduced him to Herman in the hopes that some of
the latter's learned good manners would influence him.
Predictably, Lily mistook Johann for Herman and went off
with the growling giant to a motel to relive their honeymoon.
Johann was explained as one of the original Dr. Frankenstein's failures, made prior to Herman.   Although Herman

Fred Gwynne as the lovable Herman Munster in the CBS-TV
series <u>The Munsters</u>.

was originally intended to be <u>the</u> Frankenstein Monster,
purists argue that this later version is in fact the celebrated
creature.   Actually, Johann was conceived during the second
year of the program and intended only for this one episode,
perhaps to be forgotten and leaving Herman with his previous status.

Herman himself became transformed into different
creatures.   In one episode, Herman was struck by a bolt
of lightning in Grandpa's laboratory and was changed into
Fred Gwynne <u>sans</u> monster make-up.   Since the family could
not live with this horrible creature, Grandpa used Herman's
original blueprints and the famous Strickfaden machinery to
recreate Dr. Frankenstein's experiment.   After being raised
to the lightning while the laboratory crackled with electrical
life, Herman emerged as a female Frankenstein monster,
with curly hair.   In the final scenes of the episode, Herman walked into a thunderstorm and was struck by lightning,
which transformed him back into his original form.

In yet another episode, Herman tried to impress his
son who was worshipping the ghoulish television personality
Zombo (Louie Nye).   Grandpa gave him a Jekyll and Hyde
type drug which gave Herman fangs and a fright wig.   Most
of the jokes about Herman kidded his origin.   "Even I can't
be in two places at the same time--at least not anymore."
"It's a good thing I've got a level head on my shoulders."
"Dr. Frankenstein made me all I am today."

During the second season of <u>The Munsters</u>, the
series lost much of the charm of the early episodes.   Herman was involved in such standard situation comedy plots
as forgetting his wife's anniversary.   By the end of the
second season in 1966, <u>The Munsters</u> went off the air.
Although the show had been cancelled, the Munster family
was not entirely dead.   Most of them had, after all, come
back to life often enough in the past.   In 1966 Universal
released a full length feature film <u>Munster, Go Home!</u>,
directed by Earl Bellamy.   The film included many of the
gags and situations from the television show and was the
first Universal Frankenstein feature released in color.   The
television cast recreated their roles in the film, with the
exception of Pat Priest who was replaced by Debby Watson
as Marilyn.

Herman received a telegram instructing him to come
to Munster Hall in England to collect an inheritance.   He

had once lived with the Munster family and from them took
his name.   After an ocean voyage in which Herman was
mostly seasick, the Munsters arrived at Munster Hall.
Freddy Munster (Terry-Thomas) wanted the inheritance for
himself and attempted to scare off the Americans.   But
they were only delighted to think that the house was haunted.
In Munster Hall, Herman and Grandpa found the base of a
counterfeiting operation, headed by a mysterious character
known only as the Griffin.   Later, Herman represented the
Munsters in a speed race, driving a car invented by Grandpa.   Riding against him was the Griffin, disguised as Roger
Morsby, the boyfriend of Marilyn and member of the family
feuding with the Munsters.   Despite sabotage, Herman won
the race and exposed the Griffin as the daughter of the
Munster's butler, Cruikshank (John Carradine).

Herman Munster in the person of Fred Gwynne ap-
peared on The Hollywood Palace.   He also appeared with
other members of the Munsters cast, riding in the famous
Munster Koach designed by George Barris in the televised
Macy's Thanksgiving Day parade in New York.   Men wearing
Herman Munster and Frankenstein rubber masks appear
regularly in the televised Hollywood Santa Claus Lane
Parade, plugging reruns of The Munsters and the Universal
Studios tour.   During the days of the show a working Munster laboratory with a dummy of Herman strapped to a
platform was part of the Universal tour.

Two novels about the Munsters were published.   The
first, simply titled The Munsters, was written by Morton
Cooper and published by Avon Books in 1964.   Cooper took
certain liberties with the characters, giving, for example,
Herman fourteen toes on each foot.   Herman wanted to win
the coveted award given to families on the television show
Family of the Week and proceeded to write a contest letter
to the station;   by some miracle, the Munsters won.   When
the weird family appeared on national television they became,
to the perplexity of the producer, overnight stars.   But
with stardom came an artificiality which caused the members
of the Munster family to act out of character.   When Herman realized that success was ruining his family he managed
to straighten matters back to "normal."   A second Munsters
book was The Last Resort, published in 1966 for the juvenile
market by the Whitman Publishing Company.

A magazine entitled The Munsters was published by
Kayro-Vue Productions in 1965.   The publication included a

number of features about the program including such short
stories as "The Munsters Go House-Haunting," by Eando
(Otto) Binder, in which the Munsters tried to scare a man
who had turned up a deed to their house and decided to move
into the place.   But they succeeded only in causing him to
laugh for the first time in years.   Glad to be out of his
melancholia, he tore up the deed.   The Munsters was intended to be a regular magazine but never saw a second
issue.   More lasting was The Munsters comic book published from 1964 through 1968 by Western Publishing Company with a total of sixteen issues.   Herman Munster appeared in an advertisement comic strip for Aurora plastic
models which appeared in various National Periodical Publications comic books while the series was on the air.
Another Munsters comic strip series was published in black
and white in England about the same time.

        The Munsters theme music was performed on a re-
cord by Billy Strange.   There have also been two Munsters
record albums.   The first of these was At Home with the
Munsters, released in 1964 by Golden Records.   It featured
bits of dialogue from the actual television shows and the
voices of the cast.   The second album, titled The Munsters,
and released by Decca in 1965, featured a rock music group
called The Munsters performing such numbers as "Frankenstein Had a Hod-Rod Car," "Herman's Place," and "You
Created a Monster."

        Don Post Studios merchandized rubber masks of all
members of the Munster family.   Aurora produced plastic
model kits of the Munsters and the Munster Koach.   Other
Munster merchandise included lunch boxes, coloring books,
View Master stereo reels, talking Herman Munster dolls,
hand puppets, ball-point pens, and dashboard dolls.   The
show is no longer in production and merchandising of Munsters items has ceased.   But The Munsters is still extremely popular and will probably be rerun on television
for many years to come.

Among Dark Shadows

        Dark Shadows was an afternoon serial running on
ABC television in the late 1960s.   Unlike most "soap
operas," Dark Shadows, produced by Dan Curtis, resurrected most of the classic monsters and fiends from legend,
literature, and the old motion pictures.   An assortment of

vampires, werewolves, zombies, mad doctors, witches, and
other fiendish creatures populated the vicinity of Massachusetts known as Collinwood.   Most of them found their way
into the great Collins mansion, the ancestral home of the
well known yet star-crossed family.   Sam Hall, the writer
of Dark Shadows, adapted Frankenstein to the small screen
in 1967.   The series was already an entanglement of varied
plots.   But Hall managed to take the basic storyline of the
original novel and incorporate it into Dark Shadows' world
of warlocks and vampires.

Barnabas Collins (Jonathan Frid), the most popular
vampire on Dark Shadows, was in an automobile accident
which rendered him unconscious.   He revived in a hospital
under the care of a strange Dr. Eric Lang (Addison Powell)
who revealed to the vampire his secret project.   Dr. Lang
had created a man out of corpses--a being he hoped to bring
to life by transferring into it Barnabas' life force and at the
same time drain off his vampire traits.   The creature was
appropriately called Adam.

Adam was portrayed by Robert Rodan, a handsome
six foot, six inch actor with wavy hair, who was also a
talented artist.   Make-up artist Vincent Loscalzo tried to
make Adam less a monster and more a tormented soul.
The character of Adam was to go back to the original Mary
Shelley concept as a rational being who cried out for the
love and understanding of an uncaring mankind.   Loscalzo
added some stitched scars to the actor's neck and already
prominent brow.   "Bascially, he took the structure of my
face and accentuated everything on it," said Rodan.   "Getting it put on is nothing--it's taking it off that gives me the
trouble."[1]

Eric Lang failed in his attempt to bring Adam to
life and was soon afterward killed by the witch Angelique
(Lara Parker).   The following week, Barnabas and his
partner Dr. Julia Hoffman (Grayson Hall, wife of the program's writer) succeeded in completing the experiment.
Although Barnabas' vampirism was cured, there was a
psychic bond between him and Adam.   If Adam perished,
Barnabas would revert to his former condition.   The portrayal of Adam was extremely close to the character
created by Mary Shelley.   Rodan managed to play the role
with a deep sensitivity, making Adam a real human being.
Never did he revert to the lumbering zombie image that
the Frankenstein Monster acquired in the later Universal
films.

Adam was confined in a cell by Barnabas and Dr. Hoffman and placed under the watch of Willie Loomis (John Karlen), who treated him badly. The giant escaped and was eventually captured by the police. He was driven off a cliff to his apparent death. But Adam returned, taking refuge in the house of blind Sam Evans (David Ford), who taught him how to speak simple phrases and was accidentally killed by the confused brute. Adam's vocabulary gradually increased until, despite his size and unsightly scars, he matured into a warm human being. When he learned of his origin, however, he became spiteful and demanded that Barnabas and Dr. Hoffman create a woman for him or feel his vengeful wrath.

The female body was created by the two novice monster-makers. They did an incredible job in assembling a perfect woman with a beautiful face, no stitches whatsoever, and long red hair. Appropriately, the female was named Eve (Marie Wallace).

Nicholas Blair (Humbert Allen Astredo), a demonic warlock, knew that he could serve his unholy Master by securing an evil life force for Eve. He managed to obtain the life force of Danielle Roget, a murderess who lived during the previous century. Unlike Adam, Eve came to life speaking fluent English and possessing a totally evil nature. She regarded Adam as stupid and when she rejected him again and again he killed her. Without his mate, Adam became a terrible monster. In desperation, he took the lifeless remains of Eve to the laboratory and tried to give her the life force of the show's main heroine, Victoria Winters (Alexandra Moltke). Barnabas entered the laboratory with a revolver, knowing that if Adam were killed he would again become a vampire. Before Adam threw the main switch to start the machinery, Barnabas fired. The supposedly dying Adam was taken under the care of Dr. T. Eliot Stokes (Thayer David). Barnabas did not become a vampire as a result of the shooting so it was presumed that Adam still lived.

The apparatus used to bring Adam and Eve to life later gave life to other characters in the series, including the long dead warlock Judah Zachary (Michael McGuire), whose severed head had been sewn back onto its body. But Adam and Eve themselves were never seen again.

Part of the story of this Adam and Eve was

photographed for a set of View Master stereo reels. An
original novel <u>The Peril of Barnabas Collins</u>, written by
"Marilyn" Ross and published by Paperback Library in 1969,
had Frankensteinian overtones. A strange Dr. Padrel
claimed that he had a method of forever curing his con-
sumptive daughter. His plan was to take her head after
she died and stitch it to a headless corpse. Then, using
a mechanical flow of blood, he would bring her back to life.
Diana, the heroine of the story, encountered the girl with the
stitched neck in the woods. A body had been stolen from a
grave and shortly afterward a head was washed up on the
shore. The mad experiment was finally proven to be a
hoax. The supposed composite girl was really a would-be
actress with stitches drawn around her neck.

Monsters on the Small Screen

The Frankenstein Monster became a local television
star in many cities during the late 1950s. In 1957, Screen
Gems released a package of "Shock" movies, consisting of
old Universal and Columbia horror films, to television stations across the country. Many stations that purchased the
films built programs around them, usually called <u>Shock
Theatre</u>, introduced by ghoulish hosts and often aided in
their comic yet grisly antics by the Frankenstein Monster.

Marvin (Terry Bennett), the host of Chicago's <u>Shock
Theatre</u> (WBKB) was eventually joined by a growling Frankenstein Monster named Shorty. On the final telecast of
the program Shorty removed his Don Post mask to reveal
another underneath. Warren Reed of Seattle's <u>Shock Theatre</u>
(KTNT) was assisted by the boyish Frankie (Paul Herlinger).
Gorgon (Bill Calfield) in Fort Worth and Dallas (KFJZ) and
Dr. Meridian in Fort Wayne, Indiana (WPTA) versions of
<u>Shock Theatre</u>, and Tarantula Ghoul (Suzanne Waldron) of
<u>House of Horror</u> in Portland, Oregon (KPTV) all had their
own Frankenstein creatures and experiments. In 1963, a
similar Los Angeles show <u>Jeepers' Creepers</u> (KCOP) brought
the artificial girl Ghoulita to life to introduce the old horror
films. The Monster's face also appeared in the commercials for the Los Angeles version of <u>Creature Features</u>.

<u>Shrimpenstein</u> (KHJ) premiered on Los Angeles tele-
vision in 1966. The mad Dr. Rudolph von Shtick (Gene
Moss) wanted to create the greatest Frankenstein Monster
of them all. He charged his creation with "ten zillion volts"

of electricity.   But because some jellybeans had dropped
into his apparatus, a miniature Shrimpenstein, a lovable
imp with a green Frankenstein face and pointed ears, came
to life.   Shrimpenstein was actually a hand puppet that
played opposite the human von Shtick.   Although an afternoon children's program, Shrimpenstein attracted an older
audience who appreciated the many in-jokes and sometimes
overly adult humor.   Perhaps it was this appeal to a more
mature audience that eventually took Shrimpenstein off the
air.   Shrimpenstein and Moss as von Shtick also appeared
on the nighttime adult talk show Moss and Thurman in which
there was no catering to the juvenile crowd.   Shrimpenstein
hand puppets, made by Tony Tierney, were sold commercially and helped retain the program's image as a children's
show.

     Boris Karloff continued to perpetuate the Franken-
stein legend on television, doing the famous Monster walk
on the Rosemary Clooney Show in 1957.   When Karloff
finished making Son of Frankenstein in 1939 he stated that
he would never again wear the make-up of the Frankenstein
Monster.   In his younger days, Karloff had many oppor-
tunities to enact the role on the screen but always refused.
It is almost miraculous, then, that Karloff consented to put
on the heavy make-up and recreate his famous role for the
"Lizard's Leg and Owlet's Wing" episode of Route 66 (CBS)
in 1962.   Karloff, Peter Lorre, and Lon Chaney appeared
as themselves in the hour-long episode.   The three terror
stars held a secret meeting at Chicago's O'Hare Inn to debate whether or not the old style monsters could scare
modern audiences.   Karloff contended that they could not.
In the latter portion of the show, Lorre in sinister garb,
Chaney as the Wolf Man, and Karloff, made-up by Ben
Lane with blue-gray greasepaint and golden electrodes in
his classic Frankenstein Monster guise, successfully scared
a group of young secretaries.   In September, 1968 Karloff
and Vincent Price played father and son mad scientists on
The Red Skelton Show (CBS).   As Dr. Nelson, Karloff
created a shrunken Frankenstein Monster and a perfect girl
robot.   Later in the show Karloff did his famous Frankenstein Monster growl.   The following month Karloff appeared
as another mad doctor on the Jonathan Winters Show.   This
marked Karloff's final appearance on television.

     Other actors who played the Frankenstein Monster
in the movies carried the role over to television.   In 1951
Lon Chaney as the Monster menaced Bud Abbott and Lou

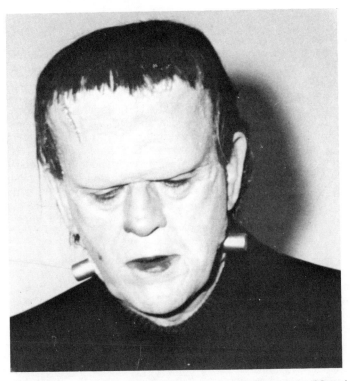

Surprisingly, Boris Karloff donned the Frankenstein Monster make-up for a 1962 CBS-TV <u>Route 66</u> episode.

Costello on the <u>Colgate Comedy Hour</u> (ABC). Glenn Strange appeared as the Monster along with Abbott and Costello and Rico Browning as the Creature from the Black Lagoon on an NBC variety show starring Sonja Henie. About the same time Strange played the fiddle in his Monster outfit on the <u>Tex Williams Show</u> (NBC). Christopher Lee played Dr. Frank N. Stein on an episode of the British spy series <u>The Avengers</u> entitled "Never Never Say Die." He created an android in his own image. The artificial man went berserk every time it heard a transistor frequency and killed the man at the source. [2]

A French television program of 1968, <u>Sur les Traces de Frankenstein</u> (translated as "On the Path of Frankenstein") followed a young girl to Geneva to research a thesis on Mary Shelley. As she visited the place where Mary wrote her novel, the girl thought a man was following her--a

man believed to be the Frankenstein Monster.   Eventually
she fled the premises.   The Monkees (NBC), a series about
four rock musicians, had four episodes dealing with the
Frankenstein Monster.   In the first of these (1967) the sinister Dr. Mendoza (John Hoyt) created a Frankensteinian
android (Richard Kyle) with electrodes protruding from his
ears.   Using some of the reliable Strickfaden machinery,
Mendoza transferred the musical abilities of the Monkees
into his giant creation.   To maintain tradition, the android
finally turned against his master.   In other episodes of the
series the Frankenstein Monster was played by Monkee
Mike Nesmith and Dick Karp.   In 1971, Rod Serling's Night
Gallery (NBC) presented a vignette titled "Junior" in which
Wally Cox was awakened in the middle of the night by his
crying baby.   The creature in the crib was a baby version
of the Frankenstein Monster (Bill Svanoe).

    Various comedy, dramatic, and information programs
featuring the Frankenstein Monster or theme include: The
Honeymooners, Leave It to Beaver, Get Smart, Here's
Lucy, The Saint, The Thin Man (mundane story with the
misleading title "Madame Frankenstein"), Lost in Space,
Le Raisins Verts (French), When Michael Calls (movie
made for television), Lancelot Link--Secret Chimp, Sesame
Street, Masquerade Party (Elsa Lanchester as the male
Frankenstein Monster), Juvenile Jury, Ralph Story's Los
Angeles, You Asked for It ("Pushbutton Frankenstein" fea-
turing a remote-controlled robot with an electric brain and
mechanical heart), 21st Century, and the special Artists
and Models Ball Beauty Pageant.

    Variety shows have used the Frankenstein Monster
so many times that it would be impossible to list all such
television appearances.   Impressionists like Frank Gorshin
have imitated Frankenstein and his Monster on such programs as the Dick Cavett Show, The Kopykats (on The ABC
Comedy Hour), and the Steve Allen Show.   Steve Allen has
used the Frankenstein Monster on many of his variety programs, the three most notable appearances, as portrayed
by comedian Louis Nye in the Universal make-up, being the
three musical spoofs entitled "Finkenstein," "Bride of
Finkenstein," and "Finkenstein Goes West," the latter
giving the Monster a horse's tail.

    In 1966 the Danny Kaye Show did a spoof with Vin-
cent Price as Dr. Frankenstein and Kaye as the Monster.
Make-up artist Steve Gokee described his work:

All our changes of make-up for the hour show must
be done during thirty-second commercials before the
sketches.   Therefore what you see here had to be in
a state of readiness to match Danny's regular make-
up and be applied within one-half minute....   I used
a special transparent flesh tape along the mask edges
(a Don Post custom studio mask was cut up and used
for the headpiece) which you can discern, to make a
quick join....   A chin strap sewn to each electrode
secured the head under the chin since it was cut out
from the lids down.   Danny's lips were painted thin
black.   Painted rubber gloves slipped on completed
the quick change.

Other variety and musical shows featuring the Fran-
kenstein Monster have been: Spike Jones, Dean Martin
Show, Jerry Lewis Show (Lewis as the Monster), Hit Parade,
Dick Clark Show, Kraft Music Hall (Steve Lawrence as
Frankenstein; Shecky Greene as the Monster), The Funny
Side (Michael Lembeck as the Monster), Carol Burnett Show,
Engelbert Humperdinck (Jerry Lewis as Frankenstein;
Humperdinck as the Monster), Lohman and Barkly, Rowan
and Martin's Laugh-In (the most notable featuring Vincent
Price as Dr. Frankenstein), the special Hurray for Holly-
wood (Don Adams as Dr. Frankenstein), Merv Griffin, and
the Marty Feldman Comedy Machine.

Perhaps the most significant animated cartoon featuring the Frankenstein Monster was "Dr. Frankenstein,"
an episode of UPA's Famous Adventures of Mr. Magoo
series of 1965.   Every week the near-sighted Mr. Magoo
appeared as a famous character out of literature.   As Dr.
Frankenstein, Magoo was totally evil, creating a bald Monster and later attempted to release an entire legion of the
creatures in order to conquer the world.   In the end, the
mad scientist and his creations were destroyed in a terrific
explosion.   The half hour story was later included with two
other episodes from the series to make a feature length
film Mr. Magoo, Man of Mystery which has been released
to television and 16mm film rental libraries.

Frankenstein, Jr. and the Impossibles was an animated cartoon series made by Hanna-Barbera Productions,
running from 1966 through 1967.   The show was designed
to capitalize on the "camp" superhero craze created by the
Batman television series.   Frankenstein, Jr. was a giant
robot with superpowers, a large "F" emblem on his chest,

and for no reason other than to conform with both the Frankenstein and superhero image, stitches and a black mask. The robot was the creation of Dr. Conroy and his son Buzz, who controlled the friendly giant with his radar-ring. Making its debut with the episode "The Shocking Electrical Monster," Frankenstein, Jr. presented such episodes as "The Deadly Living Images" in which the flying robot battled a mad scientist who was making things vanish, "The Mad Monster Maker," "The Monstermobile," and "The Pilfering Putty Monster," a total of seventeen stories. Ted Cassidy, who played Lurch on The Addams Family, did the voice of Frankenstein, Jr.

In 1968, Western Publishing Company issued a Frankenstein, Jr. comic book. Although it was intended to be a series, the title was not continued. The same publisher, under the Whitman Publishing Company banner, issued a "Big Little Book" of Frankenstein, Jr. in 1968. The story was entitled "The Menace of the Heartless Monster." Dr. Conroy found that the plans for Frankenstein, Jr. had been stolen from his mountain laboratory. A series of robberies began to take place by a creature resembling Frankenstein, Jr. and Conroy deduced that the villainous Spyclops had used the plans to create an evil robot. Kranky, the heartless robot, nearly destroyed the benevolent Franky when Dr. Conroy dropped an instant heart into his mouth and transformed him into a do-gooder.

Another animated cartoon series starring a Frankenstein type character was Milton the Monster made by Hal Seeger Productions in the mid-1960s. In a laboratory in an old house atop Horror Hill, Professor Weirdo and Count Kook tried to create a terrible monster. The professor mixed the following ingredients in a man-shaped mold: Six drops of the essence of terror, give drops of sinister sauce, and one drop of the tincture of tenderness. When he accidentally used too much of the tincture, Milton the Monster, a giant with a smoking flat head, virtually no brow at all, an enormous chin, and a voice resembling that of Gomer Pyle, was born. Milton blundered his way through the series, encountering such creatures as the evil Fangenstein. In one episode Professor Weirdo rented Milton out to the landlord who promptly ordered the imbecile to throw the professor and Count Kook out of their house. Part of the Milton the Monster show was given to a series of Fearless Fly cartoons. Professor Weirdo fulfilled his dream of creating a vicious monster in one Fearless Fly episode.

George was a scarred, scowling version of Milton and was defeated by the super-insect. A comic book <u>Milton the Monster and Fearless Fly</u> was published in 1966 by Western Publishing Company but never saw a second issue.

A lovable monster called Frankie, who spoke like Boris Karloff was one of the many monstrous stars of Filmation's hour-long <u>The Groovie Goolies</u>, a cartoon series patterned after <u>Laugh-In</u>. Frankie appeared in a number of gags and musical numbers and stories with simple plots. Usually Sabrina, the "ingenue" lead, was forced to hide the Goolies' existence from her high school friends, all of whom originated in the pages of <u>Archie Comics</u>. When the program first started on CBS a rock group called the Groovie Goolies plugged the series at the Magic Castle, a private club for magicians in Hollywood. The following year the series went to a half hour format with the new title <u>Sabrina, the Teenage Witch</u>. The usual merchandising, with items like <u>Groovie Goolies</u> coloring books, followed. [3]

Other animated cartoon shows featuring the Frankenstein Monster or theme have been: <u>Archie</u>, <u>Abbott and Costello</u>, <u>Laurel and Hardy</u>, <u>The Beatles</u>, <u>Super-Chicken</u>, <u>Tom Slick</u>, <u>Sinbad the Sailor</u>, <u>Bozo</u>, <u>Scooby Doo--Where Are You?</u>, <u>Popeye</u>, <u>Spider-Man</u>, <u>Crusader Rabbit</u>, <u>Roger Ramjet</u>, <u>Beany and Cecil</u>, <u>Snooper and Blabber</u>, <u>The Inspector</u>, <u>Casper the Ghost</u>, <u>Peter Potamus</u>, <u>The Flintstones</u>, and the titles of <u>Fractured Flickers</u>.

While the Frankenstein Monster has appeared on various television programs, the artificial man has also been employed to sell products for sponsors keeping those shows on the air. "Castle" was a television commercial for Volkswagen made by Doyle Dane Bernbach. The commercial was directed by someone who had an obvious understanding and love for the old Universal Frankenstein movies. A band of angry villagers, armed with torches and a battering ram, and led by a "Dr. van Helsing" type character, broke into the castle of a mad scientist who had created a family of Frankenstein monsters; the mad scientist escaped in a Volkswagen microbus. The commercial was extremely atmospheric with its low key lighting, black and white photography, and lack of music.

General Foods Kitchens made a commercial called "Haunted House" for Post Alpha-Bits in which the Frankenstein Monster, played by Ted Cassidy made-up as the

Universal character with a blue face and red hair, chased a group of children through a creepy mansion and finally joined them in a bowl of cereal.   The Monster also appeared in commercials for Post Sugar Crisp and Pebbles cereals.   "Frankenstein," an animated commercial for Mentholatum Deep Heating Rub made by the J. Walter Thompson Company, showed the Monster catching cold in a thunderstorm, then returning to his creator's castle where he was put to bed with his teddy bear.

In 1971, General Mills began a series of commercials for their new breakfast cereals Franken Berry and Count Chocula.   Franken Berry was a lovable monster, with a bald head decorated with guages, a factory whistle, and other attachments, and speaking like Boris Karloff with lines such as "Fiddlesticks!" and "Piffle!"   The commercials usually ended with Franken Berry and the Count huddled together in terror over the appearance of a mouse or small boy.   Franken Berry merchandise presently followed. The Frankenstein Monster (actor wearing a Don Post mask) also appeared in General Mills' Clackers cereal commercial.

The same year, Hoefer, Dieterich & Brown, Inc. made a commercial for Shasta Beverages entitled Igor and the Store.   Originally Igor was made-up by Joe Blasco in the exact image of the Universal Monster, with a greenish face and golden electrodes.   Due to copyright problems, Blasco removed the electrodes, most of the metal clamps, the cheek and forehead scars, and changed the face to bluish gray.   Igor's boots were once used by Fred Gwynne in The Munsters.   In the commercial, Igor (Chris Littler) rose from the platform in a laboratory filled with Strickfaden apparatus, stomped out of the castle in such atmospheric scenes that one might easily mistake them for stock footage from some old horror film, and crashed into a supermarket to purchase some Shasta cola for the mad doctor (Regis Cordic).   Scenes in which Igor lumbered about the castle were filmed but not used.

Joe Blasco, who has been given publicity as the "new Jack Pierce," did the make-up for a Frankenstein television commercial for Kellogg's Eggo waffles in 1971. Avery Schrieber portrayed the mad scientist while Richard Kyle was the Monster.   Kyle was made-up with a pink face, pointed ears, sparse red hair and bushy red eyebrows, and an enormous bolted screw penetrating the huge cranium.

After tugging over a waffle with the doctor, the Monster stomped off to bed, leaving a red hand clutching the product.

Other television commercials featuring the Frankenstein Monster or theme were made for Toyota automobiles ("We Can Help It" with Gino Conforti as the Monster), Ideal Toy Corporation ("Wrestle Around" with Howard Mann as Marvin the Monster), A-1 Steak Sauce ("Mad Scientist" starring Boris Karloff with the Strickfaden machinery), Ovaltine Food Products' Screaming Yellow Zonkers (character transforms into a creature resembling Frankenstein's Monster), Aurora plastic monster kits, Razzles (with an entirely original monster, with gadgets and fat, stitched cheeks), Palmolive hand cream, Colorforms, the Universal Pictures studio tour, Arrowhead Puritas bottled water (Frank N. Stine), and Los Angeles radio station KOST.

Frankenstein has been adapted to every dramatic medium. The Monster has created horror and humor on the stage, on film, tape, and "live" on the air. But he has also caused spines to tingle in that very art form which spawned him over one hundred fifty years ago.

Notes

1. "The Man Who Creates the Monsters," Afternoon TV, vol. 1, no. 4 (January 1969), p. 13.

2. Scenes from this adventure appeared in a later episode of The Avengers.

3. The Groovie Goolies starred in their own "movie" on the ABC hour-long animated series Saturday Superstar Movie. Titled "Porky Pig and Daffy Duck Meet the Groovie Goolies," the story had the monsters save their cartoon idols from a phantom who was sabotaging the movie set. For a while, the Groovie Goolies became "live" characters played by actors. Another feature of this series was "Mad, Mad, Mad Monsters," somewhat of a sequel to the film Mad Monster Party? All the famed monsters settled down with their families and were invited by Dr. Frankenstein to attend the wedding of the Monster and his newly created bride. The Monster proved his worth when he rescued her from a giant ape.

Chapter 10

THE LITERARY MONSTER RETURNS

In twentieth-century literature, the Frankenstein Monster has been a haunting figure. With the original Mary
Shelley novel in the public domain, many authors have taken
the infamous Monster and his creator and devised new
stories based on Frankenstein. Mary Shelley's novel has
itself been reworked into various new forms. In 1965 a
children's book entitled Monsters, published by Wonder
Books and written by Walter Gibson (creator of The Shadow),
featured simplified versions of Frankenstein, Dracula, and
The Strange Case of Dr. Jekyll and Mr. Hyde, with illus-
trations by Tony Tallarico. "Frankenstein and the Monster,"
as the story was titled by Gibson, was an extremely faithful
adaptation of the original novel. The story was told in the
third person. Another adaptation for young readers was
Frankenstein published in 1968 by Golden Press (Western
Publishing Company). This version, by Dale Carlson and
illustrated by Neil Boyle, began with the creation and was
mostly faithful to Mary Shelley's book. This too was told
entirely in the third person.

A version of Frankenstein with new sex scenes added
was published in Italy in the late 1960s as part of the "I
Grandi Romanzi" series. But while this edition was only
mildly sexy, a version came out in America which was
enough to arouse Mary Shelley from her peaceful rest and
come back to haunt the publishers. The Adult Version of
Frankenstein was adapted by Hal Kantor and published in
1970 by Calga Publishers. Everyone in this third person
adaptation was a sex maniac of some sort, including the
Monster, now depicted as having sharp fangs and hairy
claws. The Monster came to life demanding fulfillment of
his sexual desires and spent most of his time inflicting
himself upon everyone who crossed his path. Victor Frankenstein killed Elizabeth when he learned that she was a

288

nymphomaniac and complied with the Monster's demand that he create a woman. At last, the Monster and his ugly mate set off into the world to procreate a race of horrors. The worst thing about this version was the claim that Mary Shelley would have written Frankenstein in this lurid fashion had she not been restricted by the censorship of her time.

An updated scene purportedly from Frankenstein was included in "I Want a Ghoul ..." by Jack Sharkey, published in the September, 1971 issue of Playboy magazine. The Monster now became the dean of a college reprimanding his torch-wielding mob of destructive students.

Various novels have been issued that are adapted from Frankenstein motion pictures. The first of these was Bride of Frankenstein by Michael Egremont. The adaptation was published in England in 1936 by The Readers Library Publishing Company. A third person novelization of The Revenge of Frankenstein, by Hurford Janes, was published in London in 1958 by Panther Books. In 1966, The Hammer Horror Omnibus, published in London by Pan Books, included short novels of The Curse of Frankenstein and a new Revenge of Frankenstein, written by John Burke in the first person from Baron Frankenstein's point of view. A novelization of One More Time was published in 1970 by Popular Library.

An entire series of new Frankenstein novels by Benoit Becker was published in Paris by Angoisse in the late 1950s. The series chronicled the adventures of the Frankenstein Monster, now known as Gouroull. The novels, all of which featured the Universal Monster on the covers, include La Tour de Frankenstein (translated as "The Tower of Frankenstein"), Le Pas de Frankenstein ("The Step of Frankenstein"), La Nuit de Frankenstein ("The Night ..."), Le Sceau de Frankenstein ("The Seal ..."), all 1957, Frankenstein Rôde ("Frankenstein Prowls"), 1958, and La Cave de Frankenstein ("The Tomb of Frankenstein"), 1959.

Frankenstein '69 was a pornographic novel published by Traveller's Companion in 1969. There was little of the Frankenstein theme in this book by Ed Martin. The plot was ridiculous, with an eccentric scientist attempting to artificially impregnate a virgin. One of his accomplishments was the creation of three functioning girl robots. His sex fiend wife created her own trio of male robots. Triton, lord of the deep, and his mermaids added to the

madness of <u>Frankenstein '69</u>.   In 1972, Popular Library began a series of Frankenstein paperback novels.   <u>The Frankenstein Wheel</u>, by Paul W. Fairman, the first of "The
Frankenstein Horror Series," told of the Monster's return
from the dead to search for his artificially created mate.

A number of novels have used the Frankenstein theme
but have given other names to their mad doctors and monsters.   Edgar Rice Burroughs, the creator of Tarzan, wrote
two Frankensteinian novels, both of which were more heroic
fantasies than horror stories.   In 1913 came the first,
which he called <u>Number Thirteen</u> and which was published
as <u>A Man Without a Soul</u> in the November issue of the pulp
magazine <u>All-Story</u>.   The novel was issued as a book in
1929 with the new title <u>The Monster Men</u>.   Professor Maxon
had set up an island laboratory where he endeavored to
create men artificially in coffin-like vats.   The first of his
creations, Number One, was a hideously misshapen monstrosity.   Each of Maxon's monsters was more like a human
being until reaching Number Thirteen, a perfect man.   Number Thirteen was educated and finally led the other creatures
away from the tyranny of von Horn, Maxon's villainous assistant.   After the other monster men perished in the jungle, Number Thirteen became Bulan, a Tarzan-type hero,
who finally overcame all obstacles and won the heart of
Virginia Maxon, the professor's beautiful daughter.   When
Bulan wondered how a creature without a soul could love it
was revealed that he was not Number Thirteen at all, but
a wealthy young man with amnesia who had been placed in
Maxon's workshop.

Burroughs' second Frankenstein type novel was
<u>Synthetic Men of Mars</u>, a later and quite inferior entry to
his "John Carter" series, published in serial form in Mun-
sey's <u>Argosy</u> magazine from January 7th through February
11th in 1939.   Like Professor Maxon, Ras Thavas, the
Master Mind of Mars, was growing living beings in the
chemical vats in his laboratory.   These ugly monsters,
called hormads, at least the ones with sufficient brain
power, planned to conquer all of Mars.   Vor Daj, the hero
of the novel, had his brain transplanted in the head of a
hormad and fought to stop the creatures' plans and also to
destroy the ultimate spawn of the laboratory, a growing
monster of protoplasm which might have engulfed the entire
planet.   In the end the hero regained his own body and,
like Bulan, won the beautiful maiden.

The Greatest Adventure, published in 1929 by E. P. Dutton and Company, was John Taine's (pen name for mathematician Dr. Eric Temple Bell) novel of a lost world of prehistoric monsters, none of which could possibly have evolved in the natural way. Dr. Eric Lane, a scientist who had always dreamed of "the greatest adventure," or the creation of life by man, discovered that, as in Mary Shelley's Frankenstein, the monsters were the result of artificial creation. An early super-intelligent race had created specks of living matter which had taken a wrong course of evolution, developing into impossible travesties of Earth's great saurians.

A novel with Frankensteinian overtones was World's Fair Goblin, published in the April, 1939 issue of Street and Smith's Doc Savage magazine. Maximus, a giant man-like monster with red hair, supposedly the creation of a mad doctor, haunted the fairgrounds. Eventually the creature was exposed as a man enlarged to monstrous proportions by adrenalin. Long Tom, one of Doc Savage's agents, nearly had his brain transferred to the head of Maximus which would have resulted in the creation of a man of tomorrow.

The New Adventures of Frankenstein

A series of novels entitled "The New Adventures of Frankenstein" was written by this author and starred the original Frankenstein Monster. In the description and characterization of the Monster, I have gone back to the original Mary Shelley conception with variations to imply the motion picture character. The Frankenstein Monster stood eight feet tall and was even taller in the raised boots. The flesh, a ghastly yellow and hardly covering the muscles, contrasted with the shoulder length, black hair. The dull yellow orbs were set in whitish sockets and peered out from under a Neanderthal brow. The straight black lips would part to reveal the uneven, white teeth. Silvery electrodes protruded from each temple. A red gash, held together by stitches and strips of metal, ran horizontally across the slightly high forehead to show where the brain had been put in, and stitched scars ran the length of the right cheek, around the neck, and on each wrist and arm.

Walking about stiffly, fearing fire, and exhibiting feats of superhuman strength like the Monster of the films,

the creature also learned to speak and cry out to a humanity
whose collective soul seemed more monstrous than his own
hideous countenance.   Finding only hatred and pain where he
sought to find love, the Monster realized that men were his
eternal enemies.   Often, however, the beast would again attempt to trust his human adversaries, killing only when pro-
voked.

        In Frankenstein Lives Again, the first in the series
and a sequel to the original Frankenstein novel, a young
scientist named Dr. Burt Winslow investigated the strange
"Ice God" frozen in the Arctic wastes which he believed to
be the actual Frankenstein Monster in suspended animation
for nearly two centuries.   Mary Shelley had actually adapted
the true story related by Captain Walton to novel form and
in doing so had made a few changes.   Winslow took the
Monster to Castle Frankenstein (which was not in the Mary
Shelley book) in Ingoldstadt and revived it.   Presently the
Monster nearly killed Winslow for returning the artificial
life he so despised, then fled to the woods where he came
under the hypnotic control of Professor Dartani, the proprietor of a traveling horror show.   The entranced Monster
became Dartani's murdering agent until eventually turning on
his master and being driven by Winslow, who hurled a blazing torch in his face, off the roof of the castle to be swept
away by the river below.

        Terror of Frankenstein brought the Monster into kin-
ship with the agents of OGRE, an organization of the world's
most hideous men whose sole mission was to eradicate all
beauty from the Earth.   Burt Winslow, believing the Monster
to be still alive, journeyed to England where he and a fellow
scientist invented a superpowerful robot into whose head
Winslow's own mind could be transferred.   The robot was
built to defeat the Monster.   After a battle between the two
artificially created monsters, the creature of Frankenstein
escaped with the leader of OGRE in a flying saucer only to
be blasted by a disintegrating ray.

        Victor Frankenstein himself was resurrected by
supernatural means and forced to create a mindless army
of monsters for a world conquering foreign nation in Bones
of Frankenstein.   In this novel the Monster regained his
supposedly lost ability to speak.   Frankenstein succeeded
in giving life to six prototype monstrosities, all of which
were destroyed along with the original Monster in an explosion.

Frankenstein Meets Dracula was a sequel to Bram Stoker's Dracula and mainly dealt with the resurrection of the vampire Count and his attempt to have revenge on those responsible for his destruction, beginning with a descendant of his arch enemy Dr. Van Helsing. Dracula tried to force Winslow to transplant Van Helsing's brain into the Monster's skull by putting Lynn Powell, the doctor's fiancée under his vampiric control. Eventually the Monster learned his consciousness was to be destroyed and rammed a wooden post through Dracula's heart, pulling the building down along with him.

John Stewart, the werewolf, was introduced in Frankenstein vs. the Werewolf. The victim of a Gypsy curse, Stewart journeyed to the chateau of a strange Dr. Dorn who might be able to cure him. Dorn, however, decided it more to his liking to control both the werewolf and the Frankenstein Monster to destroy his enemies, using a mind robbing drug he invented. Both creatures finally battled each other and fell into a pool of quicksand.

In Frankenstein in the Lost World Burt Winslow flew back toward Ingoldstadt with the drugged Monster to dissect it. But he never carried out his plans. Winslow's airplane crashed atop an African plateau where prehistoric monsters and cavemen still lived. A giant gorilla called Tor, King of Beasts, nearly destroyed the Monster and took Lynn Powell for his bride until Winslow caused the volcano to erupt. Winslow and Lynn escaped in another plane while the entire plateau was destroyed by an earthquake.

Imkha-Ra, an Egyptian mummy brought back to life by a mystic scroll, tried to claim his reincarnated lost love in Frankenstein in the Mummy's Tomb. Reviving the mummies of his past followers, this evil sorcerer had at his command a legion of living dead horrors. The Frankenstein Monster saw that the reincarnated girl who had been kind to him was about to be sacrificed by Imkha-Ra in order to make her into a living mummy and lashed out at the bandaged horde, finally destroying the ancient Egyptian temple.

The Return of Frankenstein introduced Dr. Erik Frankenstein, a descendant of Victor Frankenstein, who attempted to drive off the villagers of Krausburg so that he could continue his experiments uninterrupted in the ominous Black Castle. Erik Frankenstein's creation was a patchwork

gorilla named Gorron, also sporting a horn protruding from
the forehead.   Burt Winslow and Stewart, the werewolf,
were also in Krausburg attempting to destroy the dormant
Monster which had been hijacked by Frankenstein and also
to find a cure for the werewolf curse.   The heroics were
mainly provided by the Masked Demon, a legendary mystery
hero come back to life.   The Monster was destroyed this
time by a man-made avalanche.

A descendant of Dr. Henry Jekyll appeared in <u>Fran-
kenstein and the Curse of Dr. Jekyll</u>.   Jekyll journeyed to
Krausburg hoping that his correspondent Dr. Frankenstein
had the chemicals necessary to keep him from becoming the
evil Mr. Hyde, the creature unleashed by his own experiments following his ancestor's notes.   Finding Frankenstein
dead, Jekyll kept reverting to Hyde, a condition in which
he befriended the Frankenstein Monster.   Hyde and the Monster committed horrible acts until both perished in a cave
flooded by one of the villagers.

<u>Tales of Frankenstein</u> was a slight deviation from
the series.   Not a novel, this was a collection of Frankensteinian short stories, two of which featured the original
Monster.   These were: "Frankenstein," a poem about
Victor and his creation;   "My Creation, My Beloved," in
which the deformed Gregore Frankenstein created a perfect
female who killed him out of love and put his brain in a
perfect body which she constructed;   "Crawler from the
Grave," in which the hand of another descendant of Victor
Frankenstein, also an experimenter in reviving the dead,
was cut off by grave robbers seeking its ring and crawled
after them for a terrible revenge;   "A Man Called Frankenstein," about a giant hired killer called Frankenstein who
was stabbed to death by an icepick-wielding assassin named
Dracula;   "Dr. Karnstein's Creation," in which a mad scientist, possibly a descendant of Victor Frankenstein, inadvertently created a bloodthirsty horror from vampire corpses;
the satiric "Madhouse of Death," in which a "hardboiled"
private detective found himself in a pulp magazine situation
with his brain transferred to the skull of a gorilla;   "The
Man Who Built Robots," about an inventor of a human
robot and who himself turned out to be an artificial man;
"To Be Frank,"[1] in which two employees of a motion picture studio investigated a man supposedly wearing their
copyrighted make-up, only to be killed by the authentic
article;   "Monster of the Pyramid," wherein two archaeol-
ogists encountered a supernatural monster made from

Covers of the first two Glut <u>Frankenstein</u> novels, published in Spain, 1971.

corpses to guard an Egyptian tomb; "Soul of the Matter," in which a man obsessed with a fear of death, sold his soul to the Devil for the gift of immortality and found his brain in the skull of an undying Frankenstein type creature; "The True Story of Atlantis," in which it was discovered that human life on Earth was the result of alien scientists creating Atlanteans from the parts of many living bodies; "F. R. A. N. K. E. N. S. T. E. I. N. ," about a scientist who created an android daughter and a futuristic computer capable of destroying the source of any evil; and "If One Survived," set in the distant future, in which an alien exploratory team found and revived the only living creature on the lifeless planet Earth--the Frankenstein Monster.

The eleventh book in the series <u>Frankenstein and the Evil of Dracula</u> also featured the werewolf. A scientist

named Nathan Kane attempted to eradicate vampirism from
the world.   His jealous former assistant revived Count
Dracula, who preferred to take revenge on the Frankenstein
Monster by forcing Kane to dissect him alive.   The werewolf hoped to be cured by Kane.   In the end the Monster
splashed flammable chemicals over the vampire while Kane
shot a flaming arrow through his chest.   The werewolf was
killed by a silver bullet and the Monster perished in the
burning Black Castle.

In 1971 the first two novels [see illustration] were
published in Spain by Buru Lan de Ediciones under the
titles Frankenstein Resucitado ("Frankenstein Revived") and
Frankenstein y el Robot (artwork by Esteban Maroto) with
the next nine books announced inside.   But due to strict
censorship regulations in Spain, no books after the second
title were issued.   Negotiations are now underway to pub-
lish the series elsewhere.

Frankenstein in Short Stories

As in novels, the Frankenstein concept has been
used in many short stories, the first being "Frankenstein--
Unlimited," written by H. A. Highstone, and first published
in the no. 36 (December 1938) issue of Street and Smith
Publications' Astounding Science Fiction.   Not really a
Frankenstein story, "Frankenstein--Unlimited" was set in
the future after the time in which robots did all of man's
work for him.   Before a small group of human beings
escaped to take up existence as cavemen, their lives had
been regulated by the Great Brain, a thinking collection of
factories and robots.   "Frankenstein's Twenty Cousins," by
R. S. Lerch, published in the January-February 1940 issue
of the pulp magazine Strange Detective Mysteries (Popular
Publications), was another story with a misleading title.
A short detective known as the Wedge could fit twenty different weapons into the place of his lost hand.   The Wedge
fought a gang of crooks who defied the police with their
bullet-proof armor.

More of a Frankenstein story was Wayne Robbins'
"Test-Tube Frankenstein" in the May 1940 issue of the
same publisher's Terror Tales.   A scientist named Chester
Vermis had kept some earthworm tissue alive in a jar.
The tissue fought to live and presently began to grow.   Soon
it had the ability to form itself into the semblance of another

organism.   Eventually the creature killed the scientist and
assumed the form of his friend's wife.   The lovely creature
was hacked to pieces by her husband who prayed that it was
indeed the monster that he killed.

Wayne Rogers' "I Am a Frankenstein!" in the September 1940 Terror Tales, was more in the Frankenstein
tradition.   Young Dr. Cooper reported for work to Dr.
Godfrey Kittredge, who promptly drugged him upon his arrival.   When he awoke he found Kittredge bringing the
corpse of a murderer to life via electricity.   Unable to
rebel against Kittredge in his drugged condition, Cooper
was forced to perform all manners of grisly murders and
transplants until the reanimated body was a ghastly composite.   After Cooper finally managed to impale the creature's skull, Kittredge seemingly transferred his brain into
the head of the monster.   Finally it was revealed that the
entire situation was a hoax, that "Kittredge" and the "monster" were really hired actors, and that the hypnotized
Cooper still retained his own brain and body.

Neusman Dan Bream encountered Victor Frankenstein
V in Harry Harrison's "At Last, the True Story of Frankenstein," published in the September 1965 issue of the British
magazine Science Fantasy.   Frankenstein was exhibiting a
dead white giant, with a stitched face and metal plugs pro-
jecting from the temples, supposedly the original Frankenstein Monster, in a carnival.   Asked for the true story of
Frankenstein, the reporter listened as Victor told how his
father had not been experimenting with the creation of life
but with longevity.   He had known Mary Shelley who changed
his story to suit her own conceptions.   What was known as
the Monster was really an authentic zombie animated after
death.   Frankenstein injected Bream with a special drug
that transformed him into a zombie.   The last one was
just about worn out.

"Dial 'F' for Frankenstein," by Arthur C. Clarke,
published in the January 1965 issue of Playboy, was another
story about machines rebelling against their creators.   The
creation of a world telephone system brought into effect a
vast electronic brain which began to turn upon mankind,
causing all machines to malfunction and leaving human
beings at the mercy of their inventions.   Kurt Vonnegut,
Jr.'s "Fortitude," published in the September 1968 Playboy,
was a satire written in script form.   It featured sixty-five-
year-old Dr. Norbert Frankenstein, who worked in a New

York hospital, keeping the head of Sylvia Lovejoy alive with
devices simulating human organs and systems. Although
she begged for death, Sylvia was rigged up to live at least
five hundred years. Growing old and finally realizing his
love for the disembodied head of Sylvia, Dr. Frankenstein
revealed that each one of the artificial organs could take
care of two people and willingly submitted his own head to
be wired up with hers. What a perfect marriage Frankenstein and Sylvia had, sharing the same organs, and living
happily ever after at least for the next five centuries.

"The Plot is the Thing," by Robert Bloch, published
in the July 1966 issue of The Magazine of Fantasy and
Science Fiction (Mercury Press), was about an avid movie
fan who was given a lobotomy and from then on believed
that she was a part of the old films. In Germany, she
found herself in the Frankenstein castle with the Monster
moving ever closer. In 1970, two stories submitted by fan
writers were published in Eerie (Warren Publishing Company) magazine's "Eerie Fan Fare" pages. "The Prophetic
Dream," (Eerie no. 30), by Carmen Minchella, was the
story of a young boy who had a nightmare. He dreamed
that he was big, ugly, and hated by people who trapped him
in a burning building. The boy eventually grew up to be
Boris Karloff who had the same fate in Frankenstein.

In "Reversal" (Eerie no. 32), by Michael Carlisle,
the Monster killed Frankenstein when he beheld his hideous
features in a mirror. His strength ebbing away, the beast
knew that unless he brought his maker back to life to give
him more power, he would die. "Fooled into Dating a
Female Frankenstein" was a story with a misleading title
published in the June, 1972 issue of Real Story, a romance
magazine from K. M. R. Publications. There was no monster; only an overweight girl with a deformed nose who
underwent plastic surgery and made other improvements in
herself to become a beautiful blonde who finally married
the man she loved.

The first short story utilizing the Frankenstein theme
but not the name was "The Monster Maker," by W. C.
Morrow, first published in book form in an 1897 anthology
issued by J. B. Lippincott. The story was about an old
surgeon who dabbled in mad science. A young potential
suicide paid the doctor to end his life in orderly fashion.
The scientist complied, getting rid of his head but retaining
the corpse. About three years later the police acquired a

document describing the scientist's experiments in creating
a manlike monster.   When they arrived at the doctor's home,
a giant man with a steel ball for a head killed the doctor's
wife.   Fuming with rage, the doctor tried to kill his creation with a knife.   An oil lamp was overturned, starting a
fire that destroyed both monster and maker.

     A series of Frankensteinian stories, composed of
six tales entitled "Herbert West--Reanimator" by H. P.
Lovecraft, was published from 1921 through 1922 in Home
Brew, a George Julian Houtain publication.   These were
Lovecraft's first professionally sold stories.   Written on
assignment, the Herbert West stories are considerably unlike the macabre fiction for which Lovecraft is famous.
Herbert West was experimenting with life and death after
being barred from medical school.   His first accomplishment (each experiment being a different chapter) was giving
life to a corpse which tried clawing its way back into the
grave.   West then brought the corpse of the dean of the
school, who had died of the plague, back to life as a murderous cannibal.   The third experiment delighted the racists.
A dead Negro failed to come back to life because West's
serum was intended for white men.   After being buried in
a potter's field, the black man revived and devoured a little
boy.   When a stranger died at West's doorstep, the scientist brought him to life screaming.   In his fifth experiment,
West reanimated isolated organs and combined various body
parts with reptile tissue.   A headless corpse writhed convulsively while its head, preserved in a vat, shrieked.   In
the final installment, all of the victims of West's past experiments returned, ripped apart their creator, and fled
underground.   The headless man bore with him the head of
Herbert West, reanimator.   The Herbert West series was
later reprinted in Weird Tales, a pulp magazine with a
large readership.

     In "The Synthetic Men," by Earl Repp in the Decem-
ber 1930 issue of Wonder Stories, Dr. Pontius created two
men by dissolving human skeletons in jelly-filled tubes and
bathing them in a special ray.   The two creatures, named
Joe and Jack Agar, lived.   Joe, the "good" creature, died,
leaving the evil Jack to go after the doctor's beautiful
daughter.   A police bullet ended Jack's unnatural life.
"Menace of the Metal-Men," by A. Prestigiacomo, published
in the first issue of the 1938 British pulp magazine Fantasy
(published by George Newnes), was advertised as "The
Latest and Most Thrilling 'Frankenstein' Story."   Zed Eight,

the ultimate in a long line of robots, was virtually a human being, so human that he led the other robots in a revolt against mankind.   When Zed Eight finally realized that he could never be a man of flesh and blood he led the other automatons into the Mediterranean Sea.   The cover of the magazine was more Frankensteinian, showing a scientist bringing to life a robot with a human head.

Nelson Bond's allegorical story "Another World Begins" (later retitled "The Cunning of the Beast") was published in the November 1942 issue of Bluebook and concerned an alien scientist named Yowa Eloem, who created two intelligent creatures to serve him.   When the creatures learned evil in the scientist's laboratory, Eloem was banished with them to Earth.   There his creations became Adam and Eve.   A man was almost killed in an automobile wreck in "A Matter of Principle," by E. K. Jarvis in the April 1951 issue of Fantastic Adventures (Ziff-Davis Publishing Company).   At an organs bank, he was rebuilt with parts of corpses.   Believing that he was given the brain of her former husband, his wife tried to kill him but inadvertently fell from a roof to her death.   In reality the brain transplant was unnecessary and never took place.

In "The Most Perfect Monster," by Bernard L. Elliott, in the first issue of Shock Tales (M. F. Enterprises), published in January 1959, a scientist killed a number of beautiful girls, salvaging the best parts of each and assembling them into a gorgeous woman.   The female monster came alive, killed her creator, and retaining his skillful hands, began to look around for victims that would make up her perfect man.   The story was reprinted as "The Girl and the Monster," with the new byline of "Hugo," in the first issue of Thriller (Tempest Publications), published in February 1962.

A mad scientist named Graigo went around murdering people and hacking off their heads in "Seven Victims for a Blood-Mad Ghoul," by Charles Thompson, in the August 1971 issue of Horror Stories (Stanley Publications).   Dr. Graigo's ambiguous endeavors seemed to involve reviving the head, curing his dying wife, and eventually creating a mate for her.   The hero threw acid in Graigo's face, a fire started, and the fiend died in the manner of so many mad scientists in the past.   Mary Shelley and her concept of creating life were mentioned in "Woman's Rib," a science fiction story by Thomas N. Scortia in the July 1972 issue of <u>Galaxy</u>. In this story, an aging woman created a perfect man, grown from a single human cell and suitably named Frank, to love her until she died. The theme of the story was that the created being reflects the virtues and faults of its creator.

Adam Link

Dr. Charles Link had spent twenty years creating Adam Link, a five-foot, ten-inch, five hundred pound robot. Adam Link was no ordinary automaton. He was the first robot in the history of fiction to have human emotions and the first to tell his own story:

> I will begin at the beginning. I was born, or created, five years ago. I am a true robot. Some of you humans still have doubts, it seems. I am made of wires and wheels, not flesh and blood. I am run by electrical power. My brain is made of iridium sponge.

"I, Robot" was written as a single story by Otto O. Binder (using the name "Eando" Binder) for the April 1939 issue of Ziff-Davis' <u>Amazing Stories</u>. He received a payment of $50. Binder had always been enthusiastic over the Frankenstein concept. "Adam Link was directly inspired by Mary Shelley's <u>Frankenstein</u>," Binder told this writer. "As I recall, I was just thinking about it and suddenly had an 'inspiration.' Why not substitute a robot for an organic graveyard monster? It should therefore have all the drama and pathos of the famous classic ... which it seemed to have as it brought a flood of letters, as Ray Palmer of <u>Amazing</u> then told me. "

Adam Link was like a child, whose intelligence and abilities developed with time and practical experience. Like a child, the robot learned to crawl before he could walk, to speak before he could read. When a loose transformer angle-iron struck Dr. Link on the head and killed him, Adam was immediately suspected of murdering his creator. Just as he knew a mob was forming to come destroy him, the creature that had been named after both the first man and his own creator found a book.

> Then I found the book--<u>Frankenstein</u>--lying on the desk whose drawers had been emptied untidily.

Dr. Link's private desk. He had kept this one book
from me. Why? I read it now, in a half hour, by
my page-at-a-time scanning.
   And then I understood. They thought I had "turned
Frankenstein" and had killed Dr. Link, my creator.
They had only one thought in mind, that I was a
created monster of metal who had gone 'berserk,'
lacking a soul.
   Adam Link, American citizen? No, it was Adam
Link, Frankenstein monster.

Ray Palmer, the editor of Amazing, saw the potential
in making Adam Link a series character and, backed by an
enormous amount of fan mail praising the story, insisted
that Binder do a sequel. The result was nine more Adam
Link stories, several of which won the magazine's Monthly
Merit Award: "The Trial of Adam Link" (Amazing, July
1939), "Adam Link in Business" (January 1940), "Adam
Link's Vengeance" (February), "Adam Link, Robot--Detec-
tive" (May), "Adam Link, Champion Athlete" (July), "Adam
Link in War" (December), "Adam Link in the Past" (February 1941), "Adam Link Faces a Revolt" (May), and "Adam
Link Saves the World" (April 1942).

Through the series of Adam Link Stories, the human-
ized robot stood trial for the murder of Dr. Link, was convicted but then proven innocent, and went to find his place
in a world of men. Eventually Adam discovered love and
found himself loved by a beautiful woman named Kay Temple.
A scientist built a female robot called Eve for Adam, gave
her Kay's feminine traits, then turned both robots into metal
Frankenstein monsters. When Adam regained his will that
had been controlled by the scientist, he was forced to defeat
his robot mate. Adam then disguised himself as a human
being and became an unbeatable private detective. Eve had
been changed back to her benevolent self and saw Adam intentionally tie a human being in a foot race. All the while
the robot was regarded by human beings as a Frankenstein.
After Adam and Eve destroyed a group of monstrous alien
invaders, he was no longer regarded as an electronic Frankenstein. Adam Link was awarded United States Citizenship.

In 1965, Binder revised seven of his ten Adam Link
stories and transformed them into a novel Adam Link, Robot,
published by Paperback Library, with a second chapter entitled "Frankenstein!" (Quotations in this chapter are from
the book edition.) The Adam Link stories were extremely

visual and proved to be easily adapted (by Binder himself) to the comic strip format. Three of the stories appeared in Weird Science-Fantasy (published by EC) and illustrated by Joe Orlando: "I, Robot" in issue no. 27 (1954), "The Trial of Adam Link" in issue no. 28, and "Adam Link in Business" in no. 29 (both 1955). Fantasy Illustrated, a professional quality amateur publication by Bill Spicer, ran a two-part adaptation of "Adam Link's Vengeance," drawn by D. Bruce Berry, in the first two issues (1963 and 1964). Yet a third series of Adam Link comic strips appeared in Creepy (Warren Publishing Company), all of which were again drawn by Joe Orlando: "I, Robot" in issue no. 2 (1965), "The Trial of Adam Link" in issue no. 4, "Adam Link in Business" in no. 6, "Adam Link's Mate" in no. 8, "Adam Link's Vengeance" in issue no. 9 (1966), "Adam Link, Robot Detective" in no. 12, "Adam Link Gangbuster" in no. 13, and "Adam Link, Champion Athlete" in issue no. 15 (1967).

"I, Robot" was presented on the Outer Limits (ABC) television program on 14 November 1964. Red Morgan portrayed Adam in a silvery robot costume. Unlike the character in the book who spoke like a normal human being, Adam's voice was mechanical. The television adaptation showed Adam going to trial for Dr. Link's murder and being defended by elderly lawyer Thurmen Cutler (Howard Da Silva). Convicted of murder, Adam willfully resigned himself to being executed. As he was led away from the courthouse, he saved a child from an approaching truck, but was destroyed in the attempt. The world had called Adam Link "Frankenstein." In Adam's creation in 1939, Otto O. Binder gave the world of fantasy an important and enduring character who proved himself to be more human than many of us.

More Books and His Own Magazine

The first nonfiction book to use the name "Frankenstein" in the title was published in Paris in 1935. Frankenstein, l'Age d'Or ou la Fin du Monde (translated as "Frankenstein, the Age of Gold or the End of the World"), by Jean Nocher, speculated upon the possibility of man's subjugation by the machine, a theme used in the novel Metropolis. Frankenstein & Company, by Ornella Volta, published in 1965 by the Italian publishers Sugar Editore, included the full novel Frankenstein, plus text on Frankenstein in the

theatre and on the screen.   The book also included the
original stories of The Strange Case of Dr. Jekyll and Mr.
Hyde, The Invisible Man, Dracula, The Phantom of the
Opera, and The Most Dangerous Game and notes on their
later adaptations.

     Frankenstein wie er Mordet und Lacht ("Frankenstein
How He Murders and Laughs"), edited by Edward Reavis,
published in Germany by Bürmeier and Nikel in 1968, was
an anthology of horror stories including "The Monster
Maker" and "At Last, the True Story of Frankenstein."
The dust jacket artwork featured Frankenstein Monster and
the vampire of the silent film Nosferatu combined into a
single being.   In 1969, Frankenstein, by Jean-Pierre
Bouyxou, was published in France as one of the Premiere
Plan series of books on motion pictures.   This edition primarily discussed the Frankenstein films and also mentioned
some of the other plays, television programs, and publications in which the Monster appeared.   The Children of
Frankenstein, by Herbert J. Muller, published in 1969 by
the Indiana University Press, was a treatise on technology
and its effect upon mankind.   Muller considers us the victims, the children, of our created technology turned against
us.

     James Warren, head of the Warren Publishing Com-
pany, and his editor Forrest J Ackerman, have contributed
much to perpetuating the Frankenstein legend.   In 1958,
Warren (then using the name Central Publications) and
Ackerman produced the world's first magazine devoted to
movie monsters, Famous Monsters of Filmland.   The magazine is still the most successful of its type, despite the
waves of imitations.   A frequent feature of the publication
is the "filmbook," which often gives the complete story of
some Frankenstein or other horror or science fiction film.
In 1964 Famous Monsters held an amateur movie-making
contest in which readers were to make films according to
either of two scripts written by Ackerman and supplied by
the magazine.   The first, Siegfried Saves Metropolis, was
about a robot, created by the genius Rotwang, accidentally
enlarged by a growth ray and loose in the futuristic city
Siegfried, summoned from the past, was able to destroy the
robot with his own pet dragon.   Twin of Frankenstein had
Dr. Kurt Frankenstein creating a good "twin" to the original
Monster.   The new being's face was accidentally destroyed
by acid.   When the creature's head was disintegrated by a
beam of light, Frankenstein gave him the head of his

deformed assistant.   The original Monster came back to the
laboratory, infuriated that Frankenstein was again creating
life.   Frankenstein scared off his first Monster with a copy
of Famous Monsters of Filmland.   In the end everything
was revealed as a nightmare of the Frankenstein Monster. [2]
Famous Monsters no. 35 (1965) featured an article entitled
"Fantastic Frankensteins from France," about a series of
extremely detailed miniatures of various movie Frankenstein
Monsters and scenes, made by Raphael Georges Marongiu.

In 1964 Warren published the short-lived Monster
World, a companion to Famous Monsters of Filmland, and
in 1965 the special edition magazine Monster Make-Up Hand-
book, written by professional make-up artist Dick Smith.
Attempting to recreate the Monster described by Mary
Shelley in Frankenstein, Smith made some changes for this
step-by-step lesson in how to do an original make-up.   Gregory Parker served as the model for the make-up: Smith's
Frankenstein Monster had muscles and blood vessels showing
through the skin and a metal skull plate in the place of hair.
Smith told this writer:

> This is not one of my professional make-ups.   It
> was done for a book for young amateurs to show
> them what could be achieved with the simple ma-
> terials and techniques available to them.   The basic
> materials were wax, latex, cotton, liquid make-up,
> and Knox gelatine.   For a film I would have used
> more sophisticated materials, retaining the concept
> of a transparent yellowish skin through which the
> muscles and blood vessels could be seen.

The Journal of Frankenstein, a monster magazine
aiming at an older readership, was edited and published in
1959 by Calvin Thomas Beck (under the name New World
Enterprises).   Included in this first edition was a movie
satire in script form entitled "The Return of the Son of the
Bride of Frankenstein" which included a big green monster
that consumed part of Niagara Falls.   The magazine was
not a commercial success in attempting to be a sophisticated,
adult venture and never reached a second issue.   In January
1962, Beck returned to publishing (now using the name
Gothic Castle Publishing Company) with the less "highbrow"
Castle of Frankenstein.   The magazine developed into a
publication that both the young monster fans and the more
serious students of fantastic entertainment could enjoy.
Beck also edited a paperback anthology of horror stories

<u>The Frankenstein Reader</u> which was published in 1962 by
Ballantine Books. Another one-shot publication, <u>Famous
Horrors of the Screen</u> published in the early 1960s, was
entirely devoted to photographs from the Frankenstein films.
With the Frankenstein concept so popular in modern publications, it was inevitable that the Monster would soon be featured in a medium where readers could also <u>see</u> his adventures on the printed page. Frankenstein's Monster was to
meet the comics.

Notes

1. First published in <u>Famous Monsters of Filmland</u> no. 83
    (1971).

2. Amateur Frankenstein films have been given coverage
    in magazines such as <u>Famous Monsters of Filmland</u>.
    Some of these have shown considerable imagination
    and are being distributed through colleges.   This
    writer has made a number of amateur Frankenstein
    movies over the years; they are listed in Walter
    J. Lee's Reference Guide to Fantastic Films:
    <u>Frankenstein Meets Dracula</u>, <u>Return of the Wolf
    Man</u> (1957); <u>Revenge of Dracula</u>, <u>The Franken-
    stein Story</u>, <u>Return of the Monster Maker</u> (1958);
    <u>The Teenage Frankenstein</u>, <u>Slave of the Vampire</u>,
    <u>The Teenage Frankenstein Meets the Teenage
    Werewolf</u>, <u>I Was a Teenage Apeman</u> (1959);
    <u>Monster Rumble</u> (1961); and <u>The Adventures of
    the Spirit</u> (1962).

Chapter 11

THE ILLUSTRATED FRANKENSTEIN

Heroes have been the main stars of comic books since the beginnings of the medium in the 1930s. Still there have been a number of popular anti-heroes with more appeal than the usual stock of bad guys; popular enough, in fact, to warrant their own strips and magazines. The most enduring anti-hero of the comic books remains the Monster of Frankenstein. Comic book writer and artist Dick Briefer was associated with the Frankenstein Monster for nearly fifteen years. In 1939 Briefer's Rex Dexter, Interplanetary Adventurer, a futuristic strip in Fox Publications' Mystery Men Comics (issue no. 5), featured a robot villain with a face that would leave an indelible impression on the artist. The fiendish artificial man had a squared head, straight black hair and bangs drooping over the high forehead, sunken cheeks, a wrinkled mouth, and two electrodes at the top of the head. Perhaps this showed an early desire of Briefer to utilize the movies-inspired Monster.

New Adventures of Frankenstein (known in future issues as simply Frankenstein) premiered in the seventh issue of Prize Comics published in 1940 by Feature Publications. The introduction of the Frankenstein strip was unique in that the magazine was primarily a collection of super-hero adventures. Briefer, who signed the strip with the uninspired pseudonym "Frank N. Stein" in the early installment, began the first episode with the same basic storyline of Mary Shelley's novel. Victor Frankenstein brought his creation to life in modern-day New York. Inadvertently knocking his creator unconscious, the Monster escaped the fortress-like building of his birth and fled to the countryside, where he was tormented by all that he encountered. At last he met a blind man who shared food and taught him to speak. But when the blind man's son returned he was

plagued by bullets, rocks, and clubs.   Vowing vengeance on
puny humanity, the Monster was now its most deadly enemy.

   Surely those paltry humans had reason to fear the
Monster.   Briefer depicted the brute as one of the most
ghastly interpretations imaginable.   A tremendous giant almost fifteen feet tall, the Monster had a dead white face
with terribly stitched incisions running down the center of
and across the forehead, down the neck and around the
arms, yellow teeth showing through the ripped flesh of the
mouth, eyes bulging over the bony cheeks, a twisted peg of
a nose set high between the orbs, and stringy black hair
hanging over the high forehead and high placed ears.

   As mankind's enemy the Frankenstein Monster performed such acts of villainy as tossing helpless children
into the lion cage at the zoo, then wrecking much of New
York City.   Mimicking King Kong, the Monster climbed to
the head of the Statue of Liberty.   Frankenstein himself
leaped from the crown of the Statue to cause the Monster
to lose his balance.   But the Monster caught his creator,
saving his life as police riddled the artificial body with
rifle bullets.   Victor wondered why the Monster saved him
at the cost of his own hideous life.   Suddenly the pallid
face of the living Monster crashed through the window.

> I spared you to live--to live in misery also--to
> watch and see the suffering and grief that I, your
> creation, will cause the human race.   You will
> chase me, but never get me!   I go now, always
> haunting and tormenting you!

   In the following issue of Prize Comics (1941) the
Monster was terrorizing an amusement park.   Victor
Frankenstein realized that he was wrong in tampering with
the laws of creation.   Therefore, in the tradition of the
mad scientist, Frankenstein decided to create another monster to battle with the first.   He obviously did not consider
that if the original Monster lost the fight, the world would
be plagued by an even more horrendous brute--a gigantic
crocodile man with a human brain.   Fortunately the original
creation won.   The Frankenstein Monster eventually became
the leader of the criminal underworld and was becoming
more of a calculating super-villain than a lumbering monstrosity.   A character was needed in the strip to counteract
the villainy of the Monster, and also to compete with the
super-heroes that were even more popular in the early

Forties. The character of Dr. Victor Frankenstein was not
colorful enough for the job.

In <u>Prize Comics</u> no. 11 Victor Frankenstein rescued
a young boy named Denny from a car wreck caused by the
Monster in which his parents were killed. Frankenstein's
surgical skills saved the boy, though it seemed he would
never walk again. Nearly cracking under the strain, Frankenstein finally discovered a cure for Denny. Through the
following years Denny trained himself to physical perfection,
living as the ward of Dr. Frankenstein. Donning a black
riding outfit Denny began his private war against the Monster. Because of a pin on his outfit bearing the picture of
his pet bulldog Spike, the new crusader became known as
Bulldog Denny. (Actually the name Bulldog Denny seems
to have been inspired by fictional character Bulldog Drum-
mond and his valet Denny.) At the end of this story Bulldog Denny vowed to capture the Monster.

The Monster was already losing some of his ghastly
features, as if the years in which Denny grew up gave the
ugly tissues time to heal. He was also somehow losing
much of his skyscraping height. Obviously the original version of the Monster was too formidable to be believably pul-
verized by the human Denny.

Bulldog Denny continued to battle Frankenstein (who
had acquired the name of his creator, whom Denny eased
out of the Strip) until he went to Washington for defense
work in the wartime twenty-fourth issue in 1942. Before
Denny left he called together some of the other <u>Prize Comics</u>
heroes--Yank and Doodle, the Black Owl, the Green Lama,
Doctor Frost, and the comic General and the Corporal. After
each of the heroes displayed his various talents Frankenstein
was finally subdued.

Frankenstein did not remain dormant for long. In
<u>Prize Comics</u> no. 26 a scientist named Dr. Ullrich created
a female companion and revived the original Monster. Again
the interfering humans sought to destroy what they did not
understand. When Frankenstein saw his mate burned by
their torches he killed them all and renewed his war against
humanity. The might of the Armed Forces finally captured
Frankenstein in <u>Prize Comics</u> no. 33 the following year.
Having lost his white complexion in favor of normal flesh
tone, the Monster was turned over to a Professor Carrol,
who was to effect a new life for the brute. With hypnosis,

special injections and the help of a barber, plastic surgeon, and a tailor, Carrol transformed the giant into the mild mannered "Mister Frankenstein." The world soon forgot his countless horrendous crimes. The following issues featured the revamped Frankenstein in mildly humorous adventures wherein he attended school and helped the war effort.

The Gestapo had other plans for Frankenstein. Drugged and captured, the giant was transformed by German scientists into a monstrous Nazi complete with uniform in Prize Comics no. 39 (1944). But when Frankenstein managed to escape the treatments that kept him monstrous he began to work as an undercover agent against the Gestapo. After the War, Frankenstein's adventures had him as a creature of good during the day while a ravaging Monster at night, due to the hypnotic powers of a female vampire, whom he finally drove away with garlic. Gradually the stories became more and more humorous until the strip reverted to outright comedy involving a world of absurd vampires, werewolves, and assorted characters. The series was not unlike the later television program The Munsters.

The series' popularity grew to the point where the first issue of Frankenstein comics, published concurrently with Prize Comics, appeared in 1945. The Monster was seemingly the same created back in the seventh issue of Prize Comics, since there was no break in the continuity. A new origin was given for Frankenstein in his first solo issue. A scientist, inspired by Mary Shelley's novel, created a giant Monster in the hopes of unleashing a terrible engine of death upon the world. The creature, with the same basic facial structure as the original Briefer Monster, but exaggerated to the ridiculous extreme with the nose now above the brow, only wanted to live in peace and smell flowers. After his creator was destroyed in an explosion, Frankenstein resumed the humorous life he was currently living in Prize Comics. Its issue no. 68 (1948) was the last to feature the adventures of Frankenstein. (The comic became a Western magazine with the next issue.)

In 1949, with the publication of issue no. 17, the magazine Frankenstein folded. The cover of no. 17 featured Frankenstein standing before a giant clock face and menaced by an enemy about to hurl one of the clock hands like a harpoon into his massive chest. Frankenstein seemed to be a defunct publication--until 1952 when Dick Briefer resurrected the book in its final incarnation. All the humor that had been in the feature was gone beginning with <u>Frankenstein</u> no. 18. This was the era of horror comic books and there was no room for a funny Frankenstein strip. In "The Rebirth of the Monster," two villagers broke into the ancient Frankenstein Castle in Europe, where a gust of air revived the hideous Monster created by "Henry" Frankenstein. (It is unknown why Briefer did not continue to use the name "Victor," unless he happened to have seen a re-release of the 1931 movie before producing this comic book.) The Frankenstein Monster killed both intruders, then ravaged the village.

This version was the most realistic of Briefer's Frankenstein Monsters. While still retaining the basic facial features of his original and humorous versions, the latest adaptation was the most believable. The stitches running down the center of the forehead were open so that the skull shown from beneath. The uneven teeth showed a perpetual look of hatred through the torn lips. A descendant of Frankenstein attempted to destroy the Monster. But the beast managed to escape. The young Dr. Frankenstein trailed the creature to the United States in the next issue, then disappeared from the storyline. The Monster was left alone in America to encounter a number of bizarre creatures--including zombies (in <u>Frankenstein</u> no. 20, the first to present only one Frankenstein adventure per issue), prehistoric animals, a werewolf, and living mummies.

In "The Monster's Mate" in <u>Frankenstein</u> no. 23 (1953) the Monster befriended a scarred giant woman from a circus and lived happily with her until she was killed by the usual mob of brutal villagers. His revenge was identical to that of the original Frankenstein Monster of <u>Prize Comics</u> when his mate was destroyed. Briefer delighted in repeating his plots. The Frankenstein tales of the 1950s were often reworkings of his old plots, originating in either the first or humorous series. (One story in which the Monster was encased in metal as a statue appeared in all <u>three</u> series.) "The She-Monster" in the twenty-eighth issue (1954) had a mad scientist bring a murderess back to life. But when the creature threatened the scientist's existence he destroyed her with a bomb. Again the Monster was alone to be scorned and tormented by men.

The threat of censorship loomed over the comic book industry in 1954. The Comics Code Authority was in the immediate future and horror comics would soon be banned,

Dick Briefer created his most realistic Frankenstein series during the 1950s. This page from Feature Publications' <u>Frankenstein</u> no. 23 (1953).

primarily through the efforts of Dr. Frederick Wertham, whose book Seduction of the Innocent managed to "prove" that such reading material was the cause of juvenile delinquency.   Perhaps the panic of comic book publishers resulted in the inclusion of two stories, probably tales scheduled for future issues, in each of the last three issues of Frankenstein (cover titled The Monster of Frankenstein since no. 30).   The final story, "Frankenstein and the Plant," in the thirty-third issue (1954), featured a carnivorous plant whose buds assumed the physical characteristics of its food. Again this was a rewriting of one of Briefer's humorous strips.   The cover of Frankenstein no. 33 was virtually the same as the last issue featuring the funny Monster.   (Frankenstein numbers 1 and 18 both depicted a close-up of the Monster's face, proving again Briefer's penchant for repetition.)   The Dick Briefer series of Frankenstein adventures were the most enduring.   But as the original novel was in public domain, other comic book companies capitalized on the subject.   Nearly one thousand comic books featuring the Frankenstein Monster, story, or theme have been published. Some of the more significant issues are worthy of citation.

"Spirit of Frankenstein"

The first installment of Spirit of Frankenstein began in the fifth issue of Adventures into the Unknown (1949), published by the American Comics Group (ACG), a company whose horror tales were mild compared to most of the competition, usually ending happily (for the hero, not the monsters).   The title Spirit of Frankenstein was misleading. There was, in fact, no real Frankenstein Monster or character bearing the infamous name.   Nor was there any spectre of Victor Frankenstein to haunt the strip.   The name was explained in the legend of the first episode:

> Everyone has heard of Frankenstein's Monster--the fictional creature that existed only in literature!
> But suppose, in this age of science, such a creature can be created--in the spirit of Frankenstein himself?
> Our gripping tale begins in the atomic laboratory of Dr. Daniel Warren, where a bitter old scientific aide glares at a newspaper....

The scientific aide, Dr. Lambert Pardway, resented Dr. Warren for the fame he had acquired.   Lambert saw that the instrument of his revenge might be the latest

scientific achievement of the younger Warren. Dr. Warren
was creating a giant robot, with human-like plastic "skin,"
and a bald head. The robot acted like a machine until
Pardway convinced Warren to place his, Pardway's, brain
into the creature's head after he died. Thus the robot became a veritable Frankenstein Monster, controlled by an
evil intelligence. <u>Spirit of Frankenstein</u> ran in issues 5, 6,
8, 9, 10, 12, and 16 of <u>Adventures into the Unknown</u>. During those issues the robot encountered a number of highly
unlikely (even for supernatural stories) characters, including
ghosts, a composite spirit made of the evil essences of
criminals, and in the final installment (1951), a green demon
created artificially from a spilled chemical. The short-
lived series was only slightly popular. But the original
Frankenstein Monster remained a popular ACG character,
appearing in their Comics Code approved pages even through
the late 1960s when the company folded.

The Ghostly Frankensteins

        The comic books published by EC (Entertaining
Comic) in the early 1950s were noted for their extremely
literate scripts (mostly written by Albert B. Feldstein) inte-
grated with the perfectly matching graphics of a staff of
some of the best comic artists in the business. The EC
comic books stories were illustrated short prose, usually
climaxing in a surprise ending. (Most horror comic books
have adopted the surprise ending with the monster triumphant.) Running concurrently with the Briefer <u>Frankenstein</u>
magazine, EC published a number of their own Frankenstein
stories in their magazines <u>The Haunt of Fear</u>, <u>Tales from
the Crypt</u>, <u>The Vault of Horror</u>, and <u>Shock SuspenStories</u>.

        EC's first Frankenstein-type story did not feature
the original Monster. "Monster Maker" was illustrated by
Graham Ingles (who delighted in signing his work with the
pseudonym "Ghastly") and appeared in <u>The Haunt of Fear</u>
no. 17 (1950). Doctor Ravenscar had been secretly trying
to revive the dead in his castle laboratory. Using the body
of a drowned man and the brain of his sniveling assistant,
Ravenscar brought his creation to life with the electrical
power of his equipment. The creature with its metal skull
plate fled the laboratory, inevitably leading Ravenscar to his
death. It smiled, then set out into the world of men.

        Ingles' first genuine Frankenstein story was "The

Climax of "The Monster in the Ice," drawn by Graham
Ingles, in <u>Vault of Horror</u> (1951-52). Copyright 1972 by
William M. Gaines.

Monster in the Ice," published in The Vault of Horror no.
22 (1951-52).   A mysterious figure, so horrible that it
drove all men insane, was frozen in the Artic ice.   Believing the frozen giant to be the authentic Frankenstein Monster, Gerald Dawson related the ending of the original novel
to his friend Herb Campbell, who had ordered a reluctant
Eskimo to chop the giant out of the ice.   The chopping in
the next room ceased, followed by a scream; the Eskimo
had gone mad.   Outside, the two men finally encountered
the ghastly Frankenstein Monster--with its mismatching
orbs, the stringy hair, the tusks protruding from its misshapen mouth.   The three figures, two raving mad, plunged
forever beneath the cold waters.

     Jack Davis illustrated "Mirror, Mirror, on the Wall"
in Tales from the Crypt no. 34 (1953).   Arthur Stone awoke
strapped to a platform in a laboratory.   Easily breaking his
bonds, he left the amusement park grounds to return to his
wife, finding that all who encountered him fled in terror.
His wife also ran, preferring to fall to her death from an
upstairs window than to suffer his approach.   When he returned to the doctor, Stone learned that his brain had been
placed in a stitched-together body for the mad scientist's
wax museum Frankenstein exhibit at the park.   Killing the
doctor, he saw his horrible reflection in a hall of mirrors
multiplied until he could no longer stand the shock and died.
"In Character" appeared in Shock SuspenStories no. 17 (1954).
Drawn by Reed Crandall, the story began at a testimonial
dinner for Bela Kardiff, who was made to resemble both
Boris Karloff and Bela Lugosi.   Kardiff related his career,
for which all of the men were responsible.   He told how
stardom accompanied his role as the Monster in Frankenstein.   His succeeding roles were all horror parts, including
taking both roles in Frankenstein Meets a Werewolf.   Steadily
Kardiff's career degenerated (as did Lugosi's in real life)
until he could only occasionally find work in the most abys-
mal horror productions.   Kardiff concluded his narrative by
revealing that he had become the character his guests had
created.   He had put strychnine into the drinks with which
they had toasted him.

     EC's last Frankenstein horror story was "Ashes to
Ashes," printed in The Vault of Horror no. 40 (1954-55).
This was the final issue of Vault due to the pressure put
upon publishers of horror comic books during that time.
Appropriately this Frankenstein story was illustrated by
"Ghastly" Graham Ingles.   Emil Frankenstein, the only

living descendant of the creator of the Monster, related the most tragic experiment of his infamous family. The original Frankenstein's son, in an attempt to cleanse his father's name, determined to create the perfect human being. Beginning with a blob of earth taken from a cesspool, Frankenstein created in his old age a living thing. Each succeeding Frankenstein generation developed the pulsating blob until, in Emil's time, a perfect baby girl was taken from the incubator. Years later, during a fight over the beautiful and adult "Louisa" between rival suitors, a bullet was accidentally fired into her lovely body, reducing her to a pile of decayed matter.

EC's satiric Mad comic book, edited by Harvey Kurtzman, frequently used the Frankenstein Monster. "Frank N. Stein" was published in the eighth issue of Mad (1953-54), illustrated by Bill Elder.[1] Frank N. Stein, the shortened version of Baron Francesco Napoleon Stein, with the help of his oafish assistant Bumble, created a Monster that escaped to threaten the armed might of the United States. When the Monster's face was finally revealed it was that of Hitler, complete with stitches and electrodes. At the end the Monster flapped his arms and flew away, for the brain stolen by Bumble was a bird brain.

When Mad went to the full-sized black and white format it remains today, the Frankenstein Monster made even more appearances. "Eccchh, Teenage Son of Thing," in Mad no. 40 (1958), illustrated by Wallace Wood, featured a brilliant Frankenstein Monster who created a teenage monster in the image of Elvis Presley (a favorite theme, to recur in the numerous imitations of Mad). Mad no. 85 (1964) did a spoof on Annie Get Your Gun titled "Mannie Get Your Ghoul," complete with songs, featuring the Frankenstein Monster and assorted fiends. Frank Jacobs wrote the script while Jack Richard did the artwork. Mad no. 89 (1964) featured the Monster assembling a model kit of the magazine's mascot Alfred E. Neuman, for which there was some copyright trouble with Universal Pictures.

The Marvels of Frankenstein

The greatest number of unrelated Frankenstein comic stories has been published by the Marvel Comics Group (known in the 1940s as Timely and during the 1950s as Atlas). No real continuity exists between the stories, as

was the case with the EC Frankenstein tales. During the
horror comics cycle, Atlas was EC's main rival, the stories
building to a surprise ending but stressing action and monsters rather than solid plot characterization and fine art.
Marvel's first real Frankenstein story appeared in USA
Comics no. 13 (1944). "The Curse of Frankenstein" and a
note written by Anna, Dr. Frankenstein's daughter, brought
Captain America, a superhero costumed to resemble a living
American flag, and his youthful partner Bucky to the infamous castle in Europe. Someone had revived the Monster
using the old Frankenstein records and equipment. Eventually the doctor's blind assistant attempted to have the
Monster kill the two red-white-and-blue-clad heroes, but
was himself thrown from the castle parapet by the artificial
being. Captain America then heroically rescued Anna and
lured the Monster into a quicksand bog.

A strange story "Horror at Haunted Castle" appeared
in Blonde Phantom (title changed from USA Comics) no. 14
(1947)--strange in that for no apparent explanation Baron
Frankenstein was drawn to look exactly like the Monster.
The Frankenstein castle had been removed to the United
States. The Blonde Phantom, a gorgeous masked heroine,
investigated when the castle's new owner was threatened by
the elusive Baron Frankenstein, who claimed to be after the
family treasure. Finally the Blonde Phantom defeated the
Baron/Monster and, holding him at gunpoint, discovered the
treasure in the family tomb.

With horror replacing heroes in popularity, Marvel
published "The Return of the Monster," by Syd Shores, in
Marvel Tales no. 96 (1950). An American, believing the
stories of Frankenstein to be true, journeyed to Castle
Frankenstein in Bavaria where he discovered more than he
expected. A group of fanatical scientists had captured the
latest (and last) Dr. Frankenstein and tortured him into revealing the secret of the Monster's revival. Going berserk
in the laboratory, the Monster killed the humans who had
given him new life, then lumbered away carrying Nina,
Frankenstein's daughter. Courageously the American fought
off the creature, then destroyed him in the castle's subterranean cavern with dynamite.

Marvel Tales no. 106 (1952) featured "The Monster,"
illustrated by Paul Reinman. A motion picture production
company went to the Frankenstein castle to make an authentic Frankenstein movie. The director was not content with

the gothic atmosphere and the make-up applied to Boris, the actor portraying the Monster. He insisted that the actual Frankenstein laboratory equipment be activated. Inadvertently the real Monster was revived and stalked into the scene dragging the lifeless body of Boris. Still grinding his camera, the fanatical director and the Frankenstein Monster both plunged from the castle parapet to be sucked into the quicksand below.

John Kent was another student of Frankenstein history in "The Monster's Son," published in Strange Tales no. 10 (1952), drawn by Jim Mooney. The Frankenstein Monster, after the death of his maker, created a son for himself and hid its ugly features under a life-like mask. Kent ventured to the castle after finding evidence of the existence of the Monster's son in a piece of old manuscript. After being pursued by the Monster through the mountains, Kent fell to his death. The Monster took off Kent's mask and lamented, "My son! My son!" "Vampire Maker" in Adventures into Weird Worlds no. 13 (1952) was an embellishment on the Frankenstein theme. In an Hungarian village particularly plagued by vampires, a scientist in an attempt to out-create von Frankenstein, gave life to an artificially made vampire monster that preyed upon the blood of other vampires.

The original Monster dug himself free from the earth which imprisoned him for years in "Your Name is Frankenstein," written by Stan Lee (the editor of the Marvel line of comics) drawn by Joe Manechy, and published in Menace no. 7 (1953). Desiring human companionship after so long a solitude, the creature again encountered the torches. Though he saved a husband and wife from their burning house, he was attacked by the villagers. At last the Monster lashed out at them and lumbered back to sink into the quagmire, preferring death to Mankind. The humans were the real monsters.

The final Frankenstein story in the series, published just before the arrival of the Comics Code Authority, was "The Lonely Dungeon" in Mystery Tales no. 18 (1954). Again an American went to the Frankenstein castle, now in Austria, believing that Frankenstein never created the Monster. At the castle he was given a tour by the old caretaker, who revealed that it was actually the Monster that created Frankenstein! As the American was approached by two Frankenstein Monsters, the keeper gloated, "But I made the original Monster ... and many others ... out of someone just like you! And now I'll do it again!"

Marvel published a rash of monster comic books, offshoots of their former horror magazines, in the early 1960s. Many of these, illustrated by Jack Kirby, the creator of Captain America, utilized the Frankensteinian theme of creating artificial and monstrous life. Creatures with various named like "The Thing Called ... It," "The Glob," and the monster of "Vandoom, the Man Who Made a Creature," lumbered about musty gothic castles and were pursued by torch-wielding villagers. One such monster, a growing amoeba starring in "I Created Sporr! The Thing that Could Not Die" in Tales of Suspense no. 11 (1960) was produced in the actual Frankenstein castle (which was apparently moved again, this time to the all-purpose monster haven Transylvania). In the tradition of Marvel Frankenstein stories, Sporr was lured into the inevitable pool of quicksand.

Marvel achieved its greatest successes in the late 1960s with its fresh approach to superhero comics. During this era the Frankenstein Monster made two significant appearances. A group of costumed mutants, the stars of The X-Men, fought the creature in "The Mark of the Monster," written by Roy Thomas and drawn by Don Heck for the fortieth issue (1968). Revived from the ice that imprisoned him since the climax of Mary Shelley's novel, the Monster fought the X-Men until he was destroyed by the freezing power of Iceman and exposed as an android sent to earth in the past by an alien race. No mention of androids or aliens was in "The Heir of Frankenstein," written by Stan Lee and illustrated by John Buscema in The Silver Surfer no. 7 (1969). In an attempt to destroy the hostile villagers storming his castle (now in the Alps), the new Frankenstein attempted to revive the Monster. The experiment was a failure and the Monster was apparently destroyed forever. He did, however, succeed in producing a duplicate of the Silver Surfer, a cosmic super-being, which attacked the villagers but (inevitably) was destroyed by the original.

Marvel's super-villains were constantly creating various Frankensteinian slaves to battle the legion of costumed heroes from that company. Enough of these robots and androids to form a Frankenstein Union have emerged from the laboratories and workshops of Marvel's most insidious masterminds. A more recent example is the Doomsman, a being created by Marvel's worst evil-doer Doctor Doom in a series beginning in Astonishing Tales no. 1 (1970), written by Roy Thomas and drawn by Wally Wood. After opposing his creator, the android was eventually exiled to another dimension.

New interest in horror comics flared in the early 1970s. Conforming to the relaxed restrictions of the Comics Code Authority, Marvel launched another series of diluted thrillers often using the Frankenstein format. "Mastermind," by Tom Sutton, in Chamber of Darkness no. 7 (1970) began with a passage from Frankenstein and showed the superior creature turn against his inferior creator. Igor, the assistant of Dr. Frankenstein's descendant, was glad to see his domineering master die in "Master and Slave," written by Al Hewetson and drawn by Syd Shores, published in Creatures on the Loose no. 12 (1971). Lonely, with no one to command him, Igor used Frankenstein's books to create his own being, but found to his consternation that the brain he used was none other than that of the original Baron Frankenstein. There was no opposing his monstrous master.

Marvel not only imitated the EC horror comics but also the highly successful Mad. Wild lacked the humor of the EC satire comics. In a typically unfunny story "Dr. Jackal and Mr. Hide," drawn by Bill Everett for Wild no. 1 (1954), the Monster lumbered about speaking with a Southern accent. Another Mad imitation, Marvel's in-joke magazine Not Brand Echh, presented "Frankenstein Sicksty-Nine," written by Arnold Drake and drawn by Tom Sutton for the twelfth issue (1969). This was an adaptation of the 1931 motion picture featuring lampoon versions of Marvel's regular characters. Baron von Doomstein created the Monster which threw a pretty flower child into the water-filled street gutter, carried his maker to the top of a discotheque called the Mindmill, and inevitably became a rock music star. (This ending has been used endlessly in magazine imitations of Mad.) A number of Marvel's heroes were also based upon Frankenstein, especially the original Human Torch and the Incredible Hulk. Professor Robert Horton created a living android in Marvel Comics no. 1 (1939). (Actually the character was created by artist Carl Burgos.) Upon exposure to the air the artificial being burst into flame and became known as the Human Torch. During his early adventures the Torch was a pathetic monster menacing all those that he encountered. Eventually he learned to control his flame and became a hero.

The Hulk, created by Stan Lee and Jack Kirby in The Incredible Hulk no. 1 (1962), was an adaptation of

Frankenstein and Dr. Jekyll and Mr. Hyde into a single concept upon their own admission. In an attempt to save young
Rick Jones from a gamma bomb explosion, scientist Dr. R.
Bruce Banner was caught in the blast, the result being per-
iodic transformations into a green (gray in the first story)
creature called the Hulk. The Hulk's appearance was patterned directly after the Frankenstein Monster and the
stories have stressed the alienation of the creature from
the human race. The Incredible Hulk has proven to be one
of Marvel's most successful titles. [2]

Frankenstein vs. Batman

The very first appearance of the Frankenstein Monster in a comic book was an adaptation of the film Son of
Frankenstein for the first issue of Movie Comics (1939)
published by Picture Comics (now known as National Periodical Publications, the company which pioneered the field
with such titles as Action Comics and Superman). The
adaptation was mostly faithful to the motion picture. Movie
stills combined with artwork made up the panels, the Monster having a green face.

Bob Kane's Batman and Robin, the Boy Wonder, de-
parted from their usual mystery stories in Detective Comics
no. 135 (1948) in "The True Story of Frankenstein." Professor Carter Nichols, using his technique of traveling
through time via hypnosis, ventured to the ancestral castle
of Baron Frankenstein. Ivan, the Baron's giant assistant,
stumbled into an electrostatic machine and was shocked into
a coma. Adrenalin, administered by Frankenstein's evil
cousin Count Mettern, revived Ivan as a mindless slave.
Nichols summoned Batman and Robin into the past to fight
the "monster" that was ravaging the countryside. When
Ivan's mind returned he seized Mettern and blew up the
castle. It was Batman who then related the story to Mary
Shelley, providing the basis for her novel.

House of Mystery no. 36 (1955) was the first issue of
that mild horror comic book to feature the Comics Code
seal, watering down the stories even more. The Frankenstein Monster was reduced from a living horror to a mere
mechanical man in "The Runaway Robot." Joey Frankenstein, weary of the stigma on the family name, decided to
create a beneficial robot. Inevitably the giant mechanical
boyscout fell under the control of criminals until Frankenstein

himself routed them.   A green-skinned monster resembling
that created by Frankenstein starred in "Return of the
Barsto Beast" in House of Mystery no. 116 (1961), illustrated
by Ruben Moreira.   A motion picture crew began filming the
ture story of the Frankensteinian Barsto Beast.   Inadvertently the real creature was substituted for the costumed
actor and revived by electricity.   When the monster's electrical energy was grounded, the Barsto Beast fell to a lifeless heap.

National created a Frankensteinian monster called
Bizarro, a pathetic creature with a cracked white face,
formed from lifeless matter into the image of Superboy in
Superboy no. 68 (1958).   Destroyed by Superboy, the "Thing
of Steel" was recreated as an adult in "Battle with Bizarro"
in Action Comics no. 254 (1959).   Bizarro frequently en-
countered manifestations of the original Frankenstein Mon-
ster.   Inevitably "Bizarro Meets Frankenstein," drawn by
Wayne Boring, was published in Superman no. 143 (1961).
Learning of the production of a new Frankenstein movie,
Bizarro attacked the actor portraying the Monster and set
out to prove that he was the most terrible monster of all.
In Adventure Comics no. 289 (1961), "Bizarro's Amazing
Buddies," he like Batman was given credit to inspiring Mary
Shelley to write Frankenstein.   The final creature to give
Mary Shelley inspiration was the green giant in "The Fron-
tier Frankenstein," published in Tomahawk no. 103 (1966).
A German scientist working for the British during the
American Revolution used strange jungle herbs to transform
a frontiersman into a monster.   At last, in the heat of a
blazing fire, the "monster" regained his normal shape with
the suggestion that, again, Mrs. Shelley had heard the tale.

Humorous Frankenstein Monsters have often appeared
in National's comic books.   Franklyn Stein (later changed
to Frank N. Stein) was the physical education instructor in
a strange high school first introduced in The Adventures of
Bob Hope no. 95 (1965), "Super Hip, the Sickest Super-Hero
of 'em All," written by Arnold Drake, art by Bob Oskner.
The series lasted three years.   National featured various
other continuing Frankenstein-type characters in its magazines.   King Killer, a fanged, stitched-together monster
made from corpses was a frequent villain in Will Eisner's
Uncle Sam Quarterly (published by Comic Magazines, later
to be bought out by National), first appearing in the pre-
mier issue (1941).   Robotman, featuring a robot given a
human brain, first appeared in Star Spangled Comics no. 7

(1942); another version of the character starred in <u>The</u> <u>Doom Patrol</u>, a series beginning in <u>My Greatest Adventure</u> no. 80 (1963). Solomon Grundy was a chalky-faced creature formed by bits of vegetation forming on a human skeleton lying in a bog for fifty years, producing a bizarre distortion of life in "Fighters Never Quit," by Paul Reinman in the "Green Lantern" strip in <u>All-American Comics</u> no. 61 (1944). The character haunted a number of early comic books and was revived in the late 1960s. [3] A more recent magazine, lasting only two issues, was <u>The Geek</u>, by Joe Orlando, published in 1968. It featured a dummy brought to life by light, heat, and electricity acting upon the blood- and oil-stained cloth of its body.

Stories using the Frankenstein Monster and theme were often used by other comics publishing houses. <u>Dr.</u> <u>Mortal</u>, by Godfrey Clarke, was a continuing series which began in the first issue of <u>Weird Comics</u> (1939), from Fox Publications. The mad scientist delighted in creating horrible monsters. Taking various corpses of men and lions, Dr. Mortal used his Frankensteinian laboratory to give life to a pack of savage beast-men in the second issue. The creatures were destroyed in a laboratory fire. Dr. Mortal placed a human brain in a Frankenstein robot in the third issue (1940). As the creature lumbered across the roof of a building it was destroyed by a death ray.

Dr. Sivana, "the world's maddest scientist," must have read the second installment of <u>Dr. Mortal</u>. In <u>Captain</u> <u>Marvel Adventures</u> no. 3 (1941) Sivana used the same raw materials to create his lion-man--the Beast-Ruler, who controlled animals until young Billy Batson shouted "Shazam!" and Captain Marvel flew in to knock the creature off a cliff and over a waterfall. In "Unsoo the Unseen," <u>Captain Marvel Adventures</u> no. 6, the magical super-hero tangled with a look-alike of the Frankenstein Monster until the eye of Medusa turned the fiend to marble. Classic Comics (now Classics Illustrated) devoted issue no. 26 (1945) to <u>Franken-</u><u>stein</u>. This was a faithful adaptation of the Mary Shelley novel by Ruth A. Roche, illustrated by Robert Hayward Webb and Ann Brewster. The story reads like a scene for scene breakdown of a definitive Frankenstein motion picture.

Some of the 1950s horror comics used creatures looking almost exactly like the Frankenstein Monster of the movies, but in stories not using the name. "No Grave to Hold Him" in Ace Magazines' <u>Challenge of the Unknown</u> no. 6

(1950) told of the transplanting of a scientist's brain into a body composed of sections of corpses of criminals. The criminal elements prevailed until an adjusted rheostat brought out the good side of the monster. A similar tale "Dead Man's Revenge," by Jay Disbrow, in Star Publications' Shocking Mystery Cases no. 50 (1952) concerned an artificially created monster with a criminal brain. After being given life in the laboratory, the creature killed one of his creators and then the man responsible for the death of his original body. In the end the second scientist who performed the life-giving experiment electrocuted the giant monster.

In The Ghost Rider no. 10 (1952), published by Magazine Enterprises, the white-clad Western hero met a bizarre opponent in "Ghost Rider vs. Frankenstein," drawn by Dick Ayers. After being caught in a windmill set ablaze by villagers, and escaping through a tunnel leading under a nearby graveyard, the Monster of Count Frankenstein supposedly stole a boat and sailed to America. The "Frankenstein Monster" began a campaign of murder until the Ghost Rider defeated him with his spectral tricks and unmasked the creature as a normal human being. He had adopted the guise to kill all those in the way of his acquiring a gold mine while placing the blame on the Monster.

Harvey Publications' horror comics presented several Frankensteinian stories in 1952. In "Monster Maker," published in Witches Tales no. 11 Professor Julian Arnstein gave life to a body of his own creation. Because the brain stolen by his bumbling assistant was that of a criminal the monster destroyed them both, then stalked out into the night. In "The Body Maker," published in Black Cat Mystery no. 39, a grotesque hunchbacked scientist, using Frankenstein's notes and possessed of his spirit, became a Jack the Ripper type in order to secure the parts for his perfect woman. A mad scientist created his own monster in "Graveyard Monsters," published in Tomb of Terror no. 4. After the creature came to life, the scientist's source of supply--the corpses of his enemies with their missing members--pursued him. He escaped only to be killed by the being he created.

The least violent and offensive comic books were published by Dell. Their own pledge to parents managed to get them by the Comics Code without requiring a seal of approval. As a result the tame magazines were putting that line of comics out of business. In 1963 Dell, to stay in

business, shocked the comics world--especially the parents
to whom they were pledged--by printing a series of one-
shot horror comics including Frankenstein. The Karloffian
Monster was created by Dr. Frankenstein in an imitation of
the 1931 movie. Frankenstein, his servant Fritz, and the
Monster were forced to flee their homeland to America.
The creature had been hypnotically commanded to kill by
his maker. The story ended with the Monster apparently
dying aboard a burning, sinking ship, with the hint of a
sequel. That sequel did not come until three years later
in a series illustrated by Tony Tallarico. But there were
some incredible changes. By then, super-heroes were the
fad mainly due to the popularity of the Batman television
program. Lightning struck the Frankenstein castle and revived the creature lying on a slab within. He was clothed
in a tight-fitting red costume, had a green face, and neatly
trimmed white hair. He was the Frankenstein Monster, now
incarnated as a muscular super-hero. Adopting the secret
identity of Frank Stone (from a broken rock slab containing
only the first part of the name) and wearing a life-like human mask, Frankenstein devoted his life to battling crime.
In Frankenstein no. 4 (1967), "Trouble Comes in Three's,"
Frankenstein revealed that his familiar green face was also
a mask. As for his real appearance, readers never learned
that secret. That was the final issue of Frankenstein.

The Little Monsters was a long-running series,
similar to The Munsters in format, beginning in 1964 in
Western Publishing Company's (Gold Key) Three Stooges
comic book. Later that year The Little Monsters was published as a separate magazine. The Monster family all
resembled the Frankenstein creature and was comprised of
such weird members as Mildew, his wife Demonica, and
their two children Orrible Orvie and Awful Annie. Merchandise items such as coloring books featuring the characters followed.

Various Frankenstein series have been published in
foreign comic books. Frankenstein, published by Edição la
Selva from 1959-1960, began with the Monster living in a
subterranean den of zombies and hooded madmen. Some of
the stories borrowed generously from the Briefer art and
plots. A number of artists drew the stories, which accounted for the Monster's frequent change in appearance.
Simply called Frankenstein, the giant killed without compassion and encountered any number of vampires and mad
scientists. An extremely short-lived second Frankenstein

comic book series was published in 1959 by Editora Penteado
and was labeled, for no apparent reason, "adults only." The
first story picked up after the Mary Shelley ending, with the
Monster's frozen body discovered and revived by lightning.
Unlike the first South American Frankenstein Monster, this
one could be reasoned with before violence erupted and occasionally he did good deeds.   Both series were published
in black and white in Rio de Janeiro.

       The Heap, a lumbering monster created when a pilot
fell into a vat of chemicals and based on a similar character appearing in Airboy Comics during the 1940s, met Dr.
Frankenstein's descendant in "Shadows of Satan."   Dr.
Frankenstein attempted to introduce the Heap to the world
as his creation until the brute went berserk and escaped his
laboratory.   The story appeared in The Heap no. 1, published
in 1971 by Skywald Publishing Corporation, written by Bob
Kanigher with artwork by Tom Sutton.

The Creepy Frankensteins

       As the Comics Code Authority did not apply to the
larger sized magazines, the Warren Publishing Company began a series of black and white illustrated horror magazines
in the early 1960s.   Creepy was the first comic magazine in
the Warren line and included many Frankenstein stories, the
early ones written by story editor Archie Goodwin.   "Ward-
robe of Monsters," illustrated by Gray Morrow for Creepy
no. 2 (1965), and written in this instance by Otto Binder instead of Goodwin, involved the discovery of a pharoah's tomb.
Included in the tomb were extra sarcophagi with ancient versions of a vampire, werewolf, devil, and the Frankenstein
Monster.   A greedy archaeologist, wanting all of the pha-
raoh's treasure for himself, learned that he could project
his spirit into each body to kill the other members of the
expedition.   To his consternation he found himself trapped
within the Frankenstein body forever.

       Uncle Creepy, the magazine's host, was given an
origin in "Monster Rally," drawn by Angelo Torres in the
fourth issue.   In Transylvania, Dr. Habeas, using the
methods of Frankenstein, attempted to find the secret of
immortality.   His guinea pigs were all immortal beings--a
Frankenstein monster of his own creation, a vampire, a
living mummy, and others.   Inevitably the villagers set his
laboratory ablaze.   The fire, the full moon, and the

immortality fluid all acting upon the dying monsters gave
"birth" to the infant Uncle Creepy.

A scientist used his assistant's brain for his own
Frankensteinian creation in "Monster," illustrated by Rocco
Mastroserio in Creepy no. 10 (1966). In classic tradition,
after being hounded by the usual villagers, the monster
turned upon his master and dragged him into a bog of quicksand. The hunchbacked Gypsy Hurklos wanted a new body,
which was granted him in the Frankensteinian body assembled
in "Piece by Piece," drawn by Joe Orlando for Creepy no.
14 (1967). After coming to life, the monster killed his
creator, then attacked the villagers in revenge against those
who tormented Hurklos. In a bizarre climax the mutilated
corpses emerged from their graves to call back the organs
that had been stolen from them. Only the hideous head of
the monster was later found.

A scientist blackmailed a student whom he caught
cheating on a test into helping him secure the parts for a
female monster in "The Frankenstein Tradition," drawn by
Mastroserio for Creepy no. 16. The student obtained most
of his parts from victims he killed in the Whitechapel dis-
trict of London where he became known as Jack the Ripper.
In the following issue's "Image in Wax," illustrated by Tom
Sutton, wax statues of the Frankenstein Monster and other
horrors came to life to enact their evil. Jorgo, a former
clown became the Friendly Frankenstein on a television
children's show in "Frankenstein is a Clown," written by
Bill Warren with art by Carlos Garzon in Creepy no. 36
(1970). After a fatal car accident, Jorgo's brain fell into
the surgical hands of a mad doctor who placed it in the
skull of a real Frankenstein-type monster. Back on the
television set, the intense lights warped the brain. The
monster kidnapped one of his youthful fans. Then realizing
the horror of what he had become, he leapt through a window to his death.

Eerie was Warren's followup magazine to Creepy,
again with Goodwin scripting the early tales. "Footsteps of
Frankenstein," illustrated by Reed Crandall, appeared in the
second issue (1966). Dr. Byron King visited Dr. Sebastian
in Northern England to find that he had created a living
monster. The creature's brain allowed it to function only
in a limited manner. The aged King convinced the other
scientist to transfer his brain into the monster's skull.
Sebastian performed the operation, then learned that King

was a homicidal killer wanting an all-powerful body.
As the beast stormed out to attack the villagers, the
same force which gave him life--electricity--shot from the
stormy heavens and incinerated him. "Monsterwork," art
by Mastroserio, in the next issue, was the standard plot of
a mad scientist promising to remove the hump from the
back of his assistant Otto if he helped with the creation of
his monster. The doctor then ordered his living creation
to kill Otto, but the being refused and turned against his
maker. The brain had been taken from a man on the gallows. That executed criminal was Otto's brother.

Eerie, no. 6 not only featured a full page devoted to
the creation of "The Man-Made Monster," drawn by John
Severin, but also the story "Point of View," illustrated by
Mastroserio. The inmate of an insane asylum claimed to
be Dr. Frankenstein and boasted that the stitched giant
(actually just another inmate, committed as a child) was his
Monster. When the inmates escaped in order to be free of
the cruel director of the asylum, the giant captured him.
The director awakened to find his brain in the skull of the
"Monster," put there by the laughing "Victor Frankenstein."
"The Monster from One Million B.C.," written and drawn
by Tom Sutton in Eerie no. 11 (1967), centered upon a mad
motion picture special effects man. Everyone raved about
his monsters, including the one used in the Frankenstein
films. His secret was that he took great effort to provide
the studio with the authentic creatures.

In "Monstrous Mistake," written by Bill Parente and
drawn by Barry Rockwell, in Eerie no. 19 (1968), Dr. Spool
took the brain of a jeering scientist he killed and transplanted it into a corpse. Then he brought the rotting creature with its temple electrodes to life. But Spool met a
grisly fate when he discovered that the body he had stolen
for the brain was that of a bloodthirsty werewolf. The son
of Baron Victor Frankenstein regained the brain of his
father, killed by the Monster, in "The Brain of Frankenstein," written by Fred Ott with art by Mike Ploog, in
Eerie no. 40 (1972). Young Christian Frankenstein put the
brain in his own stitched together monster. But when the
new creature was killed by a vengeful assistant, Christian
switched their brains, thereby giving his father's gray matter a less repulsive home, and leaving the assistant at the
mercy of the villagers.

Warren's third illustrated horror magazine was

Vampirella which emphasized naked or near naked girls.
The second issue (1969) featured "The Bride of Frankenstein," a full-page story by Sutton.   Bill Warren's "For
the Love of Frankenstein," with art by Jack Sparling, was
published in Vampirella no. 4 and has the basic plot of the
film La Figlia di Frankenstein, made some years afterwards.
Hedvig Krollek, the voluptuous grand-niece of Dr. Frankenstein, teased and humiliated the hunchbacked Dr. Eric Hoffstein into using his surgical skill to create a perfect male
body.   Finally she killed Hoffstein and placed his brain in
the monster's head.   When Hoffstein awakened in his new
body, he declared his hatred for Hedvig, strangled and cre-
mated her, then blew up the castle along with himself.

    Other publishers soon produced their own magazines
to capitalize on the success of the company headed by James
Warren.   Eerie Publications, edited by Carl Burgos, presented a line of horror magazines, mostly reprints of comic
book stories from the early 1950s, which would become notorious for their nauseating covers, many featuring the
Frankenstein Monster.   Weird no. 1 (1966) featured the lead
story "Frankenstein," by Roger Elwood and Burgos.   The
story was based upon the original novel.   Alienated from
the world, the Monster welcomed the bolt of lightning which
finally destroyed him.   Terror Tales, vol. 2, no. 2 (1970),
featured "The Dead Demons," in which a Frankensteinian
creature and the zombie corpses that had supplied its organs
destroyed the inevitable mad scientist, then sank beneath
the river.   "A Thing of Horror" in Tales of Voodoo, vol. 4,
no. 4 (1971), concerned a giant wooden Frankenstein monstrosity, brought to life by human blood, and eventually destroyed by fire.   Web of Horror no. 2 (1970), published by
Major Magazines, featured "The Unmasking," written by
Wilson Shard and drawn by Alfred Payan (Tony Talarico of
the Dell Frankenstein comic book).   A group of Halloween
partygoers went to a haunted house for fun, to scare the
normal people inside.   At midnight the residents removed
their human masks to reveal a group of real monsters, including that created by Frankenstein.

    Psycho, a horror magazine from the Skywald Pub-
lishing Corporation, began a series of Frankenstein in its
third issue (1971).   The first installment, "Frankenstein
Book II," began after the climax of the Mary Shelley novel,
with the Monster salvaging his maker's corpse from the icy
waters of the Arctic, taking it back to the Frankenstein
castle in Europe.   The Monster had a brilliant mind and

Page from "Freaks of Fear," the second installment of the Frankenstein series, by Sean Todd (Tom Sutton) in Psycho, no. 4. Copyright 1971 by Skywald Publishing Company.

was able to create a second living horror, transplanting
Frankenstein's head to the composite corpse he had assembled.   When the corpse was hacked to pieces by the villagers, Frankenstein's still living head was taken away by the
evil Dr. Pretorius.   In later stories, the Frankenstein
Monster went to France where he met Quasimodo, the hunchback of Notre Dame, and even the Phantom of the Opera.
Using a weird organ capable of warping time with its vibra-
tions, the Phantom inadvertently sent the Frankenstein Monster into the future.   Frankenstein, written and drawn by
Sean Todd (Tom Sutton), tried to combine elements from
the Mary Shelley novel and the Universal movies.   The
Monster spoke with the same verbosity as the character in
the novel which, when applied to a modern comic strip,
became tedius.

Magazines devoted to movie monsters have also
printed Frankenstein comic strips.   Magsyn's World Famous
Creatures no. 1 (1958) featured "The Frankenstein Fable," a
spoof.   The Curse of Frankenstein was adapted by Russ
Jones and Joe Orlando to strip form in the third issue of
Warren's Monster World (1965).   "Frankenstein '68," by
Jerry Grandenetti, was published in Major Magazines' For
Monsters Only no. 6 (1968).   After his creation, the Monster
disrupted a motion picture set.   Then, like King Kong, he
climbed to the top of the Empire State Building where he
was destroyed by lightning.   In 1969 Italy's I Classici a
Fumetti series of paperback comics featured Frankenstein.
Again this was an adaptation from the original novel, but
without the accuracy of the Classic Comics version.   The
story ended with the confrontation between creator and creature on the ice flats instead of Captain Walton's ship.   After
Frankenstein died from the cold, the Monster walked into the
icy sea.

The Frankenstein theme has been satirized countless
times in humor magazines, most of which have been imitations of Mad.   Harvey Kurtzman's Humbug no. 7 (1958) presented "Frankenstien and His Monster," drawn by Bill Elder
from Kurtzman's layouts in an extremely accurate satire on
the 1931 movie.   Mad imitations like Cracked, Loco, Frenzy,
Zany, Nuts, and Panic, to name some, frequently ran humorous Frankenstein stories, usually, it seemed, with the
redundant ending of the Monster resembling Elvis Presley.
One such magazine, Counterpoint's Thimk, introduced the
Frankensteinian Otis Dracenstein in the third issue (1958).
Otis, his wife Trixie, and children Boris and Minnie

enjoyed domestic adventures similar to The Munsters of
later years.   The stories continued through 1959.   Charles
Addams very likely patterned the giant butler of his weird
family of cartoon characters after Karloff as the Frankenstein Monster.   In 1964 the characters became the stars of
a television series The Addams Family, with Ted Cassidy
in the role of the butler, now given the name Lurch. [4]

For over thirty years the Frankenstein theme has
been a part of the illustrated story.   While super-heroes
have come and flown away, the creations of Victor Frankenstein and the hordes of mad scientists who followed him
continue to emerge from the ashes and graves of the past.

Notes

1.   Kurtzman and Elder are most recently known for their
     Little Annie Fanny strip in Playboy.

2.   The success of the Hulk has resulted in a number of
     commercially successful side ventures.   A color
     cartoon television series Marvel Super-Heroes fea-
     tured the Hulk in 1967.   The three-part episodes
     were adapted with limited animation from the actual
     stories and artwork appearing in the Hulk magazine.
     The Hulk has been the subject of records (such as
     Nobody Loves the Hulk by the Traits for Queen City
     Records), posters, T-shirts, a pizzaria in Iowa City,
     sweatshirts, stationery, mini-books, decals, stickers,
     buttons, statues, model kits (by Aurora), a paper
     back reprint of The Incredible Hulk published in
     1966 by Lancer Books, bubble gum comics and cards,
     and other paraphernalia.   A Hulk comic book was one of
     the props in the film T. R. Baskin (Paramount 1971).

3.   In October, 1971, this writer appeared on a news pro-
     gram, filmed for television in Mexico, as Solomon
     Grundy.   The film was taken at the masquerade ball
     at the first Witchcraft and Sorcery Convention in Los
     Angeles.

4.   "Lurch" was merchandized in the usual paraphernalia that
     accompanies popular television series, including a Capi-
     tol record called The Lurch by Cassidy, lunch boxes,
     toys, and the like.   In 1972 the Charles Addams versions
     of the entire family appeared as cartoon characters in an
     episode of Scooby Doo (CBS).

Chapter 12

FRANKENSTEIN STRIKES AGAIN AND AGAIN ... AND AGAIN

Frankenstein's Monster has proven himself to be most durable. His image has been captured by all popular media and more people have heard of the hideous creature than they have of many current political giants. The most popular exhibits in wax museums seem to be those in the "chamber of horrors." While the horrors were usually limited to torture devices and infamous historical figures, more recently the Frankenstein Monster, Count Dracula, and other characters from horror fiction have assumed that place of honor. The House of Wax on Fisherman's Wharf in San Francisco features the Monster, basically the Karloff version from Bride of Frankenstein. A Frankenstein Monster quite closely resembling Karloff sits in a chair in a Tokyo wax museum. The Movieland Wax Museum in Buena Park, California, recreated a scene in the windmill from the 1931 Frankenstein. [1]

Madame Tussaud's Hollywood Wax Museum first exhibited an original Frankenstein Monster with curly hair, more resembling Cesare from Das Kabinett des Dr. Caligari, but later replaced it with a new dummy wearing a Don Post/ Glenn Strange custom mask. The versions in Tussaud's Royal London Wax Museum in Chicago's Old Town and at St. Petersburg Beach, Florida, were variations on the Karloff Monster. A Karloffian wax dummy of the Monster carried a wax child in an exhibit at the New York World's Fair in 1964. Ted Selay of Vincetown, New Jersey, formerly a set designer at Republic Pictures, constructs six-foot seven-inch statues of the Monster while Hollywood's House of Horrors rents out a dummy of the Monster for parties and other affairs. The Haunted House, a Hollywood nightclub, featured a mechanical dummy of the Monster made by Don Post and Sky Highchief in 1966. Cortlandt B. Hull's Witch's Dungeon in Bristol, Connecticut, includes exhibits of the Monster and Dr. Niemann (from <u>House of Franken-stein</u>), using Post masks.   Dummies of the Monster have also haunted the "spook house" rides at amusement parks like Coney Island in New York.

Don Post made his first Frankenstein Monster rubber mask in 1948 for Glenn Strange's personal appearances with <u>Abbott and Costello Meet Frankenstein</u>.   Universal author-ized Post to commercially make and sell the masks.   In the 1950s Post made a full-head Karloff Frankenstein mask and a full-face Strange mask, both painted green, the color which stuck with the public.   During the 1960s he increased the quality of his masks with several gray, custom masks, one taken from a mold of Glenn Strange's face and a newly sculpted one of Karloff as the Monster and Dr. Niemann. He also made a pair of Frankenstein Monster hands.   While Don Post made the only authorized Frankenstein masks other companies created inferior and often completely orig-inal versions of the Monster in rubber or cheesecloth (some with printed costumes for young children) which flood toy and novelty stores every Halloween.   Ellis Berman, who worked on the make-up in <u>The Ghost of Frankenstein</u>, did his own commercial mask of the Monster, basing it on the Universal character.

Cafe Frankenstein was a coffee house in Laguna Beach, California in the 1950s.   A stained glass window of the Monster, by Burt Shonberg, became the trademark of this establishment which served such drinks as Frankenstein Cap and Hot Chocolate au Frankenstein.   The cafe was once drawn into the comic strip <u>The Tootles</u>, by Baers.   An etching of the Frankenstein Monster hangs on the wall of the Pan American Building's "Flicker Room" at the Los Angeles International Airport.   Restaurants all across the country have been named Frank & Stein or Frank 'n' Stein to show they sell hot dogs and beer.   A chain of Franken-stein restaurants was planned by Universal Pictures during the height of <u>The Munsters</u> popularity.   The project never materialized.   Perhaps Universal feared the customers might worry over the origin of their meat.

Record albums have featured the Frankenstein Mon-ster.   <u>Famous Monsters Speak</u> (A. S. Records, 1963), writ-ten by Cherney Berg, had the voice of Gabriel Dell as the Monster supposedly on crude records made by Dr. Franken-stein recently discovered.   In the style of dramatic radio the Monster related his "birth," his vow to kill all mankind,

his love for a girl, the added electrical shocks given by his
creator, his escape from chains, and his killing of Dr.
Frankenstein, growling, "I warn you, no one is safe from
me! Which one of you is next?" Themes from Horror
Movies (Coral, 1960), by Dick Jacobs and his Orchestra,
included P. Dessau and Hans J. Salter's title music from
House of Frankenstein in a new rendition.   Commentary on
the Monster and pieces of dialogue from Frankenstein,
Bride of Frankenstein, Son of Frankenstein, and House of
Frankenstein were presented by Boris Karloff from a script
by Forrest J Ackerman in An Evening with Boris Karloff
and His Friends.   Ackerman also recorded Music for Ro-
bots (1962), scripted by Frank Coe, featuring commentary
on Metropolis and a short dramatization of a "Metallic
Frankenstein."   The soundtrack of the Frankenstein movie
Mad Monster Party? was made available by RCA.   In 1971
Dick Gregory's album Frankenstein (Sugar Bear) kidded
society.   Strictly musical albums have also used the Frankenstein Monster, including: Power Records' series by
"Frankie Stein" (Introducing Frankie Stein and His Ghouls,
Shock! Terror! Fear!, Ghoul Music, Monster Melodies,
and Monster Screams and Dance Music);   The Original
Monster Mash (Garpax), with Bobby "Boris" Pickett (imita-
ting Karloff, Lugosi, and others) and the Crypt-Kickers
with such numbers as "Monster Mash," "Rabian--the
Fiendage Idol," "Graveyard Shift," "Skully Gully," "Monster
Minuet," "Transylvania Twist," "Sinister Stomp," "Monster
Motion," "Monster Mash Party," "Irresistible Igor," and
"Bella's Bash."   Monster Rally by Hans Conreid featured
the Monster and a musician named "Frank N. Stein";   a
rock group called The Electric Mouse featured an album
song about going to Frankenstein's castle, while Bill Cosby
used the character on a Fat Albert record;   Spike Jones in
Stereo (also in Hi-Fi, from Warner Brothers) used the Mon-
ster especially in his lament song "Everything Happens to
Me," with Paul Frees imitating Karloff;   Monster Shindig
(Hanna-Barbera), by Danny Hutton (later to become one of
the Three Dog Night);   and Monster Dance Party (Capitol),
by Don Hinson and the Rigormorticians, with "Riboflavin-
Flavored, Non-Carbonated, Polyunsaturated Blood" and
"Monster Jerk" in an imitation of the Pickett records.
Single records featuring the Frankenstein Monster include:
"Frankenstein's Den" (Ebb), by the Hollywood Flames;
"Dinner with Drac" (Cameo), by John Zacherle (who became
Zacherly on New York television's Shock Theatre);   "Mon-
ster's Holiday," by Pickett (later recorded by Lon Chaney);
"Merlin Jones" and "The Scrambled Egghead" (Buena Vista) by

"Annett" (Funicello);   "Frankenstein Twist" (Philles), by the
Crystals;   Frankenstein and Johnny;   "Will the Real Frankenstein Please Stand Up" by the Zanies;   and the French "Sur-
boum chez Dracula," "Frankenstein," "Frankenstein et Dracula," and Paul Dewitt's "Frankenstein Tromp."   The lyrics
to a song "Oh, My Darling Frankenstein" appeared in a
1960s issue of the folk music magazine Sing Out.

    Various film companies have made condensed ver-
sions of Frankenstein films available as home movies in
numerous editions--sound or silent;   black and white or
color;   16mm, 8mm, or Super 8.   Castle Films has released Frankenstein, Bride of Frankenstein, Son of Frankenstein, Frankenstein Meets the Wolf Man, House of Frankenstein (with a second part titled Doom of Dracula), and
Abbott and Costello Meet Frankenstein.   Americom has released The Curse of Frankenstein (with a second part titled
The Birth of Frankenstein).   Columbia has made available
The Revenge of Frankenstein.   I Was a Teenage Frankenstein, Frankenstein Meets the Space Monster, Frankenstein
Must Be Destroyed, and the cartoon Frankenstein's Cat may
be purchased from Ken Films.   Frankenstein's Daughter
(with a second part titled She Monster of the Night) is sold
by Entertainment Films.   And the cartoon Magoo Meets
Frankenstein can be bought from United Arista.

    With the dawning "monster craze" in the early 1960s,
Aurora created a plastic Frankenstein Monster assembly kit.
The success of the model kit inspired a number of monster
kits from that company, including the Bride of Frankenstein,
Frankenstein's Flivver (the Monster sitting in a bizarre
automobile), the king-sized Big Frankie with movable arms,
plus the Munsters and the Munster Koach.   Various advertisements have used the Frankenstein Monster.   The Monster (made-up model) advertised General Electric flashbulbs
in 1964.   Paul Ford wore the greenish make-up and sat
afraid in a chair in an ad for Smirnoff Vodka in 1968.   A
dummy of the Monster showed the effect of colored lights
in a 1970 ad for General Telephone and Electronics.   A
1970 ad drawn by Gahan Wilson showed the Monster wearing
Esquire Socks.   In 1971 he helped sell Doral cigarettes.

    Frankenstein's Monster seems to be eternally a com-
mercial product.   He has been the gimmick in Frankenstein
key chains, belt buckles, tie clips, Little Monster Cookies,
fan clubs, posters (some that glow in the dark), bubble gum
cards (including the series You'll Die Laughing drawn in

the late 1950s by Jack Davis), greeting cards, a bald and
fanged Frankenstein Monster that loses its pants and blushes,
iron-ons, transfers, wallets, wall placques, toys that walk
or bob their heads, Horrorscope Movie Viewer (with flip
books of the Monster), Frankenstein head radio speaker,
rings, bracelets, necklaces, bubble bath, oil paint by
numbers sets, Frankenstein Mystery Game, puzzles,
loose-leaf binders, dart boards, make-up kits, decals,
socks, stamps, handkerchiefs, spoons, calendars, statues,
coloring books, T-shirts, drinking mugs, banks, shopping
bags, View-Master stereo reels, rubber automobile mirror
ornaments, pencil sharpeners, coats of arms, sweat shirts,
35mm color slides, birthday cakes, cardboard Bride of
Frankenstein dolls with paper clothes, card games, bicycle
flaps, Mon-Stirs swizzle sticks, buttons, and candy.

    The appeal of the Frankenstein Monster and theme is
certainly unique.   The story has been told through all popular media since its first publication in 1818 and seems to
indeed possess all the eternal life sought by Percy Shelley
and given by Victor Frankenstein.   Surely it is strange for
a creature made from parts of corpses to be so appealing
and to have captured an entire generation of children too
young to have seen any of the Universal Frankenstein movies
when they still had general runs in movie theatres.   Perhaps the appeal lies with current news items about highly
sophisticated computers, heart transplants, and the quest
for scientists to discover the origins of life.   But more
important, the appeal lies with our own identification with
the Monster, basically a human character, misunderstood
and despised by all, according to his real creator Mary
Shelley.   Everyone of us has felt such paranoia whereby
we are not treated as we believe we should be by our peers.
In that sense the title of David Cramer's article for the
April, 1970 issue of Go is most appropriate: "We Are All
Frankenstein." Perhaps therein lies the true appeal of
Frankenstein.

<u>Note</u>

1.   The scene is included in a color, 8mm souvenir film
        entitled <u>Movieland Wax Museum</u>, available in camera
        stores, drug stores, and other places selling photo-
        graphic supplies.

AFTERWORD

As I stated in the Preface, there would probably be numerous films, stories and the like which would be announced or completed between the end of the writing of The Frankenstein Legend and its publication. Now, reading proof, I see how correct I was! Since, however, this is only an Afterword, I'll just briefly mention some of the more important of these new entries.

In 1972, Hammer Films went into production of Frankenstein and the Monster from Hell, directed by Terence Fisher, and starring Peter Cushing as the Baron and Dave Prowse as the Monster. American-International announced two titles, Blackenstein (The Black Frankenstein) and The Fall of the House of Blackenstein, while independent producer Frank Seletri went into production of The Return of Blackenstein, with electrical devices by Strickfaden. Frankenstein 1980, made in Italy, featured a muscle-bound monster named Mosaico equipped with a self-destruct mechanism by Dr. Frankenstein. After killing his maker, Mosaico had but 48 hours to live. A Spanish version of the original Frankenstein was announced. The Monster was featured in the English Count Downe, starring Ringo Starr, the Italian House of Freaks, starring Rossano Brazzi as Count Frankenstein, and Schooling, a Yugoslavian cartoon (all 1973). And the American-International film Konga became known in Germany as Konga--Frankensteins Gorilla.

Regarding the "silent Frankensteins," it has been learned that a Danish version of The Golem was made in 1916, directed by Urban Gad, and Des Golems letztes Abenteuer ("The Golem's Last Adventure") was made in Austria in 1921 by Sascha-Film. And a version of The Golem was planned in the 1930s to star Boris Karloff. The Golem fought the Nazis in "Thou Shalt Not Kill," a story illustrated by Neal Adams in National's Weird War Tales #8 (1972). There was also an hour-long radio dramatization of

The Cabinet of Dr. Caligari on WNIB-FM radio (Chicago) on
11 January 1972.

On stage in 1972, the Monster was featured in the
H. R. Puff 'n' Stuff live show.   There was also a rock
instrumental record called "Frankenstein," by Edgar Winter,
and a new restaurant in San Francisco called "Frankenstein's."

In 1972, Gallery Press published Monster Sex Tales,
featuring a number of pornographic Frankenstein stories:
"The Birth of Frankenstein," by Ronna Fronk, told of sexually repressed Victor Frankenstein who used a pervert's
brain in his Monster and brought it to life by sexual stimu-
lation;   "A Perfect Crime," by Johan Krumholtz, had the
Monster kill a thief;   "Frankenstein: Raging Sex Monster,"
by Lorna Dunne, had the creature rape a young woman;   and
in "Igor," by Enoch Rosengarten, the beast found a woman
who enjoyed his brutal love-making.   "Rape! Monster! Rape!"
by Frederick Fallon, in the February 1973 issue of Gem
magazine, was about a woman sexually aroused by a man in
a Frankenstein's Monster costume.   More in the family line
was Franklin Stein, a charming book by Ellen Raskin, published by Atheneum in 1972, about a lonely boy who built a
monstrous friend out of junk.   Recently discovered is "Make
Me a Monster" in the first issue of Riot, an Atlas comic
book published in 1954.   A Frankenstein-type monster became smart enough to kill his creators and use the parts
of their bodies in building his own friend.

Marvel Comics began a series of books entitled The
Monster of Frankenstein, written by Gary Friedrich and illustrated by Mike Ploog, in what may become the finest
Frankenstein comics series of all.   The white-faced Monster
is characterized as by Mary Shelley.   The first issue is
dated January 1973.   National lauched its own series, The
Spawn of Frankenstein, written by Marvin Wolfman and drawn
by Mike Kaluta, in the February 1973 issue of The Phantom
Stranger (number 23).   The Monster is portrayed as a
greenish, partially decomposed corpse.   The sixth issue
(winter 1973) of The Occult Files of Dr. Spektor, a feature
created and scripted by this writer for Gold Key, features
"The Dungeon of Frankenstein," drawn by Jesse Santos.   In
this one the Monster returns to force Frankenstein's descendant to create his mate.

Finally, Dan Curtis presented a two-part (90 minutes
each) television adaptation of Frankenstein on the "ABC Wide

World of Entertainment" in January 1973, starring Robert
Foxworth as Victor and Bo Svenson as "The Giant." Svenson
had long blond hair and a scarred face and played the role
with faithfulness to the Shelley character.   The taped teleplay
reasonably followed the original novel.

Obviously, the Frankenstein Monster is immortal.

D F G
February 1973

INDEX ["F" indicates "Frankenstein" throughout]

356

359

361

365